THE LIBERAL PARTY AND THE ECONOMY, 1929–1964

OXFORD HISTORICAL MONOGRAPHS

The *Oxford Historical Monographs* series publishes some of the best Oxford University doctoral theses on historical topics, especially those likely to engage the interest of a broad academic readership.

The Liberal Party and the Economy, 1929–1964

PETER SLOMAN

OXFORD
UNIVERSITY PRESS

Great Clarendon Street, Oxford, OX2 6DP,
United Kingdom

Oxford University Press is a department of the University of Oxford.
It furthers the University's objective of excellence in research, scholarship,
and education by publishing worldwide. Oxford is a registered trade mark of
Oxford University Press in the UK and in certain other countries

First Edition published in 2015

Published in the United States of America by Oxford University Press
198 Madison Avenue, New York, NY 10016, United States of America

British Library Cataloguing in Publication Data
Data available

ISBN 978–0–19–872350–9

Acknowledgements

This book started life as an Oxford D.Phil. thesis, and I have accumulated many academic debts over five years of research. The greatest is to my supervisor, Dr Ben Jackson, who has been generous with his time and wisdom and provided incisive and constructive feedback on a long series of drafts. I am also very grateful for the advice and encouragement of Dr Matthew Grimley and Professor Jim Tomlinson, who examined the thesis; Dr Jane Garnett, who conducted confirmation of status; Dr John Davis at The Queen's College; and Dr Michael Hart, Professor Tomoari Matsunaga, and the anonymous reader for Oxford University Press, who kindly read and commented on the manuscript. Thanks, too, to my fellow graduate students—especially Dr Sam Brewitt-Taylor, Dr Kit Kowol, Ms Lise Butler, and Dr Aled Davies—for their comradeship over the years, and to the seminar and conference participants who have listened to and engaged with parts of the argument. This book has been greatly improved by their ideas, criticisms, and suggestions. Those shortcomings which remain are, of course, my own responsibility.

The project was made possible in the first place by funding from the Arts and Humanities Research Council, with some additional small grants from the Dowager Countess Eleanor Peel Memorial Trust. I am grateful to both organizations, and also to the Warden and Fellows of New College, Oxford, who elected me to a post-doctoral research fellowship in 2012 and so enabled me to prepare the text for publication. It's also a pleasure to thank the veteran Liberal activists who have shared their experiences with me, the librarians and archivists who have helped me gain access to archival materials, and the friends in various places who put me up during research visits.

I am grateful to the following institutions and individuals for permission to quote from unpublished works in which they hold or administer the copyright: the British Library of Political and Economic Science, the Conservative Party, the Parliamentary Archives, Dr Malcolm Baines, Mrs J. M. R. Brown, Dr Gideon Calder, Mrs Elspeth Chowdharay-Best, Mrs Joanna Clement-Davies, Sir Christopher Harris, Dr Michael Hart, the Marquess of Lothian, Mr Derick Mirfin, Professor W. G. Runciman, Mr Charles Simon, Viscount Thurso, and Lord Wallace of Saltaire. Crown Copyright material is reproduced under the terms of the Open Government Licence and the Open Parliament Licence. I also thank the Bodleian Library, the Borthwick Institute for Archives at the University of

York, the National Library of Wales, and the Master and Fellows of Trinity College, Cambridge for allowing me to quote from works in their possession, and the Macmillan Trustees for permission to draw on material in the Macmillan papers. I have made every effort to trace other copyright holders, but will be glad to rectify any omissions in future printings. Some of the material in Chapter 2 has previously appeared in *Historical Research* under the title 'Can we conquer unemployment? The Liberal party, public works, and the 1931 political crisis', and I am grateful to the journal's editors for permission to reproduce it.

Last but not least, I thank my parents, Richard and Susan Sloman, and my brother Ben for their love and support over the years. What I owe to them can hardly be repaid here.

Contents

Abbreviations

AJES	*American Journal of Economics and Sociology*
BLPES	British Library of Political and Economic Science
CBH	*Contemporary British History*
EHR	*English Historical Review*
EJ	*Economic Journal*
HDE	*Huddersfield Daily Examiner*
HJ	*Historical Journal*
IEA	Institute of Economic Affairs
JLDH	*Journal of Liberal Democrat History*
JLH	*Journal of Liberal History*
JMK	*The Collected Writings of John Maynard Keynes*, ed. D. E. Moggridge and Elizabeth S. Johnson (30 vols, 1971–89)
L&L	*Land & Liberty*
LM	*Liberal Magazine*
LN	*Liberal News*
LPO	Liberal Party Organisation
LSE	London School of Economics
MG	*Manchester Guardian*
NLF	National Liberal Federation
NLYL	National League of Young Liberals
PEP	Political and Economic Planning
RRG	Radical Reform Group
TNA: PRO	The National Archives: Public Record Office
TCBH	*Twentieth Century British History*

Introduction: The Wilderness Years

The historiography of twentieth-century British politics has long been shaped by the theme of Liberalism in decline, but from the perspective of the early twenty-first century it is the resilience of the Liberal political tradition which appears more striking. The Liberal Democrats' return to government after the 2010 general election capped a remarkable recovery from the position of near-extinction in which the Liberal Party found itself in the early 1950s. Coalition with the Conservatives has brought its own difficulties for the party, so it would be premature to suggest that the mould of two-party politics has been permanently broken, but for the time being British Liberalism is back.[1]

The Liberal Party has never been short of historians, but scholarly interest has long focussed—with good reason—on the Victorian and Edwardian periods when the party of Lord John Russell and Viscount Palmerston, William Gladstone and H. H. Asquith dominated the political scene. During the 1960s, 1970s, and 1980s research by both 'high' and 'popular' political historians transformed our understanding of the nineteenth-century Liberal Party and the reasons for its eclipse by Labour in the early twentieth century, but most of this work did not make it past 1929. It is only in the last twenty-five years that scholars have begun to explore the Liberal Party's fortunes after its relegation to third-party status, and to analyse the party's organization, policy, personalities, and culture during its years of survival and revival.[2] The deposit and cataloguing of the party's archive at the London School of Economics in the late 1980s has been one important catalyst for this wave of research; the formation of

[1] This study follows the common practice of using a capital L to denote the political tradition associated with the Liberal Party and Liberal Democrats, and a small l for liberalism as a political philosophy.

[2] Malcolm Baines, 'The Survival of the British Liberal Party, 1932–1959' (Oxford D.Phil. thesis, 1989); Geoffrey Sell, 'Liberal Revival: Jo Grimond and the Politics of British Liberalism, 1956–1967' (London Ph.D. thesis, 1996); Don MacIver (ed.), *The Liberal Democrats* (Hemel Hempstead, 1996); Ruth Fox, 'The Liberal Party 1970–1983: Its Philosophy and Political Strategy' (Leeds Ph.D. thesis, 1999); Garry Tregidga, *The Liberal Party in South-West England Since 1918: Political Decline, Dormancy and Rebirth* (Exeter,

the Liberal Democrat History Group and its quarterly *Journal of Liberal History* has been another. Most recently, the appearance of *The Orange Book* (2004) and the re-emergence of overt ideological conflict within the Liberal Democrats has prompted new interest in the party's ideas and policy.[3] This book is intended to contribute to the growing literature on twentieth-century Liberalism by providing, for the first time, a detailed analysis of how British Liberals thought about economic questions during the years of the Keynesian revolution and the development of a mixed and managed economy in Britain: that is, roughly between the 1929 and 1964 general elections.

Quite apart from its contemporary political resonances, the Liberal Party's economic thought in this period deserves the historian's attention for three main reasons. Firstly, although the party was no longer entrusted with the nation's economic destiny in the way it had been under Gladstone and Asquith, it could still exert a significant influence on the course of events. David Lloyd George's 1929 proposal to 'conquer unemployment' through loan-financed public works launched Keynesianism onto the British political agenda, whilst in 1931 the Liberals' belief that unemployment benefit cuts were necessary to keep sterling on the gold standard helped bring the National Government into being. At the other end of our period, the Liberal revival under Jo Grimond added to the pressure on Harold Macmillan to reorient his government's economic policy around indicative planning, modernization, and growth. In between, the party canvassed support for free trade, demand management, and wider property ownership, and helped shape the dynamics of economic policy debate at Westminster, in the press, and on the hustings. A study of Liberal economic policy enriches the historian's understanding of the range of policy options that were canvassed in Britain in these years and the political context in which public policy choices were made. It thus provides a new angle on long-standing controversies over the existence of a 'Keynesian revolution' in British policy-making, the political significance of economic planning, the

2000); Mark Egan, 'The Grass-roots Organisation of the Liberal Party, 1945–1964' (Oxford D.Phil. thesis, 2000), published as *Coming into Focus: The Transformation of the Liberal Party, 1945–64* (Saarbrücken, 2009); Richard S. Grayson, *Liberals, International Relations, and Appeasement: The Liberal Party, 1919–1939* (2001); David Dutton, *A History of the Liberal Party since 1900* (Basingstoke, 2004; second edition, 2013); Matthew Cole, 'The Identity of the British Liberal Party, 1945–62' (Birmingham Ph.D. thesis, 2006); Robert Ingham and Duncan Brack (eds), *Peace, Reform and Liberation: A History of Liberal Politics in Britain 1679–2011* (2011).

[3] See especially Kevin Hickson (ed.), *The Political Thought of the Liberals and Liberal Democrats since 1945* (Manchester, 2009), and Tudor Jones, *The Revival of British Liberalism: From Grimond to Clegg* (Basingstoke, 2011).

emergence of perceptions of relative economic decline, and the nature and extent of Britain's post-war 'consensus'.[4]

Secondly, the Liberal Party's economic thought is significant because the party's engagement with contemporary economic opinion did not end with its exclusion from power. Up to the middle of the twentieth century, as Andrew Gamble has noted, 'economists with an orthodox training who became interested in the problems of political economy naturally gravitated to the Liberal party': its traditional support for free markets and its progressive middle-class culture made it a very congenial political home.[5] The roll-call of economists who supported the party in our period is an impressive one, and includes both self-defined radicals and market liberals: John Maynard Keynes, William Beveridge, Dennis Robertson, Walter Layton, Roy Harrod, Michael Fogarty, Frank Paish, and Alan Peacock all advised Liberal leaders or stood for Parliament as Liberal candidates at one point or another. As a result, the mid-twentieth-century Liberal Party offers a valuable case study of how economists engaged with party politics in the early Keynesian era and how politicians received, understood, and used economic ideas, complementing similar work by Nigel Harris, Elizabeth Durbin, Noel Thompson, Jim Tomlinson, Richard Toye, and Ewen Green on Labour and the Conservatives.[6]

Thirdly, an examination of Liberal economic thought and policy sheds new light on the Liberal Party as a political organization during its wilderness years—its leadership, identity, strategy, and policy-making processes—and on the age-old ideological question of British Liberalism's orientation towards the state. In spite of the many important theses, books, and biographies that have emerged in recent years, the Liberal Party of the 1930s, 1940s, and 1950s is still imperfectly understood, and

[4] The literature on these questions is vast, but the most important works include Alan Booth, *British Economic Policy, 1931–49: Was There a Keynesian Revolution?* (1989); Daniel Ritschel, *The Politics of Planning: The Debate on Economic Planning in Britain in the 1930s* (Oxford, 1997); Jim Tomlinson, *The Politics of Decline: Understanding Post-War Britain* (Harlow, 2000); and Glen O'Hara, *From Dreams to Disillusionment: Economic and Social Planning in 1960s Britain* (Basingstoke, 2007).

[5] Andrew Gamble, 'Liberals and the economy', in Vernon Bogdanor (ed.), *Liberal Party Politics* (Oxford, 1983), 191–216, at 200.

[6] Nigel Harris, *Competition and the Corporate Society: British Conservatives, the State and Industry*, 1945–1964 (1972); Elizabeth Durbin, *New Jerusalems: The Labour Party and the Economics of Democratic Socialism* (1985); Noel Thompson, *Political Economy and the Labour Party: The Economics of Democratic Socialism, 1884–2005* (1994; second edition, 2006); Jim Tomlinson, *Democratic Socialism and Economic Policy: The Attlee Years, 1945–1951* (Cambridge, 1997); Richard Toye, *The Labour Party and the Planned Economy, 1931–1951* (Woodbridge, 2003); Ewen Green, 'The Conservative Party and Keynes', in E. H. H. Green and D. M. Tanner (eds), *The Strange Survival of Liberal England: Political Leaders, Moral Values and the Reception of Economic Debate* (Cambridge, 2007), 186–211.

policy is one of the most significant lacunae.[7] Manifestos and pamphlets make it easy enough to see which policies the party espoused at any given point, but give little sense of where those ideas came from, how Liberal thought developed over time, or where internal divisions lay. Article-length surveys of Liberal economic policy by Andrew Gamble and Duncan Brack have captured the main trends in the party's thought very effectively, but they are inevitably somewhat light on the details of policy-making; the same might be said of David Dutton's highly readable general history of the party.[8] As a result, the historian lacks the evidential base needed to answer some crucial questions about the character of twentieth-century British Liberalism: for instance, about the long-term impact of New Liberal ideas, the party's response to Keynesian economics, the relationship between Gladstonian classical Liberalism and the neoliberal movement, and the role which policy choices played in Liberal decline and revival.

SOCIAL AND CLASSICAL LIBERAL NARRATIVES

In the absence of a comprehensive study, historians and political scientists have quite naturally interpreted the Liberal Party's economic thought during the mid-twentieth century through the lens of the evidence they have encountered. This practice has given rise to two contrasting narratives about the party's ideological trajectory, both structured around the dichotomy between 'classical' and 'social' forms of Liberalism which has become commonplace in recent years. One interpretation sees the Liberals as the party of Keynes and Beveridge, the consensus party par excellence, and the midwife of the managed economy and welfare state which emerged in Britain after 1945. According to this view, the party had completed the transition from classical to social Liberalism by the early twentieth century, amid widening suffrage and growing concern for 'the condition of the people'.[9] In the social Liberal vision, as characterized by W. H. Greenleaf, the state ceased to be a 'necessary evil' and became a 'vital instrument of reform':

[7] The Liberal Party's leaders in this period have been well served by biographers: John Campbell, *Lloyd George: The Goat in the Wilderness, 1922–1931* (1977); Bernard Wasserstein, *Herbert Samuel: A Political Life* (Oxford, 1992); Gerard J. de Groot, *Liberal Crusader: The Life of Sir Archibald Sinclair* (1993); Alun Wyburn-Powell, *Clement Davies: Liberal Leader* (2003); Michael McManus, *Jo Grimond: Towards the Sound of Gunfire* (Edinburgh, 2001); Peter Barberis, *Liberal Lion. Jo Grimond: A Political Life* (2005).

[8] Gamble, 'Liberals and the economy'; Duncan Brack, 'Political economy', in Hickson (ed.), *Political Thought*, 102–17; Dutton, *A History of the Liberal Party since 1900*.

[9] See, for instance, Alan Bullock and Maurice Shock (eds), *The Liberal Tradition from Fox to Keynes* (1956); W. H. Greenleaf, *The British Political Tradition* (3 vols, 1983–7), ii, part two.

> Liberalism was still formally concerned with countering tyranny and maintaining freedom but the specific objects involved were being radically transformed. The external restraints which had now to be removed were not the cramping effects of arbitrary authority and outmoded privilege but those conditions which inhibited the full life for the mass of citizens, the poverty and distress brought about by unregulated economic growth and technological change.[10]

Once Liberals had abandoned classical strictures against state activism, it was relatively easy to abandon classical economics and to support interventionist measures which were designed to tackle poverty and unemployment. On this reading, classical Liberals were a dying breed by the inter-war years, and the neoliberal movement which emerged from the 1930s onwards had little to do with the Liberal Party. Both modern Liberal Democrats such as Conrad Russell and neoliberal activists such as Arthur Seldon have had good reasons for favouring this narrative.[11] Few specialist scholars would state the case quite so baldly, but historians of political thought such as Greenleaf and Michael Freeden have also tended to see twentieth-century Liberalism in these broad terms.[12]

A second interpretation has been found more convincing by political historians, and especially by those who have studied the Liberal grassroots and the party's behaviour during the 1931 political crisis. Here Andrew Thorpe, Duncan Tanner, Ross McKibbin, and Malcolm Baines deserve particular mention.[13] These historians have been impressed by the persistence of Gladstonian beliefs among Liberal activists during the 1930s and 1940s, and by the party's commitment to free trade and sound finance in the midst of the great depression. The bourgeois social profile of Liberal activists and MPs and the prevalence of 'anti-socialist' cooperation in inter-war elections seem to bear out the party's intrinsic conservatism. From this perspective, the radicalism of Keynes and Beveridge represents, at best, a social Liberal current which *competed* with the classical tradition (and frequently lost out), and, at worst, a symptom of the party's desperation and opportunism in the face of electoral decline. It is therefore hardly

[10] Greenleaf, *British Political Tradition*, ii, 27.

[11] Conrad Russell, *An Intelligent Person's Guide to Liberalism* (1999), 57–69; Arthur Seldon, 'Economic scholarship and political interest: IEA thinking and government policy', in *The Collected Works of Arthur Seldon*, ed. Colin Robertson (7 vols, Indianapolis, 2004–5), vii, 43–68.

[12] Greenleaf, *British Political Tradition*, ii, 142–85; Michael Freeden, *Liberalism Divided: A Study in British Political Thought, 1914–1939* (Oxford, 1986).

[13] Andrew Thorpe, *The British General Election of 1931* (Oxford, 1991); Andrew Thorpe, *Parties at War: Political Organisation in Second World War Britain* (Oxford, 2009); Duncan Tanner, 'The strange death of Liberal England', *HJ*, 37 (1994), 971–9; Ross McKibbin, *Parties and People: England, 1914–1951* (Oxford, 2010); Baines, 'Survival'.

surprising that Keynes and Beveridge undertook their most important work outside the Liberal Party.

Each of these interpretations has much to commend it, but both are liable to harden into caricature, and stated in their strongest forms they cannot both be true. The fuller account of Liberal economic thinking developed in this book enables us to move beyond them and to resolve some of the difficulties they pose. Drawing on a wide range of sources, including private papers, party publications, and the press, this study emphasizes the diversity and complexity of the Liberal Party's economic traditions and traces their development in the light of changing economic, political, and intellectual contexts. Whilst recognizing that policy choices are often shaped by calculations of personal or party advantage and that Liberal policy-making in this period was frequently spasmodic and confused, it nevertheless seeks to take the party seriously both as a site in which ideas were 'filtered by rooted languages, traditions and expectations' and as a vehicle which carried ideas into the electoral arena.[14] For reasons of space and coherence the analysis is focussed on the official Liberal Party, not on defectors or liberals in other political groups. Readers interested in the formation of the Liberal National Party will find much of interest in chapters 2 and 3, but in view of David Dutton's recent study no attempt is made to document its later fortunes here.[15]

THE LIBERAL PARTY AFTER 1929

Before proceeding to the main body of the analysis, it may be helpful to make some general comments about the character of the twentieth-century Liberal Party, its place in the British political system, its intellectual heritage, its engagement with economic ideas, and how we should define Keynesianism and neoliberalism. The remainder of the introduction considers these five subjects in turn.

The Liberal Party as it existed in the middle decades of the twentieth century was a shadow of its Victorian and Edwardian self, with dwindling parliamentary representation and little realistic prospect of returning to major-party status. Tensions between Asquithians and Lloyd Georgeites, and the 1931 secession of Sir John Simon's Liberal Nationals, damaged the party's cohesion in the inter-war period, and ambitious MPs and activists continued to defect to both the larger parties in later years. Nevertheless,

[14] Ewen Green and Duncan Tanner, 'Introduction' to Green and Tanner (eds), *Strange Survival*, 1–33, at 11.

[15] David Dutton, *Liberals in Schism: A History of the National Liberal Party* (2008).

the Liberal Party remained an independent political institution with its own identity and its own internal discourse. It maintained the trappings of a national party inside and outside Parliament, with a London headquarters, annual assemblies, and a large network of constituency associations, and probably had more than 250,000 members at the beginning and end of our period, if we include its women's and youth organizations. Even at its nadir in the early 1950s, the Liberal Party still had more members, ran more candidates, returned more MPs, and won more votes than the Communist Party of Great Britain ever managed.[16] The Liberals also enjoyed significant press support, notably from the *News Chronicle* (1930–60) and *Manchester Guardian*, various regional titles, and *The Economist*. None of these newspapers was slavishly loyal and they became less so over time, but they could usually be relied on to give the party a sympathetic hearing.

The Liberal Party's organizational structure was a holdover from the late Victorian period, especially before it was reformed in 1936; in the terms coined by Maurice Duverger, it was effectively a cadre party with a mass wing.[17] The party's parliamentary leaders historically controlled both policy and strategy, and oversaw organization and finances through the Liberal Central Association, which was run by the chief whip. The National Liberal Federation had emerged as a representative body for English and Welsh Liberals during the Gladstonian era, but its organizational capacity waxed and waned with the party's fortunes in the country, and it faced an ongoing battle to assert the authority of its policy resolutions. The new party constitution adopted in 1936 introduced a more coherent and democratic structure, creating a Liberal Party Organisation in place of the NLF and granting the annual Assembly the right to determine party policy, but the Scottish Liberal Federation and the Liberal Parliamentary Party both remained autonomous. In practice, successive Liberal leaders proved able to define the structures through which policy ideas were

[16] Reliable national membership figures do not exist before the 1950s, but the Women's National Liberal Federation (later the Women's Liberal Federation) claimed 100,000 members in 1928, and the National League of Young Liberals 30,000 in the following year, so 250,000 seems a plausible overall estimate for the start of our period. Liberal membership bottomed out at around 76,000 in 1953, before climbing to 351,000 in 1963; the CPGB's peaked at 56,000 in 1942. See Pat Thane, 'Women, liberalism and citizenship, 1918–1930', in Eugenio F. Biagini (ed.), *Citizenship and Community: Liberals, radicals, and collective identities in the British Isles, 1865–1931* (Cambridge, 1996), 66–92, at 68; *The Liberal Year Book for 1929* (1929), 7; *LN*, 19 March 1964, 1; and Andrew Thorpe, 'The membership of the Communist Party of Great Britain, 1920–1945', *HJ*, xliii (2000), 777–800, at 781.

[17] Maurice Duverger, *Political Parties: Their Organization and Activity in the Modern State* (1954). For a recent overview of organizational development, see Sarah Whitehead and Duncan Brack, 'Party organisation from 1859', in Ingham and Brack (eds), *Peace, Reform and Liberation*, 373–86.

developed throughout the period in question, whether through ad hoc meetings between senior Liberals and outside experts (in the late 1920s and 1930s), a shadow cabinet (known as the Liberal Party Committee in the 1940s and 1950s), or policy panels on which the leader could draw (in the Grimond era); they were also well placed to determine the content of election manifestos. One consequence was that Liberal policy-making was a male-dominated exercise, with only a handful of women—most notably, Violet Bonham Carter and Megan Lloyd George—wielding significant influence in their own right. The Women's Liberal Federation was an important element of the mass party and could not be ignored by the party leadership, but it tended to focus most of its energies on what it saw as female issues: women's rights, public health, social welfare, and the cost of living.[18]

Until the Liberal revival began in earnest in the late 1950s, the Liberal Party in the country continued to resemble in microcosm the party of the Edwardian period. The Liberal business elite included both traditional free traders, whose interests mostly lay in the City of London and the export industries, and more progressive industrialists such as the Cadbury and Rowntree families, whose philanthropy helped sustain the Liberal press.[19] The party also drew significant support from the London professional classes, including lawyers and retired civil servants and diplomats, and from the universities, where the Liberal clubs—especially at Oxford and Cambridge—remained valuable recruiting grounds. Constituency Liberal Associations were often dominated by middle- and lower-middle-class Nonconformists, with solicitors, small traders, and farmers figuring most prominently, though of course there were significant regional variations.[20] Party organization tended to be weakest in the inner cities (with the notable exception of parts of London's East End), in mining areas, and in those parts of rural England where Labour had broken through; conversely, it was usually strongest on the Celtic fringe and in the textile towns of the Pennines, which together accounted for all six of the party's MPs in 1951, 1955, and 1959. This pattern began to change as the Grimond revival gathered pace, with the party's new members and local government strength found increasingly

[18] Thane, 'Women', 81–92; Cole, 'Identity', 123–36.

[19] G. R. Searle, 'The Edwardian Liberal Party and business', *EHR*, xcviii (1983), 28–60; Paul Gliddon, 'The political importance of provincial newspapers, 1903–1945: The Rowntrees and the Liberal press', *TCBH*, xiv (2003), 24–42.

[20] A. H. Birch, *Small-Town Politics: A Study of Political Life in Glossop* (Oxford, 1959), 53–60; Margaret Stacey, *Tradition and Change: A Study of Banbury* (1960), 38–56; Tregidga, *Liberal Party in South-West England*; Matt Cole, *Richard Wainwright, the Liberals and Liberal Democrats: Unfinished Business* (Manchester, 2011).

in south-east England, seaside resorts, and the London and Manchester suburbs.[21]

THE LIBERAL PARTY IN THE PARTY SYSTEM

The Liberal Party's political development during the mid-twentieth century can only be understood in the context of its broader environment. '[T]he Liberal Party exists', Vernon Bogdanor wrote in 1983, 'in a political and electoral environment which is alien to it.'[22] If this was true in the 1980s, it was almost certainly truer in the middle decades of the twentieth century, when the party was reduced to a handful of seats in the Commons. The electoral problem was Britain's first-past-the-post system, which encouraged political polarization; the political problem was the strength of Labour and Conservative support after 1918, based largely on class identities and the ways in which these parties managed to construct or identify with them. As Ross McKibbin has argued, class became 'the dominant variable' in political alignments in this period, steadily squeezing out the influence of religion, region, and nationality: 'What primarily determined political allegiance was ideological–sociological identification: a sense among voters that their party stood for the world as they understood it and wished it to be.'[23] Many of the Liberal Party's difficulties stemmed from the basic fact of its third-party status and its lack of a distinct class appeal.

There was, to be sure, nothing very inevitable about the Conservative–Labour duopoly which emerged after the First World War, or the electoral dominance of class. Yet once it was established, this duopoly was exceptionally difficult for the Liberal Party to puncture, as the experience of the 1929 election showed; and the progressive nationalization of electoral choice, driven partly by Labour's expansion and partly by the growing influence of radio, made the Liberals' task even harder.[24] By the early 1950s the party was only really competitive in about a dozen constituencies. It is perhaps no coincidence that the long-awaited Liberal revival finally began at a time when class-based identities were starting to weaken and electoral swings were starting to become less uniform.

Within the structure of mid-twentieth-century British politics, however, Liberals retained some control over their party's fortunes. The party's inter-war collapse stemmed partly from the feud between Asquith and

[21] On local government see Egan, *Coming into Focus*, 164–86.

[22] Vernon Bogdanor, 'Conclusion: The Liberal Party, the Alliance, and the future', in Bogdanor (ed.), *Liberal Party Politics*, 275–84, at 275.

[23] McKibbin, *Parties and People*, 185, 193.

[24] Tregidga, *Liberal Party in South-West England*, 206–8.

Lloyd George, and was exacerbated by the Simonite split; if the party had held together it might have remained a much more formidable third force. Equally, the Liberals' refusal to lie down and die—or align permanently with one of their rivals—had important implications for the wider political scene, making it harder for the Conservatives to monopolize the anti-socialist vote (though they came close to doing so in the 1930s and 1950s) and for Labour to establish itself as the sole heir of British radicalism. As one of the few spheres in which Liberals' agency was complete, policy-making figured prominently in their efforts to ensure the party's survival. Liberal politicians and activists hoped that a cogent and distinctive policy programme would attract new support and bring about an electoral recovery; more soberly, they recognized that failure to develop policy would destroy the party's remaining credibility as a political movement. Jo Grimond thought that '[t]he main task of a party must be to say what its aim is, how it sees politics developing, what will happen if a voter votes Liberal'.[25] Party policy provided MPs and candidates with material for their speeches, and helped recruit members and activists by showing that Liberal principles were relevant to contemporary problems.[26] Liberals also sought to shape the climate of opinion by keeping traditional Liberal ideas (such as free trade) alive and putting new ones (such as Common Market membership) on the political agenda. Of course, the adoption of such policies by Labour and Conservative governments was not a cause for unmitigated celebration, since it reduced the political space that Liberals could claim as their own.

POLITICAL AND ECONOMIC IDEAS

The Liberal Party's ongoing commitment to policy-making partly reflected the extent to which it saw itself as a party of ideas. Liberal ideas did not derive from a fixed ideology, as Marxian socialism was often (rightly or wrongly) believed to, but nor was Liberalism wholly open-ended; rather, Liberals tended to define their creed historically. As Michael Bentley has argued in his study of *The Liberal Mind*, 'Liberalism always involved, and sometimes amounted to, an implicit language about the past and how the present had grown out of it.'[27] Victorian and Edwardian Liberalism bequeathed principles, currents of thought, and rhetorical tropes to

[25] *The Guardian*, 2 Sept. 1971, 12.

[26] Duncan Brack, 'Liberal Democrat policy', in Don MacIver (ed.), *The Liberal Democrats* (Hemel Hempstead, 1996), 85–110, at 85-6, 101–2.

[27] Michael Bentley, *The Liberal Mind, 1914-1929* (Cambridge, 1977), 14.

the mid-twentieth-century party. Most obviously, the conception of Liberalism as a progressive creed with an emancipatory mission, extending the bounds of 'freedom' and 'citizenship' to the whole community, remained powerful throughout this period. So, too, did the political commitments which had distinguished Liberalism in Gladstone's time, including internationalism, civil libertarianism, opposition to sectional interests, and concern for the welfare of the masses. Even when Liberals understood these commitments in different ways, they remained common ideological property.

We have already noted the tendency for analysis of Liberal political thought to be framed around a binary distinction between classical and social varieties of Liberalism. In many respects, this is a useful distinction, not least because so many Liberals and Liberal Democrats have understood their politics in these terms since at least the 1950s. Used casually, however, it runs the risk of collapsing diverse economic and political debates into a single frame, depending on which Liberals were on the right or left of a particular argument. If we are to avoid this problem, we need to *historicize* the concepts of classical and social Liberalism, recognizing that they have been constructed and reconstructed over time, and also to *disaggregate* them into their constituent parts: ideological differences, particular modes of thinking about the economy and the role of the state, and more specific policy commitments.

The ideological element in the classical–social Liberal distinction has been analysed at length by scholars, and is relatively well understood.[28] In broad terms, it seems fair to identify classical Liberalism with liberal political thought as it developed up to John Stuart Mill, with its emphasis on 'negative' liberties, and social Liberalism with Mill's later writings and the thought of T. H. Green and the New Liberals, who added the concept of 'positive' freedom. In the former vision, the state's role was mainly one of upholding order and securing the civil and political rights of its citizens; in the latter one, the state also took on the task of facilitating and promoting their development. Even here, however, the distinction is not always easy to apply. What, for instance, should we make of the distributist strand in Liberal thought, with its emphasis on spreading power and property more widely so that citizens can become independent of the state?

If the dichotomy of classical and social Liberalism is just about defensible at an ideological level, it is much too blunt to capture the complexity of economic policy debate. At least four main currents of economic thought may be identified in the twentieth-century Liberal Party: classical political

[28] Greenleaf, *British Political Tradition*, ii, part two; Michael Freeden, *Ideologies and Political Theory: A Conceptual Approach* (Oxford, 1996), part two.

economy and the Georgist, New Liberal, and constructive approaches which developed in the late Victorian and Edwardian periods. These four traditions are explored in detail in chapter 1, and provide an analytical framework for the study as a whole. Keynesianism might be considered a fifth current of economic thought, which could be synthesized with other Liberal traditions in a variety of ways—as later chapters will show.

THE TRANSMISSION OF ECONOMIC IDEAS

One of the main challenges for any historian of economic policy is to establish the sources of new ideas and the lines of transmission. The temptation to attribute policy changes to theoretical developments is particularly strong in this case, since the period from the 1930s to the 1960s was a golden age for British economists' reputation and influence, as Roger Middleton has shown.[29] Nevertheless, what Middleton calls the 'rationalist fallacy' is as misleading in respect of a political party as it is in relation to policy-making in Whitehall.[30] Liberal policy-making was messier and more complicated for several reasons. Firstly, economic ideas are always mediated through interests, institutions, and ideologies.[31] In any party, policy choices are likely to be shaped by the political context, including internal power relations, electoral strategy, and the party's prior commitments. As Terence Hutchison once noted, all politicians are prone to 'select from and distort' economists' ideas 'and infuse them with their own political purposes'.[32]

Secondly, like most of their counterparts in other parties, many Liberal politicians were ill-equipped to engage directly with economic theory. Only five of the ninety-nine Liberal MPs elected during our period held economics degrees, of whom four (including Jo Grimond) were Oxford PPEists.[33] Beveridge was a professional economist before he entered the Commons, and Keynes and Walter Layton sat as Liberals in the House

[29] Roger Middleton, *Charlatans or Saviours? Economists and the British Economy from Marshall to Meade* (Cheltenham, 1998).

[30] Middleton, *Charlatans*, 4.

[31] Andrew Gamble, 'Ideas and interests in British economic policy', *CBH*, x (1996), 1–21.

[32] T. W. Hutchison, *On Revolutions and Progress in Economic Knowledge* (Cambridge, 1978), 284.

[33] The other PPEists were Richard Acland, Frank Byers and Mark Bonham Carter; the fifth economics graduate was R. T. Evans, MP for Carmarthen 1931–5, who had lectured at the University College of South Wales. Sir Percy Harris learned some economics at Cambridge in the 1890s as part of the History tripos, and found that Marshall's *Principles of Political Economy* 'stood [him] in good stead in after years': Sir Percy Harris, *Forty Years in and out of Parliament* (1947), 16.

of Lords, but these men had many other interests besides Liberal policy. In any case, as George Peden has pointed out, theory has never been the only form of economic knowledge which policy-makers value; practical economic experience and 'informed opinion' are in many respects more useful.[34] In line with Peden's argument, the Liberal politicians featured here paid close attention to the policy views expressed in broadsheet newspapers, the bank reviews, and *The Economist* (whose Liberal links dated back to the campaign against the Corn Laws), and took advice from economic and financial journalists such as Graham Hutton and Christopher Layton as well as from academics. Some Liberal-supporting businessmen, financiers, and agriculturalists also contributed their expertise to party policy-making.

Thirdly, we must recognize the intermittent nature of economists' involvement in the Liberal Party. Alfred Marshall had enjoined economists to have 'cool heads but warm hearts', and public-spiritedness propelled many into the public sphere, where they found policy work a rewarding complement to academic research.[35] However, economists also faced countervailing pressures, including the fear that party political activity would undermine their professional reputations and the suspicion that their energies would be better spent elsewhere. This 'opportunity cost' consideration became more significant as the Liberal Party declined, non-party groups and think-tanks proliferated, and the British government became more receptive to economists' advice. After 1929, the cluster of economists who had advised the Liberal Industrial Inquiry disintegrated, and Keynes found he could achieve greater influence as a freelance. In the 1930s the Liberals had nothing to rival the New Fabian Research Bureau, where Evan Durbin, Hugh Gaitskell, and other young socialist economists developed new policies for Labour, and when William Beveridge and Roy Harrod sought careers as Liberal politicians in 1944–5 it was partly because they felt rejected by Whitehall. Frank Paish and Alan Peacock, who advised Clement Davies and Jo Grimond after the war, were more committed to the party, but the overall impression is one of economists drifting in and out of Liberal politics according to their own interest in giving advice and politicians' interest in receiving it. Consequently, it was left to the politicians to turn economic ideas into workable policy programmes.

Finally, as Keynes noted at the end of the *General Theory*, there is almost always a time lag between the emergence of economic ideas and their

[34] G. C. Peden, 'Economic knowledge and the state in modern Britain', in S. J. D. Green and R. C. Whiting (eds), *The Boundaries of the State in Modern Britain* (Cambridge, 1996), 170–87.

[35] Alfred Marshall, *The Present Position of Economics* (1885), 57.

translation into policy. Keynes believed that ideas ruled the world 'after a certain interval; for in the field of economic and political philosophy there are not many who are influenced by new theories after they are twenty-five or thirty years of age'.[36] As Paul Samuelson later pointed out, the reaction to Keynes' magnum opus suggested that this was as true of academic economists as of anyone else.[37] One of the advantages of studying Liberal policy over a long span is the opportunity it gives to trace intellectual changes across two or three generations, and to see how Keynesian ideas came to be incorporated into economic 'common sense'.

KEYNESIANISM AND NEOLIBERALISM

The economic traditions which the Liberal Party carried forward from the early twentieth century are defined and analysed in the next chapter. At this point, however, it is worth interrogating the concepts of Keynesianism and neoliberalism further, both because their meanings have been widely debated by scholars and because one major theme of this book is the extent to which Liberals managed to hold these apparently antagonistic discourses together.

Keynesianism is perhaps the most contested concept in the history of economic thought, straddling as it does the worlds of theory, policy, and political debate. The difficulty for the historian stems partly from the way in which Keynes' own ideas developed over time as he sought a robust theoretical basis for the discretionary macroeconomic policies he had long favoured, and partly from the fact that 'Keynesianism' began to take on a life of its own at a very early stage.[38] From a theoretical perspective it is tempting to take the *General Theory* as a benchmark for Keynes' mature thought, but even this is problematic because economists have interpreted that book in very different ways. Broadly speaking, mainstream Keynesians have used Keynes' 1937 articles on 'How to avoid a slump' and his 1940 treatise *How to Pay for the War* to justify a hydraulic interpretation of the *General Theory* on the lines suggested by John Hicks' famous IS–LM diagram, which modelled the relationship between interest rates and real output.[39] By contrast,

[36] John Maynard Keynes, *The General Theory of Employment Interest and Money* (1936), 383–4.

[37] Paul Samuelson, 'Lord Keynes and the General Theory', *Econometrica*, xiv (1946), 187–200.

[38] Peter Clarke, *The Keynesian Revolution in the Making, 1924–1936* (Oxford, 1988); Axel Leijonhufvud, *On Keynesian Economics and the Economics of Keynes* (1968).

[39] Don Patinkin, 'In defense of IS–LM', *Banca Nazionale del Lavoro Quarterly Review*, xliii (1990), 119–34. The IS-LM model first appeared in John Hicks, 'Mr Keynes and the classics—A suggested interpretation', *Econometrica*, v (1937), 147–59.

post-Keynesian economists—including Keynes' Cambridge colleagues Joan Robinson and Richard Kahn—have placed much greater emphasis on a 1937 article in the *Quarterly Journal of Economics*, in which Keynes suggested that the problem of uncertainty and the difficulty of forming accurate expectations in a money economy formed the kernel of his thesis.[40]

In the field of policy, the historian faces the rather different problem of judging how important the *General Theory* actually was. For one thing, Keynes had been a prominent advocate of loan-financed public works for more than a decade before 1936, and many of his fellow economists seem to have supported this policy during the depression on fairly conventional neoclassical grounds.[41] For another, the adoption of demand-management policies in Britain during the 1940s was shaped by a range of influences besides Keynesian theory, including the development of national income accounting by Colin Clark and Richard Stone, the Treasury's receptiveness to new methods of inflation control in wartime, and the relatively stable international environment provided by the Bretton Woods system.[42] The significance of the *General Theory* therefore lay not so much in introducing new policy ideas, as in providing a developed theoretical rationale for abandoning the classical assumption that the economy had a long-run tendency to full-employment equilibrium. Before 1936, public works had generally been advocated as a prudential means of reducing unemployment in a world of market imperfections; thereafter demand deficiency came to be seen as a more fundamental problem.

To the student of the politics of economic policy, the rise of Keynesianism as a political discourse is as important as the influence of Keynes' theoretical ideas. 'Keynesianism' is therefore used relatively loosely here, to refer not only to the particular analysis of the *General Theory* but also to the broader policy approach with which Keynes' name became associated—that is, the manipulation of aggregate demand to achieve full employment or a favourable trade-off between unemployment and inflation. However, we can add nuance to this discussion by distinguishing between three main varieties of Keynesianism: the 'proto-Keynesian' policies which Keynes developed before he had formed his theory of effective demand, which lacked the theoretical grounding of the *General Theory* and were mainly conceived as short-term measures; the 'liberal Keynesianism' of IS–LM and the 'neoclassical synthesis', which focussed on the use of

[40] John Maynard Keynes, 'The general theory of employment', *Quarterly Journal of Economics*, li (1937), 209–23; Clarke, *Keynesian Revolution*, 302–4; Luigi Pasinetti, *Keynes and the Cambridge Keynesians: A 'Revolution in Economics' to be Accomplished* (Cambridge, 2007).

[41] Hutchison, *On Revolutions*, 121–74.

[42] Jim Tomlinson, *Problems of British Economic Policy 1870–1945* (1981), 120–34.

fiscal and monetary policy to manage demand; and 'interventionist Keynesianism', which sought to buttress demand management policies with controls over private investment, trade and capital flows, and wages. The distinction between liberal and interventionist Keynesianism roughly corresponds to the difference between the 1944 White Paper on *Employment Policy* and Beveridge's private report on *Full Employment in a Free Society*.[43]

'Liberal Keynesianism' features prominently here, both because the neoclassical synthesis was so influential in the early post-war period and because its non-interventionist bent fitted well with British Liberals' historic commitment to free markets. Nevertheless, it is worth emphasizing that some of its exponents were more strictly Keynesian than others. Roy Harrod and James Meade, for instance, followed Keynes in regarding fiscal policy as the main tool of demand management, but Meade differed from Keynes in believing that policy should act directly on consumption as well as investment.[44] Treasury officials and free-market economists such as Lionel Robbins, meanwhile, regarded monetary policy as a useful means of curbing excess demand, despite Keynes' strictures to the contrary.[45] Post-war economic management was thus more 'Keynesian' in its analytical focus on influencing aggregate demand than in the methods by which it sought to achieve this. Indeed, as Robin Matthews and Jim Tomlinson have pointed out, the question of running deficits to maintain full employment did not really arise in the 1950s and 1960s because the world economy was so buoyant.[46]

Neoliberalism is a problematic concept for a different reason. In common usage, the term is generally used to describe the strong preference for market forces over state intervention espoused by economists such as Friedrich Hayek and Milton Friedman and think-tanks such as the Institute of Economic Affairs, which has underpinned efforts to 'roll back the state' around the world since the 1970s. Leading figures in the neoliberal movement, such as the IEA's long-standing editorial director Arthur Seldon, have tended to portray its history in heroic terms: a small band of free-market thinkers, formed in a reaction against post-war 'collectivism', eventually changed the terms of debate in politics and academia and

[43] For 'liberal Keynesianism', see Booth, *British Economic Policy*, 107–21, and Scott Newton and Dilwyn Porter, *Modernization Frustrated: The Politics of Industrial Decline in Britain since 1900* (1988), 120–32.

[44] Booth, *British Economic Policy*, 93.

[45] Clarke, *Keynesian Revolution*, 322–3.

[46] R. C. O. Matthews, 'Why has Britain had full employment since the war?', *EJ*, lxxviii (1968), 555–69; J. D. Tomlinson, 'A 'Keynesian revolution' in economic policy-making?', *Economic History Review*, second series, xxxvii (1984), 258–62.

paved the way for the Thatcher and Reagan revolutions.[47] Many studies of neoliberalism have echoed this narrative; Richard Cockett's *Thinking the Unthinkable* is perhaps the best British example.[48]

During the last few years, however, a number of scholars have emphasized the need to set the neoliberal movement more firmly in its historical context and to be sensitive to change over time. As Philip Mirowski and Dieter Plehwe have argued, neoliberalism is best understood as a 'thought collective' which developed in Europe and the United States in the 1930s and 1940s, became centred on the Mont Pèlerin Society from 1947 onwards, and has become increasingly cohesive and ambitious as its political influence has grown.[49] Ben Jackson and Angus Burgin have shown that early neoliberalism was a broad church, whose exponents found it much easier to agree on what they were against—namely, socialist economic planning—than on what they were for.[50] Several of the progenitors of the neoliberal movement (especially Walter Lippmann, Henry Simons, and Hayek) believed that a positive liberal agenda was needed to counter the appeal of socialism, and were willing to support discretionary economic management, robust anti-trust policies, and limited forms of state social welfare provision in order to legitimate the capitalist system. Some of Britain's leading free-market economists, such as Lionel Robbins, also supported moderate Keynesian policies in the 1940s.[51] This moderate and reformist strand of neoliberalism forms a striking contrast with the more dogmatic anti-interventionism preached at the time by Ludwig von Mises and more recently by Friedman and his disciples.

Heroic accounts of the British neoliberal movement tend to imply that the Liberal Party as a whole proved immune to neoliberal arguments, subscribing as it did to 'the post-war Fabian–Keynesian–Beveridge collectivist consensus'.[52] Recognizing the diversity of early neoliberal thought, though, opens up the possibility that a more fruitful interaction may have taken place. After all, many Liberals welcomed Keynesian economics as an alternative to a planned economy, and remained passionately committed

[47] Seldon, 'Economic scholarship'.

[48] Richard Cockett, *Thinking the Unthinkable: Think-Tanks and the Economic Counter-Revolution, 1931–1983* (1994; paperback edition, 1995).

[49] Dieter Plehwe, 'Introduction', and Philip Mirowski, 'Postscript: Defining neoliberalism', in Philip Mirowski and Dieter Plehwe (eds), *The Road from Mont Pèlerin: The Making of the Neoliberal Thought Collective* (Cambridge, Mass., 2009), 1–42, 417–55.

[50] Ben Jackson, 'At the origins of neo-liberalism: The free economy and the strong state, 1930–1947', *HJ*, liii (2010), 129–51; Angus Burgin, *The Great Persuasion: Reinventing Free Markets since the Depression* (Cambridge, Mass., 2012).

[51] Keith Tribe, 'Liberalism and neoliberalism in Britain, 1930–1960', in Mirowski and Plehwe (eds), *Road*, 68–97.

[52] Seldon, 'Economic scholarship', 55.

to free trade and competitive markets. Some of the economists and financial journalists who kept the free-market tradition alive during the 1930s, 1940s, and 1950s were Liberal advisers or supporters, and if early neoliberals like Seldon and Arthur Shenfield felt that their talents were under-appreciated by the party, they were less isolated ideologically than they sometimes suggested. Only during the 1960s, as neoliberals' hostility to state intervention hardened and the Liberal Party moved leftwards, did the two groups finally dissociate themselves from each other. Seldon and others focussed their energies on reshaping informed opinion through the IEA, and found that the most receptive audience for the anti-statist ideas they canvassed increasingly lay among Conservatives.[53]

With these definitions in place, we may embark on the analysis proper. Chapter 1 sets the scene by distinguishing four main economic traditions within the early twentieth-century Liberal Party and tracing their development up to 1929. The rest of the book is structured chronologically, reflecting the contingent and path-dependent nature of economic policy debate. The various strands of the argument are then pulled together in the conclusion.

[53] John Meadowcroft and Jaime Reynolds, 'Liberals and the New Right', *JLH*, no. 47 (2005), 45–51.

1

Economic Inheritances

British Liberalism is a historical movement at least as much as it is a philosophical creed. It has no shortage of great texts, from John Locke's *Two Treatises on Government* to John Stuart Mill's *On Liberty* and L. T. Hobhouse's *Liberalism*, which provide inspiration for Liberal political activity. Yet the political purchase of these texts derives largely from their contribution to the long Whig–Liberal struggle to control executive power and challenge privilege, which can be dated back to the seventeenth century. Every generation of Liberals stands in some sense in the shadow of the party's past, its choices informed by the commitments into which its predecessors have entered.

The place of economic ideas in this Liberal tradition can be viewed in different ways. The early modern historian and Liberal Democrat peer Conrad Russell believed that British Liberalism was an essentially political movement to which economics was extraneous. Partly because Liberalism antedated the discipline of economics, Russell insisted that 'the party does not have an economic philosophy', but 'brought to economics a mixture of pragmatism and a series of philosophical convictions such as attachment to equal competition and support for the underdog, whose origins in party thinking lie well outside economics'.[1] Though Russell's argument has much to commend it, it risks understating the extent to which economic ideas have embedded themselves within the party's identity. If the Liberal Party has lacked an economic philosophy, it has nevertheless played host to several economic traditions which have been believed to have a distinctively Liberal pedigree.

During the mid-nineteenth century, the Liberal Party's economic horizons were dominated by classical political economy. However, the Gladstonian identification of Liberal politics with classical economics never went unchallenged, and by the Edwardian period at least three alternative approaches to economic policy had emerged within the

[1] Conrad Russell, *An Intelligent Person's Guide to Liberalism* (1999), 57.

party: Henry George's single tax, the ethical and communitarian approach of the New Liberals, and the 'constructive' proposals developed by centrist Liberals. This chapter explores the economic inheritance of inter-war Liberals by sketching the development of these four traditions, in very broad outline, up to the First World War, and then examining how they structured Liberal policy debate in the 1920s.

CLASSICAL ECONOMICS

The classical tradition which provided the starting point for Liberal economic analysis in the early twentieth century can be traced directly to the work of the classical economists: Adam Smith in the 1760s and 1770s, David Ricardo and his contemporaries—Thomas Malthus, Jean-Baptiste Say, James Mill, Robert Torrens and Nassau Senior—a generation later, and John Stuart Mill, J. E. Cairnes, and Henry Fawcett in the Victorian era.[2] The classical economists were not a homogeneous group, but there were significant connections between them, and they shared a belief that the market had 'an inherent tendency towards self-adjustment', which rested, of course, on assumptions of perfect knowledge and accurate expectations.[3]

The central concern of the classical economists—especially Smith, Malthus, McCulloch, and John Stuart Mill—was economic development or growth. Though growth was not always an unmitigated good, Smith and those who followed him had little doubt that the expansion of agricultural and industrial production would ultimately enrich the society concerned and improve the living standards of its members. Classical theories of development took a variety of forms, but most of them included the same essential features: a stable legal and political environment in which investment could take place, the accumulation of capital for investment through saving, and the expansion of markets through trade and exchange, which facilitated greater specialization. The process of growth was likely to cease eventually, as a falling rate of profit made further investment unremunerative, but new inventions, capital exports, cheaper food, and cyclical instability could help delay the advent of this 'stationary state'.[4]

The common perception that the classical economists were wedded to a doctrine of laissez-faire contains a good deal of caricature. As Lionel

[2] D. P. O'Brien, *The Classical Economists Revisited* (Princeton, 2004), 3–6.

[3] T. W. Hutchison, *On Revolutions and Progress in Economic Knowledge* (Cambridge, 1978), 125.

[4] O'Brien, *Classical Economists Revisited*, 248–87.

Robbins pointed out in the 1950s, the classical vision of a market order presupposed a strong framework of law, which would underpin property rights and prevent the development of monopolies.[5] Most of the classical economists were also willing to recognize a role for the state in the provision of public goods such as roads, harbours, public health, elementary education, and defence.[6] Nevertheless, the classical economists did regard the laissez-faire principle as a sound guide to policy in most cases. Impressed alike by the effectiveness of the market as an allocative system and by the propensity for government to be captured by vested interests, the classical economists tended to argue that government could best contribute to economic welfare by removing obstacles to the efficient operation of markets. This was most obviously true in the case of international trade, where protectionist measures such as tariffs, quotas, and subsidies seemed to prevent nations from realizing the benefits of specialization. Smith's case for free trade in terms of absolute advantage was strengthened by Ricardo's doctrine of comparative advantage and John Stuart Mill's theory of reciprocal demand.[7] Within the domestic economy, too, preferential treatment of particular industries seemed likely to retard growth by diverting resources away from their most productive uses.

The classical economists were similarly opposed to government interference with the wage bargain, at least for adult workers. This reflected a theory of wages, profits, and rents which grew out of Smith's *Wealth of Nations* and received its most distinctive form in Ricardo's *Principles of Political Economy*, although later classical economists challenged important aspects of the Ricardian model. For the short run, Smith and Ricardo suggested that wages depended on the size of the wage fund—that is, the stock of previously accumulated capital available for paying wages—and the labour supply. For the long run, Ricardo drew on Malthus' theory of population to suggest that wages would tend to settle at subsistence level.[8] This did not necessarily rule out real wage increases, but it did suggest that such increases could only be sustained if population growth was restrained through delayed marriage or birth control.[9] It also suggested that attempts to fix wages above the market equilibrium, either by the state or by workers through trade unions, were likely to increase unemployment.[10] (Conversely, many classical economists were prepared

[5] Lionel Robbins, *The Theory of Economic Policy in English Classical Political Economy* (1952), lectures II, III and VI.

[6] O'Brien, *Classical Economists Revisited*, 327–55.

[7] O'Brien, *Classical Economists Revisited*, 205–47.

[8] O'Brien, *Classical Economists Revisited*, 127–37.

[9] Robbins, *Theory*, 73–9.

[10] Robbins, *Theory*, 103–4.

to countenance trade union activity to prevent employers holding wages *below* equilibrium level—at least in theory.[11])

The classical economists believed that the economic system itself, like factor and product markets, possessed strong self-equilibrating tendencies. This vision of the macroeconomy rested on three main theoretical claims, which Keynes would sharply criticize in his *General Theory*. Firstly, following Smith's lead, the classical economists believed that the interest rate adjusted automatically to keep saving and investment in balance. Secondly, they assumed that demand was necessarily sufficient to maintain economic activity at full-employment level, a belief usually expressed in terms of Say's law of markets: that general over-production is impossible, because supply tends to create its own demand.[12] Thirdly, the classical economists denied or neglected the possibility of hoarding, and tended to accept a quantity theory of money. Together, these three doctrines suggested that there was no need for government to act to establish macroeconomic equilibrium. Indeed, government action was potentially counter-productive, because the creation of public debt was liable to reduce private investment, add to the burden of future taxation, and so depress economic activity. Ricardo's famous doctrine of equivalence, which held that 'individuals wrote down the capitalized value of their income streams to allow for future payments of debt service taxes', was not widely supported, but all the classical economists shared his opposition to peacetime deficits.[13]

THE LIBERAL PARTY AND THE CLASSICAL TRADITION

The classical economists' attitude to the state was coloured by a suspicion that any government would succumb to the temptation to interfere with the economic system, to the detriment of the nation's ultimate interest, unless it was constrained from doing so by a framework of rules and institutions. This view fitted well with the long-standing Whig commitment to limited and accountable government. During the agitation against the Corn Laws it was radicals such as Richard Cobden and liberal Tories such as Sir Robert Peel who applied classical doctrines most confidently, but the realignment of British politics after 1846 brought Whigs, radicals, and Peelites together, and William Gladstone's budgets in the 1850s and

[11] O'Brien, *Classical Economists Revisited*, 341–2.

[12] As Roger Backhouse has pointed out, most classical economists except Ricardo recognized that this was a general tendency rather than an immutable law: Roger Backhouse, *A History of Modern Economic Analysis* (Oxford, 1985), 49–53.

[13] O'Brien, *Classical Economists Revisited*, 312–9.

1860s established free trade, balanced budgets, and low taxation as the orthodox political economy of the new Liberal Party.[14] Of course, these policy choices must be seen as political as well as economic ones, as recent historians have emphasized. Peel and Gladstone's very public efforts to rein in government intervention and establish an equitable fiscal constitution strengthened the legitimacy of the British state, and also contributed to the cross-class appeal of mid-Victorian Liberalism.[15]

Central to Gladstonian political economy was the discipline provided by the gold standard, first established in Britain in the eighteenth century and revived after 1815. For the classical economists, the gold standard served as an invaluable instrument of adjustment, which held exchange rates stable and imposed an apparently automatic link between price levels and interest rates.[16] The gold standard also helped safeguard government rectitude, since in conjunction with the 1844 Bank Charter Act, which linked the note issue to the Bank of England's gold stock, it prevented deliberate inflation of the currency.[17] By the late nineteenth century it was hallowed by its antiquity, and though proposals for its replacement with a bimetallic standard enjoyed some backbench support, they were given short shrift by Liberal ministers. As Anthony Howe has put it, '[t]he gold standard, like free trade, seemed part of the social contract upon which the Victorian state was based, with advantages not lightly to be jeopardized to assuage farmers and faddists.'[18]

Classical political economy coexisted in the nineteenth-century Liberal Party—and, indeed, in the Victorian political nation more generally—with a social reforming impulse which drew strength in different ways from utilitarianism, ethical or religious disquiet at the condition of industrial society, and the exigencies of social administration. Up to the mid-Victorian period, reformers' energies were largely absorbed by campaigns for criminal justice reform, women's property rights, and open access to the professions on the one hand and sanitary and public health legislation on the other; most of this was quite compatible with classical doctrines. From the 1860s onwards, however, four broad developments—the growth of professional 'expertise' and 'social science', the emergence of working-class Liberalism and 'Lib–Labism', the intellectual turn towards

[14] H. C. G. Matthew, 'Disraeli, Gladstone, and the politics of mid-Victorian budgets', *HJ*, xxii (1979), 615–43.

[15] Martin Daunton, *Trusting Leviathan: The Politics of Taxation in Britain, 1799–1914* (Cambridge, 2001); Eugenio F. Biagini, *Liberty, Retrenchment and Reform: Popular Liberalism in the Age of Gladstone, 1860–1880* (Cambridge, 1992), 84–138.

[16] Joseph Schumpeter, *History of Economic Analysis* (1954), 732.

[17] Backhouse, *History*, 49–50; Robbins, *Theory*, 29–32.

[18] Anthony Howe, *Free Trade and Liberal England, 1846–1946* (Oxford, 1997), 203.

Idealism and 'positive liberty' associated with T. H. Green, and the marginal revolution in economic theory—began to push Liberal thought and practice in a more interventionist direction.[19] Gladstone's moralistic and constitutional brand of Liberalism largely held interventionism at bay during the 1870s and 1880s, but advanced Liberals' disillusionment with laissez-faire precepts was nevertheless increasingly apparent.

The advent of the 'New Liberalism' around the turn of the century and the policies pursued by the Campbell-Bannerman and Asquith governments after 1905 demonstrate the growing eclecticism of Liberal economic thought, but it is nevertheless important to underline the continuing purchase of classical ideas within the party.[20] In the international sphere, Edwardian Liberalism remained decidedly orthodox, defending free trade against tariff reformers in the 1906 and 1910 general elections and maintaining the gold standard. Recent historians have rightly emphasized that Liberals valued free trade for ethical and political reasons—as a means of raising working-class living standards, protecting government from the influence of vested interests, and promoting peace—as much as for specifically economic ones.[21] Even so, free trade could never be a purely ethical commitment, since every restatement of the free-trade case implicitly reaffirmed the value of specialization and trade and highlighted the possibility that government intervention could harm the welfare of the people.

In domestic policy, the Edwardian Liberal governments departed from Gladstonian orthodoxy in several important respects. In the field of taxation, the simplicity of Gladstone's proportional income tax was lost when Asquith introduced a higher rate for unearned incomes in 1907; two years later Lloyd George added a super-tax, imposed land taxes, and steepened the scale of Sir William Harcourt's death duties. Old age pensions and contributory national health and unemployment insurance schemes marked the beginnings of a recognizable 'welfare state'. The sanctity of the wage bargain was disturbed by the Trade Boards Act 1909, which provided for the establishment of minimum wages in industries with 'sweated' or weakly unionized labour, and the Coal Mines (Minimum Wage) Act 1912 extended the trade boards model to

[19] Lawrence Goldman, *Science, Reform, and Politics in Victorian Britain: The Social Science Association 1857–1886* (Cambridge, 2002); Margot Finn, *After Chartism: Class and Nation in English Radical Politics, 1848–1874* (Cambridge, 1993); Michael Bentley, *The Climax of Liberal Politics: British Liberalism in Theory and Practice 1868–1918* (1987).

[20] For a valuable overview of Liberal policy in this period see Ian Packer, *Liberal Government and Politics, 1905–15* (Basingstoke, 2006), 121–41.

[21] Frank Trentmann, *Free Trade Nation: Commerce, Consumption, and Civil Society in Modern Britain* (Oxford, 2008), 33–80; Biagini, *Liberty, Retrenchment and Reform*, 84–138.

the strike-plagued coal industry.[22] Finally, the Development Fund and Road Fund established in the 1909 budget provided funds for investment in land reclamation, afforestation, smallholdings, agricultural and scientific education, and roads, which could be timed to counteract the fluctuations of the trade cycle—a significant step towards discretionary economic management.[23]

In political terms, these reforms made an important contribution to the redefinition of Liberalism as a constructive force, willing to use state power and interfere with private property rights in the interests of the larger community; they can also be seen as the beginnings of the twentieth-century transformation of the British state. Nevertheless, it is clear that most Edwardian Liberals thought they were modifying Gladstonian political economy rather than abandoning it. Progressive taxation could be justified by an elastic interpretation of Adam Smith's canon of proportionality, by the neoclassical concept of diminishing marginal utility, or simply by the need to fend off pressure for tariffs; and though 'caves' of Liberal backbenchers formed to resist the land tax provisions of the 1909 and 1914 budgets, these only managed to muster twenty or thirty votes.[24] Unemployment and health insurance also enjoyed broad support within the party, perhaps because they were not expected to interfere with the operation of demand and supply in any significant way.[25] Despite the introduction of trade boards, ministers strongly resisted Labour demands for a general minimum wage, which they believed would be 'in defiance of both economic laws and principles, and of experience'—as junior trade minister H. J. Tennant told the Commons in 1911.[26] Perhaps most tellingly of all, H. H. Asquith remained a fiscal hawk, insisting that loan financing should be restricted to those assets which would produce sufficient revenue to service and redeem the debts incurred—the so-called 'Asquith doctrine'. The Development Fund and Road Fund were therefore financed mainly by taxation.[27] If Liberals were increasingly willing to sanction departures from

[22] Sheila Blackburn, *A Fair Day's Wage for a Fair Day's Work? Sweated Labour and the Origins of Minimum Wage Legislation in Britain* (Aldershot, 2007), 91–117.

[23] José Harris, *Unemployment and Politics: A Study in English Social Policy, 1886–1914* (Oxford, 1972), 334–46.

[24] Daunton, *Trusting Leviathan*, 138–47, 330–74; Bruce K. Murray, *The People's Budget 1909/10: Lloyd George and Liberal Politics* (Oxford, 1980), 178–81; Ian Packer, 'The Liberal cave and the 1914 budget', *EHR*, cxi (1996), 620–35.

[25] This point is suggested by H. V. Emy, *Liberals, Radicals and Social Politics, 1892–1914* (Cambridge, 1973), 157.

[26] Hansard, HC (series 5) vol. 24, cols. 1919–24, at 1919 (26 April 1911).

[27] G. C. Peden, *The Treasury and British Public Policy, 1906–1959* (Oxford, 2000), 38–40.

laissez-faire principles in the period before 1914, there remained an underlying presumption in favour of a limited state and market forces.

GEORGISM

Henry George has been described with some justification as 'the last of the classical economists'.[28] Like Karl Marx, he developed radical proposals for the elimination of poverty and injustice within a largely Ricardian framework, whilst criticizing Ricardo sharply at some points.[29] Unlike Marx, however, George believed that his proposals were broadly compatible with classical principles; indeed, twentieth-century Georgists frequently argued that the taxation of land values would obviate the need for most other forms of state intervention.

In his 1879 book *Progress and Poverty*, George sought to explain the apparent paradox that wages were continuing to tend to subsistence level in spite of rapidly increasing productive capacity. His explanation focussed on the land problem. Inverting Ricardo's view of rent as the residual which remained after wages and profits were paid, George argued that high rents reduced the amount available to pay labour and capital; he also noted that, since the supply of land was fixed, economic progress and rising demand increased rents and brought windfall gains to landowners. As a solution, George proposed that the state should tax the site value of land, thereby encouraging its most productive use, discouraging speculation, and preventing landowners from benefiting from the values created by communal action. With the benefit of this new source of revenue, the state would be able to reduce or abolish existing taxes on industry and labour.

George was a San Francisco newspaper editor, not an academic, and his economics was largely self-taught. Partly for this reason, few professional economists took his ideas seriously, and those who did were generally critical: Alfred Marshall, for instance, argued that George had misunderstood the classical writers and exaggerated the importance of rent as a cause of poverty.[30] *Progress and Poverty* nevertheless made an enormous impact on both sides of the Atlantic. About 100,000 copies had been sold in Britain by the end of 1883, and a series of speaking tours during the 1880s boosted George's profile further.[31]

[28] Terence M. Dwyer, 'Henry George's thought in relation to modern economics', *AJES*, xli (1982), 363–73, at 366.

[29] Bernard Newton, 'The impact of Henry George on British economists, I', *AJES*, xxx (1971), 179–86, esp. 180–1.

[30] Bernard Newton, 'The impact of Henry George on British economists, II', *AJES*, xxx (1971), 317–27, at 320–2.

[31] Newton, 'Impact, I', 179.

George's political impact is best understood in the context of the much broader debate about land ownership which took place in late nineteenth-century Britain. The land question, long a concern of British radicals, grew in political salience during the 1870s and 1880s as a result of the activities of English land reform groups and the agitation of Irish tenants and Scottish crofters for fair rent, free sale, and fixity of tenure.[32] The proposals canvassed by reformers, however, were diverse and even contradictory, ranging from the Cobdenite vision of 'free trade in land' to John Stuart Mill's call for taxation of the 'unearned increment' in rent and Alfred Russel Wallace's campaign for land nationalization. George's approach was different to all these schemes, though at first it was widely regarded as a variant of nationalization. Perhaps sensibly, Liberal ministers focussed on resolving Irish and Scottish grievances and later on expanding smallholdings, which seemed popular with agricultural labourers.[33]

During the 1880s George developed a devoted following in Britain, organized in the English and Scottish Leagues for the Taxation of Land Values, and by the end of the decade the single tax was clearly identified as a radical Liberal cause, with particularly strong grassroots support in London and Glasgow. In 1889, taxation of land values was endorsed by the Council of the National Liberal Federation, and two years later it appeared in the NLF's Newcastle Programme, sealing its Liberal credentials in spite of Gladstone's scepticism.[34] Thereafter, land value taxation figured prominently in Liberal election addresses, appealing especially to urban Liberals as a solution to housing shortages and the growing problem of local government finance.[35] When J. H. Whitley formed a Land Values Parliamentary Campaign Committee after the 1906 election, no fewer than 280 Liberal and Labour MPs joined within three months. However, only a handful of these members seem to have been out-and-out single taxers. Many more favoured land nationalization, whilst others seem to have regarded land values as a useful revenue source (and the appropriate basis for municipal rating) without sharing Georgists' belief in their wider economic significance.[36]

Under Asquith's government, land reform became central to the Liberal Party's strategy for social change. The land taxes introduced in the 1909

[32] Roy Douglas, *Land, People and Politics: A History of the Land Question in the United Kingdom, 1878–1952* (1976), 21–95.

[33] Paul Readman, *Land and Nation in England: Patriotism, National Identity, and the Politics of Land, 1880–1914* (Woodbridge, 2008), 23–6; see also the essays in Matthew Cragoe and Paul Readman (eds), *The Land Question in Britain, 1750–1950* (Basingstoke, 2010).

[34] Douglas, *Land*, 111–14.

[35] Readman, *Land and Nation*, 26–8.

[36] Emy, *Liberals, Radicals, and Social Politics*, 209.

budget featured prominently in the 1910 elections, when Liberal meetings across the country ended with the Georgist song 'The Land', and Lloyd George intended to base the party's appeal at a putative 1914 election on the recommendations of a Land Enquiry Committee chaired by his friend Arthur Acland.[37] However, there are good reasons for thinking that Liberal enthusiasm for land taxes in 1909–10 derived mainly from their symbolic significance as an assault on landed power, rather than from a considered appraisal of their likely economic effects. During this period, as Paul Readman has argued, the Liberal case for land reform 'drew more heavily on history'—and especially on myths of enclosure and dispossession—'than it did on abstract political economy'.[38] The Asquith government could thus maintain the rhetoric of land reform after 1910, even as its policy focus moved away from the taxation of land values.

The experience of the 1910 elections seems to have convinced Lloyd George of the political salience of the land issue, but not that the solution lay in Georgist measures. Although many Liberal MPs favoured an expansion of the land taxes, Lloyd George opted instead for a more direct engagement with wages, rents, tenants' rights, and land ownership, as Ian Packer has shown.[39] In the rural report of the Land Enquiry Committee, written largely by Seebohm Rowntree, minimum wages for agricultural labourers formed the keystone of a wide-ranging interventionist policy, which also included regulation of rents and the creation of land courts to give farmers security of tenure.[40] The committee's parallel report on urban land proposed that existing local rates should be transferred gradually to site values, but it rejected a national land value tax, and the weight of its proposals lay elsewhere: in requiring local authorities to ensure adequate housing provision for their working-class residents and establishing an urban minimum wage so that they could afford to pay the rents.[41] Although some land tax advocates found it prudent to support the Land Enquiry's recommendations, it seems clear that Georgist ideas were on the retreat within the Liberal Party by 1914.[42]

Georgist Liberals would never regain the influence they had enjoyed in the Edwardian period. The 1909 land taxes were repealed by the post-war coalition, leading land-taxers such as Josiah Wedgwood and

[37] H. V. Emy, 'The Land Campaign: Lloyd George as a social reformer, 1909–14', in A. J. P. Taylor (ed.), *Lloyd George: Twelve Essays* (1971), 35–68.

[38] Readman, *Land and Nation*, 151.

[39] Ian Packer, *Lloyd George, Liberalism and the Land: The Land Issue and Party Politics in England, 1906–1914* (Woodbridge, 2001).

[40] Land Enquiry Committee, *The Land: The Report of the Land Enquiry Committee* (2 vols, 1913–14), i.

[41] Land Enquiry Committee, *The Land*, ii.

[42] Packer, *Lloyd George*, 113.

R. L. Outhwaite defected to Labour, and when Lloyd George returned to the land issue in the 1920s he eschewed the single tax in favour of proposals for 'cultivating tenure'.[43] Nevertheless, Georgist activists managed to maintain a vocal presence within the Liberal Party during the inter-war period. True believers like Ashley Mitchell were well entrenched in local and regional Liberal organizations, especially in Scotland and Yorkshire, and could point to NLF resolutions from 1889 onwards as evidence that land value taxation was orthodox Liberal policy. Though few Liberal MPs were committed to the full Georgist programme, most could be persuaded to support the idea of transferring property rates on to site values, or the introduction of a land tax as a replacement for other sources of revenue. It was in this sense that the Liberal Party remained a land-taxing party in the inter-war years.

NEW LIBERALISM

Of greater importance than Georgism for the Liberal Party's long-term development was the New Liberalism which emerged at the turn of the twentieth century, and the tradition of left-leaning Liberalism which stemmed from it. 'New Liberalism' is, of course, frequently used as shorthand for the Liberal Party's broad turn towards state intervention in this period, but in the realm of political thought the term refers more specifically to the ideas developed by the Liberal intellectuals who gathered around *The Nation*, the *Manchester Guardian*, and the Rainbow Circle in the 1890s and 1900s, which Michael Freeden, Peter Clarke, and Stefan Collini have meticulously documented.[44] Though the boundaries of this group are difficult to draw, it is clear that J. A. Hobson, J. M. Robertson, and L. T. Hobhouse were its most significant thinkers. After the First World War, much of the common purpose of the New Liberals was lost, as the group fractured between Labour and Liberal camps. What survived was a distinctive way of thinking about the state and its role in the economy which militated against the rigid application of classical precepts, and which would continue to influence Liberal MPs and activists during the decades that followed.

[43] Michael Dawson, 'The Liberal land policy, 1924–1929: Electoral strategy and internal division', *TCBH*, ii (1991), 272–90. The policy agreed at the 1926 Land Conference made only a brief reference to site value rating: Douglas, *Land*, 193.

[44] Michael Freeden, *The New Liberalism: An Ideology of Social Reform* (Oxford, 1978); Peter Clarke, *Liberals and Social Democrats* (Cambridge, 1978); Stefan Collini, *Liberalism and Sociology: L. T. Hobhouse and Political Argument in England, 1880–1914* (Cambridge, 1979).

New Liberal thought is perhaps best understood as an attempt to recover the idea of the fullest development of the individual's potential, which Mill had elevated into the highest Liberal principle, from the classical and utilitarian assumptions in which it had become embedded.[45] Drawing on the work of his Oxford tutor T. H. Green, Hobhouse argued that man was necessarily a social being, and that citizens' rights should therefore be considered relative to the welfare of the society in which they were exercised.[46] He also contended that individuals' personalities were most perfectly developed when they were in harmony with each other, and regarded the state both as an expression of harmony and solidarity between citizens and as an instrument for bringing it about.[47] Hobson went further, developing an influential view of society as an organism in which the state functioned as a conscious mind, deriving and pursuing the general will.[48] In both formulations, the old contractarian view of the relationship between the state and the individual was replaced by an emphasis on the state's ability to represent the community and the individual's dependence on the state.

With the notable exception of Hobson, the New Liberals' originality as political theorists was not matched in the field of economic theory. Their enduring contribution to Liberal thinking about the economy lay rather in establishing three priorities. Firstly, they insisted that economics should be subordinate to ethics. 'The trunk of the tree of Liberalism', Herbert Samuel declared, 'is rooted in the soil of ethics.'[49] Hobson strongly disputed the validity of many of the 'laws' of classical political economy, but even if these laws were empirically valid he could not accept them as a basis for action because they paid insufficient attention to the welfare of the people. The fundamental problem with classical economics, which neoclassical economists had only partly rectified, was that it focussed too narrowly on the production of marketable wealth, and correspondingly neglected consumption, non-marketable activities, and non-economic motivations. For Hobson, following John Ruskin, economic ideas had to be judged instead in terms of their implications for human feelings and social utility.[50]

Secondly, the New Liberals insisted that the welfare of the individual should be judged in terms of the welfare of society as a whole. This priority

[45] Michael Freeden, *Ideologies and Political Theory: A Conceptual Approach* (Oxford, 1996), 178–225.

[46] Freeden, *New Liberalism*, 66–7.

[47] L. T. Hobhouse, *Liberalism* (1911), 116–66.

[48] Freeden, *New Liberalism*, 105–9.

[49] Herbert Samuel, *Liberalism* (1902), 6.

[50] J. A. Hobson, *The Social Problem* (1902), 17–38, 51–69; Freeden, *New Liberalism*, 99–102.

stemmed directly from their organic view of society and their communitarian view of the relationship between the individual and the state. The New Liberals were much readier than classical Liberals to assert that certain resources and revenues properly belonged to society, and that the state was also justified in taking other revenues from individuals—for instance, through taxation—to use for communal purposes.[51] In Hobson's hands, Mill's idea of unearned increment was developed into the broader concept of 'surplus', covering all payments to land, labour, and capital which exceeded the return they would receive in a competitive market; this provided a useful justification for graduated income tax, differential taxation of unearned incomes, death duties, and land taxes.[52] The New Liberals were also keen to emphasize the reciprocal obligations which existed between the individual and the state, symbolized on the one hand by progressive taxation and on the other by the state's provision of a national minimum for all citizens.[53] In this communitarian vision, both the nationalization of basic industries and collective provision for basic needs could be considered logical and desirable.[54]

Thirdly, the New Liberals argued that the distribution of wealth was at least as important as its production, and was a matter in which the state should take an interest.[55] 'The central point of Liberal economics', Hobhouse contended, 'is the equation of social service and reward.'[56] This view stemmed both from the New Liberals' ethical approach and from their belief in state action, and provided an important point of contact with the burgeoning Labour movement. Although neither Hobhouse nor Hobson favoured strict equality of incomes, both men were adamant that the market distribution of income was unjust, since it failed to take sufficient account of either needs or effort.[57] Progressive taxation and a national minimum seemed to offer the best means of reducing inequality and ensuring basic needs were met under a capitalist system. Of course, the Asquith government's social reforms made only modest progress in this direction, but the principles involved were important ones, and these policies were hailed by New Liberals as important steps towards social justice.[58]

[51] Hobhouse, *Liberalism*, 189–202.

[52] T. W. Hutchison, *A Review of Economic Doctrines, 1870–1929* (Oxford, 1953), 123–7.

[53] Freeden, *New Liberalism*, 135–6, 163–5.

[54] Freeden, *New Liberalism*, 70–4; Ben Jackson, 'Socialism and the New Liberalism', in Ben Jackson and Marc Stears (eds), *Liberalism as Ideology: Essays in Honour of Michael Freeden* (Oxford, 2012), 34–52.

[55] Freeden, *New Liberalism*, 128–34.

[56] Hobhouse, *Liberalism*, 209.

[57] For a full discussion of Edwardian debates over distributive justice, see Ben Jackson, *Equality and the British Left: A Study in Progressive Political Thought, 1900–64* (Manchester, 2007), part one.

[58] Freeden, *New Liberalism*, 195–244.

The ethical, communitarian, and egalitarian emphases of the New Liberalism were all evident in the movement's most significant contribution to economic theory, namely Hobson's theory of underconsumption. Hobson, like George, was largely self-taught and gloried in his reputation as an economic heretic, attributing the criticisms of orthodox economists to prejudice, dogmatism, or class interest.[59] As Keynes acknowledged in the *General Theory*, the core of Hobson's achievement lay in his recognition that capital accumulation was determined by actual or expected consumer demand rather than the availability of savings.[60] Hobson combined this insight with the empirical observation that an individual's propensity to save increased as his income rose, and argued that the income inequalities which existed in late nineteenth-century Britain served to depress consumption below the level at which resources would be fully employed. By reframing the economic problem in this way, Hobson could show that the redistribution of income through taxation, social welfare provision, and high wages would not inhibit production but increase it. In times of high unemployment, relief works could also play a useful role in increasing demand.[61]

Hobson's underconsumptionism received little credit from orthodox economists until Keynes' *General Theory* simultaneously legitimated and moved beyond it, and within the Liberal Party only fellow New Liberals such as J. M. Robertson and Percy Alden seem to have accepted Hobson's analysis in its entirety.[62] The basic *idea* of underconsumption, however, circulated more widely, and if it did not directly inspire the Asquith government's redistributive fiscal policies it provided a very convenient rationale for them.[63] Hobson's arguments proved even more influential in the Labour Party. As José Harris has noted, 'the idea that unemployment was caused by shortage of demand. . . was central to the unemployment policy of the I.L.P. from 1895 onwards', and formed the basis of the 'Living Wage' proposals of the 1920s, which Hobson helped develop.[64]

After 1914 the New Liberalism gave way to a looser left-Liberal tradition in the context of Liberal decline and progressive fragmentation, as Michael Freeden has vividly shown.[65] During this period, attitudes to the

[59] J. A. Hobson, *Confessions of an Economic Heretic* (1938); Donald Winch, '"A composition of successive heresies": The case of J. A. Hobson', in Donald Winch, *Wealth and Life: Essays on the Intellectual History of Political Economy in Britain, 1848–1914* (Cambridge, 2009), 297–331.

[60] John Maynard Keynes, *The General Theory of Employment Interest and Money* (1936), 368.

[61] Hutchison, *Review*, 413–4.

[62] See especially Percy Alden, *The Unemployed: A National Question* (1905). Robertson developed a similar analysis to Hobson in *The Fallacy of Saving* (1892).

[63] Harris, *Unemployment*, 319, 367.

[64] Harris, *Unemployment*, 235.

[65] Michael Freeden, *Liberalism Divided: A Study in British Political Thought, 1914–1939* (Oxford, 1986), 9–14.

state became more cautious, as New Liberals reacted against the militaristic character of much state intervention during wartime and the Labour Party's adoption of a state socialist objective (in its 1918 constitution) which seemed to lack organic grounding. Most strikingly, Hobhouse gave vent to his long-standing anti-Hegelianism in a pointed critique of Idealist philosophy, which he believed neglected individual freedom, regarded individuals as part of the universal, and failed to distinguish adequately between the state and society.[66] At the same time, the defection of Hobson and other radicals to Labour weakened the New Liberals' personal influence within the Liberal Party. By the 1930s, Herbert Samuel was one of only a handful of Liberal politicians who still engaged directly with New Liberal thought, and younger left-wing Liberals such as Megan Lloyd George and Richard Acland made little effort to draw on Hobson and Hobhouse's theories.[67]

Even so, New Liberal ideas exerted a substantial ongoing influence on the Liberal Party. The New Liberal view of the state as the instrument of the community, uniquely able to facilitate individual development and establish the common good, continued to shape the thinking of the Liberal left in the inter-war years, while the concepts of positive liberty and social justice became commonplace. Henceforth, economic proposals would be judged in ethical as well as economic terms, and on the basis of their likely impact on distribution as well as production. In this way, New Liberal ideas provided important validation for the reformist instincts of a younger generation.

CONSTRUCTIVE LIBERALISM

In his influential study of inter-war liberal thought, *Liberalism Divided*, Michael Freeden has contrasted the 'left-liberalism' of Hobson and Hobhouse with 'centrist-liberalism':

> an older, capitalist, commercial and more individualist tradition that re-emerged strongly as a reaction to economic and institutional weaknesses in the 1920s, seeking liberal hope in past images of man and society, though often attached to new institutional and technical solutions.[68]

[66] L. T. Hobhouse, *The Metaphysical Theory of the State: A Criticism* (1918).

[67] Samuel's study of *Belief and Action: An Everyday Philosophy* (1937) combined a defence of piecemeal state intervention with a rejection of the Hegelian doctrine of the living state. The Liberal activist Harold Stoner, who attempted to revive interest in Green and Hobhouse during the Second World War, thought Acland was philosophically shallow: see Bodleian Library, Oxford, MS. Balfour 69/2, Harold Stoner to Lancelot Spicer, 10 August 1942.

[68] Freeden, *Liberalism Divided*, 13.

As an analytical framework for studying liberal ideology this distinction has much to commend it, but Freeden's centrist-liberals cannot be said to have been influenced by a single economic tradition. Rather, the 'older, capitalist, commercial and more individualist' tradition of classical economics was refracted through a concern to develop 'new institutional and technical solutions' to economic problems. This may be termed constructive Liberalism—although, of course, Liberals of all stripes were liable to emphasize that their proposals were 'constructive'. Much more than Georgism or New Liberalism, constructive Liberalism drew momentum from developments in mainstream economic theory. Ethical concerns were not wholly absent, but the emphasis of the constructive tradition lay in the development of practical remedies for the shortcomings of the market.

In very broad terms, the intellectual antecedents of constructive Liberalism can be traced back through mid-Victorian 'social science' to Benthamite utilitarianism. More specifically, however, it was the welfare economics developed by the early neoclassical economists in the 1870s and 1880s that made a constructive Liberalism possible. In the work of W. S. Jevons, Henry Sidgwick, Alfred Marshall, F. Y. Edgeworth, and A. C. Pigou, we find a new awareness of the ways in which imperfect information, externalities, unequal bargaining power, and the existence of public goods prevented markets from working as effectively as classical theory suggested, and a corresponding receptiveness to compensatory state action.[69] All of these economists recognized the risks which government intervention entailed, but the cumulative effect of their work was to weaken the force of classical strictures against intervention in a wide range of fields.

The possibility of reconstituting Liberalism on an interventionist basis was recognized by Joseph Chamberlain, but the Home Rule split took him out of the party. A more sustained attempt to develop a constructive Liberalism came from the Liberal Imperialists who clustered around Lord Rosebery at the turn of the century. The Liberal Imperialists were distinguished not only by their support for the Second Boer War, but also by a conviction that the party needed to shed its 'faddism' and demonstrate its moderation in order to regain power.[70] Though personally '[u]ninterested in economics', Rosebery was impressed by evidence of national inefficiency, and urged the Liberal Party to respond by shifting its focus from

[69] See especially W. S. Jevons, *The State in Relation to Labour* (1882); Henry Sidgwick, *The Principles of Political Economy* (1883); and A. C. Pigou, *The Economics of Welfare* (1920).

[70] H. C. G. Matthew, *The Liberal Imperialists: The Ideas and Politics of a Post-Gladstonian Elite* (Oxford, 1973), 125–35.

Gladstonian 'measures of emancipation' to 'measures of construction'.[71] Younger Liberal Imperialists such as Asquith and R. B. Haldane became enthusiastic advocates of technical education, industrial arbitration, and measures to organize the labour market; and although Rosebery never regained the wider influence he sought, many of his followers later received high office under Campbell-Bannerman.

The imperialistic tone of Rosebery's 'national efficiency' rhetoric initially repelled more orthodox Liberals, but over time concern for efficiency spread across the party.[72] Probably the most committed exponent of a constructive policy in the Edwardian Liberal Party was the Germanophile MP and chemical manufacturer Sir John Brunner. Brunner's economic vision was one in which the state worked to establish the conditions under which private enterprise could flourish, notably by investing in infrastructure, education, and scientific research and by promoting harmonious industrial relations. At his most radical, Brunner was prepared to support nationalization of the railways in order to reduce freight transport costs.[73] From a rather different perspective, Seebohm Rowntree's investigations into urban poverty focussed attention on the poor physical condition of the working class, a problem which had already been highlighted by military recruiters during the Boer War.[74]

The Asquith government's interventionist policies were no doubt motivated by a humanitarian desire to eliminate poverty and unemployment, as well as by concern for efficiency. The shape which those policies took, however, generally owed more to constructive ideas than New Liberal theories. Labour exchanges and trade boards were characteristically constructive measures, designed to remedy market failures and remove specific sources of distress; the Development Fund and Road Fund involved infrastructure spending, on the Brunner model, which also promised to reduce unemployment; and Lloyd George's land campaign of 1913–14 similarly comprised a series of targeted interventions. Even the unemployment and health insurance schemes, which can be seen to have embodied the New Liberal principle of reciprocal obligation, were more proximately influenced by continental models and a pragmatic response to social need.

[71] John Davis, 'Primrose, Archibald Philip, fifth earl of Rosebery and first earl of Midlothian (1847–1929)', *Oxford Dictionary of National Biography* (60 vols, Oxford, 2004), xlv, 370–83, at 380; Rosebery at Glasgow, 10 March 1902, quoted in Matthew, *Liberal Imperialists*, 140.

[72] G. R. Searle, *The Quest for National Efficiency: A Study in British Politics and Political Thought, 1899–1914* (Oxford, 1971), 101–6.

[73] Stephen Koss, *Sir John Brunner: Radical Plutocrat, 1842–1919* (Cambridge, 1970), 189–99, 232–3.

[74] B. Seebohm Rowntree, *Poverty: A Study of Town Life* (1901).

LIBERALS AND THE ECONOMY IN THE 1920S

Classical Liberalism: Restoring 1914

The First World War destroyed both the cohesion of the Edwardian Liberal Party and the Gladstonian economic order which it had upheld. With an unprecedented commitment to a large continental army, the Asquith government found it necessary to borrow heavily for the war effort. Currency notes ceased to be backed by gold, gold exports were severely restricted, and Britain was eventually forced to abandon the gold standard.[75] The McKenna duties of 1915 represented a significant departure from free trade, and their retention by the Lloyd George coalition after the war—along with the introduction of 'safeguarding' for key industries and a measure of imperial preference—suggested that the pre-war 'open door' was closed for good.[76] Direct controls on wages, prices, production, and investment were imposed in the core war industries, and backed up by food rationing, labour conscription, and Excess Profits Duty.[77] Internationally, the war left a legacy of unstable exchange rates, reparations, and inter-Allied war debts which politicians and central bankers spent most of the next decade trying to resolve.[78] At home, rising trade union membership and the growing strength of the Labour Party put nationalization and 'socialism' firmly on the political agenda.[79]

As wartime prosperity and a post-war boom gave way to mass unemployment after 1920, politicians of all parties sought remedies. Of the Liberal Party's four main economic traditions, it was the classical and constructive strands which offered the most credible guides to policy. Proponents of classical economic theory could plausibly attribute Britain's economic malaise to the accumulation of interferences with the market system which the war had brought. In consequence, the post-war period witnessed a revival of sorts for classical political economy within the Liberal Party and among Britain's broader policy-making elite, which emphasized the need to restore pre-war institutions. This restorationism was symbolized by the decision to return sterling to the gold standard at its pre-war parity of $4.68, recommended by the Cunliffe Committee in 1918, accepted by the Lloyd George coalition in 1919, and implemented

[75] Peden, *Treasury*, 74, 80–3, 98–9, 112. [76] Howe, *Free Trade*, 280–1.

[77] Sidney Pollard, *The Development of the British Economy, 1914–1950* (1962), 42–62.

[78] These efforts are documented in Robert W. D. Boyce, *British Capitalism at the Crossroads, 1919–1932: A Study in Politics, Economics, and International Relations* (Cambridge, 1987).

[79] Duncan Tanner, *Political Change and the Labour Party, 1900–1918* (Cambridge, 1990), 351–417; Kenneth O. Morgan, *Consensus and Disunity: The Lloyd George Coalition Government, 1918–1922* (Oxford, 1979), 213–35.

by Winston Churchill—as a Conservative Chancellor—in 1925. The return to gold at par compelled a relatively deflationary domestic policy, involving retrenchment and dear money, and implied that high wage rates constituted the main obstacle to greater competitiveness and full employment.

Classical restorationism received its most vigorous expression from the Liberal financial elite. The City of London as a whole had been predominantly Conservative in politics since the 1880s, but it still contained a vociferous Liberal minority, as Anthony Howe has shown.[80] The banker and sometime Liberal MP D. M. Mason believed that the gold standard alone could provide a solid basis for the revival of international trade, and that temporary deflation was a price worth paying for its restoration. Mason founded the Sound Currency Association in 1919 to campaign for a return to gold and attracted support from several Liberals with City connections: Lord D'Abernon and later Earl Beauchamp served as president and Sir Charles Hobhouse, Sir George Paish, and Francis Hirst signed the group's first memorandum.[81] Many of the same men were also actively involved in the Free Trade Union, and undertook private initiatives to promote the reduction of tariffs and the settlement of war debts.[82] Orthodox economists such as Edwin Cannan provided academic validation for these efforts.[83]

Most, though not all, City Liberals took Asquith's side in the split which developed after 1916, and blamed Lloyd George's coalition for the nation's ills. Asquithian politicians, in turn, identified themselves closely with the restorationist agenda, which fitted well with their much-vaunted commitment to 'principles' and threw into sharp relief Lloyd George's tenuous attachment to free trade and balanced budgets.[84] Indeed, in Asquithian hands the concern to remove obstacles to trade meshed with a belief that rising public spending threatened the integrity of the constitution. Sir Donald Maclean's campaign against coalition 'extravagance' was followed

[80] Anthony Howe, 'The Liberals and the City 1900–1931', in Ranald Michie and Philip Williamson (eds), *The British Government and the City of London in the Twentieth Century* (Cambridge, 2004), 135–52.

[81] D. M. Mason, *Monetary Policy, 1914–1928* (1928), 24–9.

[82] For instance, Beauchamp, who would lead the Liberals in the House of Lords from 1924 to 1931, was president of the FTU, whilst Paish worked with Sir Charles Mallet, Sir Hugh Bell, and Lord Sheffield to issue a manifesto on 'Barriers to European Trade' in 1926: *The Times*, 19 October 1923, 9; BLPES, Sir George Paish papers, 1, 'My Memoirs' by Paish, n.d. [*c.*1949–51].

[83] BLPES, Edwin Cannan papers, 985, speech to Sound Currency Association AGM, 25 January 1921.

[84] On the post-war Asquithian elite, see especially Michael Bentley, *The Liberal Mind, 1914–1929* (Cambridge, 1977).

by persistent criticism of the size of the civil service and armed forces, and the relaxation of the link between insurance contributions and unemployment benefit from 1921 onwards provoked forceful demands that the scheme should be re-established on an actuarial basis. Policy discussions at the Liberal Council, founded in 1926 to resist Lloyd George's leadership, were dominated by these themes: the Council held 'Economy Luncheons' in provincial cities in order to recruit members, and published a monthly bulletin entitled *Burdens on Industry*.[85] By the end of the decade, the 'race for expenditure' which seemed to have developed between the parties led the former Foreign Secretary Viscount Grey to fear that financial control might be incompatible with mass democracy.[86]

Constructive Liberalism: the End of Laissez-Faire

Support for free trade remained a unifying bond between Liberals throughout the 1920s, but in other fields of policy constructive Liberalism provided an important alternative to restorationism. Indeed, in a sense the First World War brought the constructive tradition into its own. In its own terms, as a means of mobilizing Britain's resources for the war effort and managing a scarcity of food and raw materials, the wartime apparatus of state control appeared to have been relatively successful. Moreover, though most direct controls were dismantled after the armistice, not all of the wartime changes in the domestic economy were so easily reversed. The wartime production drive highlighted the value of scientific management and economies of scale, and set in motion a wave of consolidation in the basic industries which continued into the 1920s.[87] At the same time, the labour market was transformed by rising union membership, the expansion of unemployment insurance and the trade boards system, and the establishment of arbitration machinery under the 1919 Industrial Courts Act (which, though non-binding, helped institutionalize national pay awards).[88] Wartime experience also prompted a new interest in industrial democracy, reflected in the

[85] 'Economy Luncheons' took place during the spring and summer of 1927, and *Burdens of Industry* was launched in the autumn: University of Bristol Special Collections, Liberal Council papers, Executive Committee minute book, 1927–37, minutes of meetings, 7 April and 21 September 1927.

[86] *MG*, 15 January 1930, 5.

[87] Asa Briggs, *Social Thought and Social Action: A Study in the Work of Seebohm Rowntree, 1871–1954* (1961), 112–63, 268–77; Pollard, *Development*, 53–62, 110–25; Julian Greaves, *Industrial Reorganization and Government Policy in Interwar Britain* (Aldershot, 2005).

[88] W. R. Garside, *British Unemployment, 1919–1939: A Study in Public Policy* (Cambridge, 1990), 34–8; Pollard, *Development*, 267–72.

Whitley Committee's proposals for a system of Joint Industrial Councils to facilitate employer–employee cooperation over pay and working conditions. Although the committee's ambitions were never fully realized, the Councils covered over 3,500,000 workers by the end of 1920.[89] From a classical perspective these developments seemed likely to hamper economic adjustment, but to the progressive Liberal they offered a basis for a more rational and humane economic order.

The constructive Liberal position as it developed in the 1920s was stated most cogently in John Maynard Keynes' 1924 lecture 'The end of laissez-faire', and in the paper 'Am I a Liberal?' which he gave to the following year's Liberal Summer School.[90] Keynes' critique of the laissez-faire approach included penetrating criticism of the psychological foundations on which it rested, but at the heart of his argument lay the assertion that the economic and political context had changed since the nineteenth century. Drawing on the work of the American institutional economist John R. Commons, Keynes argued that Britain was moving from an era of abundance to one of stabilization, in which the classical model of the competitive market was rendered obsolete by the growth of large firms, trade associations, and trade unions.[91] Keynes shared the traditional Liberal fear that these corporate institutions might clash or conspire against the public interest, but he argued that conflict and conspiracy could be avoided if they were brought into harmony by the state.[92]

> The transition from economic anarchy to a regime which deliberately aims at controlling and directing economic forces in the interests of social justice and social stability, will present enormous difficulties both technical and political. I suggest, nevertheless, that the true destiny of New Liberalism is to seek their solution.[93]

As Keynes saw it, the state's harmonizing role—its 'Agenda'—in the modern economy took two distinct forms. On the one hand, it should integrate corporate bodies into the state, especially by transforming the most powerful private firms into semi-autonomous public corporations. On the other hand, it should also exercise 'directive intelligence' over the economy as a whole, through the control of currency and credit and the

89 Pollard, *Development*, 271–2.

90 In identifying Keynes' inter-war thought with the constructive tradition, rather than with New Liberalism, I follow Michael Freeden and Robert Skidelsky: Freeden, *Liberalism Divided*, 154–73; Robert Skidelsky, *John Maynard Keynes* (3 vols, 1983–2001), ii, 222–4. For an alternative perspective, see Peter Clarke, *The Keynesian Revolution in the Making, 1924–1936* (Oxford, 1988), 78–81.

91 John Maynard Keynes, 'Am I a Liberal?', in *JMK*, ix, 295–306, at 303–4.

92 John Maynard Keynes, 'The end of laissez-faire', in *JMK*, ix, 272–94, at 288–90.

93 Keynes, 'Am I a Liberal?', 305.

coordination of savings and investment.[94] If government did not take these decisions, they would not be taken at all.

The dual focus of Keynes' Agenda corresponds loosely to the two strands of constructive Liberalism which existed during the 1920s, associated respectively with Manchester and Cambridge.[95] In Manchester, the progressive Liberals Ernest Simon and Ramsay Muir were articulate exponents of institutional reforms in industry, which they believed were necessary to demonstrate Liberal vitality. Muir's book *Liberalism and Industry* (1920) outlined a wide-ranging programme of reform, including Industrial Councils to fix minimum wages in all industries, statutory limitation of the return on private capital, encouragement for profit-sharing, and the experimental transfer of the railways and coal mines to public ownership.[96] Not all of this vision was acceptable to the Asquithian Liberal leadership, but the idea of minimum wages set by Joint Industrial Councils formed the centrepiece of the Industrial Policy which the NLF adopted in 1921.[97] Later in the decade, Sir Herbert Samuel drew on similar ideas as chairman of the Royal Commission on the Coal Industry, arguing that the amalgamation of small mines, nationalization of mineral royalties, and a national wage agreement offered the best means of restoring the industry's competitiveness and taking the sting out of its industrial relations. However, much of this was unacceptable to the mine owners, while Samuel's simultaneous call for wage reductions meant that his report was also rejected by the miners.[98]

It would be wrong to suppose that the Cambridge economists neglected industrial organization. Indeed, Keynes accepted the trend towards monopoly more readily than most Liberals, and strongly advocated the rationalization of the cotton and coal industries to eliminate excess capacity.[99] Nevertheless, the idea that the government should pursue discretionary macroeconomic policies was the Cambridge economists' distinctive contribution. Here, Keynes' perspicacity and flair for controversy made him the dominant figure, although Hubert Henderson and Dennis Robertson helped refine his ideas and made important contributions of their own.

[94] Keynes, 'The end of laissez-faire', 288–92, at 292. Keynes also included population policy in the latter category.

[95] John Campbell, 'The renewal of Liberalism: Liberalism without Liberals', in Chris Cook and Gillian Peele (eds), *The Politics of Reappraisal, 1918–1939* (1975), 88–113.

[96] Ramsay Muir, *Liberalism and Industry* (1920).

[97] Stewart Faulkes, 'The Strange Death of British Liberalism: The Liberal Summer School Movement and the Making of the Yellow Book in the 1920s' (London Ph.D. thesis, 2000), 86–116.

[98] Bernard Wasserstein, *Herbert Samuel: A Political Life* (Oxford, 1992), 271–91.

[99] Skidelsky, *Keynes*, ii, 258–64.

At the core of Keynes' analysis in the 1920s lay a conviction that domestic wages were much too 'sticky' for the British economy to respond to the post-war reduction in demand by adjusting costs downwards in the way that classical theory predicted. Keynes did not deny that mass unemployment resulted from structural maladjustment, nor did he seriously challenge the classical argument that trade union power and unemployment insurance contributed to wage rigidity.[100] However, he rejected the classical remedy of using deflation to reduce wages to a level consistent with full employment, both on grounds of practicability and social justice and because he believed that prices were likely to fall faster than money wages in the short term. Instead of returning to gold at par, Keynes recommended that the British government should actively manage the currency in order to stabilize the price level, thereby tacitly accepting the devaluation which had taken place since the war and gaining the freedom to pursue a cheap money policy.

During 1923 and 1924, Keynes and his Cambridge colleagues conceived of macroeconomic stabilization mainly in terms of an active monetary policy, but Keynes was coming to believe that this was an insufficient remedy for the unemployment problem. Prompted by a lengthy controversy over unemployment in the pages of *The Nation*, Keynes emerged in 1924 as a vocal advocate of public works as a means of providing 'the stimulus which shall initiate a cumulative prosperity'.[101] Pigou had argued as early as 1908 that (*contra* Ricardo) public works would tend to reduce unemployment, because only part of the taxation used to pay for them would take funds away from productive uses.[102] Keynes added the idea that an initial stimulus would have cumulative effects, and the contention that the lack of investment demand at home was driving capital abroad and depressing domestic employment. In Keynes' view, this maldistribution of capital between domestic and overseas uses justified the financing of public works through government borrowing:

> The Chancellor of the Exchequer should devote his sinking fund and his surplus resources, not to redeeming old debt with the result of driving the national savings to find a foreign outlet, but to replacing unproductive debt by productive debt. The Treasury should not shrink from promoting expenditure up to (say) £100,000,000 a year on the construction of capital works at home, enlisting in various ways the aid of private genius, temperament, and skill.[103]

[100] Skidelsky, *Keynes*, ii, 120–4.

[101] John Maynard Keynes, 'Does unemployment need a drastic remedy?', *The Nation and Athenaeum*, 24 May 1924, reprinted in *JMK*, xix, 219–23.

[102] Hutchison, *Review*, 416–7.

[103] Keynes, 'Does unemployment need a drastic remedy?', 222.

Over the next five years Keynes steadily fleshed out this case, and felt his way towards the argument that state intervention was needed to bring savings and investment into balance, which he would theorize in his 1930 *Treatise on Money*.[104] In the meantime, as a result of the return to gold, Keynes' public works policy was burdened with the additional task of counteracting the depressive impact of an overvalued currency and high interest rates. Decoupled from monetary reform, public works became a stand-alone solution for unemployment.

Liberals responded to Keynes' two reflationary proposals in contrasting ways. On the monetary question, the party's concern about the gold standard's impact on the export industries was largely outweighed by its instinctive support for Gladstonian orthodoxy. Asquith acknowledged that Keynes' case for a managed currency contained 'much that [was] attractive', but was more impressed by the political and psychological advantages of returning to gold, not least because it would help re-establish Britain as 'the financial centre of the world'.[105] The Hull MP J. M. Kenworthy—who would later defect to Labour—also argued that Churchill's decision was 'absolutely right' because it would provide a stable basis for trade:

> If it may mean a little more deflation and a little unemployment temporarily, we have got to go through that stage, and we ought to have done it long ago . . . There are advantages and disadvantages, but the advantages are in favour of an export trading nation like this.[106]

The chemical magnate Sir Alfred Mond was much more critical, and David Lloyd George subsequently accused the government of acting in a 'premature and precipitate' fashion, but the parliamentary party nevertheless agreed to give qualified support to Churchill's policy.[107]

Mainstream Liberal opinion was rather more receptive to Keynes' public works proposals, partly because they fed into an existing current of interest in 'national development' which dated back to the 1909 Development Act. Lloyd George had briefly contemplated launching a £250,000,000 public works programme to tackle unemployment in 1921, before being persuaded by coalition colleagues that this would be unsound; as George Peden has pointed out, this idea closely prefigured his 1929 policy.[108] The 1923 Liberal manifesto called for the government to use the national

[104] Clarke, *Keynesian Revolution*, 83–7.

[105] *MG*, 10 March 1925, 10, and 2 May 1925, 14.

[106] Hansard, HC (series 5) vol. 183, cols. 688–91, at 688, 691 (4 May 1925).

[107] Hansard, HC (series 5) vol. 183, cols. 191–206 (29 April 1925); *MG*, 11 July 1925, 17, and 5 May 1925, 10.

[108] G. C. Peden, 'The road to and from Gairloch: Lloyd George, unemployment, inflation, and the "Treasury view" in 1921', *TCBH*, iv (1993), 224–49. I am grateful to the anonymous OUP reviewer for drawing this point to my attention.

credit 'on enterprises that would permanently improve and develop the home country and the Empire', such as roads, power generation, and land drainage, and Keynes' 1924 call for the state to help facilitate domestic investment was immediately echoed by Asquith.[109] The Liberal case for public works up to 1929 was perhaps less radical than it seemed, since the frequent insistence that capital spending must be 'productive' constrained the range of suitable projects, and the question of loan-versus-tax financing was not always addressed. Nevertheless, it is clear that many Liberals had already begun to turn away from the Ricardian equivalence principle which had constrained fiscal activism in the nineteenth century.

Britain's Industrial Future

During the early 1920s both the Manchester Liberals and the Cambridge economists involved in the Liberal Summer School identified with the party's Asquithian wing, but over time Lloyd George began to rehabilitate himself in radical eyes. The enquiries into *Coal and Power* and *Land and the Nation* which Lloyd George funded in 1923–5 helped to re-establish his progressive credentials, whilst alienating more traditional Liberals and ex-coalitionists who regarded them as steps towards socialism.[110] The crucial moment, though, followed the 1926 General Strike, when Asquith and his allies attempted to use his non-attendance at a shadow cabinet meeting as grounds for expelling him from the party. Keynes was convinced that Lloyd George was right, not only on the procedural question but in his even-handed attitude towards the strike, which contrasted with Asquith's support for the government's position.[111] Thereafter, the Summer School Liberals worked constructively with Lloyd George. Within a month of the General Strike, the former Prime Minister had agreed to finance an Industrial Inquiry, chaired by the editor of *The Economist* (and former Cambridge economist) Walter Layton, which would enable the radical Liberals to develop a comprehensive economic policy.

The Liberal Industrial Inquiry, and the report on *Britain's Industrial Future* (the 'Yellow Book') which it produced, brought together the two strands of constructive Liberalism and added Lloyd George's own reforming instincts. The membership, organization, and deliberations of the inquiry have been documented so thoroughly elsewhere that it hardly

[109] *Liberal Party General Election Manifestos, 1900–1997*, ed. Iain Dale (2000), 41; *NLF Proceedings, 1924* (1924), 90.

[110] Dawson, 'Liberal land policy'.

[111] On this incident, see John Campbell, *Lloyd George: The Goat in the Wilderness, 1922–1931* (1977), 136–56.

seems necessary to discuss them here.[112] Nevertheless, the Yellow Book's contents are important, since it represented the culmination of the constructive thought of the previous thirty years. It is no exaggeration for Michael Freeden to claim that 'the result of the Yellow Book was to incorporate state interventionism decisively within liberal ideology as no document had ever done before'.[113]

The Yellow Book's main thesis was fundamentally that of Keynes' paper on 'The end of laissez-faire': that as industrial units grew in size, and the limitations of the market became more apparent, '[t]he scope of useful intervention by the whole Society' was 'seen to be much larger than was formerly supposed'.[114] In line with this principle, the authors outlined an expansive role for the state in restoring the British economy to health. At macro level, the report proposed an Economic General Staff to advise the government on economic policy, a census of production to inform government decisions, closer public control of the Bank of England, more deliberate regulation of the volume of credit, a new budgetary distinction between capital and current spending, and a Board of National Investment to organize government investment, issue bonds for domestic investment, and vet overseas loans. At micro level, it proposed an extensive system of industrial democracy and joint consultation based on the Whitley Councils, Works Councils, and trade boards, with minimum wages fixed in each industry, official encouragement for profit-sharing, and a representative Council of Industry at the system's apex. Trade unions would remain important, but the system of wage determination would become much less adversarial. Large monopolistic firms would be forced to register as 'Public Corporations' and subjected to stringent publicity requirements, or else would be turned into 'Public Concerns' on the model of the Port of London Authority and the BBC. Linking the macro and the micro were the proposals for national development which gave the Yellow Book its immediate political force. A Liberal government would use a wide-ranging programme of capital works to reduce unemployment, financed by borrowing, a betterment duty, and land value taxation.

The Yellow Book's interventionist approach placed it firmly in the constructive tradition. Most strikingly, its treatment of the large firm broke firmly with the traditional Liberal hostility to monopolies and collusive behaviour:

> In modern conditions a tendency towards some degree of monopoly in an increasing number of industries is, in our opinion, inevitable and even, quite

[112] Faulkes, 'Strange Death', 236–72; Campbell, 'Renewal'.
[113] Freeden, *Liberalism Divided*, 118.
[114] Liberal Industrial Inquiry, *Britain's Industrial Future* (1928), xix.

> often, desirable in the interests of efficiency. It is, therefore, no longer useful to treat trusts, cartels, combinations, holding companies, and trade associations as inexpedient abnormalities in the economic system.[115]

The natural monopoly power enjoyed by public utilities (such as electricity) and the railways seemed to the authors of the Yellow Book to justify public ownership. Outside these fields, however, monopolies would be left in private hands, and the public interest safeguarded by publicity and inspection, with the Board of Trade able to fix prices 'in exceptional circumstances' where monopoly power was abused.[116] The report also proposed that trade associations which represented more than half of an industry should receive official recognition, and—in certain circumstances—the right to organize other firms. Although some liberal economists criticized the Yellow Book's tolerant attitude towards monopoly, none of these proposals faced serious opposition at the special NLF conference held to consider the report.[117] The implicit tension between the acceptance of monopolies and trusts and the party's free-trade commitment was left largely unexamined.

CONCLUSION

The endorsement of the Yellow Book by the NLF in March 1928 signalled the ascendancy of the constructive approach to economic policy within the Liberal Party, and marked the culmination of a movement away from classical Liberalism which had begun in the 1890s. Traditionalist Liberals, including the Liberal Council, viewed the report with deep suspicion, but there was no concerted attempt to rally opposition; indeed, Sir John Simon signed it, and Walter Runciman eventually gave his qualified approval.[118] The extensive involvement of academic economists in the Inquiry, including D. H. MacGregor and Hubert Phillips as well as Keynes, Henderson, Robertson, and Layton, seemed to give its conclusions

[115] Liberal Industrial Inquiry, *Britain's Industrial Future*, 93.

[116] Liberal Industrial Inquiry, *Britain's Industrial Future*, 96.

[117] *MG*, 10 March 1928, 15, and 29 March 1928, 6. The proposal that firms should be required to share financial information with Works Councils proved more controversial, but was carried 215–78. Francis Hirst tried to amend the resolution on trusts to demand abolition of the statutory monopoly in the dye industry, but abandoned his amendment after an intervention by the chairman.

[118] Liberal Council papers, Executive Committee minute book, 1927–37, minutes of meeting, 21 February 1928. For Runciman's qualified endorsement of the Yellow Book, see *MG*, 28 March 1928, 12. Michael Dawson has suggested that Asquithians accepted the Yellow Book partly because it was less inflammatory than Lloyd George's agricultural proposals: Dawson, 'Liberal land policy', 289.

expert authority, whilst radical MPs and candidates, progressive industrialists like Seebohm Rowntree and E. H. Gilpin, and women Liberals such as Margery Corbett Ashby were also enthusiastic.[119] There were therefore good reasons for thinking that the weight of opinion within the Liberal Party had moved decisively in an interventionist direction.

Nevertheless, constructive Liberalism was ascendant rather than dominant for three reasons. Firstly, proponents of classical restorationism remained influential, even though they declined to challenge the Yellow Book head-on. The Liberal Council—with more than 800 members—provided an important centre for resistance to Lloyd George, and its leaders offered only grudging support for his policies; its literature pressed for public economy and lower taxation, and the by-election candidates which it sponsored tended to campaign on traditional Liberal themes.[120] More generally, the Gladstonian canons of sound money and balanced budgets, restated forcefully by D. M. Mason and Francis Hirst, were still the guiding principles of the financial community and the Treasury.

Secondly, free trade remained an article of faith for Liberals, and party propaganda in the late 1920s relentlessly criticized the Conservative government's safeguarding duties, the protectionist Dyestuffs Act, and the beet sugar subsidy.[121] Constructive Liberals insisted that the Yellow Book's proposals for industrial organization were compatible with a free-trade regime, but it could equally be argued—from a classical perspective—that the institutionalization of monopolies and trade associations was bound to retard the workings of the free market and distort the allocation of resources. Liberals certainly remained suspicious of private concentrations of economic power, and of proposals for the state to assist particular industries by legislation or subsidy. During the 1930s, Liberals would make clear that their support for amalgamations in the interests of efficiency did not extend to restrictive measures, such as output quotas, which were intended to push up prices.

Finally, it is clear that the intellectual basis for a wholesale repudiation of the classical inheritance was not yet fully formed. 'At the opening of the 1930s', G. L. S. Shackle later noted, 'economic theory still rested on

[119] MacGregor was Professor of Political Economy at the University of Manchester; Phillips was a former head of economics at the University of Bristol, and served as the Inquiry's economic adviser and secretary. For Corbett Ashby, see *MG*, 28 March 1928, 12.

[120] Notably, Harcourt Johnstone at Westbury in 1927 and Hilda Runciman at St Ives in 1928: *MG*, 18 June 1927, 13, and 20 February 1928, 9. For Liberal Council membership, see Liberal Council papers, Executive Committee minute book, 1927–37, minutes of meeting, 22 June 1927.

[121] Parliamentary Archives, Graham White papers, WHI/1/1/32, 'Free Trade Facts', and WHI/1/1/77, 'The Sugar Beet Scandal', Liberal Publication Department leaflets, n.d. [late 1920s].

the assumption of a basically orderly and tranquil world.'[122] In micro-economics, Piero Sraffa, Joan Robinson, and Edward Chamberlin were only beginning to shake the primacy of the idea of the perfectly competitive market; in macroeconomics, as Robert Skidelsky has shown, 'Keynes rejected laissez-faire as a policy before he developed a convincing economic theory explaining why laissez-faire would not work.'[123] Classical precepts, as modified by the neoclassical economists, continued to provide the parameters within which economic debate was joined. As long as this was the case, the Liberal Party's support for state intervention and fiscal activism was bound to be somewhat contingent, and open to revision in the light of changing circumstances.

[122] G. L. S. Shackle, *The Years of High Theory: Invention and Tradition in Economic Thought, 1926–1939* (Cambridge, 1967), 5.
[123] Skidelsky, *Keynes*, ii, 219.

2

The Liberals, Keynes, and the Slump, 1929–31

The Yellow Book reads like a compendium of the economic expertise of the 1920s, but it had a highly political purpose: to give intellectual credibility to the revival of Liberal fortunes which Lloyd George was trying to set in motion. On the eve of the 1929 general election, it was joined by a striking pledge to 'conquer unemployment' within one year through loan-financed public works, which can be seen in retrospect as a landmark in the development of a Keynesian policy approach. Although the hoped-for Liberal revival only half-materialized, Lloyd George and his colleagues emerged from the election holding the balance of power. Moreover, when economic malaise gave way to financial and political crisis in 1931, the Liberals would play a central role in the fall of Ramsay MacDonald's Labour administration and the formation of a National Government. These years were difficult, even traumatic ones for Liberal politicians and activists, but there can be no doubt that the party occupied centre stage.

Political debate in the 1929 Parliament was dominated by the unemployment question, joined during 1931 by the linked issue of public finance. Following on from Lloyd George's pledge, the Liberals focussed their energies on pressing the case for public works on the Labour government, and only on rare occasions—such as the debate over the Coal Mines Bill in 1929–30—did they gain the opportunity to promote the broader reorganization proposals outlined in the Yellow Book. In this sense, the constructive Liberal agenda of 1928 was narrowed at an early stage to the question of whether domestic reflation could be undertaken successfully. It is therefore inevitable that this chapter should focus on macroeconomic themes.

Lloyd George's 1929 unemployment policy and Liberal involvement in the formation of the National Government have attracted significant scholarly attention to the party in this period. In his seminal 1967 study of *Politicians and the Slump*, Robert Skidelsky held up *We Can Conquer Unemployment* as the sort of proto-Keynesian policy which could have mitigated the depression, if only MacDonald and his colleagues had taken it up. John Campbell set the policy in the context of Lloyd George's tortuous efforts to regain office in *Lloyd George: The Goat in the Wilderness*, and Peter Clarke showed how John Maynard Keynes' involvement in Liberal policy-making shaped his own economic thought in *The Keynesian Revolution in the Making*.[1] However, the sharp contrast which Skidelsky drew between the Liberal Party's radicalism and the Labour government's caution has been undermined by subsequent research. In an important 1975 article, Ross McKibbin convincingly argued that the intellectual and institutional obstacles to the adoption of a radical reflationary policy in 1929–31—the theoretical immaturity of Keynesian ideas, ingrained assumptions about the need to balance the budget and keep sterling on the gold standard, and the power of the Bank of England and the Treasury—were much more formidable than Skidelsky had recognized. MacDonald and his colleagues accordingly deserved a more sympathetic judgment.[2] During the 1980s and early 1990s, the Liberal Party's attachment to radical economic policies also came under greater scrutiny, as Michael Hart, Andrew Thorpe, and Philip Williamson highlighted the depth of Liberal divisions in the 1929 Parliament and the hold which the Gladstonian canons of sound finance, free trade, and the gold standard retained over many Liberals' thinking.[3] Long before financial crisis hit in August 1931, Thorpe argued, the party had set aside its 1929 policy and reverted to 'an unreconstructed and unattractive Gladstonianism'.[4]

The belief that Liberal support for public works was shallow and short-lived pervades the recent historiography of the 1931 crisis. In some cases, historians have gone even further, and argued that the party's advocacy of a proto-Keynesian programme in 1929 was essentially insincere. According to Herbert Samuel's biographer, Bernard Wasserstein, Lloyd George's 'eclectic, unorthodox, opportunist mind' found public works inherently attractive, but the Liberal leader 'no more believed in Keynesianism on principle than the Celt in him believed in leprechauns'. Samuel, meanwhile, 'paid lip-service' to the Yellow Book, but 'his economic thinking remained fundamentally unaffected by Keynes'.[5] In a

[1] John Campbell, *Lloyd George: The Goat in the Wilderness, 1922–1931* (1977); Peter Clarke, *The Keynesian Revolution in the Making, 1924–1936* (Oxford, 1988).

[2] Ross McKibbin, 'The economic policy of the second Labour government, 1929–1931', *Past and Present*, lxviii (1975), 95–123.

[3] Michael Hart, 'The Decline of the Liberal Party in Parliament and in the Constituencies, 1914–1931' (Oxford D.Phil. thesis, 1982); Andrew Thorpe, *The British General Election of 1931* (Oxford, 1991); Philip Williamson, *National Crisis and National Government: British Politics, the Economy and Empire, 1926–1932* (Cambridge, 1992).

[4] Thorpe, *1931*, 62.

[5] Bernard Wasserstein, *Herbert Samuel: A Political Life* (Oxford, 1992), 312.

similar vein, Duncan Tanner singled out Samuel, Sir Donald Maclean, and Sir John Simon as three Liberal leaders who, though publicly endorsing the national development plans, 'had not believed in them for a moment'. In consequence, Tanner argued,

> The Liberals' support for Keynesian proposals did not result from a unique receptiveness to new ideas (by contrast with the hide bound old Labour party). It stemmed from political desperation. Unhappy with proposals for increased expenditure, most Liberals dropped Keynes as quickly as possible after the 1929 election, and not simply because circumstances were changing.[6]

A slightly different version of this argument accepts Lloyd George's sincerity, but emphasizes the extent to which the Yellow Book, the unemployment pledge, and the attempt to develop an alliance with the Labour government were personal initiatives to which other Liberals were only weakly committed. This interpretation emerges especially from Ross McKibbin's recent survey of *Parties and People*, and fits well with his argument that the National Government's formation and the 1931 Liberal split transformed the three-party system of the 1920s into a polarized system dominated by an anti-socialist bloc. According to McKibbin, discontent with Lloyd George's leadership reflected the fact that the party had fought the 1929 election 'on a programme neither the majority of its voters nor its MPs believed in', and the 'fundamentally anti-socialist' orientation of most MPs and activists meant that Sir John Simon, not Lloyd George, was 'the representative Liberal leader'.[7] It was therefore entirely natural both that the Liberals would insist on an orthodox policy when financial crisis hit in August 1931, and that half the party's MPs would follow Simon into a permanent alliance with the Conservatives at the October general election.

This chapter reconstructs economic debates within the Liberal Party during the 1929 Parliament in order to assess the merits of the foregoing interpretation. It shows that Liberal politicians did revert to a classical analysis during the depression, but that much of the party did so gradually and reluctantly and remained committed to the idea that public works could alleviate unemployment in certain circumstances. The vocal espousal of restorationist principles by the Liberal Council, and Lloyd George's political need to keep right-wing Liberals on side, help explain the party's emphasis on retrenchment during the spring and summer of 1931, but the practical difficulties involved in carrying through

[6] Duncan Tanner, 'The strange death of Liberal England', *HJ*, xxxvii (1994), 971–9, at 975, 977.

[7] Ross McKibbin, *Parties and People: England, 1914–1951* (Oxford, 2010), 67, 92.

fiscal reflation during an economic crisis were hardly less important. In other words, Liberal economic radicalism was not wholly insincere, and foundered not only on internal division but also on the immaturity of the developing Keynesian alternative and growing awareness of the policy constraints which the British government faced.

WE CAN CONQUER UNEMPLOYMENT AND THE 1929 GENERAL ELECTION

The 1929 general election campaign was dominated by Lloyd George's pledge that, if returned to government, the Liberals would reduce unemployment to 'normal proportions' within one year by means of a £250,000,000 programme of loan-financed public works, without additional cost to the taxpayer. The possibility of reducing unemployment through national development works had been discussed in *Britain's Industrial Future*, and it seems to have been Seebohm Rowntree, who chaired the party's Unemployment Committee, who came up with the idea of making a specific time-limited commitment.[8] This idea was taken up by Lloyd George as a means of attracting voters' attention during the election, and especially of winning working-class voters back from Labour.[9] The committee's detailed proposals, written up by Rowntree's assistant William Wallace, were published under the title *We Can Conquer Unemployment*, and Keynes and Hubert Henderson wrote a spirited pamphlet, *Can Lloyd George Do It?*, which affirmed the pledge's practicability.[10]

Peter Clarke has called attention to the fact that the economic justification which Keynes offered for national development works evolved significantly between the publication of *We Can Conquer Unemployment* in March 1929 and the general election in May, in the face of the intellectual assault mounted on the pledge by ministers and Treasury officials.[11] *We Can Conquer Unemployment* suggested that government investment would increase employment by causing frozen savings, which had accumulated in banks as time deposits during the years of depression, to be directed to more productive uses. By the spring of 1929, however, Keynes was well aware of the limitations of this argument, and began to argue

[8] Stewart Faulkes, 'The Strange Death of British Liberalism: The Liberal Summer School Movement and the Making of the Yellow Book in the 1920s' (London Ph.D. thesis, 2000), 276.

[9] Williamson, *National Crisis*, 29–30.

[10] Liberal Party, *We Can Conquer Unemployment: Mr Lloyd George's Pledge* (1929); J. M. Keynes and H. D. Henderson, *Can Lloyd George Do It? An Examination of the Liberal Pledge* (1929).

[11] This paragraph is based on Clarke, *Keynesian Revolution*, 83–102.

instead that aggregate investment had to be brought into equilibrium with savings. One way of achieving this was to impose a temporary embargo on foreign loans; another was to raise Bank Rate, and so make domestic investment more attractive. At the same time, Keynes was feeling his way towards the idea which Richard Kahn would shortly conceptualize as the multiplier effect: that an initial government investment in national development projects would generate new resources for consumption and investment through successive rounds of spending.

During the 1920s, Keynes frequently suggested that he regarded public works as a second-best strategy for economic recovery, made necessary by the inflexibility of wages and other production costs. In principle, the best means of eliminating the abnormal unemployment which had developed since 1920 was a reduction in money wages to make the export industries more competitive, but this was likely to be resisted furiously by the trade unions, and in any case Keynes doubted whether wage cuts would or could be implemented on an equitable basis.[12] In working out theoretical foundations for Lloyd George's pledge, Keynes seems to have become more firmly convinced of the intellectual deficiencies of the orthodox approach as well as of its impracticality. If a public works programme could stimulate cumulative rounds of spending leading to the restoration of prosperity, perhaps this offered the *first-best* rather than the *second-best* solution to unemployment. This was more or less where Keynes ended up by the time he drafted the *General Theory* in the mid-1930s, his earlier doubts about classical theory having been buttressed by his development of the concept of the liquidity trap and the theory of effective demand.[13]

The specificity of Lloyd George's pledge, its reliance on loan finance, and its implicit invocation of a multiplier effect marked it out from earlier public works proposals. Nevertheless, the 1929 Liberal programme is best regarded as a proto-Keynesian one, because it stopped short of the *General Theory* in several important respects. Firstly, the Liberal pledge was presented as an emergency policy for dealing with abnormal unemployment in the context of economic rigidities, and Lloyd George remained convinced that 'the permanent problem' of unemployment could only be solved 'by the restoration of our general trade'.[14] Secondly, the case for public works was conditional on their likely impact on business and financial confidence. Keynes and Henderson argued that public works would

[12] Robert Skidelsky, *John Maynard Keynes* (3 vols, 1983–2001), ii, 202, 297.

[13] Clarke, *Keynesian Revolution*, 256–310.

[14] Liberal Party, *We Can Conquer Unemployment*, 6–8; David Lloyd George, speech in London, 1 March 1929, quoted in Hansard, HC (series 5) vol. 226, col. 2200 (25 March 1929).

create 'a mood favourable to enterprise and capital extensions' in the economic circumstances then prevailing, but they did not claim such a policy would be appropriate in every situation.[15] Thirdly, to defuse allegations of financial unsoundness, Lloyd George played down the net spending increase which the programme involved, and framed it as a *transfer* of resources from unemployment benefit payments to 'productive' public works.[16] Finally, Lloyd George's emphasis on the practical value of investment in roads, telephones, and agriculture made it possible to conceive of public works as a supply-side measure, which would 'equip [the nation] for successfully competing with all its rivals in the business of the world'.[17] In this sense, the new Liberal proposals stood firmly within the party's existing discourse of 'national development'.

In retrospect, there are good reasons for questioning whether Lloyd George's pledge was achievable. Econometric models of the likely impact of the £250,000,000 investment programme have produced widely varying results, but the weight of opinion suggests that it would have been too small to eliminate abnormal unemployment in one year, especially given the countervailing impact of the Wall Street Crash and the practical difficulties involved in putting men to work on infrastructure schemes.[18] Perhaps more damagingly, Roger Middleton has pointed out the difficulties which the Liberals would have faced in carrying through a large fiscal stimulus without imposing restrictions on trade and exchange, or leaving the gold standard. Strong import demand and unprecedented peacetime borrowing might well have caused 'a capital flight of gigantic proportions'.[19] It was partly for this reason that Keynes became an advocate of tariffs and import controls in 1930.

Despite these objective shortcomings, Lloyd George's pledge was well-received by most of the Liberal Party—or, at least, by that section of it which accepted his leadership. Candidates and activists were no doubt attracted by the electoral potential of a radical employment policy, but they also seem to have been impressed by the economic arguments advanced by Keynes and the party's other advisers, whether or not they fully understood them. An analysis of election addresses by E. A. Rowe has shown that all Liberal candidates mentioned unemployment, and no fewer than 79 per cent of them gave the issue special emphasis, compared with 47 per cent of their Labour and 30 per cent of their Conservative counterparts. Fifty-two

15 Keynes and Henderson, *Can Lloyd George Do It?*, 25.

16 *MG*, 27 March 1929, 5.

17 *MG*, 2 March 1929, 13.

18 For a recent overview of this literature, see Roger Middleton, 'British monetary and fiscal policy in the 1930s', *Oxford Review of Economic Policy*, xxvi (2010), 414–41.

19 Roger Middleton, *Towards the Managed Economy: Keynes, the Treasury, and the Fiscal Policy Debate of the 1930s* (1985), 179.

per cent of Liberals also mentioned Lloyd George's pledge directly, whilst 37 per cent emphasized that the party's plans were 'detailed' and 'expert'.[20] The evidence available suggests that most active Liberals supported the pledge, in many cases enthusiastically. Public criticism emanated mainly from the party's Asquithian elite and other Gladstonian traditionalists.[21]

The position of the Asquithian elite deserves careful elucidation. It seems clear that most members of this group inclined towards classical restorationism, and shared in the scepticism towards public works which was prevalent in Whitehall: in particular, they doubted that public works could be organized quickly, and feared that they would exacerbate unemployment by damaging business confidence.[22] Walter Runciman and Sir John Simon were the best-known exponents of this position. Speaking at Penzance in August 1928, Runciman argued that Britain's economic malaise could largely be attributed to the post-war growth of public spending, which had damaged the nation's credit and kept the rate of interest high; later in the year, he told the Commons that the 'large public works' previously undertaken had 'brought very little return', and the nation had 'passed from the stage' where public works could solve the unemployment problem.[23] Similarly, Simon used a speech in September to warn that the Liberals would look 'like a cheap-jack in a fair' if they claimed to offer a 'patent remedy' to 'sweep away unemployment without question and without delay', a comment which Conservative propagandists would quote extensively during the election campaign.[24] However, both Runciman and Simon were willing to accept public works as *part* of an unemployment policy, especially if they were remunerative and helped to reduce industry's costs; and this common ground allowed them to smooth over their differences with Lloyd George as the election neared. Runciman offered a qualified endorsement of the Liberal proposals, noting that well-conceived development schemes could 'mop up . . . surplus labour, add to the national wealth, and increase our national equipment', whilst Simon was impressed by *Can Lloyd George Do It?* and extolled the virtues of public works in a radio broadcast.[25]

[20] E. A. Rowe, 'The British General Election of 1929' (Oxford B.Litt. thesis, 1959), 198, 208.

[21] For instance, J. E. Allen and Sir Charles Mallet in *The Times*, 21 March 1929, 12, and 25 April 1929, 17. Francis Hirst was more conciliatory: see *MG*, 4 March 1929, 12.

[22] The importance of these practical considerations in the 'Treasury view' has been highlighted by Jim Tomlinson and Roger Middleton: Jim Tomlinson, *Problems of British Economic Policy 1870–1945* (1981), 76–91; Middleton, *Towards the Managed Economy*, 149–65.

[23] *The Times*, 4 August 1928, 14; Hansard, HC (series 5) vol. 222, cols 273–82, at 275 (8 November 1928).

[24] *The Scotsman*, 4 September 1928, 8.

[25] *MG*, 12 March 1929, 7, and 28 May 1929, 4; Jason G. Howard, 'The British General Election of 1929' (Cambridge Ph.D. thesis, 1999), 211.

The logic of the Asquithian position was neatly stated by Sir Donald Maclean in a March 1929 speech at Launceston. Maclean distinguished between the *policy* of national development and Lloyd George's *pledge*, declaring that the policy itself was sound but that he was not prepared to predict how many jobs could be created within a given time frame.[26] This was very similar to the stance which *The Economist* had taken, and after Viscount Grey echoed it on 10 April—with the caveat that public works should not 'prejudice' private-sector expansion by disturbing 'the money market or the labour market'—it became the conventional Liberal Council line.[27] Mackenzie Livingstone, who had represented the Western Isles since 1923, retired from Parliament in protest at the pledge, and the Council's honorary secretary, Vivian Phillipps, was almost deselected as candidate for West Edinburgh because of his vocal criticism of it, but these were exceptional cases.[28] Most Asquithian candidates sidestepped the pledge and emphasized the party's long interest in national development with varying degrees of enthusiasm.[29] Up to a point, this was electoral hedging, motivated by a desire to maximize the Liberal Council contingent in the new Parliament and avoid being blamed for electoral failure; but it is also indicative of the fact that the party's division was at root one of personality rather than policy. The fundamental obstacle to Liberal unity was neither the unemployment policy nor even the 'gimmicky' pledge, but Lloyd George's leadership, the influence of his ill-gotten fund, and the belief that he was liable to abandon the party's principles for political advantage.[30]

HOW TO TACKLE UNEMPLOYMENT

The electoral impact of the unemployment pledge fell far short of what the Liberal leadership had hoped, especially in industrial areas, where Labour performed very well. Michael Hart has concluded from this 'that Keynesian economics was, as yet, no match for the class-consciousness of labour/trade unionism'; Philip Williamson, that the Conservative and

[26] *The Times*, 28 March 1929, 16.

[27] Liberal Council, *Report of the Annual Meeting. . . 1929* (1929), 4–16, at 9. For *The Economist*'s judgment, see *Economist*, 9 March 1929, 487.

[28] *MG*, 25 April 1929, 5; *The Scotsman*, 4 April 1929, 8.

[29] Bodleian Library, Oxford, Conservative Party Archive, PUB 229/5 (election addresses, 1929), 14/42 (Barbara Bliss, East Grinstead), 14/80 (F. C. Thornborough, Swindon), and 18/74 (Godfrey Collins, Greenock).

[30] Barbara Bliss in *New Outlook*, no. 59 (November 1966), 34–7, at 35.

Labour leaderships successfully portrayed the pledge as an election stunt which Lloyd George could not be trusted to carry out.[31] Overall, Labour won 287 seats, the Conservatives 260, and the Liberals fifty-nine—one of which was lost immediately when William Jowitt agreed to become MacDonald's Attorney-General. Lloyd George had achieved his minimum objective of holding the balance, but the other leaders' determination to avoid negotiating with him meant that the Liberals remained on the opposition benches. In private, Lloyd George revealed a willingness to abandon the idea of loan-financed public works, but publicly he pressed it strongly on the new Labour Cabinet; indeed, Liberal criticisms of the government revolved around its poor unemployment record.[32] Even if, as Williamson suggests, '[t]he Liberal leadership's politics were about survival. . . and only conditionally about economic radicalism', the 1929 election campaign had woven the idea that government could reduce unemployment firmly into the party's political identity, and it could not easily be removed.[33]

Lloyd George had hoped to work constructively with a Labour government, but MacDonald's intransigence left him in a reactive posture as he tried to force it to come to terms. For the first year of the new Parliament, Lloyd George engaged in tactical manoeuvring which exposed the Liberal Party's divisions and alienated MPs who should have been his allies. Part of the problem was poor communication with the parliamentary party: for example, Williamson believes that Lloyd George's objective during the Coal Mines Bill debates in the winter of 1929–30 was to force the government to acknowledge its need for Liberal support, but left-wing Liberal MPs such as Ernest Simon feared that he was trying to bring the government down.[34] At the same time, Runciman and other Asquithian MPs sought to sabotage Lloyd George's strategy by voting repeatedly with Labour.[35] Disaffection came to a head at parliamentary party meetings in March 1930, after Lloyd George had controversially decided to abandon opposition to the Coal Mines Bill, and in July, after he had imposed a party line on the Finance Bill which would have caused the government's defeat if Liberal backbenchers had not rebelled.[36] Thereafter, Lloyd George's pursuit of an arrangement with Labour became somewhat more open, and opposition to his leadership came increasingly from right

[31] Hart, 'Decline', 363; Philip Williamson, '"Safety first": Baldwin, the Conservative Party, and the 1929 general election', *HJ*, xxv (1982), 385–409.

[32] Williamson, *National Crisis*, 109; Hansard, HC (series 5) vol. 231, cols 657–770 (4 November 1929).

[33] Williamson, *National Crisis*, 31.

[34] Williamson, *National Crisis*, 110.

[35] Jonathan Wallace, 'The Political Career of Walter Runciman, 1st Viscount Runciman of Doxford (1870–1949)' (Newcastle upon Tyne Ph.D. thesis, 1995), 309–23.

[36] Manchester Archives, Ernest Simon papers, M11/11/5, Parliamentary Diary 1929–33, section A, fols 21–2, entry for 10 July 1930.

wingers who opposed a Lib–Lab alliance; but his earlier manoeuvrings had permanently damaged confidence in his leadership, and dissipated much of the sense of moral purpose which had characterized the party's 1929 election campaign.

The winter of 1929–30 witnessed a ballooning of unemployment in Britain, resulting from the international economic contraction which followed the Wall Street Crash. W. R. Garside, using Charles Feinstein's statistics, estimates that the total number of unemployed workers in Britain rose from an average of 1,503,000 in 1929 to 2,379,000 in 1930—an increase of more than 50 per cent.[37] The increased scale of the unemployment problem, and concern that loan-financed public works might damage rather than improve business confidence, prompted a renewed focus on the classical diagnosis of Britain's post-war malaise. Asquithian traditionalists, such as Viscount Grey, predictably revived their calls for orthodox policies, but concerns about private-sector confidence now extended well beyond these usual suspects.[38] Even Keynes, who had redirected his energies from the Liberal Party to the government's Economic Advisory Committee, seems to have grown more pessimistic about public works by the summer of 1930, believing that 'the effect of [the Liberal national development schemes] on unemployment and business psychology would be very small compared with what their effect would have been before the world depression began'.[39] Keynes' preferred solution at this stage was to introduce a temporary revenue tariff so that British producers could gain the domestic market, a course of action which free-trade Liberals were unwilling to contemplate.

It was in this economic climate that MacDonald invited the Liberals to discuss unemployment and agricultural policy with the government in June 1930. The Liberals held several meetings with ministers and officials during the summer and early autumn and, after the discussions broke down, published revised proposals under the title of *How to Tackle Unemployment* in October.[40] Significantly, Lloyd George did not really engage Liberal MPs in this process, nor did he turn to the Liberal Summer School. Instead, he enlisted Seebohm Rowntree and Lord Lothian, a Liberal peer and former member of his wartime 'garden suburb', to assist him in bringing the previous year's plans up to date, and engaged the young lecturer

[37] W. R. Garside, *British Unemployment, 1919–1939: A Study in Public Policy* (Cambridge, 1990), 5.

[38] Liberal Council, *Report of the Annual Meeting . . . 1930* (1930), 10–14.

[39] National Archives of Scotland, Lothian papers, GD40/17/140/456–8, 'The Views of Mr J. M. Keynes', memorandum by G. C. Allen, n.d. [summer 1930], at fol. 458.

[40] On these policy discussions see David Marquand, *Ramsay MacDonald* (1977), 543–70, and the correspondence and papers in TNA: PRO, T 161/303 and PREM 1/108.

G. C. Allen as an economic adviser. Allen's task was to look over preliminary proposals which Lloyd George, Lothian, and Rowntree had sketched out and to solicit the opinions of 'distinguished professional economists' on the unemployment question.[41] During the summer of 1930 he sounded out Keynes, Henderson, Edwin Cannan, Ralph Hawtrey, Henry Clay, Sir Josiah Stamp, and several Liberal merchant bankers. Sir Arthur Salter, the former head of the League of Nations' economic section, also provided advice via Lord Lothian.

Allen began his enquiries 'deeply pessimistic' about the impact public works could have on unemployment, and the economic opinions he gathered confirmed his pessimism.[42] For Cannan and Salter, mass unemployment mainly reflected the rigidity of the British economy, and the only solution was to make it more flexible by reducing taxation, reforming unemployment insurance, and persuading the trade unions to accept wage cuts.[43] Clay, who was working at the Bank of England, accepted the theoretical case for public works but was impressed by the practical difficulties, and placed more faith in the reduction of costs and rationalization of the basic industries.[44] As we have seen, Keynes also seemed to be moving away from the 1929 programme. The Liberal bankers, meanwhile, emphasized the need for public economy, and for the government to pursue policies which would maintain confidence in sterling.[45]

Lord Lothian shared Allen's scepticism about public works, as he indicated in a memorandum for Lloyd George, because he felt that 'palliatives, short-cuts, and "raids"' would not deal with the fundamental causes of depression. Lothian believed that high wage levels, high taxation, and the expansion of the social services were sapping 'the vitality of the productive machine', and had little confidence that public works could stimulate private-sector employment:

> A programme of public works, however well devised, cannot save or vitally improve the position unless at the same time the mainsprings of private enterprise are functioning freely. Public works can act as a balancing wheel and can improve the general national equipment in certain important and well defined fields. But the vital thing is the buoyancy of the great machine

[41] G. C. Allen, 'Economic advice for Lloyd George', in G. C. Allen, *British Industry and Economic Policy* (1979), 196–207, at 200.

[42] Allen, 'Economic advice', 200.

[43] Lothian papers, GD40/17/134/129–38, 'Sir Arthur Salter's Memo', n.d. [June 1930].

[44] Lothian papers, GD40/17/135/156–7, Clay to Lothian, 12 August 1930, and GD40/17/135/158–67, 'Committee on Finance and Industry. Memorandum by Professor Henry Clay on Unemployment Since the War', 3 July 1930.

[45] Allen, 'Economic advice', 204.

> of private enterprise, which can absorb or throw out of work hundreds of thousands of men and women in a few weeks, according to whether it is active or stagnant.[46]

In a second memorandum, Lothian added that Britain risked being pulled into a vicious cycle of rising unemployment benefit rolls and a rising tax burden, which might provoke a flight from sterling. The contemporary economic crisis which Australia was experiencing seemed to demonstrate the consequences of failing to bring production costs down.[47]

The strategy for economic recovery which emerged in *How to Tackle Unemployment* was an awkward hybrid between the 1929 proposals and the classical approach which Allen and Lothian's advice implied. The Liberals continued to advocate a bold public works policy to deal with the cyclical element in unemployment and the decline of agriculture, and claimed that £250,000,000 of loan-financed investment in roads, agriculture, regional development, housing, and telephones would directly create 650,000 jobs within a year of implementation—despite the government's insistence that such a programme was wholly unrealistic.[48] The 'refractory million' of structural unemployment which Britain had experienced since the war, however, could only be dealt with by reducing production costs in order to restore the competitiveness of British exports. The Liberals proposed that firms should seek to reduce their costs by 10 per cent or more through rationalization, efficiency measures, and the abolition of restrictive practices, and that the government should give a lead by cutting public spending by one-tenth, reforming the tax system, and tackling the growing cost of unemployment benefit.[49] Skidelsky has claimed that the spending cut 'was by no means an integral part of the policy' but merely a concession to concern about business confidence, yet this is unconvincing: Allen later recalled that a direct attack on wage rates was omitted only because Lloyd George knew the Labour government would not accept it.[50] It is difficult to avoid the conclusion that the orthodox analysis of unemployment was regaining its hold on Liberal thinking as faith in the effectiveness of public works diminished.

46 Lothian papers, GD40/17/134/88–116, memorandum by Lothian on the unemployment problem, 10 June 1930, at fols 88, 98, 103.

47 Lothian papers, GD40/17/135/185–96, 'Unemployment', memorandum by Lothian, 1 September 1930, at fol. 195.

48 David Lloyd George, the Marquess of Lothian, and B. Seebohm Rowntree, *How to Tackle Unemployment: The Liberal Plans as laid before the Government and the Nation* (1930), 85–7; TNA: PRO, PREM 1/108/290–9, MacDonald to Lloyd George, 10 October 1930.

49 Lloyd George et al., *How to Tackle Unemployment*, 7–31.

50 Skidelsky, *Politicians*, 227; Allen, 'Economic advice', 205–6. This point has been recognized by Michael Hart: Hart, 'Decline', 380.

Despite this shift, the Liberal Party's public commitment to national development had been recast rather than abandoned. Lloyd George used the annual meetings of the NLF at Torquay in October 1930 to report on his discussions with the government, and emphasized that there was no inherent contradiction between capital investment and public economy.[51] In the debate on national development, the East Dorset MP Alec Glassey made a homely call for the government to adopt the Liberal plans:

> We are shivering with cold when there's coal in the cellar, wood on the pile, and matches on the chimney shelf. The Liberal proposals are to lay a fire in the grate and put a match to it.[52]

James Blindell, MP for Holland-with-Boston and a future Liberal National, predicted that this policy would form 'the basis of the Party's next appeal to the country'.[53] In political terms, at least, there was no turning back.

THE FRIENDS OF ECONOMY AND THE 'LANDSLIDE TOWARDS PROTECTION'

Although *How to Tackle Unemployment* seems to have been well received by NLF delegates, not all Liberals were willing to support Lloyd George's policy. Two major challenges emerged during the course of 1930. Firstly, Grey's criticism of post-war public spending at the Liberal Council annual meeting in January sparked a movement for public economy which gained momentum among City Liberals during the year.[54] In July, *The Times* printed a 'Manifesto on National Economy' signed by eleven—mostly Liberal—businessmen, financiers, and journalists, including Sir Hugh Bell and Lords Cowdray and Leverhulme, and Sir Ernest Benn began to construct a non-party 'Friends of Economy' campaign, which would call attention to the dangers of rising government spending.[55] The Friends of Economy movement was finally launched in January 1931, in parallel with a Liberal Council campaign run by Harcourt Johnstone, which had Grey and Runciman at its head. The two initiatives were poorly coordinated, but both served to demonstrate the purchase which classical ideas still enjoyed among the Liberal elite.[56]

Grey and Runciman's antipathy to Lloyd George was so well known that they posed little direct threat to his leadership. In any case, Grey was

[51] *NLF Proceedings, 1930* (1930), 37–55. [52] *NLF Proceedings, 1930*, 32.
[53] *NLF Proceedings, 1930*, 33. [54] *MG*, 15 January 1930, 5.
[55] *The Times*, 16 July 1930, 9, and 7 August 1930, 12.
[56] University of Bristol Special Collections, Liberal Council papers, Executive Committee minute book, 1927–37, minutes of meeting, 21 January 1931.

nearly seventy and going blind, whilst Runciman was increasingly preoccupied by his business interests and announced in February 1931 that he would not stand for Parliament again.[57] Sir John Simon, who had held himself aloof from the Liberal Council, was a much more credible potential leader. Simon had suspended his doubts about public works during the 1929 election campaign, but his economic instincts were conservative, and by 1930 he was perturbed by Lloyd George's pursuit of a Lib–Lab arrangement.[58] As a strong critic of trade union power, Simon was especially alarmed at the prospect that Lloyd George might allow the government to repeal the 1927 Trade Disputes Act in exchange for electoral reform. In October 1930 Simon wrote to Lloyd George, declaring that the protracted effort to win policy concessions from MacDonald had proved fruitless and that he had lost confidence in the government; in November he led four other Liberal MPs—including erstwhile chief whip Sir Robert Hutchison—in support of a Conservative motion of censure; and shortly afterwards he used a speech in his Spen Valley constituency to advocate 'drastic and vigorous economy'.[59] Simon amplified his call for retrenchment in January 1931, when he told a meeting at South Molton in Devon that rising spending, taxes and debt were hampering recovery. In particular, the unemployment insurance scheme had to be restored to an actuarial basis in order to lighten the burden on the taxpayer.[60]

From the offices of the Liberal Council, Johnstone and Phillipps urged Simon to join their economy campaign.[61] Backed by the prestige of Grey and Runciman, and committed to restoring the party 'to its old standard of straightness and honour', Simon could 'leave Ll.-G. standing with a mere rump of venal hangers-on'.[62] Simon, however, was an ambitious man, and seems to have viewed Asquithian intrigue as a futile endeavour. Instead, Simon was already discussing with Neville Chamberlain the possibility of developing a bloc of right-leaning Liberal MPs, who would help defeat the government and install the Conservatives in office.[63] The price of cooperation with the Conservatives was support for protection, but Simon was willing to compromise on this point. 'I have not been dogmatic over economic policy', he explained to his friend Lord Inchcape, 'for I do

57 Williamson, *National Crisis*, 212.

58 David Dutton, *Simon: A Political Biography of Sir John Simon* (1992), 102.

59 *MG*, 6 November 1930, 9, and 17 November 1930, 14; *The Times*, 17 November 1930, 19.

60 *LM*, xxxix (1931), 122–4.

61 Bodleian Library, MS. Simon 249, fol. 102, Phillipps and Johnstone to Simon, 1 December 1930.

62 MS. Simon 249, fol. 110, Phillipps to D. R. Evans, 16 December 1930.

63 MS. Simon 249, fols 45–6, note by Simon, 1 December 1930.

feel I want here to get an impartial survey and fresh guidance from those who know.'[64]

The tariff issue posed the second challenge to Lloyd George's policy. By the autumn of 1930, free traders were alarmed by indications of growing support for protection, including the apparent success of Lord Beaverbrook's Empire Crusade, a 'Bankers' Manifesto' in favour of tariffs, and signs of disillusionment with free trade in the trade union movement.[65] This 'landslide to protection' mostly took place outside the Liberal Party, but Liberals were not wholly immune to it. Most significantly, the 1930 Liberal Summer School witnessed a robust debate over protection, sparked by Ernest Simon's suggestion that buying a British-made motor car, rather than an American-made one, was bound to have a beneficial effect on domestic employment. Simon's choice of example was telling, since Britain's motor industry, covered by the McKenna duties, was one of the few industries that had visibly benefited from protection during the 1920s. Moreover, as Frank Trentmann has pointed out, Edwardian tariff reformers had used the motor car to symbolize the modernity of their cause.[66]

Ernest Simon's critique of orthodox free-trade theory may be viewed as an extension of constructive Liberal thinking to the trade question. Sir Walter Layton insisted that buying a British rather than an American-made car would have no impact on employment, but Keynes told Simon that this was 'obviously absurd'; J. A. Hobson also endorsed Simon's iconoclasm, and even Ted Scott of the *Manchester Guardian* felt that Simon had identified a weak point in the free-trade case.[67] Simon believed that the existence of a 'permanent surplus of unemployed labour' made free-trade theory inapplicable, and suggested a temporary revenue tariff of 10 per cent.[68] Though he subsequently abandoned his call for a revenue tariff, Ernest Simon remained the most articulate left-wing critic of free trade in the Liberal Party, as the debate over renewal of the Dyestuffs Act in the winter of 1930–1 showed. He opposed the government's decision to allow the protective Dyestuffs Act, passed in 1920 for a ten-year period, to lapse, but failed to persuade the Liberal leadership to press for renewal. Simon was particularly frustrated by the attitude of deputy leader Sir Herbert

[64] MS. Simon 67, fols 23–4, Simon to Lord Inchcape, 21 November 1930, at fol. 23.

[65] Skidelsky, *Politicians*, 227–31.

[66] Frank Trentmann, *Free Trade Nation: Commerce, Consumption, and Civil Society in Modern Britain* (Oxford, 2008), 43, 323–4.

[67] E. D. Simon, 'Some questions about free trade', *Political Quarterly*, i (1930), 479–95, at 479; Trinity College Library, Cambridge, Layton papers, 75/21(2), Hobson to Simon, 21 October 1930, and 75/1, E. T. Scott to Layton, 5 August 1930.

[68] Simon, 'Some questions about free trade', 481, 490–2.

Samuel, whom he regarded as 'a 'religious' Free Trader of the worst type', 'utterly unable to consider a question of this sort scientifically and on its merits'.[69]

Samuel may have been a dogmatic free trader, but Lloyd George certainly was not. He consistently defended free trade as Liberal leader, but Asquithians did not forget that it was his coalition which had introduced safeguarding duties after the war, or that rumours of his conversion to protection had circulated widely in 1923 before Baldwin's decision to call a tariff election rallied him to the free-trade flag. The main reason Lloyd George's commitment to cheap food could never become 'religious' was that it was combined with a concern for agricultural prosperity and employment which urban Liberals—and economists—found difficult to understand.[70] The Liberals' growing reliance on agricultural constituencies, where they performed well in 1929 but were always vulnerable to protectionist sentiment, added an electoral dimension to this concern. During 1930 rural Liberal MPs called for new measures to ward off agricultural depression, and Lloyd George urged the Minister of Agriculture to investigate the 'dumping' of foodstuffs by foreign producers at below cost price.[71] These comments led some observers to believe, probably rightly, that the Liberal leader would accept tariffs if the political situation demanded.[72] Yet his dominant strategy in this period required him to emphasize the importance of free trade for economic recovery, not downplay it, and his sally against dumping is probably best seen as a tactical manoeuvre to defend an exposed position. Indeed, free trade would become a more prominent theme of Lloyd George's speeches as Lib–Lab cooperation intensified.

THE ECONOMICS OF A PROGRESSIVE BLOC

The months between the publication of *How to Tackle Unemployment* in October 1930 and the onset of financial and political crisis in the following summer saw the formation and consolidation of a semi-secret alliance between the Liberals and the Labour government, which moved forward

[69] Ernest Simon papers, M11/11/5, Parliamentary Diary 1929–33, section A, fol. 37, entry for 4 December 1930.

[70] Lothian papers, GD40/17/253/772–3, E. D. Simon to Lothian, 18 October 1930.

[71] *MG*, 22 March 1930, 17, and 20 November 1930, 15.

[72] MS. Simon 249, fols 18–27, 'The Fiscal Controversy in Relation to the Political Parties', memorandum by D. R. Evans, November 1930, at fol. 25; see also TNA: PRO, PREM 1/108/394–6, 'Luncheon with Mr. Lloyd George', note by Christopher Addison, 3 October 1930.

by fits and starts as Lloyd George secured the policy concessions he needed to make the arrangement palatable to his party. Frank Owen claimed in his 1954 biography of Lloyd George that, by the early summer of 1931, the Liberal leader expected to enter the Cabinet in an imminent reshuffle, creating a coalition government which perhaps two-thirds of Liberal MPs would have supported.[73] In line with Owen's claim, Philip Williamson has argued convincingly that the developing alliances between Lloyd George and MacDonald, on the one hand, and Sir John Simon and the Conservatives, on the other, pointed towards the emergence of a political system polarized around two blocs.[74] Lib–Lab cooperation was underpinned by the development of a shared approach to economic policy. At the same time, however, underlying differences of perspective meant that this alliance rested on fragile foundations.

In November 1930, following Simon and Hutchison's rebellion in the debate on the Address, Lloyd George and Samuel sought the support of Liberal MPs and peers for a formal two-year pact with the government, covering unemployment and agricultural policy, unemployment insurance, Trade Disputes Act repeal, and the alternative vote. This outline deal was not well received, and even when Lloyd George proposed a less ambitious one-year pact he could not secure enough support to make it worth pushing the issue to a vote.[75] However, it seems clear that many of those who disliked the idea of formal cooperation with Labour were still keen to avoid an election. Sir Donald Maclean, MP for North Cornwall, 'felt greatly perturbed at the probable result of an early Tory victory on Free Trade and Disarmament', and the Marquess of Crewe was 'prepared to contemplate some sort of bargain for the sake of Free Trade', while Isaac Foot and Sir John Tudor Walters, who opposed a time-limited pact, believed the Liberals should keep Labour in office provided it pursued an acceptable policy.[76] Similar sentiments were expressed by Liberal candidates and activists, and even—in the spring of 1931—by Viscount Grey, who was grudgingly impressed by Philip Snowden's efforts to control public spending.[77] The prospect of a formal pact

[73] Frank Owen, *Tempestuous Journey: Lloyd George, His Life and Times* (1954), 717.

[74] Williamson, *National Crisis*, 229–52.

[75] MS. Simon 249, fols 5–8 and 15–16, memoranda by Simon on meetings of leading Liberals, 20 and 27 November 1930.

[76] MS. Simon 249, fols 5–8, memorandum by Simon on meeting of leading Liberals, 20 November 1930, at fols 7–8; MS. Simon 249, fols 15–16, memorandum by Simon on meeting of leading Liberals, 27 November 1930.

[77] MS. Simon 249, fols 48–56, manuscript report of Liberal candidates' meeting, 4 December 1930; Manchester Archives, Lancashire, Cheshire and North Western Liberal Federation papers, M390/1/7, minute book, 1928–31, 'Report of Conference of Chairmen and Secretaries held 22 November 1930'; Liberal Council, *Report of the Annual Meeting . . . 1931* (1931), 6.

with Labour seemed likely to split the party, and Asquithians felt that Lloyd George's manoeuvrings made the party look like 'hucksters in the political market-place'.[78] Nevertheless, the threat which a Conservative victory posed to free trade provided a powerful justification for Lloyd George's general strategy.

The first months of 1931 witnessed fierce parliamentary clashes over Trade Disputes Act repeal, which ended in the withdrawal of the government's bill following a Liberal revolt in committee stage. *Inter alia*, this episode showed the reluctance of Liberal MPs to subordinate issues of principle to wider strategic aims, and allowed Sir John Simon to start cultivating a following among the party's dissidents.[79] At roughly the same time, however, Lloyd George was at last winning economic policy concessions from the government, reflecting both MacDonald's growing recognition of the parliamentary arithmetic and a new readiness on Lloyd George's part to play down his differences with Labour. Commons debates on retrenchment and unemployment on 11 and 12 February demonstrated how far the Liberal and Labour leaderships were prepared to coalesce around a shared short-term agenda. After Conservatives put down a motion for 11 February censuring the government for its failure to restrain the growth of public spending, the Liberals consulted with the Cabinet and then tabled an alternative motion which called for a committee to be established to propose economies. The Liberal motion, moved by Maclean, was carried with Labour support, and Sir George May was appointed as the committee's chairman. The establishment of the May Committee suited MacDonald and Snowden's needs, since it seemed likely to help them win Cabinet consent for a reduction in unemployment benefit spending; it also enabled Lloyd George to show Asquithians that their demands for public economy could be met in the framework of Lib–Lab cooperation.[80]

The debate on unemployment on 12 February revealed an even more striking rapprochement. Sir Herbert Samuel moved a motion which reiterated the Liberals' demand for national development works, but broke with the 1929 policy by declaring that the Liberals would be happy for the schemes to be financed piecemeal out of loans and economies, if it was felt that a large development loan would disturb the money markets. Samuel also stated emphatically that public works would have to be accompanied by 'a restoration of industry and the opening of foreign markets' if recovery

[78] Viscount Cowdray in Liberal Council, *Report of the Annual Meeting. . . 1931*, 4.
[79] Williamson, *National Crisis*, 203–13.
[80] Williamson, *National Crisis*, 218–22, 237–41.

was to be sustained in the long run.[81] Lloyd George acknowledged that the motion embodied 'substantially the same programme' as that outlined in Labour's 1928 manifesto *Labour and the Nation*, and it is quite reasonable to interpret this debate—as Philip Williamson does—as the point at which 'the Liberal leadership capitulated to the Labour position and buried *We Can Conquer Unemployment*'.[82] It should be emphasized, however, that the Liberals accepted the practical and intellectual framework for public works set by the Labour government precisely so that they could secure a significant expansion of activity within it. National development was still a Liberal cause; the difference was that Lloyd George was now committed to working with the government to put schemes into practice. Progress was slow in the face of budgetary constraints and mutual misunderstandings, but the government eventually agreed to take up a rural house-building scheme championed by Sir John Tudor Walters, which Lloyd George was able to hail as the first fruit of cooperation at the NLF annual meetings in May.[83]

Snowden attempted to cement the emerging alliance in his April budget by introducing a penny-in-the-pound annual tax on site values. At first this was welcomed by Liberals as an attempt to revive the spirit of 1909, but it backfired badly as its details became clear and by the end of May a vocal section of Liberal opinion was agitating against it. Sir John Simon complained that Snowden's tax failed to distinguish between unearned increment and the values which landowners created through their own enterprise, whilst Liverpool industrialist Sir Benjamin Johnson felt that it was 'a penal exercise in confiscation'.[84] Alarmed by the prospect of a full-blown Liberal revolt, Lloyd George declared that the 'double taxation' of land which had already been subject to income tax under Schedule A was unjust, and organized an amendment to the Finance Bill which would have allowed landowners to offset income tax payments against their land tax liability.[85] After a lengthy stand-off with the government, a compromise was reached in which the incidence of double taxation was

[81] Hansard, HC (series 5) vol. 248, cols 631–46, at 643 (12 February 1931).

[82] Hansard, HC (series 5) vol. 248, cols 725–34, at 728 (12 February 1931); Williamson, *National Crisis*, 209.

[83] TNA: PRO, HLG 68/21, Thomas Johnston to MacDonald, 1 April 1931; CAB 23/67/4, Cabinet conclusions, 20 May 1931; *MG*, 16 May 1931, 9. The Housing (Rural Authorities) Act 1931 was a more modest measure than Tudor Walters had hoped, but he chaired the Advisory Committee which oversaw its implementation before it was emasculated by the National Government: Hansard, HC (series 5) vol. 254, cols 2011–15 (7 July 1931), and vol. 255, col. 2446 (30 July 1931).

[84] *MG*, 20 May 1931, 9; *The Times*, 29 May 1931, 15. The Eighty Club of Liberal speakers also passed a critical resolution: *MG*, 19 June 1931, 18.

[85] *MG*, 12 June 1931, 9.

greatly reduced but the principle was not conceded. Sir John Simon, Sir Robert Hutchison, and Ernest Brown then resigned the Liberal whip in protest at the party's apparent humiliation, and several Liberal grandees including Lord Rosebery and Lord Stanley of Alderley announced their withdrawal from active politics.[86] Snowden and Lloyd George clearly mishandled the land tax proposals, but the fundamental problem was that Simon wanted a pretext for a split, while many elite Liberals were unwilling to accept the Georgist principle that land was different from other forms of property. The result was that a policy initiative which should have strengthened the Lib–Lab alliance instead temporarily destabilized it.

Sir John Simon's secession from the Liberal ranks over the land tax in June 1931 might have attracted a larger following if he had not converted to protection in March, on the grounds that a revenue tariff was necessary to balance the budget.[87] This move cut Simon off from most of his potential supporters, including Asquithians such as Grey and Maclean, and aided Lloyd George's efforts to clothe his pro-Labour strategy in the free-trade mantle. After facing down his critics at a party meeting in March and at the NLF meetings at Buxton in May, Lloyd George launched a national campaign in defence of free trade, and persuaded some erstwhile dissidents to participate in it.[88] A few free traders, most notably Ernest Brown, felt the land tax humiliation so keenly that they were prepared to follow Simon in June in spite of his altered fiscal views, but most of those who opposed Lib–Lab cooperation were repelled by Simon's new line: throwing over free trade in pursuit of an alliance with the Conservatives involved an even greater surrender of Liberal independence than Lloyd George's strategy implied.[89] Suspicion of Lloyd George ran deep, but it would be quite wrong to conclude from this, as Ross McKibbin does, that Simon had become '[t]he representative Liberal leader'.[90]

Liberal support (or consent) for Lloyd George's strategy in the spring of 1931 rested, then, on quite definite economic policy foundations: the defence of free trade and the emergence of compatible Liberal and government positions on public finance and national development. The crucial question is whether this policy convergence was likely to provide a permanent basis for cooperation; and this should probably be answered in the negative. The problem which confronted the Liberal and Labour leaders was not merely that disagreements over policy details (like the

[86] *The Observer*, 28 June 1931, 19; *The Times*, 26 June 1931, 14, and 3 July 1931, 9.

[87] *The Times*, 4 March 1931, 8.

[88] Churchill Archives Centre, Cambridge, Thurso papers, I 20/2, Sinclair to C. E. Taylor, 26 May 1931.

[89] For Brown's position, see *HDE*, 29 June 1931, 2.

[90] McKibbin, *Parties and People*, 92.

land tax) and external shocks (like the European financial crisis which developed in July) were liable to destabilize the Lib–Lab alliance, but that MacDonald and Snowden's belief in the necessity of retrenchment was not shared by the Labour Party at large. The May Committee's recommendations for spending cuts were due to appear over the summer, and there was clearly a significant gap between the response which the Liberal Party expected from Snowden and that which Labour MPs and the trade union movement would allow him to deliver.

THE MAY REPORT AND THE AUGUST CRISIS

In a sense, the crisis of August 1931 was the moment Lloyd George had feared and Sir John Simon had hoped for, when the incompatibility of the two parties' attitudes and instincts became starkly apparent. By August, however, neither Lloyd George nor Simon was really able to shape the party's behaviour directly: Simon had left the parliamentary party, stage right, and Lloyd George was bed-ridden, recuperating from a serious illness in late July and an operation to remove his prostate gland. The influence of both men was indirect, setting the political parameters within which the party's acting leader, Sir Herbert Samuel, and his colleagues acted. In particular, the danger that other MPs would join Simon, Hutchison, and Brown as independent Liberals made it imperative for Samuel to retain the confidence of the party's right wing.

The May Committee's report was received by the government in the last week of July, and Snowden sent advance copies to Baldwin and Samuel, asking them to consult their colleagues about it.[91] The majority report, signed by all but the Labour members of the committee, estimated that on current trends the budget deficit for 1932–3 would hit £120,000,000, and recommended that this gap should be closed by £25,000,000 of additional taxation and £96,500,000 of new economies. Most controversially, £66,500,000 would be saved from the unemployment insurance scheme by reducing benefit rates by one-fifth, increasing contributions, and imposing a means test on transitional benefit.[92] Similar changes had recently been proposed by the Royal Commission on Unemployment Insurance, but the cuts which May envisaged were more drastic.[93] When these recommendations were published on 31 July, Liberal reaction was ambivalent, as

[91] Snowden also gave a copy to Walter Runciman: Wallace, 'Walter Runciman', 325–6.
[92] For a succinct account of the May Committee's work, see Williamson, *National Crisis*, 267–73.
[93] Cmd. 3872, *First Report of the Royal Commission on Unemployment Insurance* (1931).

a glance at the main Liberal newspapers shows. The *Manchester Guardian* agreed that it was 'life and death' for Britain to balance her budget and maintain her credit, but pointed out that the proposed savings on unemployment insurance seemed to go well beyond what was necessary to make the Unemployment Fund solvent. The newspaper also argued that the proposed cuts would only be equitable if an equivalent sacrifice was imposed on higher-income groups:

> The proposals of the Economy Committee do not, taken by themselves, constitute a truly national effort. The brunt of them falls upon specific classes of men and women, and those not the strongest to sustain the load . . . To make the economies suggested without some kind of additional direct taxation would be neither just nor adequate.[94]

In similar vein, *The Economist* noted that the committee's estimate of a £120,000,000 deficit 'rather seriously overpaints the gloom of the immediate budgetary prospect' because it included £50,000,000 of sinking fund payments and £40,000,000 of borrowings for the Unemployment Fund, which were not normally counted as government expenditure. The paper also sympathized with the complaint of Labour nominees Arthur Pugh and Charles Latham, in their minority report, that the committee had articulated an inadequate conception of equality of sacrifice and failed to meet even this principle. Yet the budgetary situation had to be dealt with, and *The Economist* hoped that the government would use the majority report as its starting point in devising a scheme which would distribute sacrifices fairly across the community.[95]

Many progressive Liberals seem to have agreed that the May Report was 'suspiciously one-sided'.[96] The most widely canvassed alternative was a 'National Treaty' for an all-round reduction in costs and wages, on the lines proposed by Keynes, Reginald McKenna, and other radicals in their addendum to the report of the Macmillan Committee on Finance and Industry, and recently implemented in Australia in an attempt to solve that country's difficulties.[97] This had two major advantages over the May Committee's proposals: it would spread sacrifices more widely and would directly improve the competitiveness of British exports by reducing labour costs. At the Liberal Summer School in Cambridge on 31 July, Sir Walter Layton and Ernest Simon both came out in favour of a National Treaty to introduce cuts, by agreement, in all wages, salaries, and benefits, in

94 *MG*, 1 August 1931, 10.

95 *Economist*, 8 August 1931, 255–6. The *News Chronicle*'s assessment was similar: see *NC*, 1 August 1931, 6.

96 *MG*, 11 August 1931, 8.

97 Cmd. 3897, *Report of Committee on Finance and Industry* (1931), 190–209, esp. 200.

the incomes of the 'rentiers class', and in retail prices.[98] Layton developed this idea further in private correspondence with Snowden, and suggested that it should also involve a special tax on fixed-interest-bearing securities and the raising of a large loan to shore up sterling.[99] The treaty idea was a powerful one, and won support from the dramatist Reginald Berkeley and the Liberal journalist Elliott Dodds.[100] Ramsay Muir, speaking at the Guildford by-election on 21 August, put a particularly radical slant on it, arguing that an emergency tax on the yield of securities could 'practically wipe out the Budget deficit' and suggesting that low earners should be insulated from measures to reduce real wages to 1929 levels.[101]

The significance of the National Treaty option lay in the way it allowed its exponents to combine political radicalism with a relatively orthodox analysis of Britain's economic problems. Muir and other progressive Liberals remained committed to public works and the wider interventionist agenda outlined in the Yellow Book, but their interest in a National Treaty suggests that they recognized the difficulty of pursuing domestic reflation in the context of an international financial crisis.[102] Conversely, the growing atmosphere of crisis made the classical solution of wage reductions, which even Keynes had suggested was the best policy in theory, seem more politically feasible. By reducing incomes and prices across the board, a National Treaty held out the prospect of reconciling economic orthodoxy with social justice and so making retrenchment acceptable to the Labour movement. However, neither MacDonald and Snowden nor the Liberal leadership showed much interest in the idea, perhaps because it would have required complex negotiations with employers and trade unions. As a result, the crisis measures which the government drew up in August 1931 were focussed on the much narrower issue of the budget deficit.

Snowden's initial plan for dealing with the May Report was to use the summer recess to agree an economy package within government, and then present it to the Liberal and Conservative leaders for approval. After discussing the general situation with senior colleagues on 29 July, Samuel indicated to Snowden that the Liberals were prepared to support the government 'in any practicable measures of economy which they may take': cuts which were acceptable to Labour ministers were also likely to be

[98] *NC*, 1 August 1931, 2.

[99] Layton papers, 101/4, Layton to Snowden, 11 August 1931, and 101/7, Layton to Snowden, 16 August 1931. In his second letter, Layton also advocated mobilization of Britain's foreign investments.

[100] *NC*, 3 August 1931, 2; *British Weekly*, 20 August 1931, 403.

[101] *NC*, 22 August 1931, 2.

[102] For Muir's continuing enthusiasm for the Yellow Book, see *NC*, 3 August 1931, 2.

acceptable to them.[103] However, there were already signs that Britain was vulnerable to the financial instability that had recently thrown Germany into crisis, and the flight from sterling which began on 5 August forced the government to respond to the May Report more quickly than it had intended.[104] Between 12 and 23 August, Snowden and MacDonald held an exhausting series of meetings with their Cabinet colleagues, the Liberal and Conservative leaders, and Sir Ernest Harvey and Edward Peacock of the Bank of England in an effort to produce a mutually acceptable programme of spending cuts and tax increases. It was at this point that Lloyd George's incapacity made itself felt, for some Liberals—such as the chief whip, Sir Archibald Sinclair—seem to have been willing to accept a relatively modest austerity package in order to keep Labour in office.[105] Samuel, though, chose Sir Donald Maclean to accompany him to the Downing Street meetings, partly because he was able to attend at short notice and partly because (as he told Sinclair) 'Donald has been our protagonist on the economy question'.[106] Samuel's choice of Maclean was significant, because he was a long-standing deficit hawk with City connections and had already indicated an inclination to work with the Conservatives to secure deep retrenchment.[107] From outside the talks, the Marquess of Reading also urged Samuel to adopt a tough line.[108]

Virtually all politicians and economists, including Keynes, agreed in August 1931 that the ordinary budget should be balanced and that sterling should be kept on the gold standard. (Keynes, at this stage, proposed to suspend the sinking fund, continue borrowing for the Unemployment Fund, and impose a revenue tariff to help eliminate the ordinary deficit.[109]) The question at issue was *how* budgetary balance would be achieved, and here Samuel and Maclean's position reflected a mixture of political and economic judgments. Firstly, it was essential to ensure that the Labour government did not try to plug the deficit with heavy new taxation or a revenue tariff, both of which would be unpopular with Liberals and seemed likely to inhibit economic recovery.[110] Secondly, Samuel believed that a package of measures which left unemployment benefit untouched

[103] Parliamentary Archives, Samuel papers, SAM/A/78/3, memorandum by Samuel, 13 August 1931, containing copy of Samuel to Snowden, 29 July 1931.

[104] Williamson, *National Crisis*, 285–90.

[105] See for instance Thurso papers, III, 3/5, Sinclair to Samuel, 14 August 1931.

[106] Thurso papers, III, 3/5, Samuel to Sinclair, 18 August 1931.

[107] *The Times*, 13 August 1931, 12.

[108] British Library, MSS Eur. F118 (Reading private papers), fol. 7, note by Reading, n.d. [August 1931].

[109] *New Statesman and Nation*, 15 August 1931, 189–90.

[110] Bodleian Library, dep. c. 468 (Maclean papers), fol. 116, Maclean to Lady Maclean, 18 August 1931.

would not be perceived as fair by the upper and middle classes. Thirdly, Samuel and Maclean recognized that the composition as well as the size of the deficit-reduction package would influence the response of the financial markets. On this point, the Liberal leaders deferred to the judgment of the Bank of England, and accepted its view that only a cut in unemployment benefit could stem the run on the pound.[111]

In the light of these considerations, Samuel and Maclean—along with Neville Chamberlain and Samuel Hoare for the Conservatives—told MacDonald and Snowden on 20 August that an unemployment benefit cut was an 'indispensable' component of an economy scheme.[112] This, of course, was also MacDonald and Snowden's view, though they faced strong resistance from Cabinet ministers. Nevertheless, as Williamson notes, it represented a significant shift by the Liberals away from the position of critical support for the government which they had previously maintained, and it is at least conceivable that a more flexible attitude might have allowed Labour to stay in office.[113] On the other hand, it is not at all clear that the modest economy programme which the Cabinet was prepared to support would have been sufficient to save sterling.

THE NATIONAL GOVERNMENT

With the Cabinet unable to agree on a cut in unemployment benefit, the Labour government fell on 24 August. During the preceding days, Samuel's consultations with Maclean, Lloyd George, and other Liberals had confirmed his view that both party and national interests would be best served by the formation of a National Government under MacDonald's leadership.[114] Samuel recommended a National Government to the King, and MacDonald and Baldwin were persuaded to assent. Samuel became Home Secretary and Reading Foreign Secretary within MacDonald's new Cabinet of ten, and several other Liberals received posts outside it. Maclean was appointed President of the Board of Education, Sinclair Secretary of State for Scotland, and Lothian Chancellor of the Duchy of Lancaster.

After the October 1931 general election, when he broke with the main body of the Liberal Party, Lloyd George portrayed the August crisis as a coup by the party's 'Whigs', who had never liked the 1929 pledge and were 'glad of this opportunity of throwing it over'.[115] The crisis certainly showed

[111] Samuel papers, SAM/A/77/7, 'Course of Events—August 20th–23rd, 1931', memorandum by Samuel, 23 August 1931; Williamson, *National Crisis*, 316–7.

[112] Samuel papers, SAM/A/77/7, 'Course of Events'.

[113] Williamson, *National Crisis*, 310.

[114] Williamson, *National Crisis*, 335.

[115] *MG*, 2 November 1931, 4.

the continuing influence of the party's Asquithian elite, and brought the Liberal Council 'back into the centre of Liberal party politics'.[116] Maclean, 'the perfect representative of that older type of Liberalism', had brought classical concerns about rising public expenditure to bear on the Liberal negotiating position, and Runciman later congratulated him on making retrenchment 'the keystone'.[117] When Liberal MPs, peers and candidates met to endorse the new government at the National Liberal Club on 28 August, Viscount Grey attended to pronounce his blessing, and even Sir John Simon sent a message of support.[118] The inclusion of the aged Crewe at the War Office added to the atmosphere of Asquithian restoration.

It would, however, be wrong to interpret Liberal support for the National Government wholly in these terms. Samuel himself was no Asquithian, and remained in touch with Lloyd George during the crisis; he also received strong backing from the Liberal shadow cabinet, and the party meeting on 28 August—attended by approximately 250 Liberals—passed a resolution approving of his actions with just one dissentient, who was not an MP.[119] Samuel's claim that Lloyd George fully supported the National Government was somewhat exaggerated, since the bed-ridden leader was frustrated at the way 'foreign financiers' were being allowed to dictate government policy; but he had no problems with the benefit cut, and as he was unable to develop an alternative strategy he publicly backed the new administration and allowed his son Gwilym to join it.[120] Lloyd George also ensured that recent critics of his leadership, such as Sir John Simon and Ernest Brown, did not receive office.[121] Following Samuel and Lloyd George's lead, most progressive Liberals accepted the economy programme as a disagreeable necessity and focussed their energies on making it as equitable as possible.[122] One MP, Frank Owen, publicly accused the party leadership of betraying Liberal principles, but among the parliamentary party this stance was exceptional.[123]

[116] Williamson, *National Crisis*, 354.

[117] Stuart Hodgson in *NC*, 26 August 1931, 6; Bodleian Library, dep. c. 468 (Maclean papers), fols 143–6, Runciman to Maclean, 25 August 1931, at fol. 143.

[118] *MG*, 29 August 1931, 11, 15.

[119] Samuel papers, SAM/A/78/3, memorandum by Samuel, 13 August 1931; *NC*, 24 August 1931, 2; *MG*, 29 August 1931, 11.

[120] Campbell, *Lloyd George*, 298; Samuel papers, SAM/A/77/12, Lloyd George to Samuel, 25 August 1931.

[121] British Library, MSS Eur. F118 (Reading private papers), fols 131–3, memorandum by Reading on meeting with Lloyd George, 11 September 1931.

[122] For instance, Percy Harris in Hansard, HC (series 5) vol. 256, cols 450–8 (11 September 1931).

[123] Hansard, HC (series 5) vol. 257, cols 83–7 (28 September 1931).

The National Government largely took over the economy scheme which had been proposed by MacDonald on 22 August and rejected by the Labour Cabinet.[124] Snowden's emergency budget on 10 September reduced unemployment benefit rates by one-tenth, increased insurance contributions, means-tested transitional benefit, and cut public sector salaries by between one-tenth and one-fifth; it also raised taxes on beer, tobacco, petrol, and entertainments, and increased direct taxation by £57,000,000 through higher rates and lower allowances.[125] The rhetoric used by MacDonald, Snowden, and other ministers was that of equality of sacrifice; the justification for the benefit cut was that prices had fallen in recent years, so that the real value of benefit would still be slightly above its 1929 level.[126] Following advice from Henry Clay, ministers also argued that working- class living standards would have been hit much more sharply if Britain had been forced off the gold standard.[127]

Liberal concerns about the National Government's policy took two main forms. Their overriding concern was that its rhetoric of equal sacrifice should be borne out by its measures. At times, this led Liberals to oppose specific cuts which they perceived to be unjust, especially the 15 per cent cut in teachers' salaries, which the party's Education Advisory Committee condemned on the grounds that it exceeded the sacrifice required from most other public servants.[128] The government eventually agreed to reduce the teachers' pay cut to 10 per cent in late September, following the departure from the gold standard.[129] More commonly, however, Liberals sought to spread sacrifices more widely. Within government, Lothian urged a special effort to show 'that the rich as well as the poor are going to bear their fair share of the burden'. He supported the cuts in social spending, but he argued that ministers should also impose a capital levy to cancel £2,000,000,000 of war debt, which would 'permanently balance . . . the budget' and facilitate some targeted tax reductions 'or an expanded programme of national development to absorb the unemployed'.[130] Samuel and Neville Chamberlain considered the idea, but Sir Ernest Harvey of the Bank of England warned that it might precipitate a renewed flight from sterling. The government settled instead for increasing

[124] Williamson, *National Crisis*, 362–7.

[125] *MG*, 11 September 1931, 9.

[126] *The Times*, 26 August 1931, 10; Hansard, HC (series 5) vol. 256, cols 297–312 (10 September 1931).

[127] Lothian papers, GD40/17/143/31–3, 'The Pound and the Gold Standard', memorandum by Clay, 25 August 1931.

[128] *NC*, 3 September 1931, 2.

[129] *NC*, 22 September 1931, 1.

[130] British Library, MSS Eur. F118 (Reading private papers), fols 112–7, Lothian to Samuel, 25 August 1931, at fol. 113.

the tax differentiation against unearned income and reviving plans to convert war loan to a lower rate of interest.[131]

Liberals outside the government sought to keep the National Treaty idea alive more explicitly. In mid-September, faced by the prospect of 'a catastrophic fall in the £' and keen to stave off 'a dog fight election' over tariffs, thirteen prominent Liberals including Layton, Rowntree, and the financial journalist Norman Crump drew up a memorandum on 'Liberalism and the Crisis of the £' which Lothian circulated to senior Liberal ministers.[132] The memorandum argued that the collapse of international confidence in Britain stemmed not only from her budget deficit but, more fundamentally, from her weak export position. '[A]n all round reduction of British money costs of the order of from 10 to 20%' was therefore essential. Devaluation and protection were possible means of achieving this, but both were unacceptable: the former because it would destabilize the international financial system, the latter because it would require extensive government intervention and undermine efforts to reduce tariffs worldwide. The inescapable conclusion was that the government should seek to cut domestic costs by reducing wages, salaries, capital, rents, and prices 'on some generally agreed scale', perhaps through 'a deal with the T.U.C.'.[133] 'Liberalism and the Crisis of the £' was rendered out of date when sterling was forced off the gold standard on 21 September, and historians' verdicts have not been sympathetic: Williamson, for instance, takes it as evidence that the 'Liberals had almost nothing new to offer' and that 'Keynes's influence had . . . been virtually erased'.[134] Yet this neglects the purchase which the National Treaty idea held among Liberals as a way of giving meaning to 'equal sacrifices' and laying a sound foundation for recovery.

A second, and subsidiary, Liberal concern involved the treatment of public investment within the economy programme. In contrast to his acceptance of the unemployment benefit cuts, Lloyd George was infuriated by the proposed reductions in capital spending, especially on smallholdings, land reclamation, and other agricultural projects.[135] Liberal ministers such as Lothian and Graham White, the Assistant Postmaster-General, took a

[131] Williamson, *National Crisis*, 364–5.

[132] Lothian papers, GD40/17/144/57–67, 'Liberalism and the Crisis of the £', n.d. [*c.*16 September 1931], fol. 58, and GD40/17/144/54, Crump to Lothian, 18 September 1931.

[133] Lothian papers, GD40/17/144/57–67, 'Liberalism and the Crisis of the £', fols 60, 64, 65.

[134] Williamson, *National Crisis*, 396.

[135] Samuel papers, SAM/A/77/12, Lloyd George to Samuel, 25 August 1931.

similar attitude.[136] Outside government, the authors of 'Liberalism and the Crisis of the £' proposed to continue 'a wise policy of national development', whilst Philip Oliver, MP for Manchester Blackley, lamented that the need 'to go slow with schemes of national reconstruction' was the Liberals' 'part of the sacrifice'.[137] Clearly, then, national development retained a prominent place in the party's political economy during the 1931 crisis. It is indicative of the Liberals' reduced bargaining power after the National Government was formed—and the political difficulties involved in finding savings elsewhere—that deep capital cuts went ahead anyway.

By the time the National Government went to the polls in October 1931, the issue of protection was coming to dominate political debate and split the Liberal Party, a development which will be explored in the next chapter. However, it would be wrong to leave behind the 1931 political crisis without noting that Britain's departure from the gold standard in September transformed the context in which economic policy was made. Most obviously, the devaluation of sterling improved the competitiveness of British exports and reduced the need for a direct attack on costs; as Nicholas Dimsdale has observed, concern with wage rates as a cause of unemployment largely disappeared in the 1930s.[138] The final quarter of 1931 witnessed a modest revival in manufacturing, concentrated in the export industries, though this was rapidly choked off by trade restrictions and competitive devaluations; Keynes meanwhile concluded that protection was no longer really necessary.[139] Over time, the departure from gold also facilitated a shift to cheap money, with the reduction of Bank Rate from 6 per cent to 2 per cent between February and June 1932 followed by a massive conversion of war loan to 3½ per cent stock. Cheap money, in turn, was central to the private house-building boom which led a sustained (if regionally concentrated) domestic recovery.[140] The National Government still showed little interest in public works, perhaps partly because it perceived a trade-off with low interest rates.[141] Nevertheless, there are good reasons for believing that a Keynesian programme would

[136] Lothian papers, GD40/17/143/26–8, Lothian to Samuel, 31 August 1931, at fol. 27, and Graham White papers, WHI/5/8/35, notes for speech in Birkenhead, n.d. [October 1931].

[137] Lothian papers, GD40/17/144/57–67, 'Liberalism and the Crisis of the £', fol. 63; Thurso papers, III, 3/5, Oliver to Sinclair, 27 August 1931.

[138] N. H. Dimsdale, 'Employment and real wages in the inter-war period', *National Institute Economic Review*, no. 110 (November 1984), 94–103.

[139] G. D. N. Worswick, 'The sources of recovery in the UK in the 1930s', *National Institute Economic Review*, no. 110 (November 1984), 85–93, at 87–9; *The Times*, 29 September 1931, 15.

[140] Worswick, 'Sources of recovery', 89–91.

[141] For perceptions of a trade-off, see Middleton, *Towards the Managed Economy*, 165–71.

have been more practicable and more effective under the post-1931 regime of managed exchange rates than under the gold standard.

CONCLUSION

The evidence presented in this chapter demonstrates that senior Liberals drew back from their support for loan-financed public works during the 1929 Parliament, and returned by 1931 to a largely classical analysis of Britain's economic difficulties. However, it does not bear out the notion that the Liberal Party's embrace of Keynes' ideas in 1929 was purely opportunistic, nor does it suggest that the party's shift in policy can be attributed wholly to factional machinations, despite Maclean's prominence in the Downing Street talks. Asquithians were the most enthusiastic supporters of retrenchment and cost reductions, but by the time the crisis hit other Liberals were also moving in that direction.

Why, then, did the Liberals revert to orthodox policies? Three reasons may be identified. Firstly, Liberal confidence in the practicability and efficacy of a large-scale public works programme was shaken after 1929 by worsening economic circumstances and the government's continued opposition. The cyclical downturn which followed the Wall Street Crash caused Liberals to question whether public works would stimulate private-sector activity in the way Keynes had suggested, and advice from informed economists confirmed their growing doubts. Lloyd George and his colleagues continued to champion public works as one element of a vigorous anti-slump policy, but the task of finding appropriate projects for the Labour government to invest in brought them face to face with the practical difficulties involved, and even Ernest Simon felt that Lloyd George's 'desperate search for development work' was leading him to back unsound schemes.[142] The possibility that a large development loan might destabilize the financial markets also came to be taken more seriously. As the facts changed, then, the Liberals changed their minds about how government could best promote recovery. Interest in a National Treaty to bring down production costs paved the way for the party to embrace retrenchment when the crisis hit. As Samuel explained to the Commons after the National Government was formed, the austerity programme was difficult for Liberals to stomach, since—quite apart from its distributional impact—it would 'add to existing unemployment' by 'lessening effective

[142] Ernest Simon papers, M11/11/5, Parliamentary Diary, 1929–33, section C, fol. 9, entry for 15 July 1931.

demand and diminishing the call for goods'. Yet in view of the mounting budget deficit and the pressure on sterling, there was 'no alternative'.[143]

Secondly, as Michael Hart has pointed out, the Liberals' economic radicalism was undermined by the fragmentation of the group of experts which had given Lloyd George's pledge much of its authority:

> Whereas in 1929 the Liberal programme had received the active support of progressive businessmen, academics and economists, this consensus quickly broke up. By late 1930 or early 1931 when Lloyd George, Rowntree and Lothian argued their case in committees with Labour ministers and civil servants none of either Keynes, Henderson, [Robert] Brand or [Sir Josiah] Stamp any longer agreed with the 1929 proposals with which their names were associated.[144]

Keynes' rapidly shifting views were especially difficult to follow, in view of his conversion to protection, his distinction between first-best and practical policies, and his willingness to put his name to an eclectic variety of proposals. By contrast, orthodox economists offered a relatively consistent prescription for unemployment which fitted with classical theory, economic 'common sense', and the views of the Treasury and the Bank of England. To some extent, therefore, the story of 1931 is one of the Liberal Party coming back into line with the views of the dominant policy community in Whitehall and the City of London.

Thirdly, the events of 1931 brought to the surface the tension between the Liberals' deep-seated commitment to economic internationalism and their desire to bring about domestic reflation. Although Keynes had made clear during the 1920s that his policy implied a reorientation of the British economy towards production for the home market, Liberals had preferred to emphasize the compatibility of national development with international trade and to ignore the difficulties involved in pursuing unilateral reflation in the most open economy in the world. The party's conduct during the 1931 crisis showed that it was unwilling to sacrifice the institutions of economic internationalism—the gold standard, free capital movement, and free trade—in order to facilitate an expansive fiscal policy. In the Liberal vision, a stable and integrated world economy seemed to be a prerequisite for sustained prosperity, which was not to be sacrificed lightly for short-term gain.

Most Liberal leaders were satisfied that the party had done the right thing in 1931, and that the painful but temporary cuts provided a firm foundation for recovery. By the time the free-trade ministers resigned

143 Hansard, HC (series 5) vol. 256, cols 537–54, at 539–40 (14 September 1931).

144 Hart, 'Decline', 369.

from the National Government in September 1932, Sir Archibald Sinclair later asserted, '[c]onfidence had been restored, the Budget had been balanced, huge conversions of War Loan had been effected, the blessing of cheap money had been conferred upon industry, and the national credit had been restored'.[145] However, none of this helped the party politically. The 'Labour-against-the-rest' structure of the 1931 election campaign sealed the party's identification with the retrenchment programme, and except on the trade issue the Liberal leaders made little effort to distinguish themselves from the Conservative line.[146] Left-leaning voters were alienated by the cuts, conservative Liberals developed new loyalties to the National Government, and half the party's MPs followed Sir John Simon into a pro-tariff Liberal National Party. If the Liberal Party was to survive in this difficult environment, Samuel and Sinclair would need to make a compelling case for Liberal independence—and work out how the party's commitments to free trade, balanced budgets, and public works could fit together.

[145] *NLF Proceedings, 1934* (1934), 20.

[146] On the Liberal campaign in the 1931 election, see especially Thorpe, *1931*, 219–54, and Wasserstein, *Herbert Samuel*, 329–34.

3

Defending Economic Internationalism, 1931–5

The crisis which loomed over the Liberal Party during the 1929 Parliament broke after the National Government was formed, and would dominate Liberal politics for the rest of the 1930s. From October 1931 onwards, British Liberalism was split three ways, with Sir John Simon and the Liberal Nationals seceding rightwards and Lloyd George and his family breaking away on the left. Sir Herbert Samuel was left with the unenviable task of maintaining party cohesion as the official Liberals moved from the National Government to the backbenches, and then into opposition. In a political and intellectual climate which appeared increasingly inhospitable to Liberalism, hopes of a large-scale revival faded from view, and the party focussed its energies on strengthening and consolidating existing Liberal support. However, the bleakness of the Liberal Party's electoral record in the 1930s should not obscure vital elements in its thought. If this was a 'decade of dormancy' for liberal ideology, as Michael Freeden has suggested, the Liberal Party itself nevertheless responded creatively to the challenges which unemployment, protection, and overseas dictatorships posed.[1]

Within a year of the National Government's formation, the free-trade regime which Britain had maintained since 1846 had been decisively abandoned. As Frank Trentmann has powerfully suggested, the switch to a protectionist regime partly reflected the displacement of the free-trade idea from progressive political culture since the First World War: as voters polarized on class lines, free trade shrank from a moral cause which embodied democratic and internationalist principles into a narrowly technical policy.[2] The readiness with which Sir John Simon and his followers

[1] Michael Freeden, *Liberalism Divided: A Study in British Political Thought, 1914–1939* (Oxford, 1986), chapter 9.

[2] Frank Trentmann, *Free Trade Nation: Commerce, Consumption, and Civil Society in Modern Britain* (Oxford, 2008), part two.

accepted protection bears out Trentmann's argument. Among those who remained in the Samuelite ranks, however, the tariff controversy of 1931–2 sparked a renewed commitment to open markets, which reflected ethical and economic commitments as well as the political imperative of maintaining a distinct Liberal identity. The 'general apathy' towards free trade which Trentmann detects among the 1930s electorate was not for want of trying by the Liberals.[3]

The combined effect of the Simonite defections and the introduction of tariffs was to reaffirm the centrality of free trade to the Liberal Party's political economy. Classical ideas about the 'fundamental' causes of depression and unemployment retained the force they had regained in 1930–1 and made Liberals more critical of state intervention at home than they had been during the Yellow Book period. At the same time, as Richard Grayson has shown, Liberals drew incisive connections between protectionist economic policies and the growth of aggressive nationalism in the political sphere, and urged that the British government should recognize the 'interdependency' of nations, initiate economic disarmament, and work for the enforcement of international law.[4] Public works and other constructive ideas could sit alongside this internationalist agenda, but they were bound to be conceived more modestly than they had been in the late 1920s. Until the *General Theory* provided a developed theoretical basis for economic management, Liberals were left to graft Keynesian policy ideas uneasily on to a largely classical intellectual framework.

THE ANATOMY OF THE SIMONITE SPLIT

When the National Government was formed, it was envisaged by all parties as a short-term combination to deal with the financial emergency, after which the parties would fight an election in the normal fashion.[5] By mid-September 1931, however, the political prospect had changed significantly. On the one hand, the vehemence with which the Labour Party opposed the economy programme alarmed ministers, and made the prospect of going to the polls as a National Government seem more attractive, especially for MacDonald and Snowden.[6] On the other hand, it became

[3] Trentmann, *Free Trade Nation*, 345.

[4] Richard Grayson, *Liberals, International Relations, and Appeasement: The Liberal Party, 1919–1939* (2001).

[5] Parliamentary Archives, Samuel papers, SAM/A/77/11, 'Memorandum written at the Conference at Buckingham Palace, August 24th 1931'.

[6] Philip Williamson, *National Crisis and National Government: British Politics, the Economy and Empire, 1926–1932* (Cambridge, 1992), 387–401.

increasingly apparent that Britain's balance of trade deficit was undermining her efforts to remain on the gold standard. Conservatives resumed their agitation for tariffs, and Simon and a number of other Liberal MPs joined in.[7] Most significantly, Walter Runciman relaxed his commitment to free trade, and argued that the trade balance should be corrected by a temporary embargo on luxury imports. The Liberal ministers seem to have been disposed to compromise in order to hold the National Government together, but free traders outside Parliament mobilized rapidly to discourage this, with the Liberal Free Trade Committee—led by Francis Hirst—warning Samuel that a luxury import ban would not be accepted by the party.[8] The departure from the gold standard on 21 September strengthened free traders' confidence that import restrictions were unnecessary, but by this time Conservative pressure for protection was difficult to stem, and Simon and his allies were actively canvassing Liberal support: indeed, twenty-eight Liberal MPs signed a 'memorial' organized by Leslie Hore-Belisha, which promised MacDonald backing for any measures he deemed necessary to restore the nation's trade and finances.[9] In early October, aware of the electoral rout that Liberals would face if they opposed the National Government, Samuel agreed to fight an election on the formula of a 'free hand' for ministers to introduce protective measures, provided an impartial inquiry found them necessary to redress the trade balance.[10] Simon could not object to this formula, but his preparations for a separate group of Liberal National candidates had proceeded too far for a split to be averted.[11] Lloyd George, on the other hand, felt Samuel had been hoodwinked, and raised his standard in opposition.

The formation of the Liberal National Party can only be adequately understood if it is recognized that it took place in the context both of an economic crisis and of a looming general election. The claim that members of the National Government parties should set aside their previous ideological commitments and consider possible remedies for Britain's trade deficit on their objective merits, which formed the basis for the Hore-Belisha memorial, was a compelling one; indeed, it underlay the appeal for a 'free hand' on which the National Government fought

[7] For instance, Henry Morris-Jones and Ernest Brown: *The Times*, 16 September 1931, 6, and 18 September 1931, 6.

[8] Williamson, *National Crisis*, 394–7; National Archives of Scotland, Lothian papers, GD40/17/143/40, Raymond Jones to Lothian, 15 September 1931, with enclosures (fols 41–5); see also Samuel papers, SAM/A/81/13, E. H. Gilpin and ten others to Samuel, 30 September 1931.

[9] Williamson, *National Crisis*, 435–6.

[10] Williamson, *National Crisis*, 441–5.

[11] Bodleian Library, Oxford, MS. Simon 68, fol. 163, Simon to Ramsay MacDonald, 5 October 1931.

the election. The Simon group appears to have had a particular appeal for MPs who had previously been disillusioned with Lloyd George's leadership or were aggrieved by their failure to receive government office, such as Ernest Brown and Geoffrey Shakespeare. MPs and candidates were also attracted by the Conservatives' readiness to give Liberal Nationals a free run against Labour, and by the large election fund which Simon and his organizers built up.[12] Conversely, those Liberals who could secure local Conservative support without joining the Simonites had little reason to do so, and several successful candidates—such as Joseph Leckie in Walsall and Joseph Maclay in Paisley—took an essentially Simonite line on the tariff question whilst professing allegiance to Samuel.[13] Runciman, who had been offered a Cabinet post by MacDonald if he stayed in Parliament, also tried to avoid taking sides.[14] Only in the weeks and months after the election would the divisions between the Simon, Samuel, and Lloyd George groups harden.

Notwithstanding the electoral considerations which shaped Liberals' behaviour in October 1931, and the cross-currents which existed between the different groups, it is possible to identify an economic policy basis for the Simonite split. The *sine qua non* of membership of the Liberal National Party was a diminution of free-trade conviction, expressed in a willingness to support the National Government 'in any measures found to be necessary for national recovery without regard to fiscal theories and prepossessions'.[15] This could stem from at least three different sources. Firstly, among right-wing Liberals, the choice between remaining with Samuel and following Simon was largely a question of priority, a judgment on the relative importance of maintaining the National Government in office and defending free trade. Those old Asquithians who regarded free trade as vital, such as Richard Holt and Francis Hirst, tended to remain in the official party; those who shared Viscount Grey's view that retrenchment was

[12] All nine Liberal MPs who had enjoyed straight fights with Labour in 1929 became Liberal Nationals, and several other candidates declared themselves Simonites during the campaign as the price of local Conservative support: MS. Simon 69, fol. 8, W. Devenport Hackney to Richard Soper, 21 October 1931; fols 36–8, Sir Robert Hutchison to Simon, 'Sunday evening' [October 1931]; and fols 9–10, Hackney to William Mabane, 21 October 1931. On finance, see especially *The Observer*, 11 October 1931, 16.

[13] For a valuable study of the brokerage of local pacts between Liberals and Conservatives in 1931, see Nick Smart, 'Constituency politics and the 1931 election', *Southern History*, xvi (1994), 122–51. For Leckie, see John Ward, 'The development of the Labour Party in the Black Country (1918–1939)' (Wolverhampton D.Phil. thesis, 2004), 295; for Maclay, *The Scotsman*, 23 October 1931, 11.

[14] Jonathan Wallace, 'The Political Career of Walter Runciman, 1st Viscount Runciman of Doxford (1870–1949)' (Newcastle upon Tyne Ph.D. thesis, 1995), 330–8.

[15] MS. Simon 68, fols 158–61, notes by Simon on meeting establishing Liberal National group [5 October 1931], at fol. 158.

the dominant issue were more likely to become Liberal Nationals (though Grey himself did not).[16] In the provinces, middle-class Liberals whose Liberalism derived from cultural identity rather than ideological conviction tended to be impressed by the claim that the government deserved unequivocal support.[17]

Secondly, Liberal MPs representing agricultural constituencies disproportionately followed Simon. This was especially noticeable in wheat-growing East Anglia, where six out of seven sitting Liberal MPs became Liberal Nationals. Initially, there had been some doubts about whether Simon's advocacy of a tariff included provision for agriculture, and James Blindell (who championed the interests of the potato industry) sought assurances on this score before joining the Liberal National group.[18] Another agricultural Liberal National, Richard Russell, became a strong advocate of a wheat quota, which he believed would give farmers a stable income and bring more land into cultivation.[19] With the benefit of Conservative support, Liberal National MPs in agricultural seats were re-elected with enormous majorities.

Thirdly, and perhaps most surprisingly, some of those who joined the Liberal National group were economic radicals whose willingness to support tariffs stemmed from a broader commitment to government intervention. Clement Davies, for instance, later explained that he had joined the Simon group because he thought free trade was 'a very narrow and out-of-date question' and accepted the case for reciprocal tariff bargaining.[20] Even more striking was the attitude of William Mabane, elected as Liberal National MP for Huddersfield in 1931, who had opposed the return to the gold standard but took the financial crisis as evidence that government needed to restructure the British economy. 'To the serious student of economics or politics,' Mabane argued, 'nothing is more obvious than that, as the century progresses[,] national planning, and later international planning, of our economic and industrial life will become the only accepted road to progress and stability.'[21] Although Mabane remained sceptical of full-blown protection, his belief in planning led him to the view that 'one of the proper functions of Government was to control,

[16] For Grey's views, see *NC*, 19 October 1931, 3.

[17] Barry M. Doyle, 'Urban Liberalism and the "lost generation": Politics and middle class culture in Norwich, 1900–1935', *HJ*, xxxviii (1995), 617–34.

[18] MS. Simon 68, fols 132–5, Blindell to Simon, 26 September 1931. For Blindell's efforts to aid potato farmers, see *MG*, 9 December 1929, 12.

[19] MS. Simon 70, fols 28–32, 'Agriculture', memorandum by R. J. Russell, 8 December 1931.

[20] National Library of Wales, Clement Davies papers, C/1/16, Davies to Stanley Clement-Davies, 3 November 1943.

[21] *HDE*, 26 August 1931, 3.

either by prohibition or by some form of tariff, the direction of our imports'—especially in the context of a large trade deficit.[22] Throughout the National Government years, Mabane would make it clear that he considered the Simonite approach more radical, more interventionist, and more faithful to the spirit of the Yellow Book than the Samuelites' free-trade position.[23] From this perspective, the National Government's tariff policy was the fulfilment of the constructive Liberalism of the 1920s.

The rump Liberal Party which Samuel led was similarly diverse. On the one hand, the departure of the party's more pragmatic right wingers meant that free-trade zealots such as Francis Hirst bulked larger than previously, and the 1931 election brought several orthodox Asquithians back to the Commons, including Walter Rea, Harcourt Johnstone, and D. M. Mason. With Rea and Johnstone in charge of the whips' office, Vivian Phillipps appointed chairman of the Liberal Publications Department, and Lloyd George in self-imposed exile, the Liberal Council began to wind down its independent activities, though it would continue to produce traditionalist propaganda until the Second World War.[24] The loss of Lloyd George's fund also increased the party's financial dependence on wealthy Asquithians. On the other hand, the Liberal left wing was also proportionately strengthened by the defections, though some radicals looked to Lloyd George to provide an alternative rallying point and help rebuild links with Labour.[25] Finally, Samuel had to deal with those who remained in the official party through inertia despite sympathizing with Simon's fiscal views. This group included Grey and Reading, as well as MPs like Leckie and Maclay, and formed a significant obstacle to the adoption of an overt anti-government line.

THE TRADE DEBATE OF 1931–2

The eleven months that passed between the October 1931 general election and the Samuelites' resignation from the National Government in September 1932 were some of the most uncomfortable in the Liberal Party's history. The seventy-two Liberals returned in the election split almost equally between Samuel and Simon, with Lloyd George, his children Gwilym and Megan, and his son-in-law Goronwy Owen sitting as

22 *HDE*, 30 September 1931, 4.

23 See for instance West Yorkshire Archive Service, Kirklees, William Mabane papers, DD/WM/2/13, Mabane to Elliott Dodds, 4 April 1938.

24 University of Bristol Special Collections, Liberal Council papers, Executive Committee minute book 1927–1937, minutes of meetings, 31 January 1934 and 22 October 1936.

25 Samuel papers, SAM/A/84/15, Harcourt Johnstone to Samuel, 30 November 1931.

independent Liberals on the opposition benches. At leadership level, the party's division was confirmed when the Simonites received government office from MacDonald, declined to take the Liberal whip, and began to establish a national organization.[26] Simon replaced Reading as Foreign Secretary, while Runciman took on the task of introducing protection as President of the Board of Trade. In the country, divisions hardened more slowly, and all three groups were represented at the NLF meetings at Clacton-on-Sea in April 1932. However, this made it harder for the Samuelites to act as a cohesive force, as Lloyd George and his allies sought to exploit grassroots disaffection with the Liberal ministers' compromises over protection.[27] Liberal loyalties were divided, confidence in the party's effectiveness waned, and some activists such as the former MP George Thorne decided that their energies could be better spent in the service of non-party groups such as the League of Nations Union.[28]

The 'doctor's mandate' on which the National Government fought the 1931 election included an understanding that a permanent system of tariffs would not be introduced without an impartial inquiry. With a huge Conservative majority in the Commons and the free traders outnumbered in the new Cabinet, this turned out to be a Cabinet Committee on Fiscal Policy, chaired by Neville Chamberlain, on which Samuel and Philip Snowden struggled to make their objections to protection heard; Liberals understandably complained that this was hardly impartial.[29] In the meantime, the government set about erecting temporary restrictions on trade in an attempt to reduce the trade deficit. Within weeks of the election, the Cabinet agreed to introduce legislation giving the Board of Trade powers to levy duties on goods being imported in 'abnormal quantities'. Samuel did not even attempt to resist this, and only one Liberal MP—D. M. Mason—voted against the Abnormal Importations (Customs Duties) Bill at its second reading on 18 November.[30] Shortly thereafter, Minister of Agriculture Sir John Gilmour announced plans for a tariff on non-essential horticultural products and a wheat quota. Again the Liberal ministers were acquiescent, saving their energies for the looming struggle over the general tariff. When the Wheat Bill came before the Commons, Sir Archibald Sinclair defended it as a 'temporary lifebuoy' to

[26] David Dutton, *Liberals in Schism: A History of the National Liberal Party* (2008), 52–4.

[27] For Simonite representation at Clacton, see *MG*, 7 April 1932, 8.

[28] Churchill Archives Centre, Cambridge, Thurso papers, III, 54/1, George R. Thorne to Miss Bridgwater, 3 February 1932.

[29] For the tariff debate within the National Government, see Barry Eichengreen, *Sterling and the Tariff, 1929–32* (Princeton, 1981).

[30] Bernard Wasserstein, *Herbert Samuel: A Political Life* (Oxford, 1992), 337–9; Hansard, HC (series 5) vol. 259, cols 953–9, 979–92 (18 November 1931).

the farmers while they adjusted to changed market conditions, a striking departure from the blanket opposition to quotas which the Liberal Party had traditionally expressed.[31] The Import Duties Bill agreed by the Cabinet in January 1932, which embodied a general tariff, was a step too far for the Samuelites and Snowden, who offered MacDonald their resignations. Lord Hailsham, however, suggested that collective responsibility might be suspended so that the free-trade ministers could speak and vote against the bill, and Samuel eagerly seized on this proposal.[32] For an administrative politician like Samuel, remaining at the Home Office was doubtless more attractive than leading a small band of free traders in opposition.

Samuelite opinion outside Parliament was vocally opposed to the government's protectionist measures, and during the winter months there began a wide-ranging mobilization which encompassed the NLF leadership, young Liberals, some backbenchers, the Liberal press, the Lloyd George group, and Cobdenite purists like Francis Hirst. In December 1931 the NLF executive urged that protection should be resisted 'at the earliest opportunity', and the agreement to differ greatly heightened grass-roots disquiet: by the end of March 1932 the Union of University Liberal Societies, the National League of Young Liberals, and the Scottish and Welsh Liberal Federations had all passed resolutions calling on the Liberal ministers to resign.[33] Heavyweight support for the free traders came from free-market economists at the LSE, including the distinguished group—chaired by Sir William Beveridge and including Lionel Robbins, John Hicks, and Arnold Plant—which had produced *Tariffs: The Case Examined* in 1931.[34] Edwin Cannan's Sidney Ball lecture on 'Balance of Trade Delusions', delivered at Oxford in November 1931, was also widely read and quoted by Liberals.[35] In substance, these economists offered a restatement of the classical case for free trade, arguing that the adverse balance would redress itself automatically and that protectionist measures were bound to inhibit economic adjustment and wealth creation. Those Liberals who were more wary of classical reasoning could draw heart from Dennis Robertson's address to the 1931 Liberal Summer School, which had argued that the existence of unemployed resources did not invalidate

[31] Hansard, HC (series 5) vol. 262, cols 1068–78, at 1074 (1 March 1932).

[32] Samuel papers, SAM/A/87/7, 'Course of Political Events—January 18th–23rd 1932', memorandum by Samuel, 25 January 1932.

[33] *NC*, 17 December 1931, 2, and 28 March 1932, 8; Tom Stannage, *Baldwin Thwarts the Opposition: The British General Election of 1935* (1980), 87.

[34] Sir William Beveridge et al., *Tariffs: The Case Examined* (1931).

[35] *MG*, 14 November 1931, 16; BLPES, Cannan papers, 1031/181–2, Leif Jones to Cannan, 19 December 1931, and 1032/76, Ramsay Muir to Cannan, 7 March 1932.

the free-trade case, and from the fact that Keynes had turned against protection after the departure from gold.[36]

The free-trade mobilization of 1931–2 derived a measure of coherence from free-trade theory and the task of rallying opposition to protection, but it did not comprise a unified movement with a single strategy. Rather, a number of different groups may be identified. For Hirst and the LSE economists, the survival of the Liberal Party seems to have been almost incidental to the main objective of preserving Britain's free-trade system. By contrast, Lloyd George and radical Liberal economists such as Hubert Phillips were less firmly committed to open markets, but were infuriated by the Samuelite ministers' apparently supine support for the National Government's measures. Liberal MPs such as Harry Nathan and Sir Percy Harris, who represented Bethnal Green, meanwhile found their free-trade convictions reinforced by an awareness of the impact tariffs would have on their working-class constituents. There were some important linkages between these different groups: for instance, Nathan was both an ally of Lloyd George and a member of the Liberal Free Trade Committee, and worked with Phillips to draft amendments to the Import Duties Bill.[37] Even so, the overall impression is that of a cacophony of voices urging Samuel and his colleagues to oppose protectionist policies.

In Parliament, it was Harris and Nathan who set the tone of Liberal opposition to protectionist legislation, harrying the government to omit certain articles—especially foodstuffs—from the scope of the measures. Harris led four other Samuelite MPs in opposition to the Horticultural Products Bill in December 1931, strongly criticizing the inclusion of potatoes and tomatoes in the list of luxury foodstuffs on the grounds that these figured prominently in the working-class diet.[38] Later, when the Import Duties Bill came to the Commons, Nathan convened a group of Liberal MPs to mount line-by-line opposition.[39] Opposition to the Wheat Bill, in defiance of a party whip, brought Liberal MPs for industrial seats together with the ultra-orthodox Mason and the Lloyd George group. As Herbert Holdsworth, MP for Bradford South, put it, it was 'an evil thing to tax the food of the poor', and the quota would simply 'bolste[r] up an uneconomic industry at the expense of those least able to bear the burden'.[40] This was, of course, a line of argument which had been used extensively by free

[36] For Robertson's address, see *MG*, 1 August 1931, 15.

[37] Thurso papers, II, 54/1, 'In Defence of Free Trade', Liberal Free Trade Committee annual report, June 1932; *MG*, 14 April 1932, 18.

[38] Hansard, HC (series 5) vol. 260, cols 870–6 (30 November 1931) and cols 1883–6 (9 December 1931).

[39] *NC*, 8 February 1932, 2, and 13 February 1932, 2.

[40] Hansard, HC (series 5) vol. 262, cols 1205–9, at 1209 (2 March 1932).

traders in the Edwardian period, but it took on an added urgency in the political climate of the early 1930s.[41] If Liberal MPs could not compete with Labour in promising to increase or maintain working-class incomes, it was the very least they could do to try to keep the cost of living down.

Robert Bernays, Liberal MP for Bristol North, argued in the *News Chronicle* that the approach of the general tariff had rallied wavering free traders to the cause.[42] This may have been true in some contexts—Oxford University Liberal Club claimed a doubling of membership, to 300, over the winter of 1931–2—but few of those who had defected to the Simonites returned, and differences over strategy threatened to divide the party further.[43] Samuel, Sinclair, and junior minister Isaac Foot used the agreement to differ to make vigorous speeches against the Import Duties Bill in the Commons, but the overwhelming Conservative majority ensured that the bill passed easily and made the Liberals look impotent. The prospect of a split was heightened when Lloyd George returned to the political fray in March with a speech condemning the Liberal ministers' complicity in the Wheat Bill, and a series of area conferences organized by the NLF confirmed Ramsay Muir's belief that the party's future would be jeopardized if its leaders stayed in the government much longer.[44]

Liberal tensions came to a head in April 1932 at the NLF meetings at Clacton. The NLF executive had tabled a resolution which strongly reaffirmed the party's commitment to free trade but avoided calling on Samuel and his colleagues to resign, fearing that this would resemble the TUC's 'dictation' to the late Labour ministers. Delegates supported this resolution and voted down a critical amendment, but they nevertheless made clear their belief that the party should dissociate itself from the government at the earliest possible opportunity.[45] Gwilym Lloyd George was loudly cheered when he rose to move the Free Trade resolution, and Violet Bonham Carter was accorded a similar reception when she declared that she felt 'betrayed' by MacDonald's failure to deliver the 'open, impartial, expert inquiry' into tariffs which he had promised.[46] Bonham Carter went on to warn the Liberal ministers that the agreement to differ could not be long sustained:

> Our leaders may wave the Free Trade flag—we hope they will continue to wave it—but it can only fly at half mast so long as it is nailed to the Front Bench of a Protectionist Government.[47]

41 Trentmann, *Free Trade Nation*, 34–40, 87–100.

42 *NC*, 2 February 1932, 1.

43 *NC*, 18 March 1932, 8, and 9 April 1932, 2.

44 *NC*, 17 March 1932, 1; Samuel papers, SAM/A/155(VIII)/48, Muir to Samuel, 22 April 1932.

45 *NLF Proceedings, 1932* (1932), 47–67.

46 *NLF Proceedings, 1932*, 28.

47 *NLF Proceedings, 1932*, 30.

With an eye on the forthcoming Imperial Economic Conference at Ottawa, delegates unanimously backed an amendment moved by Hirst, which declared that any multi-year trade agreement with the Dominions would represent an unconstitutional interference with Parliament's right to control taxation.[48] The NLF executive meanwhile pronounced itself independent of the government, pledged to fight protection in the country, and—in a move inspired by Lloyd George's secretary Thomas Tweed—assumed responsibility for party propaganda and by-election campaigns from the whips' office, which was suspected of collusion with the Conservatives.[49] At times, the mood of delegates towards the party leadership became heated, with shouts of 'Quota, quota' when Herbert Holdsworth praised Samuel's principled defence of free trade and cries of 'No whips' when party organization was being discussed.[50] The meaning of Clacton, the *News Chronicle* concluded, was plain: 'Nothing can disguise the fact that that the chief part of the Liberal Party is in opposition to the Government of which they are now members.'[51]

Clacton marked the emergence of a new assertiveness on the part of the Liberal grassroots, inspired by the belief that Liberal parliamentarians were unreliable guardians of party policy. It also meant that Samuel and his colleagues were bound to resign if the Ottawa conference in August established a permanent system of imperial preference—which it did. All of the Liberal ministers agreed that the Ottawa agreements were unacceptable, and a summer by-election victory in the marginal seat of North Cornwall (held by Sir Francis Acland following the death of Sir Donald Maclean) made the prospect of fighting the government seem less forbidding.[52] However, Samuel was determined to keep the party's 'Whigs' in the fold, and delayed his decision for a month whilst he consulted with Grey, Crewe, and other Liberal grandees.[53] Worse, when the Liberal ministers finally resigned in September they remained on the government benches in deference to these peers and those MPs, such as Joseph Leckie, who had refused to cross the floor.

Samuel's cautious party management in 1932 meant that the Liberals missed the opportunity to make a clean break with the National Government and develop a distinctive line in opposition. Harold Storey of the *Liberal Magazine* hoped that the resignations would inaugurate

48 *NLF Proceedings, 1932*, 36–8.

49 *MG*, 30 April 1932, 17; Parliamentary Archives, David Lloyd George papers, LG/G/85/3, 'Miss Stevenson', note by Tweed, 21 April 1932.

50 *MG*, 30 April 1932, 17.

51 *NC*, 30 April 1932, 6.

52 Wasserstein, *Herbert Samuel*, 355.

53 Extensive correspondence relating to these consultations may be found in Samuel papers, SAM/A/89.

'an open and relentless battle which will not cease until the stupid carcass of Protection once more lies stricken on the field'; but the failure to cross the floor meant that the battle was only half-joined, and the ex-ministers lacked the energy and the resources needed to prosecute this fight.[54] The Samuelites' dispute with Lloyd George continued to fester, Harry Nathan grew disaffected and defected to Labour, and some Liberals who supported Samuel's line in 1932, such as Robert Bernays, lost their free-trade zeal as the difficulty of mounting an effective campaign against Ottawa became apparent.[55] When the Liberals eventually crossed the floor in November 1933, the party management issues had to be faced all over again, and a clutch of Liberal MPs—including Leckie and Bernays—decided to remain government supporters. In the meantime, as Banffshire MP Sir Murdoch McKenzie Wood pointed out, the party faced 'the worst of all worlds', dissatisfied with the direction of government policy but unable credibly to assail it.[56]

BLICKING AND THE WORLD ECONOMIC CONFERENCE

The difficulties involved in pursuing public works in the 1929 Parliament, and the tariff debate of 1931–2, focussed Liberals' attention on the need to remove economic distortions in order to achieve a permanent solution to unemployment. Despite the National Government's claims, Liberals were adamant that the new protectionist regime exacerbated the unemployment problem by favouring agriculture, and those industries which produced for the home market, over the export trades which were concentrated in the depressed areas. Milner Gray, who had been Parliamentary Secretary to the Ministry of Labour in 1931 and subsequently became chairman of the NLF executive, estimated in 1935 that the government's trade policy had made unemployment 500,000 persons higher than it would otherwise have been.[57] Even in theory, protection could only increase employment at the cost of pushing the standard of living down. The overriding imperative for a Liberal policy was to unblock the channels of trade at home and abroad so that goods could flow freely and the proper relationship between demand and supply could be restored.

[54] *LM*, xl (1932), 451.

[55] *The Diaries and Letters of Robert Bernays, 1932–1939: An Insider's Account of the House of Commons*, ed. Nick Smart (Lampeter, 1996), 11–12, 89–100.

[56] Samuel papers, SAM/A/95/4, Sir Murdoch McKenzie Wood to Samuel, 31 October 1933.

[57] *NLF Proceedings, 1935* (1935), 49.

The implications of the National Government's measures for Liberal policy were worked out in October and November 1932 in two weekend conferences at Blickling Hall, Lord Lothian's house in Norfolk. Along with the Liberal ex-ministers, and prominent activists such as Gray and Ramsay Muir, Lothian invited a number of policy experts: Sir Walter Layton, Dennis Robertson, and Seebohm Rowntree to advise on economic policy, Sir William Beveridge to advise on unemployment insurance, and Sir Francis Acland to provide agricultural expertise.[58] No formal manifesto followed the Blickling meetings, but the arguments developed there formed the basis of Liberal policy for the rest of the Parliament—including the brief statement issued when the party went into opposition (November 1933), Samuel's 'Liberal Address to the Nation' (March 1934), and the NLF pamphlet *The Liberal Way* (May 1934).[59] It is therefore worth exploring what the Blickling policy entailed.

The only active research economist among the Blickling participants was Dennis Robertson, who had been a close ally of Keynes during the 1920s but offered his own distinctive analysis of economic fluctuations.[60] In a memorandum he wrote for the Liberal leaders, Robertson argued that the post-1929 slump in world trade had resulted from the collapse of an American over-investment boom, which—in conjunction with a rapid improvement in agricultural productivity—led to 'a catastrophic fall in prices' and widespread reductions in money incomes.[61] The problems of war debts, exchange restrictions, tariffs in creditor countries and maldistribution of gold had exacerbated the fall in prices, but these were 'really rather symptoms than initiating causes'. Robertson doubted whether fluctuations in investment and prices could be eliminated altogether, but urged that monetary policy should be used 'to damp them down as far as possible, and to promote . . . the stability of trade and employment'—a policy which could be pursued most easily if Britain remained off the gold standard. At the same time, Robertson warned that monetary policy was likely to have little impact on economic activity outside the housing sector until general economic prospects and expectations of profit began to

[58] Sir Arthur Salter was invited to the October meeting, but does not seem to have attended: Lothian papers, GD40/17/269/909–10, Sinclair to Lothian, 8 October 1932.

[59] Samuel was keen to produce a full-scale manifesto at Blickling, but Lothian judged this inappropriate and plans for a volume of essays proved abortive: Lothian papers, GD40/17/146/95–8, Lothian to Samuel, 13 December 1932, and G40/17/146/99–100, Samuel to Lothian, 13 December 1932.

[60] Gordon Fletcher, *Dennis Robertson* (Basingstoke, 2008).

[61] Thurso papers, II, 75/1, 'Notes on Monetary Policy' by D. H. Robertson, December 1932. Robertson's emphasis on the boom as a cause of the slump echoed Austrian trade-cycle theory, as Lionel Robbins noted: see Susan Howson, *Lionel Robbins* (Cambridge, 2011), 270.

recover. Robertson therefore argued that the government should stimulate consumption and investment more directly, as confidence permitted, through public works or tax cuts.[62]

The Liberal politicians present at Blickling largely accepted the substance of Robertson's analysis, including his scepticism towards the gold standard and his emphasis on the need for coordinated international reflation.[63] Following Lothian's lead, however, they tended to describe Britain's economic problems in more classical terms, partly because this enabled them to keep tariffs at the forefront of the policy debate, and perhaps also because some of their number had never abandoned restorationist assumptions. 'Why are we in this present confusion?', Lothian asked rhetorically.

> Primarily because, owing to the war and its consequences, the nations have, by political action, profoundly deranged the adjustment of supply and demand through the free play of enterprise in the market which was the basis of pre-war prosperity.

Lothian argued that world prosperity in the 1920s had been stimulated artificially by 'exceptional' American lending, and could not be sustained when that lending ceased. 'The only real remedy' for depression, therefore, was the classical one: to 'set free the wheels of trade and enterprise, and allow the operation of price in the markets of the world to adjust demand and supply as in the past'.[64]

The most distinctive element of the Blickling analysis (though not a particularly new one) was the close link which the Liberals drew between the problem of economic dislocation and the growth of political nationalism. International economic policy was seen as a facet of international relations. As Ramsay Muir put it:

> All over the world a conflict is being waged between those who recognise and accept the interdependence of all peoples, classes and interests, and make this the governing factor in their outlook and policy; and those whose outlook is dominated by the selfish concerns of nations, classes, vested interests. The predominance of the latter has been the main cause of the world's distresses. The victory of the former might quickly bring the world into an era of assured peace and widely diffused prosperity.[65]

[62] Thurso papers, II, 75/1, 'Notes on Monetary Policy'.

[63] For instance, Samuel noted after Blickling that it was 'impossible to foresee' when Britain might return to gold, since this would have to be preceded by settlement of tariffs and war debts: Thurso papers, II, 75/1, 'Monetary Question', memorandum by Samuel, December 1932.

[64] Lothian papers, GD40/17/146/116–21, 'Liberalism and the Recovery of Prosperity', memorandum by Lothian, January 1933, at fols 117, 118, 119.

[65] Thurso papers, II, 75/1, 'Policy Memorandum' by Ramsay Muir, 7 November 1932.

This contrast between nationalist and internationalist policies would be a mainstay of Liberal rhetoric throughout the 1930s. For Muir and Layton, the problem lay in the failure of nations to recognize their interdependency; for Lothian, 'international anarchy' could only be solved by strengthening the rule of international law and ultimately creating a world federation.[66] As the decade wore on, Liberals became adamant that economic nationalism was a major cause of Europe's growing political tensions. The ultimate justification for internationalist policies was the Cobdenite one that nations which traded with each other would not fight each other.

The Liberal leaders recognized that world free trade could not be re-established overnight, but felt that the World Economic Conference scheduled to take place in London in the summer of 1933 offered a rare opportunity to initiate a movement towards cooperation. Indeed, one of the Samuelites' objections to the Ottawa agreements was that they would tie the National Government's hands at the conference and hamper efforts to seek tariff reductions from other nations.[67] Samuel argued that Britain should use the conference to pursue 'economic disarmament' across a wide front, and seek the abandonment of export subsidies and quantitative restrictions (such as quotas) along with tariff reductions.[68] The most practical proposal, canvassed by Layton and taken up by Samuel, was that Britain might organize a group of low-tariff and free-trade nations, with tariffs against each other of no more than 10 per cent, as a first step towards wider free trade.[69] The Ouchy Convention agreed by Belgium, Luxembourg and the Netherlands in June 1932 provided a model for such a group, but had foundered when other governments (including the United Kingdom's) refused to waive the most-favoured-nation rights they enjoyed under earlier agreements. Effective progress towards freer trade therefore required not only a reorientation of the National Government's policy from bilateral to multilateral trade bargaining, but also a general agreement to take a more flexible attitude towards most-favoured-nation clauses.[70]

In retrospect, it seems unlikely that the line of policy the Liberals suggested would have prevented the World Economic Conference from

[66] Grayson, *Liberals, International Relations, and Appeasement*, 33–6, 40–50, 148–50; Marquess of Lothian, *Liberalism in the Modern World* (1933).

[67] Samuel papers, SAM/A/89/84, resignation letter by Liberal ministers to Ramsay MacDonald, 28 September 1932.

[68] *MG*, 7 February 1933, 4.

[69] *MG*, 7 February 1933, 4. Layton had first canvassed this idea at the 1932 Liberal Summer School: *LM*, xl (1932), 393–4.

[70] The Liberals used a Commons debate in March 1933 to press the case for low-tariff groups and most-favoured-nation revision: Hansard, HC (series 5) vol. 275, cols 1967–80, 1980–5, 2028–38 (15 March 1933).

ending in failure. As Barry Eichengreen and Marc Uzan have pointed out, the conference was stymied from the start by the Roosevelt administration's reluctance to discuss war debts and specific tariff rates, and by the basic conflict between French demands for currency stabilization and the British and American governments' commitments to monetary reflation.[71] However, the Liberals felt, perhaps justifiably, that the conference could have made some progress on tariff reduction if British ministers had taken a lead.[72] Instead, Neville Chamberlain and Walter Runciman reaffirmed their bilateralist position and used the conference 'as a forum for self-justificatory pronouncements on the British route to trade liberalisation'—as Tim Rooth has shown.[73] For Samuel, at least, the National Government's refusal to consider multilateral action belied its professed desire to bring world tariffs down.

The idea of a low-tariff group was unpopular with grassroots Liberals, and sparked a rebellion at the 1933 NLF meetings amid fears that it would blur the party's message; young candidate Frances Josephy complained that it was 'pure Simonism and nothing else'.[74] The revolt was defeated by 254 votes to 210 after Sir Francis Acland emphasized that the group would not prevent Britain returning to free trade, but suspicions remained that the ex-ministers were 'not quite sound' on the issue.[75] Conversely, senior Liberals such as Lothian believed that activists were too ready to dismiss the importance of securing tariff reductions from other nations.[76] The idea that Britain would have to return to free trade by stages, so that protected industries could adjust to the new competitive environment, was less controversial, but the leadership still had to contend with calls for a future Liberal government to 'sweep away all protectionist duties and quotas' as soon as possible.[77] A handful of committed restorationists, led by D. M. Mason and Sir George Paish, also pressed for an early return to the gold standard.[78]

[71] Barry Eichengreen and Marc Uzan, 'The 1933 World Economic Conference as an instance of failed international cooperation', in Peter B. Evans, Harold K. Jacobson, and Robert D. Putnam (eds), *Double-Edged Diplomacy: International Bargaining and Domestic Politics* (Berkeley, Calif., 1993), 171–206.

[72] *MG*, 21 June 1933, 5; Hansard, HC (series 5) vol. 280, cols 791–7 (10 July 1933).

[73] Tim Rooth, *British Protectionism and the International Economy: Overseas Commercial Policy in the 1930s* (Cambridge, 1992), 159–60.

[74] *MG*, 19 May 1933, 6.

[75] Lothian papers, GD40/17/274/318, Percy Heffer to Lothian, 7 December 1933.

[76] Lothian papers, GD40/17/274/319–20, Lothian to Heffer, 8 December 1933.

[77] Elliott Dodds, in *NLF Proceedings, 1934*, 49. *The Liberal Way*, drafted by Muir, acknowledged the need for a gradual return to free trade: NLF, *The Liberal Way* (1934), 54–5.

[78] Hansard, HC (series 5) vol. 280, cols 804–10 (10 July 1933); *NLF Proceedings, 1935* (1935), 37–9.

PROTECTIONISM AND PLANNING

The emphasis which Liberals placed on economic nationalism as a cause of depression and unemployment represented an important point of contact with the free-market economists at the LSE. Lionel Robbins, for instance, read Lothian's discussion of 'international anarchy' with 'the most complete agreement', and wondered whether 'the connection between the nationalist madness and economic interventionism might not have been even more strongly underlined'.[79] The need to re-establish a stable international order and restore the workings of the price mechanism formed the main policy prescription of Robbins' 1934 book *The Great Depression*, though he diverged from Samuel and Lothian in advocating a restored gold standard and firmly rejecting public works.[80]

Another parallel between the Liberals and the LSE economists lay in their forceful critiques of the National Government's efforts to buttress tariff protection with production quotas and marketing schemes, especially in relation to agriculture.[81] The restrictive nature of the National Government's policies made the Liberals more sceptical about state intervention in the domestic sphere and proposals for 'planning' than they had been in the 1920s. The contrast with the Yellow Book was perhaps more apparent than real, since Liberals had always emphasized that industrial reorganization should aim to reduce costs rather than raise prices; indeed, it was on this ground that they had opposed and amended the Labour government's Coal Mines Bill in 1929–30.[82] The party also remained committed to the Yellow Book's proposals for industrial democracy, minimum wages, the conversion of monopolies to public corporations, and the regulation of trusts and cartels.[83] Nevertheless, the National Government's measures forced Liberals to attend more closely to the possibility that state interference would exacerbate economic dislocation, and in the years after Ottawa the dangers of planning became a major Liberal theme.

The idea of statutory agricultural marketing schemes first gained currency in the 1920s, as a means of strengthening farmers' market power

[79] Lothian papers, GD40/17/276/571–2, Robbins to Lothian, 25 January 1934, at fol. 571.

[80] Lionel Robbins, *The Great Depression* (1934).

[81] For Robbins' views on agriculture, see Lionel Robbins, 'The planning of British agriculture', *Lloyds Bank Limited Monthly Review*, no. 57 (November 1934), 458–69.

[82] M. W. Kirby, 'Government intervention in industrial organization: Coal mining in the nineteen thirties', *Business History*, xv (1973), 160–73; Hansard, HC (series 5) vol. 233, cols 1293–1311 (17 December 1929).

[83] NLF, *The Liberal Way*, 127–35, 162–78.

vis-à-vis distributors and retailers and enabling farmers to even out price fluctuations. On this basis, and in the context of Lib–Lab cooperation, Lloyd George's Liberals backed the Agricultural Marketing Act of 1931, which reached the statute book before the Labour government fell. Under the National Government, however, statutory marketing took on an overtly protectionist and restrictive cast. The Agricultural Marketing Act of 1933 empowered the Minister of Agriculture to reorganize any branch of the agricultural industry in the interests of efficiency or economic stability, and the marketing boards established for milk, hops, potatoes, pork, and bacon were explicitly intended—in conjunction with tariffs—to raise food prices permanently above world levels. Liberals were especially perturbed by the powers which the marketing boards received to fix minimum prices and penalize farmers who exceeded their production quotas.[84] The proliferation of agricultural subsidies was hardly less offensive, especially in view of ministers' parsimony in other fields. As Ramsay Muir pointed out in 1935, the contrast between the £27,000,000 spent each year supporting agricultural prices, and the £2,000,000 spent on the Special Areas, was a striking indication of the National Government's priorities.[85]

The Liberal critique of the National Government's measures centred on the charge that they were socialistic, interfering with the operation of the price mechanism and 'setting up Government, rather than the buying public, as the arbiter of which trades are to be encouraged and which repressed'.[86] The equation of restrictive planning with socialism was widely made: Samuel thought that the Agricultural Marketing Bill was 'by far the most Socialistic Measure that has been brought before Parliament in recent years', and Liberals took delight in pointing out that the Minister of Agriculture, Walter Elliot, had been a Fabian in his youth and was now putting similar ideas into practice as a Conservative.[87] More generally, the government's policies seemed to demonstrate that socialism and protectionism were two sides of the same coin. Only the Liberals could therefore be trusted to defend free enterprise.

Liberals recognized that the National Government's measures did not cause all the problems associated with full-blooded socialist planning. The problem of pricing in a planned economy, identified by Ludwig von Mises in the 1920s, presented itself in only a mild form; the practical difficulties of state-run industries were largely avoided; and private ownership

[84] Parliamentary Archives, Graham White papers, WHI/1/2/1, 'Agricultural Marketing Acts. The Liberal Party's Record', memorandum by Sir Robert Hamilton, n.d. [1934].

[85] Graham White papers, WHI/5/8/78, 'An Open Letter to the Electors' by Ramsay Muir, November 1935.

[86] Muir in *NLF Proceedings, 1935*, 7.

[87] Hansard, HC (series 5) vol. 276 cols 72–91, at 72 (20 March 1933), and vol. 278, cols 390–5 (17 May 1933).

was evidently preserved.[88] However, the differences between capitalist and socialist planning were perceived to be ones of degree rather than kind. 'You cannot take sections of industry out of the price system and put them on some other principle', Lord Lothian argued, 'without dislocating it still further.'[89] Indeed, Lothian thought capitalist planning could be more dangerous than socialist planning, precisely because it was piecemeal:

> I am not very much afraid of a straight fight at the polls between individualism and democracy at the one hand and socialist dictatorship on the other. But economic nationalism, by the unemployment and losses it creates, forces governments to try to remedy by ever-increasing interference their own mistakes . . . Our overloaded governments, while protesting that they believe in freedom are being steadily driven towards fascist economic dictatorships by the quotas, tariffs, and embargoes they put on and by the restriction and control of output at home which these measures inevitably make necessary.[90]

The restrictive National Recovery Administration codes of President Roosevelt's New Deal stood condemned on the same grounds.[91] As Robbins noted, the cumulative effect of these interventionist policies was to make the economy 'less stable, less free, less productive' than it would otherwise be.[92]

The Liberals' theoretical criticisms of planning were overlain by constitutional and political objections. Comprehensive socialist planning, as practised in the Soviet Union, again provided the negative model. As Lothian saw it, socialism 'inevitably' meant 'the end of democracy and Parliamentary government as we have known it', along with 'the end of individual freedom, of freedom of the press, of independence of the judiciary, possibly even of freedom of conscience'.[93] The Labour Party's shift to the left after 1931, and especially the growing prominence of Sir Stafford Cripps and the Socialist League, heightened Liberal fears of a socialist regime, whilst at the other end of the political spectrum Sir Oswald Mosley's British Union of Fascists posed a more obvious threat to liberty.[94] Liberals could not credibly link the National Government to totalitarian extremism, but they did believe that its policies undermined democracy, especially by delegating power to autonomous agencies outside effective parliamentary control. In addition to the agricultural marketing schemes,

[88] Ludwig von Mises, 'Economic calculation in the Socialist Commonwealth', in F. A. Hayek (ed.), *Collectivist Economic Planning* (1935), 87–130; *NLF Proceedings, 1934*, 73; NLF, *The Liberal Way*, 135.

[89] *NLF Proceedings, 1934*, 73.

[90] *NLF Proceedings, 1934*, 77–8.

[91] Keynes was also critical of the NRA codes, and urged Roosevelt to abandon restrictive policies: Robert Skidelsky, *John Maynard Keynes* (3 vols, 1983–2001), ii, 489–94.

[92] Robbins, *Great Depression*, 198.

[93] *NLF Proceedings, 1934*, 73, 74.

[94] Muir in *NLF Proceedings, 1934*, 8–9; NLF, *The Liberal Way*, 91–2.

the Unemployment Assistance Board established in 1934 aroused concern on this score.[95] As the decade drew on, the barrister and Dundee MP Dingle Foot emerged as the most forceful critic of the National Government's record on civil liberties. Echoing John Dunning's 1780 motion on the influence of the Crown, Foot complained that the power of the executive 'has increased, is increasing, and ought to be diminished'.[96]

The stridency with which the Liberals condemned the National Government's policies was liable to obscure the qualified nature of their own anti-statism. As the next chapter shows, many Liberals engaged closely with non-party planning groups such as Political and Economic Planning and the Next Five Years Group in this period, and highlighted the ways in which their proposals for industrial organization had been prefigured in the Yellow Book. Samuel himself believed that a 'merely negative' attitude to state intervention was no longer tenable.[97] Yet though Liberals did their best to differentiate between good and bad forms of planning, their explanations were not wholly convincing. If the classical analysis espoused by Lothian was right, why did it not follow that *any* form of intervention would further dislocate the market system?

NATIONAL DEVELOPMENT

The emphasis which Liberals placed on tariffs and restrictions as a cause of unemployment significantly circumscribed the claims which they could make for public works. After 1931, Samuel and his colleagues routinely argued that the remedy for unemployment must be 'primarily international', and there was likely to be 'a grave measure of unemployment so long as the international trade situation was not redressed'.[98] Liberals were also impressed by the practical difficulties involved in setting public works in motion, and sensitive to the charge that 'relief works' damaged confidence and wasted public money, which continued to be pressed by Asquithian right-wingers.[99] Moreover, despite taking advice from Dennis Robertson, the party struggled to keep up with theoretical developments in these years: for instance, Muir still spoke of putting the 'unused money'

[95] Hansard, HC (series 5) vol. 283, cols 1114–24 (30 November 1933).

[96] Hansard, HC (series 5) vol. 319, cols 1026–36, at 1026 (27 January 1937), printed as Dingle Foot, *Despotism in Disguise* (1937).

[97] Hansard, HC (series 5) vol. 300, cols 409–15, at 409 (3 April 1935).

[98] Samuel in Hansard, HC (series 5) vol. 274, cols 1242–56, at 1243 (16 February 1933); see also Hansard, HC (series 5) vol. 270, cols 224–35 (8 November 1932).

[99] Thurso papers, II, 75/1, 'From Mr Vivian Phillipps', n.d. [September/October 1933], and II, 75/5, 'Note on Liberal Policy' by Francis Hirst and others, January 1934.

which 'clogged' the banks to work.[100] Only in the late 1930s would Keynes' new concept of demand deficiency, leading to an equilibrium forming below full employment level, be widely understood.

In spite of these limitations, the Liberals were adamant that the national development schemes of 1929–31 should be revived and extended as circumstances permitted. Pressure for this came at first from the left of the party. At Clacton, Harry Nathan and Megan Lloyd George successfully amended the official policy declaration, 'Liberalism in a New Era', to add a reference to national development, arguing that it was established party policy and Liberal ministers should not be ashamed of it.[101] At the same time, the essay collection *Whither Britain? A Radical Answer*—written by Hubert Phillips and a group of radical candidates including Alan Sainsbury, Jules Menken and Ronw Moelwyn Hughes—argued that the state should expand its capital spending up to 'the limits of public confidence' in order to bring saving and investment into balance.[102]

Samuel and his colleagues did not share the enthusiasm for planning expressed in *Whither Britain?* or the Lloyd Georgeites' desire to rebuild links with Labour, and until September 1932 they were still enmeshed in the National Government. After the resignations, however, national development again became a major plank in the Liberal programme. A Labour motion of censure on unemployment in February 1933 gave Samuel the chance to define his party's position: pending the restoration of free trade, public works could not solve the unemployment problem, but they could alleviate it considerably if pursued on bold lines. With national credit restored and Bank Rate brought down, Samuel argued, the government had ample scope to expand its capital investment programme. The Liberal leader was encouraged by recent calls for a revival of public investment by Sir Arthur Salter and Sir Walter Layton; 'no great economist in England', he claimed, approved of the government's caution in this matter.[103] Samuel proposed that, as a first step, the government should release funds to local authorities which had prepared public works schemes, such as the Liberal-run Bethnal Green Borough Council.[104] More ambitiously, he suggested that special commissioners should be appointed to prepare schemes for housing, railway electrification, land settlement, and other projects, work with the Chancellor of the Exchequer to obtain finance,

[100] Graham White papers, WHI/5/8/78, 'An Open Letter to the Electors'; see also Philip Oliver in *NLF Proceedings, 1935*, 50.

[101] *NLF Proceedings, 1932*, 17–21. The amendment was carried unanimously.

[102] Hubert Phillips et al., *Whither Britain? A Radical Answer* (1932), 44–5, 67–9.

[103] Hansard, HC (series 5) vol. 274, cols 1242–56, at 1251 (16 February 1933).

[104] MacDonald had recently turned down a request from Bethnal Green Borough Council for help in financing relief works: *The Times*, 14 February 1933, 7.

and ensure that the schemes were carried through. Sir John Tudor Walters' work on rural housing in the latter months of the previous Labour government provided a model of how such a commissioner could operate.

Samuel's proposal for special commissioners to oversee national development schemes fitted well with the Yellow Book's proposal, revived after 1931, for a Board of National Investment which would coordinate public investment plans.[105] These two ideas formed the basis of Liberal public works policy for the rest of the Parliament.[106] The ambition and confidence of the 1929 programme were conspicuously lacking, and Liberals remained ambivalent about the idea of a large development loan, but the party placed itself firmly on the reflationary side of the unemployment debate as it developed during the 1930s.[107] As far as fiscal policy was concerned, the Liberals stood much closer to Keynes—whose articles on 'The means to prosperity' appeared in *The Times* in March 1933—than to the free-market economists at the LSE who opposed public works.[108] The main policy difference with Keynes was that the Liberals could not view experiments in 'national self-sufficiency' with equanimity.[109] Rather, Samuel and his colleagues advocated an expansionary fiscal policy within an overtly internationalist policy framework.

LLOYD GEORGE'S NEW DEAL

The Liberal Party approached the 1935 general election with a plausible economic policy programme based on free trade, free enterprise, and public works. However, its efforts to secure publicity for this programme—and to convince voters that it deserved to be taken seriously—were hampered by David Lloyd George's activities. From the moment of the Liberal split in October 1931, Lloyd George presented himself as a king over the water, committed to breaking the party's ties with the National Government and

[105] NLF, *The Liberal Way*, 123–4, 136–43.

[106] The party also suggested creating regional authorities so that local authorities could take joint action in housing, town planning, and transport: *MG*, 16 March 1934, 4.

[107] Delegates at the 1933 NLF meetings rejected grassroots calls for a development loan, and Francis Hirst was predictably hostile, but Welsh Liberals such as R. T. Evans favoured one and Sinclair was also sympathetic: *NLF Proceedings, 1933* (1933), 11–17; *MG*, 13 July 1933, 18, and 8 May 1933, 13; Thurso papers, II, 75/1, Sinclair to Walter Rea, 9 October 1933.

[108] John Maynard Keynes, 'The means to prosperity', in *JMK*, ix, 335–66. For the reception of Keynes' articles by Liberals, see Sir Percy Harris in *The Times*, 15 March 1933, 11, and Kingsley Griffith in Hansard, HC (series 5) vol. 277, cols 1295–1302 (8 May 1933).

[109] John Maynard Keynes, 'National self-sufficiency', in *JMK*, xxi, 233–46. The fullest account of Keynes' attitude to the international economy in these years is Donald Markwell, *John Maynard Keynes and International Relations* (Oxford, 2006), 140–209.

rebuilding links with Labour on the basis of the Yellow Book. As we have seen, Lloyd George assiduously fostered discontent with Samuel's leadership over the agreement to differ and the party's reticence in crossing the floor. The *Manchester Guardian* and *News Chronicle* gave the former leader sympathetic coverage, and in Wales even nominally Samuelite MPs and activists looked to him to revive the Liberal cause.[110] In January 1935, Lloyd George returned to the centre of the political stage with a speech at Bangor which, apeing Roosevelt, outlined a 'New Deal'; in June, when the National Government rejected his plans, he formed the Council of Action for Peace and Reconstruction to campaign for them. An examination of the New Deal is instructive, not least because of the contrast its proposals formed with official Liberal policy.

The conventional interpretation of Lloyd George's New Deal sees it as a personal initiative, in which the former Prime Minister sought to use Nonconformist support to regain political influence.[111] Although this interpretation is justified, the New Deal should also be understood as a manifestation of Welsh Liberal disaffection with the official party. In September 1934, Lloyd George convened an informal gathering of prominent Welsh activists, including Thomas Waterhouse, J. E. Emlyn-Jones, and future Chancellor of the Exchequer Selwyn Lloyd, at a hotel in Criccieth.[112] At this meeting, Lloyd George outlined plans for '[a]n organised effort . . . to secure a Parliament of the Left, pledged to an advanced progressive programme of Peace, Liberty and Reconstruction'. This programme, he felt, should involve large-scale public investment in agriculture, rural industries and housing, to reverse the drift of population from the land to the towns and provide 'work or sustenance for all'. A campaign organization would back Liberal candidates who accepted the programme and had a reasonable chance of victory, and would use 'organised Liberal pressure' to persuade other candidates to support it.[113]

Lloyd George assembled a group of predominantly Welsh economists, social scientists, agriculturalists, and Liberal activists at his farm in Churt, Surrey, to work out a programme over two weekends in October 1934.

[110] The six Welsh Samuelite MPs joined the Lloyd George family members in a Welsh Liberal group, with Lloyd George as chairman, in February 1933, whilst Welsh Liberal activists called for Lloyd George to return as party leader: *MG*, 15 February 1933, 9, 20 January 1933, 9, and 8 May 1933, 13.

[111] Stephen Koss, 'Lloyd George and Nonconformity: the last rally', *EHR*, lxxxix (1974), 77–106.

[112] Geoffrey Crowther of *The Economist* also attended, probably on behalf of Sir Walter Layton: see David Lloyd George papers, LG/G/141/26/5, Layton to Lloyd George, 13 September 1934.

[113] David Lloyd George papers, LG/G/153/5, Notes of conversations at Criccieth, 13–14 September 1934.

D. Caradog Jones of Liverpool University, Morgan Rees and Alun Roberts of Bangor, and Richard Stapledon of Aberystwyth were among the most active participants, but it was Lloyd George who determined the main lines of the New Deal policy. Most strikingly, Lloyd George repudiated free trade, declaring that a tariff was justified as part of a programme to put half a million more workers on the land and that no party would dare advocate a wholesale abolition of tariffs at the next election. Against protests from Stapledon, he argued that British agricultural policy should seek to enable domestic farmers to provide the whole of the nation's needs in those foodstuffs which Britain was capable of producing.[114] It was also Lloyd George who advocated a National Investment Board to ensure that sufficient capital was available to industry, and controlling boards for major industries—such as shipping, coal, and cotton—to ensure that the capital thus disbursed was wisely used.[115] In the field of public works, the Welshman revived the 1929 Liberal programme, proposing a £250,000,000 'prosperity loan' to finance two years' investment in infrastructure, agriculture, and housing. He claimed that this would create 500,000 jobs directly, and another million jobs in ancillary trades and through the multiplier effect. Taken together with measures to raise the school leaving age and expand training facilities, such a programme would reduce the unemployment rolls to a hard core of 250,000 'unemployables'.[116]

Lloyd George's reliance on Welsh academics for advice on the New Deal meant that the proposals were largely developed in isolation from the Samuelite leadership, but he did ask Layton and Lothian for comments on his draft programme, and persuaded Lothian to draft a foreign policy statement which could be combined with it.[117] Both men approved of the Keynesian element in the proposals, but criticized the neglect of the international dimension and the acceptance of tariffs. Layton was particularly unsettled by the assertion that no significant expansion of exports could be expected in the coming decade; instead, he felt, Lloyd George should clearly label his proposals as interim measures for reducing unemployment, without prejudice to longer-term aims.[118] Lothian echoed this point, and also questioned the wisdom of Lloyd George's target of returning 500,000 workers to the land. A national development programme

[114] David Lloyd George papers, LG/G/153/1, Notes of conversation at Churt, 26 October 1934 at 6.30pm.

[115] David Lloyd George papers, LG/G/153/1, Notes of conversation at Churt, 27 October 1934 at 10am.

[116] W. R. Garside, *British Unemployment, 1919–1939: A Study in Public Policy* (Cambridge, 1990), 355–6.

[117] Koss, 'Lloyd George and Nonconformity', 86.

[118] Thurso papers, II, 57/1, Sinclair to Samuel, 11 January 1935.

which related to both town and country, he argued, would stand a better chance of winning popular backing.[119]

The Samuelite attitude to Lloyd George's New Deal was necessarily ambivalent. On the one hand, Lloyd George's adoption of tariffs represented a serious departure from Liberal orthodoxy, and—together with his efforts to press the scheme on the National Government—showed how opportunistic his earlier criticisms of the Samuelites had been. The protectionist implications of the New Deal were widely criticized, and traditionalist free traders such as Francis Hirst revelled in the discomfort of Lloyd George's Liberal followers.[120] On the other hand, Liberals recognized that their former leader could hardly be ignored, and that the national development plans closely resembled the party's 1929 policy. As Sinclair pointed out to Samuel, 'the possibility of reuniting the Party roughly on the basis of the Ll. G. policy', provided it could be shorn of its protectionism, was politically very appealing; Lloyd George even told Layton that he had been offered the chance to take over the party 'lock, stock and barrel'.[121] Lloyd George's preference for independent action ruled out this option, but it also meant that Samuelites could participate in the Council of Action without committing themselves to the details of his proposals. A host of active Liberals, including Lothian, Layton, Sir Francis Acland, and Milner Gray, took prominent roles in the Council, and left-leaning Liberals and Nonconformists appear to have provided the mainstay of its support.[122] Moreover, Samuelite relations with Lloyd George became easier over time as he moved back towards a free-trade position and the Abyssinian crisis pushed foreign policy to the top of the political agenda.[123] When the election came, Samuel gave him one of the party's three radio broadcasts, and most Liberal candidates—including almost all the successful ones—signed the Council of Action's questionnaire and received its endorsement.[124]

[119] Lothian papers, GD40/17/112/97-9, Lothian to Lloyd George, 10 March 1935, at fols 97–8.

[120] David Lloyd George papers, LG/G/142/1, Emlyn-Jones to Lloyd George, 5 March 1935; Bodleian Library, Hirst papers, 64, Francis Hirst to Gertrude Hirst, 7 February 1935.

[121] Samuel papers, SAM/A/155(IX)/17, Sinclair to Samuel, 4 May 1935; Layton papers, 104/34, 'Note of conversation with Mr Lloyd George, Friday, May 17th, 1935'.

[122] Lothian papers, GD40/17/300/342–7, 'Notes of the Committee Meeting' of the Council of Action, 10 July 1935.

[123] Thurso papers, II, 57/1, Sinclair to Samuel, 14 October 1935.

[124] Stannage, *Baldwin Thwarts the Opposition*, 144–6; David Lloyd George papers, LG/G/142/2, 'List of Approved Candidates Who Have Been Returned', n.d. [November 1935]. Many Labour and some National Government candidates also signed the Council of Action questionnaire.

THE 1935 GENERAL ELECTION

The activities of the Council of Action may have raised Liberal influence and morale, but they did little to improve the party's performance at the 1935 general election. With limited financial resources and few candidates available, the Samuelites were forced to fight on a narrow front: only 159 candidates took the field, and some of these had been recruited for hopeless seats at the last minute. The tone of the Liberal appeal in the constituencies is conveyed by Tom Stannage's analysis of election addresses. Whilst peace was the dominant issue, 93 per cent of Liberals mentioned the need for free or freer trade, 70 per cent advocated some form of public works, and one-third mentioned their support for the Council of Action's programme. Compared with Labour and National Government candidates, Liberals said relatively little about taxation, the social services, or the cost of living, although some Liberal candidates engaged in heated disputes with Conservatives over the impact of protection on food prices.[125] The NLF's manifesto focussed on similar themes, following the main lines of policy developed at Blickling and embodied in *The Liberal Way*.[126]

On polling day, seventeen official Liberals were returned—about half the party's 1931 tally—together with four Lloyd Georgeites. One major problem was the appearance of Conservative rivals in industrial constituencies such as Edinburgh East, Middlesbrough East, South Shields, and Dewsbury, where Liberals had won straight fights with Labour in the unusual circumstances of 1931; another was the party's qualified support for the means test, which alienated working-class voters and seems to have contributed to Samuel's defeat at Darwen.[127] Only strong local reputations, and perhaps some tactical voting, saved Geoffrey Mander, Graham White, Kingsley Griffith, and Sir Percy Harris in their urban seats. Otherwise, except for occasional cases (such as Dundee and Bradford South) where Samuelites retained local Tory backing, the party was pushed back to rural Britain. Ex-ministers Isaac Foot and Sir Robert Hamilton were unseated at Bodmin and Orkney and Shetland respectively, but Wales held relatively strong, and three seats on the English periphery (Barnstaple, North Cumberland, and Berwick-upon-Tweed) were gained in straight fights with the Conservatives.

[125] Stannage, *Baldwin Thwarts the Opposition*, 291–2; BLPES, Josephy papers, Add. 1/8, Frances Josephy election address and National Government election leaflets, November 1935.

[126] *Liberal Party General Election Manifestos, 1900-1997*, ed. Iain Dale (2000), 56–8.

[127] Wasserstein, *Herbert Samuel*, 370–1.

CONCLUSION

Across much of the British political spectrum, the years of depression were characterized by a burgeoning interest in state intervention and planning. This chapter has shown, however, that the Liberal Party leadership moved away from the constructive Liberalism of the Yellow Book in the wake of the 1931 crisis. In this 'new era of intensified economic nationalism', free trade returned to the heart of Liberal policy, and classical doctrines were again seen to militate against government intervention in the domestic as well as the international sphere.[128] Without much direct input from economists, Sir Herbert Samuel and his colleagues worked to synthesize grassroots commitments to free trade and public works into a coherent policy. Although the Samuelites struggled to decide whether tariffs and misguided interventions had caused the depression or merely exacerbated it, they were adamant that unemployment could not be fully conquered until free trade was re-established and international cooperation restored. In the meantime, public works could create jobs directly and reinforce the wider economic stimulus provided by cheap money. This policy may have lacked a developed theoretical basis, but it neatly spanned the ground between Keynes' reflationary position and the classical-cum-Austrian analysis of Robbins and other LSE economists.

Whatever its intrinsic merits, however, the electoral impact of the policy which the Liberals developed after 1932 can only be described as negligible. Indeed, Liberal decline continued unabated at the 1935 general election. This political failure requires a threefold explanation. Firstly, the polarization of the electorate on socialist and anti-socialist lines left little political space for a Liberal alternative to develop. As Ross McKibbin has powerfully argued, the National Government enjoyed enormous success in identifying itself with the welfare of the 'public' against a Labour movement which represented the sectional interests of the unionized working class.[129] The Simonites' ongoing presence in the National Government helped substantiate its claims to moderation, and backed up Stanley Baldwin's efforts to appeal to erstwhile Liberal

[128] Thurso papers, II, 75/5, 'Notes on Parts IV and V of "The Liberal Way"' by Sinclair, January 1934.

[129] Ross McKibbin, 'Class and conventional wisdom: The Conservative Party and the "public" in inter-war Britain', in Ross McKibbin, *The Ideologies of Class: Social Relations in Britain, 1880–1950* (Oxford, 1990), 228–58; Ross McKibbin, *Parties and People: England, 1914–1951* (Oxford, 2010), 69–105.

voters.[130] At the same time, the Samuelites' complicity in the National Government's economy programme undermined their progressive credentials and alienated radical support. In this sense, the Liberals were condemned to continued decline by the structure of political allegiances which the events of 1931 had established.

The proliferation of 'middle opinion' groups in the 1930s, however, should warn us against taking the partisan polarization of that decade too much for granted. Clearly, there did exist a progressive but non-socialist element in the electorate whose support the Liberals might have won. From a second perspective, then, the Liberals' problem lay in a lack of definition, unity, and purpose. The tripartite division within Liberalism blurred the party's image, and was compounded by the Samuelites' perceived ambivalence towards the National Government: Stannage has noted that Samuel frequently sounded like an ally of Baldwin's administration even during the 1935 election campaign.[131] In these circumstances, Liberal candidates were bound to play up their personal qualities and their links with the Council of Action at the expense of party loyalties: for instance, Graham White's election address in Birkenhead East did not even mention his Liberalism.[132] A sharper break with the National Government in 1932 would have been fraught with difficulties, but it would have defined the Samuelite position much more clearly, and it might have enabled the party to attract centre-left support at a time when Labour was still recovering from 1931.

A third cause of the Liberals' failure lay in the economic environment in which the National Government's policies were implemented. On the basis of classical theory, Samuel and his colleagues believed that tariffs would raise prices and damage employment, all other things being equal; indeed, this had been the basis of the popular free-trade case since the nineteenth century. In the 1930s, however, any negative impact tariffs might have had was outweighed by the general fall in world prices and by the stimulus which devaluation and cheap money provided to employment. The Ministry of Labour's cost-of-living index fell until 1933, and did not regain its 1931 level until 1936; registered unemployment peaked in 1932 and had fallen by one-quarter by the time the election came.[133] In these

[130] Philip Williamson, *Stanley Baldwin: Conservative Leadership and National Values* (Cambridge, 1999), 50–2.

[131] Stannage, *Baldwin Thwarts the Opposition*, 158–9.

[132] Graham White papers, WHI/5/3/20, Graham White election address, November 1935.

[133] B. R. Mitchell and Phyllis Deane, *Abstract of British Historical Statistics* (Cambridge, 1962), 478, 66.

circumstances, it was difficult to claim that protection had condemned Britons to a 'little loaf', and Liberals were reduced to using counter-factual comparisons to challenge the notion that tariffs had proved successful.[134] The Liberals' efforts to revive free trade as a popular cause were thus inhibited by economic developments as well as by political ones.

[134] For contemporary recognition of this problem, see Thurso papers, II, 75/5, 'Notes on Parts IV and V of "The Liberal Way"'.

4

From 'Middle Opinion' to *Ownership for All*, 1935–9

The electoral dominance of the National Government, asserted in 1931 and reaffirmed at the 1935 general election, structured the politics of the middle and late 1930s. With Conservative policies cloaked in the language of the public welfare and the national interest, both the Labour and Liberal parties found it difficult to present themselves as credible alternative governments, while the ascendancy of Stanley Baldwin and Neville Chamberlain within the Conservative ranks meant that maverick Tories such as Harold Macmillan also found themselves excluded from power. In consequence, the 1930s saw a spate of efforts to promote cooperation between elements in the centre and left of the political spectrum. At mid-decade, 'middle opinion' initiatives such as the Council of Action, Political and Economic Planning, and the Next Five Years Group were most prominent, and focussed on canvassing non-socialist support for reflationary policies and planning measures.[1] Later, as British policy towards Hitler and Mussolini became the dominant political issue, centre-progressives sought to construct an anti-appeasement 'popular front' which would include the Labour Party and perhaps even the Communists.[2] As Daniel Ritschel has pointed out, these initiatives all had different ideological casts, and most of them sought to establish agreement on short-term policies without necessarily harmonizing participants' underlying views.[3] 'Middle opinion' was not unitary and cohesive but diverse and fragmentary.

Many Liberals engaged actively in planning groups such as the Next Five Years Group and in the campaign for a popular front. At a time of Liberal decline, non-party movements offered a valuable means of rallying

[1] Arthur Marwick, 'Middle opinion in the Thirties: Planning, progress and political "agreement" ', *EHR*, lxxix (1964), 285–98.

[2] David Blaazer, *The Popular Front and the Progressive Tradition: Socialists, Liberals, and the Quest for Unity, 1884–1939* (Cambridge, 1992).

[3] Daniel Ritschel, *The Politics of Planning: The Debate on Economic Planning in Britain in the 1930s* (Oxford, 1997), 1–19.

the political centre, challenging the National Government's foreign policy, and pressing the case for Yellow Book-style reforms. However, the Liberal leadership treated cooperative initiatives with caution, and emphasized instead the need to build up the Liberal Party as a vital and independent force. This was especially the case after Sir Archibald Sinclair succeeded Samuel as leader in 1935. In line with this strategic orientation, the main trajectory of Liberal thought continued to run away from the constructive Liberalism of the Yellow Book and towards a more individualistic appeal. The new policy synthesis which emerged in this period brought together three main currents of thought. From classical economics came a strong commitment to competitive markets; from Keynes, via the financial press, came the idea that demand management could be used to temper booms and slumps; and from the distributist movement of G. K. Chesterton and Hilaire Belloc, and the wider republican tradition, came the belief that private property ownership was the soundest basis for individual liberty and self-development. In Sinclair's hands, this liberal Keynesian synthesis was tentative and incomplete, but it clearly prefigured the direction that Liberal economic thought would take after the Second World War.

The reorientation of Liberal policy which took place in the late 1930s reflected diverse influences, and its ideological coherence should not be exaggerated. However, it is worth noting that Liberals' concern to legitimate the market order by distributing property and economic power more widely showed a strong affinity with the neoliberal movement that was beginning to develop in this period. The American journalist Walter Lippmann, who inspired a famous colloquium in 1938, was an important influence on Liberal thinking, and characteristically neoliberal concepts such as the rule of law featured prominently in the party's rhetoric. Of course, the Liberal Party was an imperfect vehicle for a neoliberal political agenda, and Lippmann's influence on the party partly reflected his moderation: unlike more radical neoliberals such as Ludwig von Mises, he regarded demand management and social insurance as quite legitimate policy measures.[4] Nevertheless, the party's interaction with early neoliberal thought makes it difficult to view the 1930s as a period of intellectual torpor.

Sinclair's leadership stabilized the Liberal Party's political position. Morale revived, and the party's central organization was reformed, so that—as Malcolm Baines has put it—the party could function 'like an orthodox party' again.[5] Sinclair's biographer, Gerard de Groot, has credited him with renewing the party's image by linking together free trade,

[4] Ben Jackson, 'At the origins of neo-liberalism: The free economy and the strong state, 1930–1947', *HJ*, liii (2010), 129–51.

[5] Malcolm Baines, 'The Survival of the British Liberal Party, 1932–1959' (Oxford D.Phil. thesis, 1989), 28.

social justice, and opposition to appeasement under the rhetorical banner of 'freedom and democracy'.[6] The electoral impact of Sinclair's new approach is difficult to quantify, and it is possible that the Liberals would have lost further ground at a general election held in 1939–40.[7] Garry Tregidga, however, has argued that Sinclair's leadership helped the party exploit growing opposition to the government's foreign and agricultural policies, making the late 1930s 'an active and even optimistic period for the Liberal Party in rural Britain'.[8] Tregidga points out that the absence of a national popular front did not prevent Lib–Lab cooperation in regions such as south-west England, where both parties stood to benefit. With a continuing reservoir of traditional support and a renewed appeal to radical voters in these areas, the Liberals enjoyed a realistic prospect of improving their electoral performance for the first time in a decade.

This chapter unpacks the debates over the Liberal Party's policy and strategy which took place in these years. The first half examines Liberals' engagement with the planning movement during the mid-1930s, and the emergence of Elliott Dodds' arguments for a more distinctive Liberal policy, based on 'ownership for all'. The second half traces the development of Liberal policy after 1935, including the *Ownership for All* report, the reception of Keynes' *General Theory*, and the party's populist campaign against the rising cost of living. A concluding section considers the implications of these developments for the party's economic position on the eve of war.

THE POLITICS OF LIBERTY

The Liberal Party's intellectual trajectory in the 1930s can only be understood in the light of the inhospitable political environment which the party faced. Labour, Conservative, and Liberal National politicians repeatedly asserted that Liberalism's task was finished; nineteenth-century Liberalism, caricatured as a laissez-faire creed, served as a rhetorical foil for planning proposals of all kinds, and Harcourt Johnstone noted that Gladstone's name was 'now more of a music-hall joke than an inspiration for youth'.[9] The growth of totalitarianism, economic nationalism, and international tensions intensified Liberals' sense of disorientation.

[6] Gerard J. de Groot, *Liberal Crusader: The Life of Sir Archibald Sinclair* (1993), 121.

[7] Baines, 'Survival', 45–6; David Dutton, *A History of the Liberal Party since 1900* (second edition, Basingstoke, 2013), 128–34.

[8] Garry Tregidga, 'Turning of the tide? A case study of the Liberal Party in provincial Britain in the late 1930s', *History*, xcii (2007), 347–66, at 365.

[9] Bodleian Library, Oxford, Hirst papers, 14, Harcourt Johnstone to Francis Hirst, 13 February 1936.

The need to justify the party's continued existence brought Liberals back to the idea of defending and expanding liberty, which became the defining characteristic of Liberal thought and rhetoric in the 1930s. To an extent, this involved a return to the older libertarian agenda espoused by traditionalists such as Francis Hirst, who used the Liberal Free Trade Committee, the Cobden Club, and a series of 'Liberty luncheons' at the National Liberal Club in 1933–4 to canvass support for Gladstonian policies.[10] Unlike most Liberals, Hirst defined liberty in almost exclusively negative terms, but his hope that 'a strong intellectual movement' would soon emerge 'against Communism and Fascism and in favour of all forms of personal liberty' was shared by many within the party.[11]

In the hands of the party's official spokesmen, the case for liberty took a more positive form. 'The most fundamental aim of Liberalism', Ramsay Muir declared in *The Liberal Way*, was

> To create the conditions in which every man and woman shall be genuinely free, enjoying a real 'equality of opportunity' to make the most and the best of their own powers of body and mind, for their own advantage and that of the community, and effectively sharing in the control of their own destinies.

The party fought on, Muir wrote, because this aim was 'still far from being realised'.[12] Sinclair put the position in similar terms. Although personal liberty was vital—he pointed out to his colleagues in 1933—Liberals had to demonstrate its relevance to 'the great mass of the electors', for whom 'unemployment and poverty' were the most obvious sources of oppression.[13] The liberty which Liberals championed therefore included 'freedom . . . from poverty and dependence' and the possession by every citizen of the means necessary to enjoy 'a free and full life'.[14]

THE LIBERALS AND THE PLANNING MOVEMENT

In the political climate of the 1930s, 'middle opinion' initiatives had an obvious appeal to Liberals. The idea of a middle way between Conservatism and socialism had long been implicit in the party's identity, and had

[10] Hirst papers, 64, Francis Hirst to Gertrude Hirst, 16 November 1933 and 2 October 1934.

[11] Hirst papers, 64, Francis Hirst to Gertrude Hirst, 28 September 1933.

[12] NLF, *The Liberal Way* (1934), 185.

[13] Churchill Archives Centre, Cambridge, Thurso papers, II, 75/1, Sinclair to Walter Rea, 9 October 1933.

[14] *NLF Proceedings, 1934*, 22.

become an explicit theme of Liberal rhetoric during the 1920s. Samuel and his colleagues believed that their party was the natural instrument of centrist politics, through which the 'great body of progressive opinion' could regain control of 'the policy of the British State' and defend liberty against extremists; but they also recognized that the Liberals were unlikely to regain major-party status in the near future.[15] Non-party and cross-party organizations offered a more promising means of building up the moderate forces.

As Helen McCarthy has recently reminded us, non-party organizations proliferated during the inter-war years. At both elite and popular levels, bodies such as the League of Nations Union mobilized citizens in support of specific causes, providing spaces for 'inclusive, pluralist participation' and helping to anchor British politics 'in the centre-ground'.[16] Liberals were particularly keen supporters of the LNU, and played a prominent role in its 1934–5 'Peace Ballot'; indeed, the Liberal scholar Gilbert Murray became the Union's defining personality, alongside the Conservative Lord Hugh Cecil. Liberals also featured prominently in the women's movement, Eleanor Rathbone's Family Endowment Society, and other civic and religious organizations: for instance, the Asquithian MP Leif Jones presided over the prohibitionist United Kingdom Alliance from 1906 to 1932, whilst Sir Herbert Samuel and James de Rothschild were prominent Zionists.

The Council of Action was not the only 'middle opinion' group which recruited within this Liberal and Nonconformist milieu. In 1934, a manifesto on 'Liberty and Democratic Leadership' drawn up by the principal of Ruskin College, Oxford, Alfred Barratt Brown, with Harold Macmillan and the National Labour peer Lord Allen of Hurtwood, attracted signatures from more than twenty Liberals of impressively diverse views.[17] Several prominent Liberals also became patrons of the 'Democratic Front' group, founded at Cambridge University in 1934 to promote progressive cooperation.[18]

Appeals to liberty and democracy could always rely on a sympathetic Liberal audience, but few advocates of centrist cooperation were

[15] *MG*, 16 March 1934, 4.

[16] Helen McCarthy, 'Parties, voluntary associations, and democratic politics in interwar Britain', *HJ*, l (2007), 891–912, at 893; see also Helen McCarthy, *The British People and the League of Nations: Democracy, citizenship and internationalism, c.1918–48* (Manchester, 2011).

[17] Parliamentary Archives, Graham White papers, WHI/6/4/7, 'Liberty and Democratic Leadership'; Bodleian Library, MS. Macmillan dep. c. 864, fols 8–11, list of proposed signatories by A. Barratt Brown, n.d. [January 1934]; Ritschel, *Politics of Planning*, 246.

[18] MS. Macmillan dep. c. 864, fols 136–7, 'The Democratic Front', n.d. [1934–5].

content to leave their activities on this relatively abstract level. For Macmillan and other progressive Tories, the defence of the democratic system was tied up with the attempt to promote economic planning. The most explicitly planning-oriented groups, such as PEP and the Industrial Reorganisation League, drew only scattered Liberal support, notably from Graham White and Seebohm Rowntree.[19] The Next Five Years Group which emerged from 'Liberty and Democratic Leadership' attracted much wider Liberal backing, but White, Geoffrey Mander, Sir Walter Layton and Geoffrey Crowther of *The Economist*, and Lothian (who wanted to give the group an anti-socialist edge) were most heavily involved.[20] *The Next Five Years*, 'an essay in political agreement' which appeared in July 1935, was widely seen as a lineal descendant of the Yellow Book. At macro level, the government would use national development spending to stabilize the trade cycle; at micro level, industries would be organized under industrial boards, created by the trade associations but with independent as well as business members. Monopolistic industries of national importance such as banking, electricity, and transport would become 'public concerns', privately owned but subject to publicity requirements and with profits and prices fixed by independent tribunals.[21] A range of social reforms, including the abolition of the household means test, higher unemployment benefits and pensions for the needy, and the raising of the school leaving age to sixteen, also endeared *The Next Five Years* to progressive opinion.

Although there was a great deal of common ground between Liberal Party policy and the 'middle opinion' manifestos, there was also an element of disjunction which some Liberals considered fundamental. Both *The Next Five Years* and PEP incorporated protectionism and industrial self-government into their visions of a mixed economy. By contrast, official Liberal policy had moved away from the Yellow Book since 1929, with a new emphasis on the importance of free trade and free markets, and efforts to promote 'planning' within the party during the early 1930s had been conspicuously unsuccessful.[22]

[19] On PEP, see John Pinder (ed.), *Fifty Years of Political & Economic Planning: Looking Forward, 1931–1981* (1981); Graham White papers, WHI/3/2/2, 'Unemployment Assistance' (PEP memorandum), 1 April 1935, and WHI/16/3/10, PEP circular on the social services, 30 December 1941. Daniel Ritschel describes Rowntree as 'the only Liberal of note' involved in the IRL: Ritschel, *Politics of Planning*, 195.

[20] *The Next Five Years: An Essay in Political Agreement* (1935), v–x; MS. Macmillan dep. c. 375, fols 177–8, 'The "Next Five Years Group"', n.d. [February 1936], and 226–32, 'Members of "The Next Five Years Group"', n.d. [May 1936].

[21] *The Next Five Years*, 70–96.

[22] *Whither Britain?* was largely ignored by the party leadership, and the Liberal Constructive Group which young activist Harold Cowen launched in 1933 gained little

This disjunction prompted the Liberal leadership to adopt a cautious attitude towards planning initiatives, including *The Next Five Years*. One hundred and fifty-three prominent personalities, including more than a dozen active Liberals, signed the book's foreword and promised 'general support' for the measures it contained, but Samuel and his senior colleagues were not among them.[23] Samuel considered *The Next Five Years* an 'able and stimulating book', which contained the kind of 'constructive policy' that the times demanded, but—along with the other Liberal ex-ministers—he felt that signing the foreword '*simpliciter*' would commit the party too closely to its contents.[24] The book's treatment of the trade question was especially unsatisfactory, since it appeared to presuppose the maintenance of protection, and proposed to replace the existing patchwork of tariffs with uniform tariff rates covering whole categories of imports. The authors' support for the revision of most-favoured-nation clauses, which would facilitate multilateral tariff reductions, only partially mitigated this problem.[25] The Liberal ex-ministers offered to write a public letter outlining their dissent, but the book's organizers decided that this would be inappropriate, and Samuel was left to define his position at the 1935 Liberal Summer School.[26]

A secondary point of difference between the Liberals and the moderate planners concerned industrial reorganization, especially in the form of the industrial self-government schemes canvassed by the Industrial Reorganisation League. Samuel's investigations into the coal industry had persuaded him that statutory reorganization was acceptable provided there were safeguards for the public interest, and he seems to have been unperturbed by the proposals in *The Next Five Years*.[27] The Wolverhampton MP Geoffrey Mander, himself a paint manufacturer, also thought that 'all these ideas found their origin consciously or unconsciously in the Yellow

traction. See National Archives of Scotland, Lothian papers, GD40/17/262/210–3, Cowen to Lothian, 2 April 1933; GD40/17/272/151–2, Cowen to Lothian, 19 April 1933; and GD40/17/272/160–1, Cowen to Lothian, 20 July 1933.

[23] The Liberal signatories included Graham White, Isaac Foot, Geoffrey Mander, and Sir Francis Acland—all MPs—along with A. G. Gardiner, H. A. L. Fisher, Gilbert Murray, Sir Walter Layton, Margery Corbett Ashby, Laurence J. Cadbury, and Seebohm Rowntree.

[24] Sir Herbert Samuel, *The Political Situation. Being the Inaugural Address to the Liberal Summer School, Cambridge, August 1st, 1935* (1935), 7, 8; Thurso papers, II, 57/1, 'The Next Five Years', memorandum by Samuel, 15 July 1935.

[25] Samuel, *Political Situation*, 7; *The Next Five Years*, 129–47; Graham White papers, WHI/3/5/30, 'The Next Five Years. Foreign Trade. Most-Favoured-Nation Clause', n.d. [1935]. In similar vein, Sinclair was impressed by PEP's output but found it difficult to see how the Liberals could work with it so long as it proceeded 'on purely protectionist lines': Thurso papers, III, 10/2, Sinclair to Samuel, 4 April 1934.

[26] Thurso papers, II, 57/1, 'The Next Five Years'.

[27] Hansard, HC (series 5) vol. 300, cols 409–15 (3 April 1935).

Book'.[28] Other Liberals, however, associated industrial self-government with the National Government's restrictive planning schemes and felt that it would give statutory sanction to monopolies and cartels. On this basis, Ramsay Muir and Elliott Dodds refused to endorse *The Next Five Years*, and added the complaint—which Samuel echoed—that the book ignored the need for industrial democracy and profit-sharing.[29]

Liberals' substantive criticisms of the planning movement were overlaid by a more political concern. Middle opinion initiatives offered a valuable means of promoting centrist cooperation, but they were also liable to blur the party's identity and divert its members' energies away from Liberal work. 'Groups, councils, programmes, questionnaires'—Samuel told the Liberal Summer School—might be excellent, but for the time being there was no means of giving electoral expression to this cooperation.[30] The Conservatives involved in *The Next Five Years* would do nothing to help Liberals win seats when the general election came, and the Labour Party showed no interest in a progressive combination. Samuel emphasized that Liberals were willing to join a centre-left alliance; but until an electoral agreement was reached, the party's main contribution would have to lie in ensuring its own survival.

'FREEDOM FOR ALL BASED ON OWNERSHIP FOR ALL'

The difficulties Liberals encountered in building centrist alliances opened up political space for an alternative strategy, based on staking out a more distinctive position. Elliott Dodds, the editor of the *Huddersfield Daily Examiner* and president of the National League of Young Liberals, was the most energetic advocate of this approach.[31] Dodds was no laissez-faire purist—he had backed the Yellow Book—but by the early 1930s he was concerned that 'the man in the street' did not know 'what kind of society' Liberals stood for.[32] Dodds tried to remedy this deficiency by drafting a 'Declaration of Liberal Faith' for the 1932 NLYL conference. The Liberal ideal, he argued, was

> [A] commonwealth of free citizens living harmoniously within itself, developing in the fullest measure its human as well as its material resources, cherishing variety rather than uniformity, assuring justice and equality of opportunity for

[28] Hansard, HC (series 5) vol. 300, cols 452–7, at 452 (3 April 1935).

[29] Ritschel, *Politics of Planning*, 266; Samuel, *Political Situation*, 7.

[30] Samuel, *Political Situation*, 11.

[31] For an overview of Dodds' life and thought, see Donald Wade and Desmond Banks, *The Political Insight of Elliott Dodds* (Leeds, 1977).

[32] Thurso papers, II, 75/1, Dodds to Walter Rea, 10 September 1933.

all, and, in the wider field of world organisation, freely co-operating with other nations to preserve peace and promote the common good.[33]

The Young Liberals adopted the declaration after debate, and Dodds then began to canvass support for his approach in the wider party.[34]

The vision of a Liberal society which Dodds sketched was a distributist and republican one, in which the ownership of personal property by citizens served as the basis for self-development and democratic participation.[35] Various intellectual sources for this vision may be identified. Dodds had been a fervent admirer of Chesterton and Belloc in his youth, and his emphasis on the social importance of 'the small man' echoed Belloc's 1912 polemic *The Servile State*.[36] Although he was a Congregationalist lay preacher, he also engaged with Catholic social thought: by the early 1940s, at least, he was reading widely in the works of continental personalists such as Jacques Maritain and Nikolai Berdyaev.[37] More broadly, the idea of spreading property ownership had significant Liberal antecedents, going back at least as far as John Stuart Mill and reflected in the Yellow Book's enthusiasm for industrial democracy.[38] Finally, Dodds was impressed by the contrast between the stringent anti-trust provisions which applied in the United States and the British government's tolerance of cartels and monopolies. In this respect, he showed an affinity with American progressivism.

Dodds' ideas received timely reinforcement from the American liberal journalist Walter Lippmann, whose books *The Method of Freedom* (1934) and *The Good Society* (1937) stemmed from his disillusionment with the New Deal.[39] Lippmann's intellectual contribution was twofold. Firstly, he offered a pointed critique of collectivism and central economic planning, and argued that a directed economy based on a comprehensive plan was bound to result in scarcity and loss of individual freedom. Lippmann believed that an evolutionary approach based on social reforms and

[33] National League of Young Liberals, *A Declaration of Liberal Faith* (York, 1932), 8.

[34] *MG*, 29 March 1932, 12.

[35] The Liberals' long-standing interest in 'ownership for all' has been analysed by Stuart White: Stuart White, '"Revolutionary Liberalism?" The philosophy and politics of ownership in the post-war Liberal Party', *British Politics*, iv (2009), 164–87.

[36] See Dodds' self-drawn calendar for 1910 with selections from Chesterton's *Orthodoxy* in University of Sheffield Special Collections, Elliott Dodds papers, box 2.

[37] Elliott Dodds papers, box 3/10, commonplace book; Elliott Dodds, *Let's Try Liberalism* (1944), 72–3.

[38] See especially John Stuart Mill, *Principles of Political Economy* (1848), book ii, chapter 1, 'On Property', and book iv, chapter 7, 'On the Probable Futurity of the Labouring Classes'.

[39] *The Good Society* received a warm review from A. G. Gardiner in the *Liberal Magazine: LM*, xlvi (1938), 109–12. For Lippmann's intellectual trajectory, see Barry D. Riccio, *Walter Lippmann: Odyssey of a Liberal* (1994), 95–138.

counter-cyclical fiscal policies offered a much more satisfactory remedy for the failings of the free market:

> I shall call it the method of free collectivism. It is collectivist because it acknowledges the obligation of the state for the standard of life and the operation of the economic order *as a whole*. It is free because it preserves within very wide limits the liberty of private transactions. Its object is not to direct individual enterprise and choice according to an official plan but to put them and keep them in a working equilibrium. Its method is to redress the balance of private actions by compensating public actions.[40]

Lippmann's critique of planning, developed cautiously in *The Method of Freedom*, became more forceful over time as he came into contact with Friedrich Hayek and the Chicago economist Henry Simons.[41] In *The Good Society* he warned that New Deal measures such as the National Industrial Recovery Act, which delegated state authority to interest groups and encouraged the restriction of production, were qualitatively equivalent to directive planning and were liable to undermine democratic government. The task for liberals, Lippmann argued, was to rehabilitate the market order by removing social and economic injustices through redistributive taxation, social insurance, demand-management policies, and the reform of corporate law.[42] All of these interventions were acceptable because they conformed to the rule of law, and provided a framework within which individuals could determine their own destinies. Lippmann illustrated this distinction by an analogy with traffic management, which Hayek later copied.[43] There was all the difference in the world between setting down the rules of the road and telling drivers where they should go.[44]

Lippmann's insistence that liberal and collectivist forms of progress were qualitatively distinct provided a useful justification for the Liberal Party's hostility to Labour, but a second element of his analysis was equally significant. Drawing on classical republican ideas, Lippmann claimed that extreme inequalities of wealth were fatal to democratic government, as economically insecure proletarians and rich plutocrats pressed their respective interests on the state. True Liberalism sought to abolish these extremes by spreading property ownership:

[40] Walter Lippmann, *The Method of Freedom* (New York, 1934), 46.

[41] Angus Burgin, *The Great Persuasion: Reinventing Free Markets since the Depression* (Cambridge, Mass., 2012), 58–60.

[42] Walter Lippmann, *The Good Society* (second edition, New York, 1943), 106–30, 203–40.

[43] On Hayek's debt to Lippmann, see Ben Jackson, 'Freedom, the common good, and the rule of law: Lippmann and Hayek on economic planning', *Journal of the History of Ideas*, lxxiii (2012), 47–68.

[44] Lippmann, *Good Society*, 283.

> It is a project to make the mass of the people independent of the state: that they may be free citizens, who need not be fed by the government, who have no impelling reason to exploit the government, who cannot be bribed, who cannot be coerced, who have no fear of the state and expect no favours.[45]

Dodds drew explicitly on Lippmann's argument in his exposition of the Liberal ideal. All Liberal policy, he argued—quoting from *The Method of Freedom*—should be orientated towards 'a society of free men with vested rights in their own living'.[46]

Under Dodds' leadership, the NLYL took a strong line against economic planning. Certainly, Liberals were not opposed to all state action, as the League's 1935 pamphlet on *Planning* explained: intervention was clearly justified 'where it is necessary to protect personal rights, to prevent exploitation, or to undertake duties which private enterprise cannot adequately discharge', such as the 'planning' of national finance, the currency, credit, and public investment.[47] Large-scale directive planning, however, would lead to regimentation, or else would fail as the state struggled to adjust production in response to changing consumer preferences. 'Freedom for all based on ownership for all' was therefore a more suitable objective.[48]

An invitation to speak at the 1935 Liberal Summer School gave Dodds the chance to put his views across to a wider audience. Here, Dodds' speech amplified the concerns which Samuel had expressed in his discussion of *The Next Five Years*. Dodds told his audience that he was 'tired of the cant of non-party', and feared that it was eroding Liberal distinctiveness:

> While they must co-operate over the widest possible field and with the largest possible number of people, the essential business was to strengthen the Liberal party, for if that was shipwrecked the whole cargo of Liberal ideas might be lost.[49]

If the Liberal Party stood for 'a jelly-like compromise between Socialism and Conservatism, wobbling first one way and then the other', Dodds argued, then Liberalism was never likely to be revived. The solution lay in the idea of ownership for all, which needed to be raised 'from the position of a parenthesis in many a Liberal speech to that of a declared and central part of Liberal policy'. Dodds emphasized that a host of Liberal policies, including free trade, taxation of land values, profit-sharing, and graduated death duties, could be presented as steps towards this goal, since they would break up large incomes, help citizens obtain 'something of [their]

[45] Lippmann, *Method of Freedom*, 100. [46] *MG*, 8 August 1935, 12.
[47] National League of Young Liberals, *Planning* (1935), quoted in *MG*, 1 May 1935, 14.
[48] *MG*, 12 June 1935, 18. [49] *MG*, 8 August 1935, 12.

own', or give employees a greater stake in the firms they worked for.[50] Dodds' call for a clearer Liberal identity came too late to shape the party's 1935 election campaign, but Sir Archibald Sinclair was sympathetic, and after the election Liberal policy would be recast along these lines.[51]

SIR ARCHIBALD SINCLAIR AND *OWNERSHIP FOR ALL*

The 1935 general election gave the Liberal Parliamentary Party a more radical complexion than hitherto. In contrast to 1931, only a handful of Liberal MPs had been elected with Conservative support, so the party was able to oppose the National Government more forthrightly; the Lloyd George family group quietly resumed the Liberal whip; and the newly elected Liberal members included two young radicals, Richard Acland and Wilfrid Roberts, who would become energetic advocates of a popular front. Sinclair only reluctantly agreed to succeed the defeated Samuel, but he rapidly burnished his parliamentary reputation with a fierce attack on Baldwin over the Hoare-Laval pact, and would punch above his weight in the Commons during the appeasement years.[52] Sir Percy Harris took over as chief whip and established a series of committees to develop policy in the Commons, whilst Sinclair appointed his friend Harcourt Johnstone—who had lost his seat at South Shields—to chair the Liberal Central Association and manage his dealings with the extra-parliamentary party.[53]

As Samuel's *de facto* deputy during the 1931 Parliament, Sinclair had been involved in the Blickling discussions and remained committed to the policy of free trade plus public works that had emerged from them. At the same time, he shared Dodds' view that it was more important to capture voters' imagination than to present a detailed programme now that the Liberals had little chance of regaining power.[54] Harcourt Johnstone pressed the same view on him at the beginning of 1936:

> I would suggest that you might seriously turn your mind towards a simplification of Liberal policy this year, and the preaching of it next year and up to the Election. I think you have a great opportunity. The country is tired of

[50] *MG*, 8 August 1935, 12, and 12 October 1935, 16.

[51] Thurso papers, II, 57/1, Sinclair to Samuel, 14 October 1935.

[52] Thurso papers, II, 57/2, Sinclair to Johnstone, 18, 19 and 20 November 1935; de Groot, *Liberal Crusader*, 116–7; on the Liberals' parliamentary performance in this period, see *MG*, 27 May 1937, 10, and *Spectator*, 14 January 1938, 39, and 6 January 1939, 3.

[53] Thurso papers, II, 60/1, 'Committees', circular by Sir Percy Harris, 12 December 1935, and II, 58/1, Sinclair to Hirst, 28 January 1936.

[54] Thurso papers, II, 75/5, Sinclair to Samuel, 16 January 1934.

the older men and is looking eagerly for a policy and a man of this generation. I should like to see fresh minds turned on to this problem and, above all, I should like the policy to be a politician's policy and not an economist's or a publicist's policy. We must consult experts, but for Heaven's sake let us give up allowing them to dictate to us what we have got to bear the burden of preaching.[55]

Sinclair approved of the approach Johnstone suggested, though he proposed a slightly different timetable. For the first half of the new Parliament, he felt, it made sense to focus on 'criticism of the Government and the exposition of the fundamental principles of Liberalism', especially peace, freedom (in its widest sense), and the rule of law. Later, the party could issue a restatement of Liberal policy, 'putting as much cutting edge on it as we can'. Sinclair regarded Dodds' idea of 'ownership for all' as a very suitable cutting edge, provided it could be fleshed out on sound lines. In particular, it seemed likely to chime with the concerns of younger voters, who objected to 'the concentration of power in the hands of a few bankers, landlords and industrialists'. If the Liberals were to challenge the appeal of socialism, they needed to show that they offered an 'alternative means' of building a fair society.[56]

Sinclair took two early steps to clarify the party's sense of purpose. First—at Muir's urging—he set in train a reorganization process, overseen by the former Indian civil servant Lord Meston, which culminated in the replacement of the NLF with a new Liberal Party Organisation.[57] This was a worthwhile reform, which improved the cohesion of Liberal organization in the country: the party organization was made more democratic, the system of district federations was regularized, and the NLYL and Women's Liberal Federation received official representation at the annual Assembly and on the LPO executive and Council.[58] The new party constitution included a preamble, drafted by Muir, which began with a ringing commitment to positive liberty:

The Liberal Party exists to build a Liberal Commonwealth, in which every citizen shall possess liberty, property and security, and none shall be enslaved by poverty, ignorance or unemployment. Its chief care is for the rights and opportunities of the individual, and in all spheres it sets freedom first.[59]

[55] Thurso papers, II, 60/1, Johnstone to Sinclair, 27 January 1936.

[56] Thurso papers, II, 60/1, Sinclair to Johnstone, 29 January 1936.

[57] Parliamentary Archives, Samuel papers, SAM/A/155(X)/41, Muir to Samuel, 17 November 1935; Thurso papers, II, 58/1, 'Report of the Liberal Reorganisation Commission', April 1936.

[58] *MG*, 14 April 1936, 5, and 18 June 1936, 10.

[59] Liberal Party, *Constitution of the Liberal Party* (1936), 3. On the authorship of the preamble, see Lord Meston, 'At the N.L.F.', in *Ramsay Muir: An Autobiography and Some Essays*, ed. Stuart Hodgson (1943), 194–8.

The preamble went on to elaborate the implications of this vision for Liberal policy at home and abroad. Liberals were committed to the League of Nations; 'a just electoral system'; free trade; 'guarantees against the abuse of monopoly whether private or public'; housing, education, and fair wages for all; 'access to land and an assurance that publicly created land values shall not be engrossed by private interests'; and, 'as a safeguard of independence, the personal ownership of property'.[60] These were 'the conditions of liberty, which it is the function of the State to protect and enlarge'.

Sinclair's second step was to underline the party's independence in the face of growing pressure for the formation of a popular front. 'The duty of the Liberal party', Sinclair told the Liberal Summer School in July 1936, 'is to build up a non-Socialist alternative to the present Government.'[61] He would repeat this line, with support from the LPO executive, for most of the next three years.[62] As an ardent opponent of appeasement, Sinclair was not opposed to a popular front per se, but in view of Labour's hostility he felt an alliance was more likely to be formed 'in the heat and pressure of events . . . than as the result of personal negotiations by a few individuals round a table'.[63] In the meantime, he explained to Harold Macmillan, Liberals had to focus on strengthening their own position. '[T]he stronger the Liberal Party is, the greater the contribution it will be able to make to the combination of Left Wing forces.'[64]

Sinclair incorporated 'ownership for all' into his rhetoric as soon as he became party leader. 'Liberal policy in all its aspects', he told the *Liberal Magazine*, was 'directed towards the diffusion of the ownership of wealth and the achievement of equality of opportunity'.[65] However, Sinclair left it to Dodds and the LPO to work out the policy in detail.[66] At the first Assembly held under the new constitution, at Buxton in May 1937, Dodds moved a resolution which declared the party 'indignantly aware of the grossly unequal distribution of property' in Britain, and established a special committee to investigate how this could be changed. Most members of the Ownership for All Committee were Liberal activists with practical rather than scholarly expertise, but Dodds, as chairman, energetically sought expert help.[67] Through Lionel Robbins, he secured the services of Arthur Seldon—then

[60] Free trade was omitted from this list in the original draft, but was added by the party convention which adopted the new constitution: *LM*, xliv (1936), 193–200, at 197.

[61] *MG*, 31 July 1936, 12.

[62] de Groot, *Liberal Crusader*, 130.

[63] *MG*, 7 April 1937, 4.

[64] MS. Macmillan dep. c. 864, fols 267–9, Sinclair to Macmillan, 19 August 1936.

[65] *LM*, xliv (1936), 89–90.

[66] Thurso papers, III, 19/3, Sinclair to Dodds, 21 June 1937.

[67] Liberal Party, *Ownership for All: The Liberal Party Committee's Report on the Distribution of Property* (1938), 1.

a young researcher and a member of the LSE Liberal Society—to act as the committee's paid secretary and write its report.[68] Robbins and several other economists, including Arnold Plant of the LSE and Albert Baster of University College, Exeter, also met and advised the committee, though they were not all committed Liberals and declined to be identified publicly with its work.[69] After a year's deliberations, the committee submitted a sixty-six-page report on *Ownership for All* to the 1938 Assembly. This was given unanimous approval, subject to a Scottish amendment which emphasized the importance of land value taxation, and passed into party policy.[70]

The significance of *Ownership for All* lay less in its detailed proposals than in the idea which it embodied.[71] The committee's economic advisers seem to have emphasized the difficulties involved in promoting small enterprise and profit-sharing, and Dodds himself later came to believe that its recommendations were too cautious.[72] Nevertheless, the report identified a series of measures by which wealth could be spread and the trend towards the concentration of economic power reversed.[73] First, death duties should be reformed, with the rate graduated according to the size of the bequest and the existing wealth of the legatee; this would 'encourage the splitting up of large fortunes' without direct state intervention. Second, monopolies and trade associations should be broken up through anti-trust legislation on the American model, company and patent law reforms, and the restoration of free trade. Only in the case of 'natural' monopolies, such as gas and electricity, was public control or public ownership really appropriate. Third, there was a pressing need to create real 'equality of opportunity', notably in education and health—a subject which was referred to a separate committee.[74] Fourth, the taxation

[68] Robbins also sent Dodds a copy of a paper by the Chicago economist Henry Simons—possibly *A Positive Program for Laissez Faire* (Chicago, 1934)—which Dodds felt contained 'a tremendous lot of useful stuff': BLPES, Robbins papers, 5/1, Dodds to Robbins, 28 October 1937. Seldon was known as Arthur Slaberdain before he changed his surname in 1939: Colin Robinson, *Arthur Seldon: A Life for Liberty* (2009), 25, 34–7, 56–7.

[69] Liberal Party, *Ownership for All*, 1; Susan Howson, *Lionel Robbins* (Cambridge, 2011), 317–8; Robbins papers, 5/10, 'Memo. on Restraining the Growth of Monopoly in England', by Dr A. S. J. Baster, 1 October 1937.

[70] *MG*, 20 May 1938, 5.

[71] Thurso papers, III, 27/1, Dodds to Sinclair, 21 March 1938.

[72] Robbins papers, 5/1, Dodds to Robbins, 13 November 1937, and 5/10, précis of Ownership for All Committee meetings at the LPO office, 18–19 December 1937; Wade and Banks, *Political Insight*, 36–7.

[73] This discussion is based on Liberal Party, *Ownership for All*.

[74] The activities of the Equality of Opportunity Committee are obscure, but it appears to have been established by the 1938 Assembly, with Dodds as its chairman and Graham White among its members: *LM*, xlvi (1938), 270; Lothian papers, GD40/17/361/211, Dodds to Lothian, 20 June 1938; Graham White papers, WHI/8/4/21, 'Equality of Opportunity Committee. Memorandum of the Health Sub-Committee', 3 January 1939.

and rating systems required reform, with the tax burden shifted from 'concealed' indirect taxes to direct taxes on income and wealth, and rates levied on land values. Fifth, the government should be sensitive to the difficulties faced by the 'small man' in agriculture and retail, and ensure that he could obtain adequate credit. Finally, firms should be encouraged (though not compelled) to give wage-earners a financial stake in the enterprise through profit-sharing and co-partnership schemes. This was a progressive Liberal agenda, which nevertheless contrasted sharply with the interventionism of the constructive tradition and the planning movement.

Ownership for All said very little about macroeconomic policy, beyond a brief reference to national development, and it did not overtly challenge the Yellow Book, but its analysis of industrial organization was very different to that of *Britain's Industrial Future*. The growth of large corporations and the existence of imperfect competition were not considered inevitable but vigorously condemned; the advantages of 'bigness' were questioned, and the perfectly competitive market was set forth as the model at which government policy should aim.[75] In this sense, the report anticipated Stephen Broadberry and Nick Crafts' argument that Britain's poor productivity performance in the 1930s stemmed partly from a lack of competitive pressures.[76] Public ownership or control was rejected unless it was absolutely necessary, since it was liable to 'create more evils than it cures'.[77] The critique of planning which had emerged within the Liberal Party during the 1930s thus received its mature expression.

The champions of *Ownership for All* may have been in the ascendant within the Liberal Party on the eve of the Second World War, but in the light of later events it is important not to overstate the report's influence. *Ownership for All* enjoyed Sinclair's patronage, and was popular with 'sturdy individualists' such as the Yorkshire textile manufacturer Ronald Walker and the journalist J. A. Spender who had disliked the Yellow Book's interventionism; it also enthused many moderate Liberals.[78] However, left-leaning Liberals tended to be suspicious of Dodds' hostility to planning, and continued to propose moderate planning on Next Five Years lines as a basis for progressive cooperation.[79] The most vocal popular fronter, Richard Acland, advocated nationalization of the coal mines and the Bank of England, and there is good reason to think that Sinclair would have accepted at least the first of these if it turned out to be the price of

[75] Liberal Party, *Ownership for All*, 9–10.

[76] S. N. Broadberry and N. F. R. Crafts, 'Britain's productivity gap in the 1930s: Some neglected factors', *Journal of Economic History*, lii (1992), 531–58.

[77] Liberal Party, *Ownership for All*, 6.

[78] Wade and Banks, *Political Insight*, 23; *LM*, xlvi (1938), 294–5; *MG*, 20 May 1938, 5.

[79] *LM*, xlvi (1938), 267–8.

stopping appeasement.[80] Clearly, then, *Ownership for All* was not considered a definitive statement of Liberal policy even to the extent that the Yellow Book had been.

THE LIBERALS AND THE *GENERAL THEORY*

In wider economic thought, the most significant development of the later 1930s was the 1936 publication of *The General Theory of Employment, Interest and Money*: the most mature statement of Keynes' thinking, and a notable theoretical advance on the *Treatise on Money* (1930) which had underpinned his policy advice during the depression. The impact of the *General Theory* on the economics profession is well known. Many younger economists, especially in Cambridge, became devoted adherents of Keynes; Dennis Robertson, Hubert Henderson and A. C. Pigou—all long-standing colleagues—reacted against his caricature of the 'classics' and some of his theoretical claims; and John Hicks and Roy Harrod worked to integrate Keynes' insights with existing neoclassical theory and develop usable 'Keynesian' models.[81]

Keynes' vigorous assault on 'classical' doctrines made it inevitable that the *General Theory* would polarize opinion. As Robert Skidelsky has argued, however, it is difficult to classify economists as 'Keynesian' or 'non-Keynesian' on the basis of their responses to the book:

> The complexity of the doctrine itself, and its ambiguous relationship to 'orthodox' economics, meant that it was never a simple question of taking it or leaving it, rather of degrees of mutual accommodation and assimilation.[82]

If this was true of the 'fellow economists' for whom Keynes wrote the *General Theory*, it was doubly so for politicians and other lay people. In relation to government policy, the new book largely fleshed out the arguments which Keynes had already been making for counter-cyclical public investment and cheap money. The multiplier effect, and the idea of balancing the budget over the trade cycle rather than year-by-year, had been developed in 'The Means to Prosperity' and had been widely understood. On the other hand, the theoretical questions which the *General Theory* raised about the determination of the interest rate, the relationship between the short and long periods, and whether Keynes' analysis

[80] Richard Acland, *Only One Battle* (1937), 153–85; Thurso papers, II, 60/1, Sinclair to Johnstone, 17 November 1936.

[81] On the reception of the *General Theory*, see Robert Skidelsky, *John Maynard Keynes* (3 vols, 1983–2001), ii, 572–621.

[82] Skidelsky, *John Maynard Keynes*, ii, 572.

of under-employment equilibrium was a special or general case had little immediate relevance to policy. As a result, the heated theoretical debates which emerged from the *General Theory* largely passed the political world by. The book's political significance lay rather in the way in which it changed policy-makers' understanding of how the economy worked, and wider perceptions of what macroeconomic policy could achieve, during the years that followed.

The short-term political impact of the *General Theory* was also muted for another reason. Keynes' new treatise represented an attempt to explain the persistence of depression by challenging classical assumptions about the self-equilibrating nature of the economic system, both at macro level and within the labour market. By the time the book appeared, though, the British economy had been recovering for more than three years, and it was far from clear that the remaining unemployment resulted from a general demand deficiency. Press and parliamentary discussions of unemployment increasingly focussed on the difficulties of the Special Areas.[83]

With southern England visibly prospering, a general stimulus seemed more likely to stoke the boom than to alleviate the regionalized distress to which the Jarrow Marchers called attention. Indeed, Keynes acknowledged this in a series of articles on 'How to avoid a slump', which appeared in *The Times* at the beginning of 1937. In 'the later stages of recovery', he argued, 'special assistance to the distressed areas' was the best way to reduce unemployment.[84] Keynes insisted, however, that the incipient boom should be tamed by restraining public investment, increasing taxation, and temporarily reducing tariffs, instead of by raising Bank Rate. He added that the government should prepare to check the next recession by planning a public works programme which could be implemented when conditions worsened.

The evidence available to the student of Liberal macroeconomic policy-making in the late 1930s is relatively limited, and it is impossible to say how many Liberal MPs read the *General Theory*. (One, Richard Acland, certainly did so, but admitted that he did not fully understand it.[85]) What is clear is that Sinclair set the party line on economic management through his speeches in House of Commons debates. The content of Sinclair's speeches suggests that he drew heavily on *The Economist* and other published sources for economic information, and backed this up through personal discussions with journalists (Sir Walter Layton and Geoffrey Crowther are the most likely candidates). As the prospect of

[83] *Economist*, 20 March 1937, 633–4.
[84] John Maynard Keynes, 'How to avoid a slump', in *JMK*, xxi, 384–95, at 385.
[85] Acland, *Only One Battle*, 185.

war grew nearer, the party also benefited from the Oxford economist Roy Harrod's move back towards the Liberal fold. Harrod had been an active Liberal in the 1920s, but was disillusioned by the party's conduct in 1931 and advised Labour through the New Fabian Research Bureau during the years that followed.[86] However, he was an enthusiastic popular fronter, and revived his Liberal links—without rejoining the party—in 1937–8.[87] In January 1938 he addressed a Liberal meeting in London on measures for avoiding a slump, and later in the year he advised Sinclair on how to respond to the budget.[88]

The Economist adopted a nuanced attitude to the Keynesian revolution during the 1930s. The case for economic management appeared in its pages in relatively orthodox terms, reflecting the paper's long association with mainstream classical and neoclassical economics and its reliance on sales in the City, whilst its editor Sir Walter Layton—like Robertson, Henderson, and Pigou—seems to have inclined to the view that Keynes had identified a particular case of demand deficiency rather than a general theory.[89] *The Economist* supported loan-financed public works in the conditions of the early 1930s, when productive projects and 'idle savings' were at hand, but it found it 'easy to imagine the circumstances' in which they might do more harm than good.[90] As the recovery gained pace in 1936–7, the paper warned of boom conditions, and emphasized the need to dampen demand, liberalize trade, and restrain credit expansion.[91] Neville Chamberlain's proposal to borrow £400,000,000 over five years for rearmament seemed particularly dangerous, since it would expand the money supply and accentuate the upswing of the trade cycle. On the proximate questions of policy, including the need for rearmament to be funded by taxation, the paper was largely at one with Keynes, but the tone of its analysis was rather different. Right up to the outbreak of the Second World War, Keynes' concern about excess demand was tempered by his fear of a new depression. In contrast, *The Economist* echoed Lionel Robbins and the Austrian tradition in suggesting that an uncontrolled

[86] Henry Phelps Brown, 'Sir Roy Harrod: A biographical memoir', *EJ*, xc (1980), 1–33, at 18.

[87] For Harrod's insistence that he had no party affiliation at this time, see his letter to a group of Conservative MPs, February 1939, in *The Collected Interwar Papers and Correspondence of Roy Harrod*, ed. Daniele Besomi (3 vols, Cheltenham, 2003), ii, 911–15.

[88] *LM*, xlvi (1938), 57–9; British Library, Add. MS. 71192 (Harrod papers), fol. 39, Alan Campbell Johnson to Harrod, 29 April 1938.

[89] David Hubback, *No Ordinary Press Baron: A Life of Walter Layton* (1985), 93–4; Ruth Dudley Edwards, *The Pursuit of Reason: The Economist, 1843–1993* (1993), 679, 709.

[90] *Economist*, 18 March 1933, 568–9; 23 January 1937, 157–8, at 158; and 1 January 1938, 1–2, at 2.

[91] *Economist*, 18 April 1936, 116–7; 2 January 1937, 1–2; and 23 January 1937, 157–8.

boom itself contained the seeds of a later slump.[92] The *News Chronicle*'s influential City editor, Oscar Hobson, took a similar approach, though he was more overtly critical of Keynes' enthusiasm for cheap money.[93]

During 1936 and 1937, Sinclair's criticisms of government economic policy closely followed *The Economist*'s. In the upward phase of the trade cycle, he argued, the state ought to pay down the national debt and restrain its expenditure, thereby strengthening its position for when the next slump came. Instead, civil spending was rising rapidly, and Chamberlain had failed to establish a sinking fund.[94] When the Defence Loans Bill came to Parliament in February 1937, Sinclair deprecated the decision to finance rearmament by borrowing, not only because armaments were 'unproductive' but also because the timing was completely wrong:

> Before ever public expenditure on this scale was thought of, economists and bankers, in their speeches and articles, were urging the Government to put on the brake of taxation, and to try to even out the trade cycle at this critical stage—for this is a well proved maxim—the bigger the boom, the sharper the slump.
>
> Now there is a real danger that after 12 months or two years our conditions will be like those of the United States of America in 1928, and into these conditions of hectic economic activity the Government propose to inject the additional and violent stimulant of a net addition of £400,000,000 worth of loan expenditure.[95]

The trade-cycle case against loan-financed rearmament disappeared in the second half of 1937, when a mild recession took hold. Nevertheless, Sinclair remained adamant that the government should have raised taxation during the earlier period. The Liberal leader also urged closer parliamentary control of government spending, in order to eliminate 'waste, bureaucratic extravagance, and profiteering in armaments' and minimize the burden of taxation and borrowing required.[96]

The Liberal Party's support for a counter-cyclical fiscal policy in the late 1930s was unambiguous. '[A]s far as we on these benches are concerned', Graham White told the Commons in 1937,

> the proposition that we are to drift from prosperity to slump and that we are unable in the present state of world development, with regard to production

[92] *Economist*, 14 November 1936, 297–8, and 2 January 1936, 1–2; Robbins, *Great Depression*, 30–54.

[93] *NC*, 15 January 1937, 12.

[94] Hansard, HC (series 5) vol. 311, cols 171–83 (22 April 1936), and vol. 322, cols 1796–1810 (21 April 1937).

[95] Hansard, HC (series 5) vol. 320, cols 1233–47, at 1234, 1244 (17 February 1937).

[96] Hansard, HC (series 5) vol. 335, cols 146–58, at 157 (27 April 1938).

> and the means of distribution, to extricate ourselves from a trade cycle, is one which we refuse to accept.

Variations in the volume of public investment, White added, 'could have a very powerful influence in staving off or levelling out fluctuations in trade'.[97] Successive Liberal Assemblies in 1937, 1938, and 1939 endorsed this view without controversy, suggesting that demand-management ideas had become embedded in the party's thinking.[98] At the same time, Liberals emphasized that the problems of the depressed areas were mainly structural rather than cyclical. Much of the blame could be placed on the government's tariff policy, which favoured home industries over the export trades; as Sinclair pointed out, it had 'brought prosperity to Birmingham at the expense of Liverpool, Glasgow, the depressed areas and our great export and maritime industries'.[99] Freeing trade and reviving exports seemed the best way to help these districts. An ancillary policy was to control the location of industry, either by restricting factory building in south-east England or by providing incentives for firms to move to the Special Areas. Sir Malcolm Stewart, the Commissioner for the Special Areas, proposed an active location of industry policy in 1936, and a Royal Commission chaired by Sir Montague Barlow developed more detailed proposals in 1938–9. The respective merits of 'positive' inducements and 'negative' restrictions on industrial location were not widely discussed by Liberals before the war broke out, but Megan Lloyd George and the Union of University Liberal Societies both declared their support for compulsory measures.[100]

THE COST-OF-LIVING PETITION

During the 1931 Parliament, economic circumstances hampered Liberals' efforts to revive free trade as a popular cause. By contrast, the conditions of the second half of the decade were much more propitious. Not only was unemployment concentrated in the export districts, but the cost of living increased rapidly in 1936–7 as a deterioration in Britain's terms of trade coincided with 'bottleneck' effects, resulting from high demand,

[97] Hansard, HC (series 5) vol. 328, cols 765–75, at 765–6, 768 (2 November 1937).

[98] *MG*, 29 May 1937, 15; 31 May 1937, 11; 21 May 1938, 8; and 12 May 1939, 7.

[99] Hansard, HC (series 5) vol. 311, cols 171–83, at 175 (22 April 1936). The same point was made by Graham Hutton: D. Graham Hutton, 'Our economic discontents', *Lloyds Bank Limited Monthly Review*, no. 76 (June 1936), 286–303.

[100] Hansard, HC (series 5) vol. 330, cols 441–8 (8 December 1937); *NC*, 13 April 1937, 13.

which were exacerbated by rearmament. Food prices jumped especially sharply, rising by more than 11 per cent between 1935 and 1937, whilst manufacturers faced higher raw material costs.[101] In these circumstances, Liberal complaints about tariffs and other import restrictions could finally gain traction.

A shift in social attitudes towards food can also be detected in this period. As Frank Trentmann has powerfully shown, the displacement of free trade from progressive political culture after the First World War partly reflected a new interest in the purity and quality of food, rather than simply its cheapness. The cheap white loaf lost the symbolic importance it had once held, and in its place 'pure and clean milk' became 'the symbol of social citizenship'.[102] Yet what Trentmann fails to notice is that British progressive opinion began to move back in the other direction during the 1930s, stimulated especially by Sir John Boyd Orr's 1936 report into *Food, Health and Income*, which drew attention to the prevalence of working-class malnutrition. Orr criticized the National Government's agricultural policy for restricting output and keeping food prices high, and also called for subsidies to be redirected to those products which had the greatest nutritional value, such as milk, eggs, fruit, and vegetables.[103] Liberals seized on Orr's findings as evidence that protection was harming the welfare of the poor, and urged the government to bring prices down.[104] A Liberal administration, Sinclair promised, would pursue 'a policy of nutrition', focussed on raising the consumption of milk and other protective foods 'which directly built up the health and strength, and the disease resisting powers of the people'.[105] As part of this policy, tariffs and quotas would be dismantled, farmers would be given greater security of tenure, and cooperative marketing schemes and a central purchasing agency would help bring distribution costs down.

The Liberals publicized their concern about food prices with a highly effective petition against the rising cost of living in the winter of 1937–8. The public response wildly exceeded Sinclair's expectations, and by the time he presented the petition to the Commons in February 1938 it bore over 800,000 signatures. In a controversial publicity stunt, the party also circulated the petition to hospital patients and staff, drawing attention to

[101] B. R. Mitchell and Phyllis Deane, *Abstract of British Historical Statistics* (Cambridge, 1962), 478.

[102] Frank Trentmann, *Free Trade Nation: Commerce, Consumption, and Civil Society in Modern Britain* (Oxford, 2008), 216.

[103] Sir John Boyd Orr, *Food, Health and Income* (1936).

[104] Hansard, HC (series 5) vol. 313, cols 1023–5 (17 June 1936).

[105] Sinclair at Trowbridge, 18 November 1938, reported in *LM*, xlvi (1938), 607–8, at 607.

an estimate that the cost of milk to voluntary hospitals had increased by £400,000 since the Milk Marketing Board was established in 1933.[106] Part of the significance of the cost-of-living campaign was that it galvanized Liberal Associations into action and reminded voters that the party was 'a force still to be reckoned with'—as former MP T. Atholl Robertson noted.[107] At the same time, the petition gave populist expression to the distinctive political economy of free markets and low prices which the Liberals had tried to revive during the 1930s. By contrast, women Labour activists who organized a similar campaign called instead for living standards to be maintained through an increase in wages.[108]

The cost-of-living petition provided a model for other single-issue Liberal campaigns during 1938 and 1939: East London Liberals, for instance, ran a campaign for better Air Raid Precautions with LPO support, while Dodds circulated a questionnaire to 20,000 small traders to canvass interest in *Ownership for All*.[109] Sinclair and Johnstone noticed that pensions aroused strong popular interest, and asked Graham White to draw up proposals for higher pensions—initially for the neediest old people—which became the subject of a petition in the spring of 1939.[110] This was, of course, overshadowed by the National Petition Campaign which Sir Stafford Cripps launched in February 1939 to promote progressive unity. Nevertheless, the Liberals' heavy use of petitions on the eve of the war revealed a new ruthlessness in exploiting popular grievances.

THE POPULAR FRONT

Although Sinclair's strategy was predicated on maintaining Liberal independence, the urgency of the international situation propelled the party towards a popular front position during 1938 and 1939. Sinclair had always been relaxed about local electoral pacts, and backed independent progressive candidates at the Oxford and Bridgwater by-elections which took place after the Munich agreement; he also maintained close links with Conservative anti-appeasers such as Winston Churchill and Anthony

[106] *LM*, xlvi (1938), 49–50.

[107] Thurso papers, II, 67/9, T. Atholl Robertson to Sinclair, 4 February 1938.

[108] *MG*, 23 February 1938, 3.

[109] Thurso papers, II, 67/3, William Allison to Johnstone, 14 October 1938; *MG*, 29 March 1939, 5.

[110] Thurso papers, II, 64/2, Sinclair to Johnstone, 7 March 1939; *MG*, 12 July 1939, 12. Johnstone was 'alarmed' at the idea of an across-the-board pension increase, and sought Lionel Robbins' advice: Thurso papers, II, 64/2, Johnstone to Sinclair, 6 March 1939.

Eden, whom he hoped would form part of a new government.[111] When the Cripps petition appeared, Sinclair joined other Liberals in supporting it, and pointed out that the Labour leadership was the main obstacle to progressive unity.[112] Later, after the fall of Prague, he issued a programme of 'Ten Points for Progressives' around which he believed anti-appeasers could unite.[113]

The hostility of Labour's National Executive Committee meant that a national electoral pact never became a realistic prospect, but Liberal preparations for the general election due in 1939–40 nevertheless seem to have been shaped by popular front assumptions. Though the party had to maintain its independence and 'national character', it made strategic sense to concentrate resources on forty or so winnable seats, most of which were bound to be in rural Britain.[114] In Devon, Cornwall, and Somerset, as Garry Tregidga has shown, Lib–Lab cooperation was already well developed, driven forward by Labour candidate A. L. Rowse and supported by some local Liberals.[115] Local agreements also operated in some other rural constituencies, such as Chertsey in Surrey, whilst Roy Harrod and A. D. Lindsay attempted to create a progressive pact in eleven seats around Oxford.[116] Although Liberal and Labour candidates would have clashed in much of the country in a 1939–40 election, the main thrust of the Liberal campaign would almost certainly have been directed to the capture of Conservative seats and the formation of an alternative government.

Significant tension clearly existed between Sinclair's efforts to accentuate the distinctiveness of Liberal policy and the pursuit of a popular front. In general, popular fronters treated *Ownership for All* with suspicion, whilst northern Liberals such as Dodds jealously guarded the party's independence.[117] Yet Sinclair negotiated this tension relatively well; indeed, his policy arguably had a sound strategic logic. With a clear commitment to personal liberty, wider property ownership, and competitive markets, the Liberals could retain a distinct identity whilst cooperating with others over short-term aims. The popular front agitation brought young people

[111] A. D. Lindsay failed to defeat his Conservative opponent Quintin Hogg at Oxford, but the *News Chronicle* journalist Vernon Bartlett gained Bridgwater from the Conservatives.

[112] de Groot, *Liberal Crusader*, 132–50.

[113] Sir Archibald Sinclair, *Liberal Policy: A Speech Delivered to the Council of the Liberal Party Organisation on the 15th March, 1939* (1939).

[114] Thurso papers, II, 64/1, 'Note of discussion at luncheon at the National Liberal Club, 21/6/38'.

[115] Tregidga, 'Turning of the tide?', 359–65.

[116] Martin Pugh, 'The Liberal Party and the popular front', *EHR*, cxxi (2006), 1327–50, at 1337; *Collected Interwar Papers of Roy Harrod*, ii, 899–900.

[117] Thurso papers, II, 64/5, 'Mr Acland's Resolution', memorandum for Sinclair, 16 May 1938.

into the party, and Liberal morale was much improved towards the end of the decade. Some old Asquithians backed appeasement, and D. M. Mason and Herbert Holdsworth MP defected to the Simonites over Munich, but the party's fragile unity otherwise held. Sinclair thus managed to keep alive the possibility of Liberal revival.[118]

CONCLUSION

The political landscape of the middle and late 1930s was kaleidoscopic in its complexity. 'Middle opinion' groups jostled with one another, Keynesian ideas stood in tension with central planning proposals, and party political divisions overlaid them all. Many Liberals participated in external groups and lent their names to the manifestos which resulted, and at the end of the decade the party itself sought a popular front. Yet amid this confusion the Liberal leadership developed a relatively clear and distinctive policy line. In consequence, the party should not be regarded as intellectually dormant, nor simply identified with 'middle opinion' views.

During the first half of the 1930s, the Liberal Party renewed its historic commitment to free trade and free markets. In the second half of the decade, the party's turn away from the Yellow Book was theorized and consolidated. In place of the constructive Liberalism of the 1920s, there emerged a new synthesis which drew on classical, Keynesian, and distributist ideas. Sinclair's Liberal Party 'put freedom first', and sought to facilitate individuals' self-development by spreading private property ownership and building up the social services. In the microeconomic sphere it stood for competitive markets, policed by the state, except in the case of genuine natural monopolies. In the macroeconomic sphere it endorsed demand management through counter-cyclical public investment, though it placed rather more emphasis than Keynes did on the need to control booms as well as slumps.

The liberal Keynesian synthesis which Sinclair presided over was, as Harcourt Johnstone had demanded, 'a politician's policy' rather than an economist's one. Sinclair's engagement with the *General Theory* seems to have been mediated through other sources, and Liberals hardly noticed that the aim of *Ownership for All* implicitly ran against Keynes' desire to euthanize the rentier.[119] Moreover, the party was unashamedly populist in its criticisms of rising prices and high public spending. This was not

[118] de Groot, *Liberal Crusader*, 149–50.

[119] John Maynard Keynes, *The General Theory of Employment Interest and Money* (1936), 374–7.

necessarily a problem, since Liberals were unlikely to be asked to form a government, and the party was still more comfortable with Keynes' basic approach—of eliminating instability in a free-market economy—than either Labour or the Conservatives. However, the party's limited engagement with economic theory in the 1930s, combined with the diversity of proposals canvassed by popular fronters, gave its new synthesis a provisional character. The experience of the Second World War would show how easily Liberal policy could be blown in a new direction.

5

Planning for War and Peace, 1939–45

The development of Liberal economic policy in the 1930s showed a coherent trajectory away from the constructive Liberalism of the Yellow Book, towards a more libertarian approach which combined demand management with free-market industrial policies and the pursuit of 'ownership for all'. This trajectory was dramatically interrupted by the Second World War. From May 1940 onwards, Sir Archibald Sinclair and other senior Liberals held office in Winston Churchill's coalition government, and devoted most of their energies to the war effort. In the meantime, the Liberal Party in Parliament and the country swung sharply to the left. Constructive and New Liberal ideas gained new purchase in the context of a generalized vogue for planning and more specific doubts about the adequacy of demand-management policies for achieving peacetime full employment. During the early years of the war, central planning proposals were widely canvassed among left-wing Liberals. Later, the party settled on a broadly Keynesian position, given an interventionist form by Sir William Beveridge in his report on *Full Employment in a Free Society* and backed up by piecemeal nationalization measures.

The present chapter offers the first comprehensive account of Liberal policy-making during the Second World War, and complements Andrew Thorpe's invaluable research into Liberal organization in this period.[1] From this analysis, three main points emerge. Firstly, it is clear that the party's internal life was significantly affected by the enforced absence of its leader. With Sinclair absorbed in government duties, Liberal policy-making became more formal and committee-based, and both activists and outside experts assumed a more prominent role than hitherto.

Secondly—and partly as a consequence of the first point—the Liberal Party shared fully in the turn towards planning and egalitarian ideas which

[1] Andrew Thorpe, *Parties at War: Political Organisation in Second World War Britain* (Oxford, 2009).

took place across British society in this period.[2] Significantly, it was not only new adherents who succumbed to planning fervour, but also more established Liberals such as Sir Percy Harris and Violet Bonham Carter (who had been a stalwart of the Liberal Council in the 1930s). The left turn which Liberal policy took during the Second World War would prove temporary, but it cannot be dismissed as a 'coup' by Beveridge and other newcomers. Indeed, the policy on which the Liberals fought the 1945 election was more obviously shaped by the views of the party at large than earlier manifestos had been, or later ones would be.

Thirdly, wartime controversies over planning brought into unusually sharp relief differences of opinion about what Liberalism was or should be. Left wingers tended to argue that economic planning was justified as a means of achieving full employment and social security, provided that the essential personal and political liberties were preserved; Beveridge's insistence that Liberalism was 'a faith, not a formula' encapsulated this view.[3] By contrast, traditionalist Liberals adopted a Hayekian critique of state intervention and sought to define Liberalism in terms of classical and Georgist policies. Moderate Liberals tried to navigate a middle way between these positions and keep the idea of 'ownership for all' alive, but they could not impose their views on the rest of the party. These wartime debates left a legacy of ideological confusion which would have to be resolved in later years.

THE LIBERALS AND THE CHURCHILL COALITION

The outbreak of the Second World War prompted a suspension of electoral hostilities and the curtailment of regular constituency activities by all three main parties, but in other respects the Liberal Party's position remained largely unchanged until the Churchill coalition was formed. Sinclair turned down the chance to join Neville Chamberlain's government, partly because he had not been offered a seat in the War Cabinet and partly because Chamberlain had not brought Labour into office, and other Liberals backed this decision, although Gwilym Lloyd George took a junior post at the Board of Trade with his father's blessing.[4] Liberals

[2] Paul Addison, *The Road to 1945: British Politics and the Second World War* (1975); José Harris, 'Political ideas and the debate on state welfare, 1940–45', in Harold L. Smith (ed.), *War and Social Change: British Society in the Second World War* (Manchester, 1986), 233–63.

[3] Sir William Beveridge, *Why I am a Liberal* (1945), 32.

[4] John Vincent, 'Chamberlain, the Liberals and the outbreak of war, 1939', *EHR*, cxiii (1998), 367–83.

subsequently became prominent critics of Chamberlain's conduct of the war, and helped rally opposition to his leadership in the Norway debate of 7–8 May 1940. One consequence was that Clement Davies, a leading anti-Chamberlainite, began to move back from the Liberal Nationals to the official party in this period.[5]

When Chamberlain fell and Churchill's coalition took shape, Sinclair became Secretary of State for Air, outside the War Cabinet but with a promise of consultation of matters of general policy.[6] In the junior ranks, Sinclair obtained office for Dingle Foot at the Ministry of Economic Warfare and for Harcourt Johnstone as Secretary for Overseas Trade (prompting a hasty by-election at Middlesbrough West so that Johnstone could return to the Commons). Gwilym Lloyd George remained in post and worked his way up the ranks, becoming Minister of Fuel and Power in 1942, but was increasingly detached from the Liberal Party. As the war went on, several other Liberals drifted into the government machine, either as junior ministers or as parliamentary private secretaries to Sinclair (in the case of Wilfrid Roberts and Geoffrey Mander). Sir Percy Harris, who deeply resented Sinclair's failure to secure him office, became *de facto* party leader in the Commons and took over responsibility for policy development.[7]

The character of the wartime coalition, and the allocation of posts within it, gave the Liberal ministers little influence over domestic policy. Sinclair's working life was dominated by the task of managing the RAF, and Foot was effectively responsible for the economic warfare effort while his superiors Hugh Dalton and Lord Selborne ran the Special Operations Executive. Johnstone's position at the Department of Overseas Trade was therefore the party's main economic post. As well as chairing the government's Shipping Committee, Johnstone was closely involved in internal discussions over post-war trade and agricultural policy, and pressed strongly for an internationalist approach. Lionel Robbins, as director of the Economic Section of the War Cabinet, and Roy Harrod, who moved in and out of Whitehall during this period, became important allies.[8] Johnstone fought particularly hard against restrictive agricultural proposals, such as the draft

[5] David M. Roberts, 'Clement Davies and the Liberal Party, 1929–1956' (University of Wales M.A. thesis, 1974), 55, 79.

[6] Sinclair had fought alongside Churchill during the First World War and was a long-standing friend, but this did not ensure a close relationship in government. See *Winston and Archie: The Collected Correspondence of Winston Churchill and Archibald Sinclair, 1915–1960*, ed. Ian Hunter (2005).

[7] Parliamentary Archives, Harris papers, HRS/1, Harris diary, entry for 16 May 1940.

[8] Susan Howson, *Lionel Robbins* (Cambridge, 2011), 392–3; Henry Phelps Brown, 'Sir Roy Harrod: A biographical memoir', *EJ*, xc (1980), 1–33, at 21–3.

international Wheat Agreement which appeared in 1941, and against the idea that agricultural subsidies should be continued in perpetuity to maintain soil fertility; instead, with Sinclair's support, he argued that subsidies should be focussed on nutritional needs.[9] The eventual adoption of a multilateral framework for post-war trade policy was a triumph for Johnstone and the Whitehall economists, including Keynes, who shared his views. Johnstone also represented the Liberals on the government's War Aims Committee, and received regular briefings from Anthony Eden on upcoming War Cabinet decisions.[10]

The policy line which Johnstone and Sinclair pursued within government was broadly consistent with the party's pre-war positions, but Johnstone's activities were intrinsically unsuitable for publicity and Sinclair returned to the Liberal fray only in occasional speeches to the LPO Assembly and Council. On major questions of policy, moreover, the Liberal ministers loyally toed the government line, most notably in the February 1943 House of Commons debate on *Social Insurance and Allied Services*, on which ministers sought to defer action until after the war. To the consternation of Liberal backbenchers and activists, Sinclair seemed oblivious to the strength of popular feeling in favour of Beveridge's scheme.[11] Nine Liberal MPs, led by Harris and David Lloyd George, voted for a critical amendment tabled by Labour's James Griffiths, and some radical activists began abortive manoeuvres to take the party into opposition.[12] Sinclair's new-found enthusiasm for reunion with the Liberal Nationals also dismayed Violet Bonham Carter, who would become president of the LPO after Lord Meston's 1943 death: at a time of growing popular radicalism, Sinclair seemed to be preparing his party for staying in coalition in peacetime, with Churchill at the helm.[13] Even relatively moderate Liberal activists felt that this would be a fatal course.

[9] TNA: PRO, CAB/66/42/8, 'Post-War Agricultural Policy. Memorandum by the Secretary of State for Air and the Secretary, Department of Overseas Trade', 13 October 1943, and CAB/65/36/9, War Cabinet conclusions, 15 October 1943; British Library, Add. MS. 71192 (Harrod papers), fol. 76, Johnstone to Harrod, 18 June 1942, and Add. MS. 72736A (Harrod papers), fols 97–101, memorandum by Harrod, n.d. [October 1943].

[10] Jaime Reynolds and Ian Hunter, '"Crinks" Johnstone', *JLDH*, no. 26 (2000), 14–18, at 17.

[11] Harris papers, HRS/2, Harris diary, entries for 10, 17, and 19 February 1943.

[12] Hansard, HC (series 5) vol. 386, cols 2049–54 (18 February 1943); Parliamentary Archives, David Lloyd George papers, LG/G/25/2/26, A. J. Sylvester to Lloyd George, 19 February 1943.

[13] *Champion Redoubtable: The Diaries and Letters of Violet Bonham Carter, 1914–1945*, ed. Mark Pottle (1998), 275–6, 293, 294. Negotiations with the Liberal Nationals began in August 1943 and continued until November 1944, but foundered over the Simonites' refusal to break with the Conservatives: see David Dutton, *Liberals in Schism: A History of the National Liberal Party* (2008), 136–9.

Grassroots disaffection with Sinclair's leadership was compounded by the perceived lethargy of party headquarters (which had been evacuated to Sutton) and by the constraints which the electoral truce placed on by-election activity. The Liberal Action Group, formed by twenty-seven activists and candidates after the 1941 Liberal Assembly, sought to deal with both these problems.[14] The group was most successful at spurring the LPO into action, as headquarters returned to central London in December 1941 and Wilfrid Roberts worked to revive local and regional Liberal organizations.[15] A public relations department was established during 1942, and the party's Reconstruction Committee, chaired by Harris, formed a number of specialist sub-committees which began to produce policy reports.[16] A steady recovery of Liberal activity and morale can be traced from mid-1942 onwards. The electoral truce, on the other hand, proved harder to challenge. Several Liberals contested by-elections as independents, and Donald Johnson and Honor Balfour almost won Chippenham and Darwen respectively in 1943, but the party as a whole was not prepared to fracture national unity.[17] The most that could be achieved was a declaration, demanded by the 1943 Assembly and finally issued by MPs in 1944, that the Liberals would fight the post-war general election as a free and independent party.[18]

The agitation for greater Liberal independence cut across the party's internal ideological spectrum. When the Liberal Action Group was formed, it took no definite line on economic policy, and moderates and anti-planners such as Elliott Dodds, Philip Fothergill, Deryck Abel, and the young Berwick-upon-Tweed MP George Grey were counted among its members.[19] Over time, the group assumed a position in favour of economic planning; in the spring of 1943 it took the name Radical Action, and at the 1945 election it issued a manifesto drafted by Tom Horabin (MP for North Cornwall since a 1939 by-election) which called for large-scale public ownership. Nevertheless, despite Sinclair's misconceptions, Radical Action was never ideologically cohesive, and the revival of

[14] Bodleian Library, Oxford, MS. Balfour 71/1, 'Resolutions passed by the Liberal Action Group at various meetings', n.d., and 68/1, Lancelot Spicer to Colonel Dew, 11 October 1943.

[15] Thorpe, *Parties at War*, 53–4, 152, 230

[16] Malcolm Baines, 'The Survival of the British Liberal Party, 1932–1959' (Oxford D.Phil. thesis, 1989), 51–2; Parliamentary Archives, Graham White papers, WHI/2/4/8, B. S. Rowntree to White, 25 July 1942.

[17] Donald Johnson, *Bars and Barricades* (1952), 208–51.

[18] Mark Egan, 'Radical Action and the Liberal Party during the Second World War', *JLH*, no. 63 (2009), 4–17, at 10.

[19] MS. Balfour 71/1, 'Resolutions passed by the Liberal Action Group at various meetings', and 71/2, report of Liberal Action Group meetings, 5–6 December 1942.

Liberalism as an independent force remained its raison d'être at least until the general election came into prospect.[20]

PLANNERS AND ANTI-PLANNERS

Two planning movements emerged within the Liberal Party during the early part of the war. The first move came from Sir Richard Acland, who had inherited a baronetcy on his father's 1939 death and broke with conventional Liberal thought in *Unser Kampf* (February 1940).[21] As he later explained to the historian Angus Calder, Acland had read the *General Theory* soon after its publication and was impressed by its demonstration that 'the automatic, self-working, laissez-faire Liberalism' he had been brought up on 'just did not work', but he did not believe that Keynes' policy prescriptions were sufficiently radical to deal with the problem he had diagnosed.[22] During the late 1930s Acland focussed on promoting progressive cooperation, but after war broke out he announced his conversion to socialism. Acland's ethical case for 'Common Ownership' of productive resources was strongly flavoured by his upbringing in West Country Liberalism, but neither his new views nor his increasingly messianic tone could be accommodated comfortably within the Liberal fold. Although Acland did not formally leave the party until September 1942, he channelled most of his energies into a series of independent bodies: the 'Our Struggle' movement (later renamed 'Forward March') which he founded in 1940, the 1941 Committee, and the Common Wealth Party.[23]

Acland's ethical approach and his conception of the state as the expression of the general will placed him loosely in the New Liberal tradition. By contrast, Clement Davies and Tom Horabin developed constructive ideas in a radical direction. Davies and Horabin formed part of a group of malcontent MPs from all parties who were dissatisfied with the prosecution of the war, and pressed for the British economy to be fully mobilized under a small War Cabinet, as in the First World War. With advice from the Hungarian émigré and Oxford economist Thomas Balogh and tacit support from Lloyd George, the malcontents called for the state to plan output in the shipping, machine tools, and munitions industries by pooling production capacity under the

[20] MS. Balfour 71/2, Lancelot Spicer to Sinclair, 12 January 1944.

[21] Sir Richard Acland, *Unser Kampf: Our Struggle* (Harmondsworth, 1940).

[22] A. L. R. Calder, 'The Common Wealth Party, 1942–1945' (Sussex Ph.D. thesis, 1967), part one, 17.

[23] Calder, 'Common Wealth', part one, 20–31.

control of regional boards.[24] Both Davies and Horabin were heavily influenced by their experience of business management in the 1930s—Davies as a director of Unilever, Horabin as managing director of Lacrinoid Ltd, which made synthetic buttons—and were impressed by the efficiency improvements which could be achieved through better organization. This version of the case for planning was severely practical. Davies and Horabin were keen to extend rationing to ensure 'fair shares', but they were not egalitarians in any strict sense, and had no principled objection to private enterprise or profit.

Under Balogh's influence, Davies and Horabin became convinced that post-war reconstruction would also require a centrally planned economy. At the 1942 Liberal Assembly, Horabin tabled proposals for a thoroughgoing planning regime, run by a Ministry of National Planning with 'power to allocate labour, plant and machinery and raw materials and to determine priorities'. The state would also ensure the adoption of modern production methods and control the joint stock banks and basic industries through public utility boards. Balogh regarded international trade and financial movements as a major source of economic instability, and favoured bilateral agreements and regional economic blocs as means of maintaining control over trade flows; Davies and Horabin followed the Hungarian in arguing that the free-trade case was no longer valid.[25]

Many Liberals were wary of these radical ideas, but Elliott Dodds bore much of the burden of resisting them. The outbreak of war did nothing to stem Dodds' zeal for 'ownership for all', and he was particularly concerned by the government's wartime policy of concentrating retail distribution in large firms, which threatened the survival of small traders. Along with the Leeds solicitor Donald Wade and contacts in the retail trade, Dodds established a Liberal Independent Traders' Enquiry Committee and later the Independent Traders' Alliance to champion the interests of the small man.[26] Arthur Seldon meanwhile wrote a report for the LPO, which claimed that the government's concentration policy was bringing about a 'drift to the corporate state'.[27] The 1941 Liberal Assembly passed a resolution on the Independent Trader, expressing 'grave concern' at the 'monopolistic tendencies' which had been operating before the war and were being 'accentuated by present conditions'.[28] The following year, Dodds persuaded the LPO executive to sponsor a resolution on Freedom

[24] David Lloyd George papers, LG/G/24/2/63, A. J. Sylvester to David Lloyd George, 8 April 1941, and LG/G/24/2/208, Sylvester to Lloyd George, 9 January 1942; see also correspondence between Balogh and Lloyd George in LG/G/2/1.

[25] BLPES, Liberal Party papers, 8/3, 1942 Assembly Agenda, 23–4.

[26] *LPO Bulletin*, no. 29 (March 1942), 4–6.

[27] *LPO Bulletin*, no. 24 (October 1941), 8.

[28] Liberal Party papers, 8/3, 1941 Assembly Agenda, 7–8; *MG*, 19 July 1941, 8.

of Enterprise which elaborated these themes, called for 'the removal, at the earliest possible date, of all controls which cannot be shown to be in the interest of the community as a whole', and warned that 'the functions of the state cannot be indefinitely extended without leading to administrative chaos and arbitrary rule'.[29] Oscar Hobson developed similar arguments in the *News Chronicle*, and several of his most pointed articles were reprinted in the LPO's monthly bulletin.[30]

Dodds' commitment to competition and private property came under fierce attack from the left. At the 1941 Assembly, Acland lambasted the Independent Trader motion, claiming that it sought to 'mak[e] a paradise for people with £500 a year' and ignored the position of 'the left-out millions'.[31] Dodds repulsed this criticism by pointing to the aim of giving ownership to all, but Horabin and Davies proved stronger opponents. At the 1942 Assembly, Horabin developed a wide-ranging critique of free-market assumptions, arguing that American anti-trust laws had been ineffective, that the growth of monopolies was 'inevitable', and that nationalization of the banks and basic industries was necessary to prevent large corporations from wielding political power. Dodds insisted that he did not stand for laissez-faire—'I cannot conceive of a more fantastic misrepresentation'—but he failed to prevent Horabin from portraying him in these terms. Viscount Samuel endorsed Horabin's claim that monopolies were inevitable in some industries, and Megan Lloyd George argued that the export trade had to be planned. Faced with an open clash of opinion, the Assembly agreed to refer both Dodds' resolution and Horabin's amendment to a policy sub-committee on the Structure of Industry, chaired by Harris.[32] This would become the hub of the party's economic policy discussions for the next year.

THE RELATION OF THE STATE TO INDUSTRY

The Liberal Party's Reconstruction Committee was established by Sir Percy Harris in March 1941, and from the start it took an interest in planning.[33]

[29] Liberal Party papers, 8/3, 1942 Assembly Agenda, 22; Borthwick Institute for Archives, University of York, Seebohm Rowntree papers, PLA/4/12, Dodds circular to LPO executive, 2 July 1942.

[30] *LPO Bulletin*, no. 19 (May 1941), 6–7, no. 28 (February 1942), 2–3, and no. 30 (April 1942), 1–2.

[31] Donald Wade and Desmond Banks, *The Political Insight of Elliott Dodds* (Leeds, 1977), 28–9; *MG*, 19 July 1941, 8.

[32] Wade and Banks, *Political Insight*, 30–1; *MG*, 6 September 1942, 8.

[33] David Lloyd George papers, LG/G/24/2/43, A. J. Sylvester to David Lloyd George, 12 March 1941.

E. H. Carr, Professor of International Relations at the University of Wales, Aberystwyth, was asked to produce a memorandum on a post-war Liberal policy, and proposed bold central planning, a national minimum income, state-controlled corporations to manage monopolistic and socially important industries, and the direction of investment and labour.[34] Carr's approach proved to be too radical for the committee to accept—Seebohm Rowntree thought it amounted to socialism—but Harris and Rowntree shared his conviction that the basic industries would have to be reorganized.[35] In the autumn of 1941, the committee began an inquiry into industrial organization, and Rowntree's assistant F. D. Stuart was despatched to investigate conditions in the staple trades.[36] An unpublished report which emerged from this inquiry, drafted by Harris, suggested that a varied approach would best suit each industry's needs: private competition for textiles, competitive public ownership for the mines, and the rationalization of iron and steel under a single public utility.[37] Nothing more seems to have come of Harris' draft, but it shows the predominantly microeconomic orientation of Liberal thinking at this stage.

In summer 1942, the Reconstruction Committee was reorganized on a more specialized basis, with a series of sub-committees deputed to examine particular fields of policy.[38] Wilfrid Roberts chaired a sub-committee on Food and Agriculture, the barrister A. S. Comyns Carr did likewise for Land and Housing, and Sir John Stewart-Wallace, a former chief land registrar, took responsibility for Money and Banking. Rowntree chaired three—on International Trade, Remuneration of the Workers, and the Status of the Workers—but Sir Percy Harris' sub-committee on the Structure of Industry was where the most heated ideological debates played out.[39] After the 1943 Liberal Assembly, the whole system was placed on a more formal footing, with a Permanent Policy Committee appointed jointly by the Liberal Parliamentary Party and the LPO, and sub-committees created and dissolved at its discretion.[40] The guiding objective throughout was to develop a detailed policy programme which Liberals could put forward when the election came.

[34] Rowntree papers, UNEM/11/1, E. H. Carr, 'Some Outlines of Reconstruction Policy', 7 May 1941, and UNEM/11/3, E. H. Carr to D. O. Evans, 24 November 1941.

[35] Rowntree papers, UNEM/11/4, notes by Rowntree on Carr's memorandum, 31 December 1941.

[36] Graham White papers, WHI/2/4/6, Rowntree to Harris, 6 January 1942.

[37] Graham White papers, WHI/2/1/4, 'Liberal Social and Industrial Reconstruction Committee. Chairman's General Report', June 1942.

[38] Graham White papers, WHI/2/4/8, Rowntree to White, 25 July 1942.

[39] Liberal Party papers, 8/3, 1943 Assembly Agenda, 1.

[40] BLPES, Beveridge papers, VI/103/2/65, LPO Seventh Annual Report to the Assembly, spring 1944, 40.

The Structure of Industry sub-committee comprised a cross-section of the Liberal establishment from London and the provinces: Harris, Rowntree, Stewart-Wallace, Bonham Carter, Lord Meston, Graham White, and the banker Sir Felix Brunner, with Geoffrey Mander representing the Liberal ministers. E. H. Gilpin, the chairman of the LPO executive, joined later on.[41] As Harris explained at the start, the sub-committee's task was to survey the evidence on planning, and consider what forms of intervention were necessary to ensure full employment in peacetime.[42] Certainly, Harris thought,

> [A]ny political party that has any pretensions to govern this country must satisfy the electorate that they have a constructive policy to prevent large-scale unemployment.[43]

The sub-committee's report, moreover, would have to 'satisfy the two sections of the party'.[44] Harris therefore asked Dodds and Horabin for memoranda of their views, and organized meetings to take evidence from both groups. Horabin and Davies turned to Balogh for assistance; Dodds turned to Seldon and Arthur Shenfield, a lecturer at Birmingham University and later a prominent neoliberal, and to Friedrich Hayek's research assistant, Ludwig Lachmann. Walter Hill and Geoffrey Crowther of *The Economist*, E. F. Schumacher of the Oxford Institute of Statistics, the social scientists Michael Polanyi and Ferdinand Zweig, and the economist Gerda Blau also provided advice for Harris and his colleagues.[45]

The possibility of a broadly Keynesian solution to the unemployment problem was recognized by Harris and his colleagues from the outset. In three articles in October 1942, Walter Hill recapitulated *The Economist*'s version of the Keynesian position: government policy should focus on raising investment to full-employment level through low interest rates and taxation allowances, backed up by direct controls through a National Investment Board, with public works kept on tap as a last resort.[46] Dodds and his colleagues were willing to accept this as a basis of agreement, although they were reluctant to control private investment and placed more emphasis on public works: the state, Dodds said, 'should come in on whatever scale was necessary to prevent mass unemployment'.[47]

[41] Rowntree papers, PLA/5/11, minutes of Structure of Industry sub-committee (hereafter S.I. minutes), 15 February 1943.

[42] Rowntree papers, PLA/5/1, S.I. minutes, 23 November 1942.

[43] Rowntree papers, PLA/4/15, 'Some Informal Notes on Planning in its Relation to Personal Freedom', by Sir Percy Harris, 14 January 1943.

[44] Rowntree papers, PLA/5/9, S.I. minutes, 8 February 1943.

[45] The relevant correspondence appears in Rowntree papers, PLA/4 and PLA/5.

[46] *The Economist*, 3, 10 and 17 October 1942, 407–8, 438–40, 472–3.

[47] Rowntree papers, PLA/4/23, 'A Policy for Liberalism', by Dodds, 24 February 1943, and PLA/5/12, S.I. minutes, 12 March 1943.

Harris, however, was unconvinced that higher overall demand would solve the basic industries' problems, and was receptive to two criticisms which Horabin, Davies, and Balogh levelled against a liberal Keynesian approach.[48] Firstly, Harris thought it unreasonable to make public authorities vary their investment in order to compensate for the impact of private firms' decisions; it made more sense to try to stabilize both public and private investment plans. Secondly, Harris was impressed by the danger that the state would run out of productive public works projects during a depression. The nationalization of certain industries, such as transport, might therefore be justified as a means of expanding the field for public investment.[49]

The Structure of Industry sub-committee was well aware of the difficulties involved in reconciling planning with Liberal principles. Polanyi, who was an early neoliberal, warned that planning would take government beyond its legitimate role of establishing and enforcing the rule of law; Zweig argued that some instability was inevitable in a free society; and the former Treasury official Sir Andrew McFadyean pointed out the danger of creating sheltered nationalized industries.[50] However, the weight of opinion ran towards greater state intervention. Prompted by White and Gilpin, and encouraged by E. F. Schumacher, the sub-committee played down the value of trust-busting and suggested that publicity requirements would prevent monopolies from exploiting the consumer.[51] Bonham Carter even sympathized with Balogh's proposal for a statutory wages policy and restrictions on strikes in order to prevent wage inflation, though Harris wisely judged it best to avoid this controversial question.[52]

Harris and the other members of his sub-committee clearly favoured an interventionist form of Keynesianism, which lay part-way between *The Economist*'s recommendations and those of the planners. However, they found it difficult to agree on detailed proposals, and faced opposition to their more radical ideas from the LPO executive. By the time the report on *The Relation of the State to Industry* finally appeared, Harris complained, its recommendations had been 'boiled down to nothing'.[53] In substance, the

[48] Rowntree papers, PLA/5/2, S.I. minutes, 4 December 1942.

[49] Rowntree papers, PLA/4/15, 'Some Informal Notes on Planning'; PLA/5/9, S.I. minutes, 8 February 1943.

[50] Rowntree papers, PLA/4/18, 'Comments on the "Draft Memorandum on a Planned Economy"', by Polanyi, n.d.; PLA/5/4, S.I. minutes, 18 December 1942; PLA/4/21, 'Government and Industry', by McFadyean, January 1943.

[51] Rowntree papers, PLA/5/12, S.I. minutes, 12 March 1943; Graham White papers, WHI/2/1/15, 'An Economic Policy for Liberalism' by Schumacher, 8 March 1943.

[52] Rowntree papers, PLA/5/5 and PLA/5/11, S.I. minutes, 18 January and 15 February 1943.

[53] Harris papers, HRS/2, Harris diary, entry for 5 May 1943.

report largely followed *The Economist*'s approach, arguing that the state's first response to a downturn should be

> to stimulate private enterprise and restore business confidence by lowering rates of interest and by increasing the amounts which industrial companies may charge for depreciation when making their returns of profits liable to income tax.

If this proved insufficient to 'take up all the slack of unused productive resources', 'the State should be called upon to restore the balance by investing in public works on a scale large enough to make up for the deficiency in private capital expenditure'.[54] In other words, public investment was still the balancing factor. The report revived the Yellow Book proposals for an Economic General Staff and National Investment Board, advocated a capital budget, and suggested that the nationalization of some natural monopolies would increase the scope for counter-cyclical public investment, but it also emphasized that the 'overwhelming part' of industry 'would remain in private hands operating under free competition'.[55] There was no reference to regulation of private investment: large firms would merely be required to report their plans to the National Investment Board so that it could calculate how much public investment would be needed to maintain full employment.

Dodds and other moderate Liberals regarded *The Relation of the State to Industry* as a satisfactory compromise, but Horabin and Davies were much less impressed, and decided to take their case to the 1943 Assembly. Horabin tabled a lengthy amendment to the executive resolution on The State and Industry, and W. J. Gruffydd (the new MP for the University of Wales) and Radical Action member Everett Jones were persuaded to add their names to a memorandum on 'A Radical Economic Policy for Progressive Liberalism', which was circulated to delegates. This document took a vigorously interventionist line, and argued that central planning would be required permanently if full employment and price stability were to be maintained.[56] In the Assembly debate, Horabin and Davies were backed up by Megan Lloyd George, who argued that the party was being paralysed by 'the shackles of a nineteenth-century philosophy'.[57] However, strong speeches from Harris, Dodds, Gilpin, and Johnstone—and a letter of support from Sir Walter Layton—carried greater weight with the delegates, and Horabin's amendment was 'decisively rejected' on a show

[54] Liberal Party, *The Relation of the State to Industry* (1943), 11.

[55] Liberal Party, *The Relation of the State to Industry*, 16.

[56] MS. Balfour 65/1, 'A Radical Economic Policy for Progressive Liberalism', n.d. [June/July 1943].

[57] *NC*, 17 July 1943, 4.

of hands. A traditionalist amendment tabled by East Grinstead Liberals, opposing *The Relation of the State to Industry* on the grounds that it was too interventionist, received even less support, and the executive resolution was carried by a large majority.[58]

The 1943 Assembly also received reports from several other policy sub-committees. The report of the International Trade sub-committee declared that free trade was a Liberal principle, and emphasized the need for international cooperation—through an International Clearing Union, an International Commodity Board, and an International Investment Board—to make it compatible with full employment.[59] The Money and Banking report rejected bank nationalization, but called for a clearer distinction between the formulation of monetary policy, which was the government's responsibility, and its implementation by the Bank of England.[60] Both of these reports fitted well with the policy outlined in *The Relation of the State to Industry*, and were comfortably approved.[61]

Seebohm Rowntree's report on *The Remuneration of the Worker* was more controversial. Drawing on his own social research and industrial experience, Rowntree proposed to abolish want by extending the trade boards system to all industries where no effective wage-fixing organization existed, giving them a brief 'to fix the highest wages the industry can afford', and setting a statutory national minimum wage at the lowest trade-board rate. Trade unions and employers would be encouraged to channel pay bargaining through Joint Industrial Councils, while 'essential industries' which could not afford to pay adequate wages would be taken over by the state and run by public boards.[62] For Dodds, Ronald Walker, and Frances Josephy, Rowntree's plan raised two problems: it took large industries (and large firms) as the model of the whole economy, and it paid too little attention to industrial democracy and profit-sharing. At the Assembly, Rowntree's resolution was amended to make Joint Industrial Councils the main wage-fixing bodies and strengthen the calls for profit-sharing and a subsistence-level minimum wage.[63] Internal debate over Rowntree's proposals would rumble on until 1945, when a compromise was finally reached.[64] Despite this wrangling, the readiness with which the party supported a national system of wage-fixing machinery shows how far interventionist ideas had regained their influence.

58 *MG*, 17 July 1943, 8.
59 Liberal Party, *International Trade* (1943).
60 Liberal Party, *Money and Banking* (1943).
61 *MG*, 16 July 1943, 6.
62 Liberal Party papers, 8/3, 1943 Assembly Agenda, 18–19.
63 Liberal Party papers, 8/3, 1943 Assembly Agenda, 20–1; *MG*, 16 July 1943, 6.
64 *LM*, liii (1945), 199; Beveridge papers, VI 18/2/58, LPO Council minutes, 18 April 1945.

Two other reports touched on issues of special sensitivity to Liberals. In *Land and Housing*, Comyns Carr's sub-committee recommended a national development plan with controls over industrial location, a house-building target of 400,000 houses a year for the post-war decade, and the creation of Fair Rent Courts to replace the Rent Restriction Acts. This report also accepted the Uthwatt Committee's recommendation that the government should nationalize development rights outside built-up areas, in order to deal with the problems of compensation and betterment, and suggested that this could be combined with the introduction of site value taxation in the towns.[65] The Food and Agriculture sub-committee proposed the continuation of guaranteed prices 'until agriculture is self-supporting', along with the creation of a Land Commission to buy land that required improvement and lease it to farmers, the reform (though not abolition) of the marketing boards, and measures to improve the living standards of agricultural workers.[66] The main thrust of the *Food and Agriculture* report was in line with the nutritionist approach which Sinclair had articulated before the war, but the commitment to guaranteed prices in peacetime was a significant new departure.

The reports adopted at the 1943 Assembly placed the Liberals in the mainstream of progressive thinking about post-war reconstruction, whilst stopping short of full-blown central planning. Most Liberals were satisfied with this position, and turned their energies to the task of popularizing the party's new platform.[67] However, the 1943 Assembly also crystallized traditionalist disaffection. Francis Hirst believed the party was drifting towards bureaucratic state control, whilst Georgists such as Ashley Mitchell and A. R. MacDougall complained that it was jettisoning its historic commitments to land value taxation and free trade.[68] On the land question itself, the Georgist position retained considerable purchase, and an attempt to amend the Land and Housing resolution at the Assembly was defeated by only thirteen votes.[69] After the Assembly, the Georgists began to rally support, notably from the Scottish Liberal Federation and the London Liberal Federation, for the repudiation of the Uthwatt proposals and the restoration of land value taxation as a core Liberal policy.[70]

65 Liberal Party, *Land and Housing* (1943).

66 Liberal Party, *Food and Agriculture* (1943).

67 For instance, Dodds developed the party's case in his book *Let's Try Liberalism*, and Lancelot Spicer of Radical Action left the Assembly impressed by the need to get Liberal ideas over to the electorate: MS. Balfour 68/1, untitled typescript by Spicer, n.d. [1943].

68 *L&L*, no. 591 (August 1943), 63; *MG*, 16 July 1943, 6.

69 *L&L*, no. 591 (August 1943), 63.

70 National Library of Scotland, Scottish Liberal Party papers, 15, resolutions for General Council conference, 6 October 1943; *L&L*, no. 594 (November 1943), 85.

The Liberal Liberty League, formed in January 1944 with Mitchell as its chairman and T. Atholl Robertson as vice-chairman, provided an institutional vehicle for this campaign.[71]

The creation of the Liberal Liberty League confirmed the breach between diehard classical and Georgist Liberals and the mainstream of the party which had been brewing for years. For Dodds and other moderates, demand-management policies and Beveridgean social insurance offered valuable means of achieving Liberal ends whilst minimizing interference with private ownership and consumer choice; for the Liberty Leaguers, these policies were dangerous panaceas, which intensified the dislocation of economic forces and failed to deal with the land question. Both groups laid claim to Walter Lippmann, though—as Dodds pointed out when the Yorkshire Liberal Federation executive discussed the Beveridge scheme—social insurance was clearly endorsed in *The Good Society*.[72] A more natural point of reference for the Liberty Leaguers was Friedrich Hayek, whose book *The Road to Serfdom* received a sympathetic review in the Georgist journal *Land & Liberty*.[73] Moderates recognized the electoral dangers of Hayekian rhetoric in this period, and viewed anti-statist fringe groups with suspicion: Dodds thought only 'a queer sort of Liberal' could be comfortable in Sir Ernest Benn's Society of Individualists.[74] By contrast, the Liberty Leaguers were happy to identify with the libertarian right, and only lamented that Hayek had not dealt with the land question.[75] Francis Hirst took a similar line, although he was not especially interested in land value taxation, and resigned from the Society of Individualists in 1944 in protest at its merger with the Conservative-dominated National League for Freedom.[76]

SIR WILLIAM BEVERIDGE AND THE 'RADICAL PROGRAMME'

The Liberal Liberty Leaguers hoped that the moderately interventionist policies adopted in 1943 would be reversed during the years that followed. Instead, they were consolidated and extended, partly through the growing

[71] *L&L*, no. 597 (February 1944), 109.

[72] West Yorkshire Archives Service, Leeds, Yorkshire Liberal Federation papers, WYL456/3, executive minutes, 10 July 1943.

[73] *L&L*, nos. 600–1 (May–June 1944), 131–2.

[74] Elliott Dodds, *The Rights of Men as Persons* (1945), quoted in Beveridge, *Why I am a Liberal*, 10.

[75] *L&L*, nos. 603–4 (August–September 1945), 150–1.

[76] Deryck Abel, *Ernest Benn: Counsel for Liberty* (1960), 125.

influence of Radical Action, partly through the leftward drift of leading Liberals such as Harris and Bonham Carter, but above all as a result of Sir William Beveridge's adhesion to the party. Beveridge brought with him an enormous popular reputation as the author of *Social Insurance and Allied Services*, a commitment to an interventionist version of Keynesianism which he elaborated in *Full Employment in a Free Society*, and a conviction that the Liberals must fight the coming election on a 'Radical Programme'.

William Beveridge had a lifelong association with the Liberal Party. As a young man he developed the Asquith government's plans for labour exchanges; in the early 1920s he attended the Liberal Summer School and wrote a Liberal pamphlet on *Insurance for All and Everything*; and as lead author of *Tariffs: The Case Examined* in 1931 he helped the party fight for free trade. As José Harris has shown, however, it would be quite wrong to regard him as a lifelong Liberal. Throughout his career, he was 'suspicious and critical of conventional party politics' and carefully guarded his independence.[77] Beveridge's views on economic organization also oscillated wildly, from Fabian-influenced reformism in the Edwardian period to an orthodox line in the 1920s and early 1930s and enthusiasm for planning during the Second World War. By the 1940s his policy views would have fitted in the Labour Party as easily as the Liberal; his differences with the Labour movement were largely cultural and attitudinal ones.

After *Social Insurance and Allied Services* appeared in December 1942, Beveridge hoped he would be asked to follow it up, either by overseeing its implementation or by investigating the related issue of how to achieve full employment. When this did not happen, he began a private full employment inquiry and made it known that he was interested in entering Parliament.[78] Violet Bonham Carter was determined that he should stand as a Liberal, and set about cultivating links with him in spite of Sinclair's reservations; in José Harris' words, the Liberals 'wooed and flattered Beveridge and eventually won him'.[79] In March 1943 Beveridge spoke on a Liberal platform at the Caxton Hall, Westminster, and discussed social security at a meeting of the party Council; later in the year he met with the Structure of Industry sub-committee, specially reconvened for the occasion, to obtain Liberal input into his full employment inquiry.[80] Beveridge was initially reluctant to commit himself to the Liberals, partly because he

[77] José Harris, *William Beveridge: A Biography* (second edition, Oxford, 1994), 118.

[78] Harris, *William Beveridge*, 432–4.

[79] *Champion Redoubtable*, 248, 316; Harris, *William Beveridge*, 445.

[80] *Champion Redoubtable*, 258–9; Bodleian Library, Hirst papers, 67, Francis Hirst to Gertrude Hirst, 19 March 1943; Beveridge papers, IXa/15/10/91, minutes of meeting with Liberal committee, 17 November 1943, and IXa/15/10/82, minutes of meeting with Liberal committee, 1 December 1943.

still prized his freedom of action and partly because he believed Sinclair favoured a post-war coalition, but Bonham Carter and her colleagues persisted with their efforts and assured him that the party would back his full employment policy.[81] No sooner had Beveridge agreed to join the Liberals than an unexpected opportunity for him to enter the Commons presented itself, when George Grey was killed in France in August 1944. Beveridge fought and won the ensuing by-election at Berwick-upon-Tweed, and soon began to stamp his mark on the party.

The White Paper on *Employment Policy* which the coalition government published in May 1944 was a cautiously Keynesian document, the product of a carefully brokered compromise between the Economic Section of the War Cabinet and more orthodox Treasury officials.[82] For the first time, the government assumed responsibility for 'a high and stable level of employment', and publicly embraced the idea of using variations in public investment and taxation to manage demand and mitigate cyclical instability.[83] This momentous shift, however, was combined with an emphasis on the importance of structural factors—the revival of world trade, the location of industry, and the mobility of labour—and with an insistence that the government did not envisage deliberate deficit budgeting. Beveridge's report on *Full Employment in a Free Society*, which he finished in spring 1944 though it did not appear until November, took a much more radical approach. Beveridge defined full employment very strictly, as an average unemployment rate of no more than 3 per cent, and insisted that this could only be achieved through 'a long-term programme of planned outlay' by the government, stabilization of private investment by a National Investment Board, and an acceptance of the need to run budget deficits, at least in slumps and possibly across the economic cycle.[84] The White Paper, he complained, was 'a public works policy, not a policy of full employment'.[85] Beveridge proposed to expand the public sector 'to enlarge the area within which investment can be stabilized directly', and suggested that the threat of nationalization could be used to control private investment plans.[86] He also followed Balogh in taking a sceptical view of the prospects for trade liberalization, and emphasized the value

[81] Beveridge papers, IXa/37/10/301, 'From April 1943–February 1945', typed copy of letter from Beveridge to Wilfrid Roberts, 28 February 1944; IXa/38/3/73, Dingle Foot to Beveridge, 25 May 1944; IXa/38/3/76, Bonham Carter to Beveridge, 2 June 1944; and IXa/38/3/88, Wilfrid Roberts to Beveridge, 1 August 1944.

[82] Jim Tomlinson, *Employment Policy: The Crucial Years, 1939–1955* (Oxford, 1987), 45–63; Alan Booth, *British Economic Policy, 1931–49: Was there a Keynesian Revolution?* (1989), 107–21.

[83] Cmd. 6527, *Employment Policy* (1944), 3, 20–4.

[84] Sir William Beveridge, *Full Employment in a Free Society* (1944), 30.

[85] Beveridge, *Full Employment*, 262.

[86] Beveridge, *Full Employment*, 271.

of bilateral agreements and regional blocs for allowing the state to ensure economic stability.

On the basis of existing Liberal policy, there were good reasons why the party might have favoured the White Paper's approach: it was more internationalist, treated public works as a balancing factor, and did not call into question (as Beveridge did) whether private ownership of the means of production was 'an essential citizen liberty'.[87] Keynesian economists such as James Meade and Roy Harrod also considered the White Paper much more realistic.[88] On the other hand, its treatment of finance seemed overly cautious, as Graham White pointed out in the Commons, and there was a strong political incentive for the Liberals to take Beveridge's line.[89] A Liberal committee chaired by Sir John Stewart-Wallace met to draw up a response to the White Paper during the summer of 1944, and drew heavily on advice from Beveridge, including proof copies of his report. Some of Stewart-Wallace's colleagues had become nervous about state intervention after reading *The Road to Serfdom*—Lady Juliet Rhys Williams, a pre-war recruit from the Liberal Nationals, was especially cautious—but this was a minority view, as the report which the committee produced in August showed.[90] The 'basic error' in the White Paper, the report argued, was its insistence on balancing the budget each year 'on orthodox 19th century lines':

> A truly balanced budget is one that brings the whole economy of the country into balance. It may frequently, and over long periods, be the duty of the Government to spend more than its income, if by so doing it can assist the maintenance of an adequate flow of purchasing power.[91]

Beveridge would still have to convince the Liberal Party at large of the merits of *Full Employment in a Free Society*, but senior Liberals outside the government were clearly already sympathetic.

It was at one stage intended that Stewart-Wallace's committee would draw up 'a positive policy on Full Employment', but this never happened.[92]

[87] Beveridge, *Full Employment*, 23.

[88] James Meade, 'Sir William Beveridge's *Full Employment in a Free Society* and the White Paper on Employment Policy (Command 6527)', in *The Collected Papers of James Meade*, ed. Susan Howson and Donald Moggridge (4 vols, 1988–90), i, 233–64; British Library, Add. MS. 72735 (Harrod papers), fol. 93, Harrod to Sinclair, 18 July 1945.

[89] Hansard, HC (series 5) vol. 401, cols 239–46 (21 June 1944).

[90] Beveridge papers, IXa/18/2/165, Stewart-Wallace to Beveridge, 21 August 1944; Rowntree papers, POV/3/4, 'Notes on White Paper on Full Employment', by Juliet Rhys Williams, n.d. [June 1944]. The report was drafted by Rhys Williams, with assistance from Geoffrey Crowther: BLPES, Rhys Williams papers, J/2/8/1, Rhys Williams to Rowntree, 28 July 1944.

[91] Liberal Party, *The Government's Employment Policy Examined: An Interim Report of the Liberal Party Committee on Full Employment* (1944), 6.

[92] Beveridge papers, VI 103/1/61, Supplement to LPO Seventh Annual Report to Assembly, 31 December 1944, 7.

Instead, Beveridge was asked to draft '[a] comprehensive resolution on Full Employment' for the Liberal Assembly which was due to take place in February 1945.[93] Beveridge's resolution followed *Full Employment in a Free Society* in all significant respects, calling for manpower budgeting, 'a long-term programme of planned outlay' by the government, and regulation of private investment through a National Investment Board. The government's external policy would seek 'the greatest possible extension of international trade' compatible with full employment and economic stability, whilst public ownership would be extended wherever 'the need to control monopolies, or the overriding importance of the industry in the national life, or the necessities of national defence' made this desirable.[94] Prominent references to workers' participation and the need to control monopolies were included as concessions to Liberal sensibilities, but it was not unreasonable for T. Atholl Robertson to ask whether Beveridge had joined the Liberal Party or the party had joined Beveridge.[95]

Though Beveridge's approach to policy-making was generally pragmatic and utilitarian, he justified his interventionist agenda in terms which he drew from the New Liberal tradition. 'The ultimate aims of Liberalism', he declared, were the same as they had always been:

> equal enjoyment of all essential liberties secured by the rule of law, material progress for the sake of increasing spiritual life, toleration for variety of opinion, the common interest of all citizens over-riding every sectional privilege at home, peace and goodwill and international trade abroad.[96]

The methods needed to achieve these aims, however, were constantly changing, and in contemporary Britain conquering 'the social evils of Want, Disease, Ignorance, Squalor and Idleness' required 'an extension of the responsibilities and functions of the State'.[97] Under his Radical Programme, he argued, all the 'essential' personal and political liberties would be preserved, and the elimination of unemployment and poverty would bring about 'more true liberty for all the people'.[98] Beveridge regarded concrete liberties, such as the 'right' to running water, as important forms of freedom.[99] Conversely, he considered Hayek's concern for the freedom of entrepreneurs misguided, because most citizens had never been able to own the means of production. He also believed that the risk

93 Beveridge papers, VI 103/1/1–3, Assembly Agenda Committee minutes, 10 October 1944.

94 Liberal Party papers, 8/3, 1945 Assembly Agenda, 25–7.

95 *L&L*, no. 610 (March 1945), 27.

96 Beveridge, *Why I am a Liberal*, 32.

97 Beveridge, *Why I am a Liberal*, 34, 33.

98 Beveridge, *Why I am a Liberal*, 33, 67.

99 Beveridge, *Why I am a Liberal*, 29.

of arbitrary government would be substantially eliminated by 'effective Parliamentary control'. In a democratic society, Liberals had 'no reason to be afraid of the State'.[100]

The interpretation of Liberal principles which Beveridge articulated in 1944–5 chimed closely with the views of many left-wing Liberals, but predictably raised hackles on the right of the party. The Liberal Liberty League was most vocally critical, and decided to force the issue at the 1945 Assembly, tabling a wrecking amendment to the Full Employment resolution and distributing a memorandum which purported to demonstrate its incompatibility with the Liberal principles of free trade, free enterprise, and land value taxation.[101] The Liberty League stood well outside the party's mainstream, but some of its concerns were shared by more moderate Liberals, especially in northern England, where free-trade sentiment remained strong and Labour was the party's main opponent.[102] 'There is a deep feeling in many quarters', claimed Juliet Rhys Williams, 'that the Party is continually being driven against its will. . . to abandon cherished principles.'[103] Dodds certainly disagreed with Beveridge's view that the maintenance of private ownership was a matter of relative indifference.[104] On the other hand, the symbolic importance of Beveridge's resolution could not be lightly discounted. If the Liberals rejected it, they ran the risk not only of alienating Beveridge but also of forfeiting their claim to be a progressive, reforming party.

Beveridge's Full Employment resolution was the centrepiece of the 1945 Assembly, and in an attempt to defuse traditionalist opposition, the party executive asked Dodds to second it. Beveridge moved the resolution with a forthright exposition of his policy, and a rebuttal of those he had previously christened 'the bow-and-arrow brigade'; Dodds followed up with a 'flank attack' in which he acknowledged his reservations but argued that the resolution deserved to pass.[105] Dodds emphasized that land value taxation and free trade could not solve unemployment by themselves,

[100] Beveridge, *Why I am a Liberal*, 37.

[101] Beveridge papers, VI 103/1/34, Liberal Liberty League circular to delegates, 27 January 1945, and VI 103/1/35, 'Full Employment at the Liberal Assembly. Memo of Notes.'

[102] For instance, the Leeds Liberal Federation had issued a 'Declaration' in 1944 which declared that the party should stand for liberty and the rule of law: Graham White papers, WHI/1/3/71, 'Liberalism: The Leeds Declaration', 12 February 1944.

[103] Rhys Williams papers, J/10/3, 'Notes on Liberal Policy in relation to the Beveridge Employment Report', by Juliet Rhys Williams, n.d. [winter 1944–5].

[104] Elliott Dodds papers, 3/10, 'Full Employment', speech to Huddersfield Soroptimists, 24 September 1945.

[105] *MG*, 18 January 1945, 6, and 3 February 1945, 6; Beveridge papers, VI 103/1/49–50, Dodds to Beveridge, 28 January 1945.

and that 'nearly all economists' agreed that demand management was also necessary. 'The question is, will more people enjoy greater liberty as a result of this policy? And to that question I, as a libertarian, give an unhesitating affirmative.'[106] Ashley Mitchell moved the Liberty League's amendment, and Commander Geoffrey Bowles accused Beveridge of importing his ideas—via E. F. Schumacher—from Nazi Germany.[107] The chorus of support for Beveridge, however, was overwhelming, and when a vote was taken only twenty of the one-thousand-or-so delegates backed the Liberty League. The Full Employment resolution was then carried with just four dissentients.[108]

The radical mood of the 1945 Assembly showed itself in other ways, too. In her presidential speech, Violet Bonham Carter placed Beveridge's policy in the tradition of social reform which her father's government had begun. Liberalism, she emphasized, was not 'a rigid, static, invariable formula' but 'a dynamic concept'; and with a post-war world to build, Liberals had to 'attack' and 'advance'.[109] This was fleshed out by a resolution which declared the party's intention to contest enough seats at the general election to offer a Liberal government.[110] Sinclair declared that the party would fight 'with a clear and distinctive policy', and paid tribute to the work which Harris and Beveridge had done.[111] The party's support for guaranteed prices was affirmed, and delegates also approved a Housing resolution, drafted by Horabin, which set a target of building 750,000 houses a year for the next five years, using licensing and controls to prioritize the house-building effort and making full use of mass-production techniques.[112] Finally, the party's internal elections showed the ascendancy of the Liberal centre-left, as Beveridge topped the poll in the election for four vice-presidents, winning support from 88 per cent of delegates in a seven-candidate contest.[113] In the poll for thirty members of the party Council, meanwhile, Dodds came first, followed by Rhys Williams and Margery Corbett Ashby, while none of the Liberty League's eight candidates were successful. Analysis of the voting figures suggests that around one-third of delegates were left-wing Radical Action supporters, but only about one-tenth sympathized with the Liberty League.[114]

[106] *LM*, liii (1945), 195.
[107] *L&L*, no. 610 (March 1945), 27–8.
[108] *NC*, 3 February 1945, 4.
[109] *LM*, liii (1945), 186–8, at 187, 186.
[110] *LM*, liii (1945), 189.
[111] *LM*, liii (1945), 200–1, at 200.
[112] *LM*, liii (1945), 199, 197. Johnstone considered the housing target unachievable, and contemplated resigning from the LPO executive to oppose it: Beveridge papers, VI 103/1/26–8, LPO executive minutes, 31 January 1945.
[113] *LPO Bulletin*, no. 63 (February 1945), 8.
[114] Beveridge papers, VI 103/1/18, results of LPO Council elections, February 1945, and VI 103/1/62, voting paper. 603 delegates cast valid votes for the vice-presidencies, of which 214 named Horabin as one of their four choices. The bottom six candidates for the Council were all Liberty League nominees, who received between fifty-five and 110 votes.

PUBLIC OWNERSHIP

The passage of the Full Employment resolution at the February 1945 Assembly did not bring debate over Liberal economic policy to an end. Although the main lines of employment policy had been agreed, Beveridge's resolution had left the Liberal stance on several key issues—wage determination, trade, and public ownership—relatively loosely defined. On all three issues, Beveridge's views were clearly more interventionist than centre-right Liberals such as Dodds and Ronald Walker were willing to accept; indeed, the *Manchester Guardian* believed that Walker and his allies had been reconciled to the Full Employment resolution 'by their confidence that the policy would lose some of its asperities during its development under vigilant Liberal eyes'.[115] Wages policy proved to be least problematic, as Beveridge had been assured by trade union leaders that a wages policy would not be necessary, and restricted himself to suggesting that arbitration clauses should be included in wage agreements to encourage restraint.[116] The Liberal Party's commitment to free collective bargaining thus survived the war without a serious challenge.

Trade policy caused greater controversy, as a result of Beveridge's insistence that the classical free-trade case no longer applied.[117] Most Liberals accepted that trade would have to be freed by multilateral rather than unilateral action, but Beveridge's rhetoric was nevertheless alarming, especially as a wartime Mass Observation survey suggested that free trade was still the party's best-known policy.[118] Hirst's Liberal Free Trade Committee waged guerrilla warfare against Beveridge's pragmatism, and found support from the top of the party, where Harcourt Johnstone and Roy Harrod were planning to use Article VII of the Anglo-American Mutual Aid Agreement (which committed Britain to work for the removal of all forms of trade discrimination after the war) to turn trade policy into a major election issue.[119] Despite Johnstone's death in March 1945, Harrod pressed forward with this strategy with Sinclair's backing, and Beveridge acquiesced in it. When the election came, the Liberals positioned themselves as aggressive multilateralists, committed to freeing trade rapidly through international agreement. For a strict free trader, this stance was a betrayal of Liberal principles, but most of the

[115] *MG*, 3 February 1945, 4.

[116] Harris, *William Beveridge*, 437.

[117] *MG*, 18 January 1945, 6.

[118] Rhys Williams papers, J/10/3, 'Notes on Liberal Policy in relation to the Beveridge Employment Report'; University of Sussex, Mass Observation Archive, File Report 1128, 'Report on the British Public's Feeling about Liberalism', 3 March 1942.

[119] Hirst papers, 68, Francis Hirst to Gertrude Hirst, 7 and 21 March 1945; Beveridge papers, VI 13/2/21–4, 'Mr R. F. Harrod's Statement', n.d. [18 July 1945], at fol. 21.

party seems to have supported it, and by the end of the campaign Sinclair was giving it so much emphasis that even Hirst was satisfied.[120]

With compromise positions at hand on these issues, the debate over government intervention in the post-war economy came to centre on public ownership. Indeed, this debate would rage into the next Parliament, as the Liberals struggled to articulate a coherent response to the Attlee government's nationalization measures. On the one hand, Horabin and Davies believed that a far-reaching extension of public ownership was necessary to raise efficiency, improve working conditions, prevent exploitation by monopolies, and provide an adequate field for public investment. Beveridge and Bonham Carter broadly shared this view, and articulated it in meetings of the party Council.[121] On the other hand, Dodds, Walker, Harrod, and Rhys Williams regarded nationalization as a last resort, which should be pursued only if monopolies could not be broken up or placed under effective public control. Dodds' suspicion of 'natural monopoly' arguments had been strengthened by Arthur Shenfield, who emphasized that competition could exist *between* as well as *within* industries: for instance, railways had to compete with road transport.[122] Most Liberals could accept the principle of a mixed economy, but it was much harder to secure agreement on the nature of the mixture.

Sinclair, returning to party politics as the war neared its end, took a middle position in this debate. In his speech to the 1945 Assembly, he argued that Liberals were not dogmatically committed to either private or public ownership, but would settle the issue 'calmly and objectively on the merits of each individual case'.[123] Seebohm Rowntree, who chaired the party's policy committees on transport and coal, took these words to heart—and produced two divergent sets of recommendations. The Transport Committee proposed in March that all railways, long-distance road haulage and passenger transport, and canals should be placed under a public utility corporation. Rowntree was impressed by the danger that the railways would develop into a private monopoly, by the difficulty of raising capital for rail modernization on the private market, and by the need to coordinate transport services.[124] By contrast, the Coal Committee recommended in its interim report in April that the mines should be placed

[120] Hirst papers, 68, Francis Hirst to Gertrude Hirst, 22 June 1945.

[121] Beveridge papers, VI 18/2/57 and 58, LPO Council minutes, 21 March and 18 April 1945.

[122] Rowntree papers, PLA/4/3, 'Notes on Private and Public Enterprise in the Post-War World', by Arthur Shenfield, n.d. [*c.*1941–2].

[123] *MG*, 5 February 1945, 3.

[124] Liberal Party, *The Future of British Transport: Proposals of a Liberal Party Committee under the Chairmanship of B. Seebohm Rowntree, C.H.* (1945).

under public control but not nationalized. Here, Rowntree felt that competition between different mines and districts was valuable, and that pressure from miners for higher wages was likely to result 'either in excessive coal prices, or else in continuous subsidies by the taxpayer'.[125]

Rowntree's pragmatic approach meant that he came under fire from both sides. When the transport report was presented to the party Council, it received support from left wingers such as Horabin and from the industrialist E. H. Gilpin, but Ronald Walker and the London activist Harold Glanville were vigorously opposed.[126] Nationalization of road transport was particularly unpopular among Liberals in Yorkshire and Lancashire, and A. S. Comyns Carr proposed amendments which would restrict nationalization to the railway companies and their holdings.[127] After two heated meetings, it was agreed to adjourn the debate *sine die*, leaving the party's transport policy unresolved.[128]

On coal, it was the left wingers' turn to be angry with Rowntree. At the Council meeting in April, Lady Dorothy Layton—wife of Sir Walter—joined Horabin in arguing that nationalization was essential to reorganize the coal industry and improve industrial relations.[129] Moderates such as Dodds found coal nationalization less objectionable than transport, but thought the case for competition between units was strong—a view which the Cardiff shipowner J. E. Emlyn-Jones vocally pressed—and were frustrated by the attitudes of those 'whose minds cease to function once they have uttered the word "nationalisation" '.[130] The Coal Committee was unmoved by radical criticisms, and resolved simply to 'try to bring out the progressive nature of the proposals' in its final report.[131] Before the final report could be submitted for approval, however, the war against Germany was over and the election campaign had begun.[132]

With an election under way, the Liberal leadership took the nationalization issue into its own hands. Beveridge drafted a memorandum of guidance for candidates on outstanding policy questions in his capacity as chairman of the Campaign Committee, though since the coal issue was so sensitive this section was drawn up in consultation with Viscount

[125] Beveridge papers, VI 13/2/173–6, 'Coal: Interim Report', 18 April 1945, and VI 13/2/123–6, 'Coal', 25 May 1945, at fol. 124.

[126] Beveridge papers, VI 18/2/57, LPO Council minutes, 21 March 1945.

[127] Beveridge papers, VI 13/2/172, Dodds to Beveridge, 13 April 1945.

[128] Beveridge papers, VI 18/2/58, LPO Council minutes, 18 April 1945.

[129] Beveridge papers, VI/18/2/58, LPO Council minutes, 18 April 1945.

[130] *LM*, lii (1944), 335–9; Rhys Williams papers, J/2/3/1, Dodds to Rhys Williams, 19 April 1945.

[131] Rhys Williams papers, J/2/3/1, Rhys Williams to Dodds, 7 May 1945.

[132] The final report was published without party approval: Liberal Party, *Reorganisation of the Coal Industry: Report of a Liberal Committee* (1945).

Samuel and approved by Liberal MPs. The compromise formula agreed was that coal should be a 'public service', run in the public interest but with a decentralized structure and no subsidy; the question of ownership was reserved for future judgment. Railways would be nationalized, along with 'the large part of road transport directly controlled by them', but otherwise road transport would be left in private ownership, and made more competitive by abolishing the licensing system established by the Road Traffic Acts of 1930 and 1934. Electric power was to be run as a public utility, whilst wholesale land nationalization was ruled out.[133] The Liberal manifesto—drawn up by Sinclair, Harris, Beveridge, and Samuel—closely followed Beveridge's memorandum, and explained that the party had judged nationalization proposals against three criteria: 'the service of the public, the efficiency of production and the well-being of those concerned in the industry in question'.[134]

This hastily constructed compromise may have been the best the party could manage in the circumstances, but clearly it did not constitute a coherent long-range industrial policy, nor was it really binding on Liberal candidates. Radical Action, on the one hand, issued its own manifesto which called for public ownership of the land, the Bank of England, coal, transport, electricity, and gas.[135] By contrast, Roy Harrod in Huddersfield only paid 'lip-service to the Liberal formula', and emphasized 'in every particular case' that nationalization would weaken trade unions' bargaining power and involve 'loss of liberty'.[136] This divergence was significant, and potentially embarrassing, as Bonham Carter found in the Wells constituency.[137] With Liberal candidates espousing radically different views on public ownership, it was difficult to believe that the party was united in its basic economic vision.

THE 1945 GENERAL ELECTION

The Liberal Party leadership pulled together after VE Day. With the European war finished, Churchill offered Sinclair and Attlee a choice between a summer election or the continuation of the coalition until the

[133] Beveridge papers, VI 14/4/81–6, 'Outstanding Questions of Party Policy', 2 June 1945.

[134] *Liberal Party General Election Manifestos, 1900–1997*, ed. Iain Dale (2000), 65; Beveridge papers, VI 13/1/19, Campaign Committee minutes, 24 May 1945.

[135] MS. Balfour 26/1, 'Radical Action Manifesto for the General Election', May 1945.

[136] Beveridge papers, VI 13/2/21–4, 'Mr R. F. Harrod's Statement', at fols 22–3.

[137] Bodleian Library, MS. Bonham Carter 231, fol. 69, Cyril Morgan to Bonham Carter, 30 June 1945.

defeat of Japan. Sinclair would have preferred an October election, but neither Churchill nor Attlee favoured this suggestion, so the election was set for 5 July and a caretaker government took office in the meantime.[138] Sinclair treated Churchill with respect throughout the campaign and kept open the possibility of a post-war coalition, which Beveridge and other left wingers thought was a mistake.[139] Nevertheless, the wartime division between ministers and other Liberals healed relatively quickly, and there were no significant internal arguments once the nationalization formula was settled. The Liberals fought the election as an independent force, with 306 candidates, and Sinclair and Beveridge toured the country to rally support for the party.[140]

The Liberal election campaign was upbeat in tone, and sometimes even revivalist. Party organization had to be improvised in many parts of the country, but enthusiasm was rarely lacking and many new activists came forward; some, indeed, would become Liberal stalwarts in later years.[141] Moderates and radicals generally worked well together, and Sinclair and Harrod's Article VII campaign tended in practice to complement Beveridge's emphasis on domestic economic policy. More than nine-tenths of Liberal candidates mentioned social security and full employment, usually with specific reference to Beveridge's two reports; this was frequently combined with strident attacks on socialism.[142] Many official Liberal candidates supported land value taxation as a policy, but without giving it the conceptual centrality desired by the Liberty Leaguers.[143] On the other hand, Ashley Mitchell ran as an independent Liberal in Batley and Morley, made opposition to Beveridge a major theme of his campaign, and managed to save his deposit.[144]

The Liberals faced different electoral circumstances in different parts of the country. On the Celtic fringe and in other rural constituencies, the Liberals were still the main rivals to the Conservatives, but Labour posed a growing threat to their hold on the radical vote. Conversely, in many urban and suburban seats, Liberal candidates appeared for the first time since 1929, and faced the challenge of demonstrating the party's continued relevance. In some areas, like the Pennine textile towns, this

[138] Gerard J. de Groot, *Liberal Crusader: The Life of Sir Archibald Sinclair* (1993), 220.

[139] Beveridge papers, IXa 38/2/137, 'My Entry to Politics', by Beveridge, August 1945; BLPES, Josephy papers, Add. 2/29, Frances Josephy to Wilfrid Roberts, 24 July 1945.

[140] Thorpe, *Parties at War*, 56; de Groot, *Liberal Crusader*, 220–5.

[141] Thorpe, *Parties at War*, 236–40; Mark Egan, *Coming into Focus: The Transformation of the Liberal Party, 1945–64* (Saarbrücken, 2009), 136.

[142] R. B. McCallum and Alison Readman, *The British General Election of 1945* (Oxford, 1947), 96–7.

[143] *L&L*, no. 613 (June 1945), 66–7.

[144] Ashley Mitchell, *Memoirs of a Fallen Political Warrior* (1974), 64.

meant reawakening traditional Liberal loyalties; in others, like London and Birmingham, the party started almost from scratch. Liberal MPs, meanwhile, had to defend the seats they had won in 1935, many of which had experienced significant population turnover in the interim. One new factor which all candidates faced was the service vote, which made up almost one-tenth of the electorate and made it unusually difficult to forecast the results.

Before the campaign began, Liberals had spoken privately of winning fifty or sixty seats, which would enable them to form 'a big wedge' in the new Parliament and build up their strength for subsequent contests.[145] The vigour of the Liberal campaign seemed to bear out these hopes, and at the very least the party expected to increase its representation.[146] In fact, when the votes were counted on 26 July, the Liberals were reduced to twelve seats, as Labour swept industrial Britain and took radical votes away from the Liberals in the rural and suburban constituencies they had hoped to win.[147] Sinclair and Beveridge, who had neglected their constituencies for much of the campaign, lost their seats, and Harris, White, Mander, and Dingle Foot were all defeated by Labour. In Scotland and urban England, the Liberals were wiped out; in Wales, the party did better, but Lloyd George's old seat of Caernarvon Boroughs fell to the Conservatives. Victories by Frank Byers in North Dorset, George Wadsworth in Buckrose, and Rhys Hopkin Morris in Carmarthen were the only compensating gains, all in straight fights with one of the other parties. Across the country, the party took 9 per cent of the vote, but came first or second in only thirty-eight constituencies, giving a narrow field for future advance.[148] Young voters seemed more receptive to the Liberal message than at any time since 1929, but they still overwhelmingly preferred Labour.[149] Conversely, some older Liberal supporters seem to have voted Conservative out of gratitude for Churchill's wartime service.[150]

[145] David Lloyd George papers, LG/G/25/3/137, A. J. Sylvester to David Lloyd George, 1 December 1944, reporting conversation with Sir Percy Harris.

[146] *The Times*, 10 July 1945, 4.

[147] I have discussed this pattern further in a recent article: Peter Sloman, 'Rethinking a progressive moment: The Liberal and Labour parties in the 1945 general election', *Historical Research*, lxxxiv (2011), 722–44.

[148] Peter Joyce, *The Liberal Party and the 1945 General Election* (Dorchester, 1995), 10.

[149] Mass Observation Archive, File Report 2261, 'The New Voters and the Old', n.d. [June 1945]; Henry W. Durant, *Political Opinion: Four General Election Results* (1949), 7.

[150] Beveridge papers, VI 13/2/6–8, 'Thoughts on the Present Discontents', by Elliott Dodds, 30 July 1945. On Churchill's efforts to appeal to Liberal voters, see Richard Toye, 'Winston Churchill's "crazy broadcast": Party, nation, and the 1945 Gestapo speech', *Journal of British Studies*, xlix (2010), 655–80.

Liberals mostly attributed their poor performance to organizational deficiencies and their failure to field more candidates, but the content of the campaign also came in for close scrutiny.[151] From the left, Beveridge complained that his efforts to give Liberalism a radical image had been undermined by the party's publicity material, which placed too much emphasis on the dangers of socialism, and by Sinclair's sympathetic attitude to Churchill.[152] Bonham Carter likewise felt that the failure to agree a radical line on coal and transport had left the party looking timid and confused.[153] By contrast, Dodds believed that the party had failed to distinguish itself sufficiently from Labour:

> We should have realised that we were competing with Labour for the anti-Conservative vote. Instead we hesitated to attack Labour and let the idea get about that our own programme was merely a milder variant of the Socialist programme.[154]

Roy Harrod shared this view, and argued that the party should have placed much more emphasis on the dangers of nationalization. 'Unless we can persuade [voters] to a horror of state control, why should they vote Liberal on a Liberal–Labour ticket? Why not Labour?'[155]

In a sense, both arguments had some force. Since most of the best prospects for Liberal gains in 1945 came in Conservative-held rural seats, and the election results revealed a sharp swing to the left, it made strategic sense to take a left-wing line; a more consistently radical image might have enabled rural Liberal candidates to squeeze the Labour vote in a way that most of them conspicuously failed to do. Moreover, it is difficult to see how Liberals could have used the nationalization issue to attack Labour effectively during a short campaign, at a time when public ownership was relatively popular.[156] On the other hand, the landslide Labour victory made it imperative to develop a more distinctive identity in future. The Liberals would no longer be able to justify their continued existence by arguing that Labour had no record of constructive achievement and was unable to win a majority on its own.

Beveridge's personal value to the Liberal Party in 1945, which was taken for granted by contemporaries, has been questioned by some historians.

[151] Thorpe, *Parties at War*, 57.

[152] MS. Bonham Carter 157, fols 41f–44, Beveridge to Bonham Carter, 10 August 1945.

[153] Beveridge papers, VI 18/2/92–7, Bonham Carter to Beveridge, 17 August 1945.

[154] Beveridge papers, VI 13/2/6–8, 'Thoughts on the Present Discontents', at fol. 7.

[155] Beveridge papers, VI 13/2/21–4, 'Mr R. F. Harrod's Statement', at fol. 23.

[156] Gallup polls in 1944–5 found that 60% of respondents supported coal mines nationalization, and 54% backed rail nationalization: see Steven Fielding, 'What did "the people" want? The meaning of the 1945 general election', *HJ*, xxxv (1992), 623–39, at 634.

Bentley Gilbert has claimed that the party's emphasis on Beveridge was a 'great tactical error', and finds support for this in the Gallup Poll's finding that only 8 per cent of Liberal voters backed the party because of Beveridge or social security.[157] More broadly, Andrew Thorpe has suggested that Beveridge's adhesion was a mixed blessing, because 'it set the Liberals up to try and rival Labour in the language of collectivism and security, when they might have been better off trying to rival the Conservatives in the language of individualism and freedom'.[158] Gilbert's point may be dismissed, because the Gallup responses seem to have been unprompted, and 73 per cent of respondents said simply that the Liberals stood for 'the middle way' or were 'the best party'.[159] Thorpe's argument carries more weight, but it is difficult to believe either that Liberal activists would have allowed the party to take an overtly anti-statist line in 1945 or that such a policy would have achieved much resonance. Beveridge gave form to the leftward turn in Liberal policy which took place during the war, but he did not single-handedly create it. Moreover, as Thorpe acknowledges, we must also take into account the energy, confidence, and publicity that Beveridge gave to the Liberal campaign.[160] All told, it seems unlikely that the Liberal Party would have performed better in 1945 without Beveridge than it did with him.

CONCLUSION

As Angus Calder has shown, Britain's collective memory of the Second World War has been structured by a series of compelling 'myths': the miracle of Dunkirk, the heroism of the Few, and the solidarity expressed in the 'Blitz spirit'.[161] Political myths emerged just as quickly and were no less powerful: thus Labour politicians tended to attribute their 1945 election victory to a wave of wartime radicalization, whilst Conservatives blamed organizational disparities and complained that voters had been ungrateful to Churchill. For many Liberals, the Second World War would appear in retrospect as a moment of ideological radicalism, when the party shed its reservations about state intervention. 'Planning was much in vogue', Jo Grimond later recalled, and 'we were all to some extent Socialists'.[162]

[157] Bentley Gilbert, 'Third parties and voters' decisions: The Liberals and the general election of 1945', *Journal of British Studies*, xi (1972), 131–41, at 136.

[158] Thorpe, *Parties at War*, 286.

[159] *Public Opinion, 1935–1946*, ed. Hadley Cantril (Princeton, 1951), 197.

[160] Thorpe, *Parties at War*, 238, 286.

[161] Angus Calder, *The Myth of the Blitz* (1991).

[162] Jo Grimond, *Memoirs* (1979), 132.

Left-wing Liberals, especially, tended to look back on 1945 with fondness—'Ah, . . . in those days we were a Radical party', Megan Lloyd George once told Alan Watkins—and to regard subsequent policy developments as a kind of betrayal.[163] When Tom Horabin joined Labour in 1947, he complained that the Liberal Party had changed its stance since the election, whereas he stood by the 1945 manifesto.[164] The party's wartime radicalism became the benchmark against which a 'drift to the right' could be identified.

The evidence presented in this chapter shows that there is much truth to this characterization. The wartime popularity of planning ideas reinvigorated constructive Liberalism, and the New Liberal conception of the state as the instrument of the community also gained new purchase. The Yellow Book's pragmatic approach to industrial organization experienced a revival, and doubts about the efficacy of demand management and free trade drove Liberals to consider radical measures for achieving full employment. Beveridge gave the Liberal left a figurehead and a policy, and his resolution based on *Full Employment in a Free Society* was carried by an overwhelming majority at the 1945 Assembly.

At the same time, the Liberal Party's leftward shift had important limitations, which radicals were prone to forget in later years. First, the Liberal ministers in the coalition were almost untouched by it, and continued to espouse a cautious version of demand management which emphasized the international dimension. Second, the party showed little appetite for central planning of the kind that Horabin and Davies advocated in 1942–3, and consistently preferred a broadly Keynesian approach. Third, free-market ideas remained strong among sections of the Liberal grassroots, especially in northern England, and ensured that nationalization proposals faced spirited resistance. Finally, the party's choice of an interventionist Keynesian policy over a liberal Keynesian one was only really settled by Beveridge's adhesion. The Structure of Industry sub-committee which met in 1942–3 had favoured an interventionist policy, but had found itself stymied by a cautious LPO executive. This might have happened again in 1944–5 if Sinclair and other moderate Liberals had not been influenced by the need to satisfy Beveridge and maximize his electoral value to the party.

The political situation which developed in wartime was essentially artificial. After the war ended, the Liberals found themselves back in opposition, facing for the first time a majority Labour government. They also faced a very different economic environment to the one which wartime

[163] Alan Watkins, *The Liberal Dilemma* (1966), 38.

[164] *The Times*, 28 November 1947, 6.

discussions had assumed, in which inflation and the balance of payments were the most pressing problems and Beveridge's target of 3 per cent unemployment would come to be regarded as relatively cautious. In this context, liberal Keynesianism and 'ownership for all' would gain a new appeal, and the party's wartime radicalization would prove to be temporary rather than permanent.

6

Clement Davies and Liberal Keynesianism, 1945–56

The decade which followed the Second World War was the Liberal Party's nadir, a period in which—as David Dutton has put it—the party stood 'on the brink of oblivion'.[1] Labour's landslide victory in 1945 pushed the Liberals to the margins of political debate, and the defeat of Sinclair and Beveridge made it harder for them to gain a hearing. An attempted revival under new leader Clement Davies ended in disaster at the 1950 general election, and in 1951 and 1955 only six Liberal MPs were returned, five of them without Conservative opposition. Successive electoral reverses battered Liberal morale, and the party's membership, central income, and representation on local councils all hit bottom in the early 1950s.[2]

The late 1940s and early 1950s were also marked by acute divisions within the party. A long dispute over electoral and political strategy caused severe ructions up to 1951, and no sooner had the prospect of Liberal–Conservative cooperation been killed off—by Davies' refusal to join Winston Churchill's peacetime government—than the party stumbled into an open conflict over agricultural policy, provoked by a group of diehard free traders, and a separate debate on industrial co-ownership.[3] 'If you attended our Liberal Party Committees, or the meetings of the Parliamentary Party, or saw the correspondence that I receive', Davies wrote to Gilbert Murray in one moment of weakness,

[1] David Dutton, 'On the brink of oblivion: The post-war crisis of British Liberalism', *Canadian Journal of History*, xxvii (1992), 425–50.

[2] William J. L. Wallace, 'The Liberal Revival: The Liberal Party in Britain, 1955–1966' (Cornell University D.Phil. thesis, 1968), 268, 190, 271.

[3] On efforts to build alliances in the late 1940s, see Dutton, 'On the brink', and Robert Ingham, 'A retreat from the left? The Liberal Party and Labour 1945–55', *JLH*, no. 67 (2010), 38–44.

> I believe that you would come to the conclusion that there is no Party to-day but a number of individuals who, because of their adherence to the Party, come together only to express completely divergent views.[4]

A steady stream of defections culminated in Megan Lloyd George, Dingle Foot, and Wilfrid Roberts joining Labour in 1955–6 on the grounds that the Liberal Party had forfeited its radicalism. All in all, it is hardly surprising that historians have characterized these years as ones of decline, division, and incoherence.

The strategic tensions and electoral failures of the post-war decade have coloured perceptions of Liberal policy-making under Clement Davies' leadership. Malcolm Baines, for instance, has identified free trade and co-ownership as the twin planks of Liberal economics after the war, though both divided the party, and suggests that Davies was committed to a 'simplistic' Welsh radicalism which left him ill-equipped to reconcile the party's right and left wings.[5] Robert Ingham has likewise seen the factional conflict between extreme free traders and the left-wing Radical Reform Group which structured intra-party debate in the 1950s as a symptom of Davies' weakness.[6] Though he could be an effective parliamentarian and committee chairman, his cautious style, erratic political career, and reputation for emotionalism and verbosity made it difficult for him to establish his authority over the party.[7]

This picture of a chronically divided Liberal Party, squabbling over free trade and co-ownership until Grimond restored discipline and purpose, contains a good deal of truth, but there is a danger of overstating it. Disputes over policy and strategy in the late 1940s were serious and debilitating, especially at parliamentary and leadership level, but they did not prevent the party in the country from achieving a modest organizational revival. Conversely, the battle between the free traders and the Radical Reform Group was mainly played out in Assembly debates and in the pages of the *Liberal News*, not in Parliament, where the small band of Liberal MPs became more cohesive after 1951. Above all, the sound and fury of these debates should not be allowed to obscure the extent to which the advent of a Labour government at home and the Cold War abroad prompted a revival of the libertarian and distributist conception of Liberalism which Dodds and Sinclair had outlined in the 1930s. Before

[4] National Library of Wales, Clement Davies papers, J/3/26i, Davies to Gilbert Murray, 11 May 1950.

[5] Malcolm Baines, 'The Survival of the British Liberal Party, 1932–1959' (Oxford D.Phil. thesis, 1989), 93–5, 124.

[6] Robert Ingham, 'Battle of ideas or absence of leadership? Ideological struggle in the Liberal Party in the 1940s and 1950s', *JLH*, no. 47 (2005), 36–44.

[7] Robert Ingham, 'Clement Davies: A brief reply', *JLDH*, no. 26 (2000), 24–5.

very long, the interventionist Liberalism of the war years had given way to a more mature version of the liberal Keynesian synthesis, which relied on fiscal and monetary policy to maintain full employment and treated nationalization and planning with deep scepticism.

Liberal policy development in the early post-war period was centred on the Liberal Party Committee, which had been established in 1944 as a 'safety-valve' for party opinion with MPs, LPO office-holders, and policy experts among its members.[8] Davies turned the Committee into a *de facto* shadow cabinet, and used it to try to unite the party around a common policy. On economic questions, he took advice from Roy Harrod, the journalist Graham Hutton, and especially Frank Paish of the LSE, who became the party's official economic adviser and chaired an Economic Advisory Committee—dominated by LSE staff and graduates—during the 1950s.[9] The liberal Keynesian approach which Davies and his advisers evolved was unpopular with left-wing parliamentarians, but leading LPO figures such as Philip Fothergill and Sir Andrew McFadyean strongly supported it, and after 1950 the new MPs Donald Wade, Jo Grimond, and Arthur Holt added further ballast to the party's centre ground.

The structure of this chapter is designed to draw out the coherence of the Liberal Party's economic policy in the early post-war period, as well as its limitations. The first part sketches in outline the trajectory of Liberal thought after 1945 and the political context in which Liberal policy-making took place. The following sections trace the party's turn towards liberal Keynesianism in three main fields of policy in the late 1940s and early 1950s: nationalization and industrial policy, economic management, and social welfare provision. The final part of the chapter then considers the challenges to the new policy which emerged after 1950 from the extreme free traders and the Radical Reform Group.

THE 'DRIFT TO THE RIGHT'

The twelve Liberal MPs elected in 1945 were a highly disparate group. About half of them were instinctive rural radicals, who strongly sympathized with the new Labour government: Megan Lloyd George, Tom Horabin, and Emrys Roberts fell firmly into this category, and

[8] Churchill Archives Centre, Cambridge, Thurso papers, VII, 1/2, fols 49–50, Sinclair to W. R. Davies, 29 October 1945, at fol. 49.

[9] The committee comprised Paish, Hutton, Alan Peacock, Gilbert Ponsonby, Paul Bareau of the *News Chronicle* and George Schwartz of the *Sunday Times*, and met periodically in Paish's room at the LSE: BLPES, Liberal Party papers, 5/16, committee membership file, 1958–60, fol. 58; Sir Alan Peacock, letter to the author, 1 April 2012.

Clement Davies, Wilfrid Roberts, W. J. Gruffydd, and Edgar Granville were normally to be found taking leftist positions. The other half tended to be more moderate, but also more idiosyncratic: thus Gwilym Lloyd George was already working with the Conservatives, and drifted out of the Liberal orbit in these years, whilst Rhys Hopkin Morris took a firmly individualist line and proved to be virtually unwhippable. The new parliamentary party chose Davies to act as its chairman, and hence as party leader, until Sinclair could return to the Commons (which he never did).[10] Davies in turn appointed his friend Horabin as chief whip and indicated that the party would adopt a constructive attitude towards the Attlee government's measures.[11]

The emergence of Davies and Horabin in leadership roles horrified those Liberals who had sparred with them during the war. Violet Bonham Carter regarded them as 'lunatics and pathological cases' who hampered the party's efforts to be taken seriously, whilst Elliott Dodds feared that they would try to lead it 'into the Labour fold'.[12] Sinclair was equally alarmed by Davies' left-wing instincts, and though he was determined to avoid 'back-seat driving' he hoped that the new leadership would soon start to develop a critique of Labour.[13] The early portents were not promising, but over time Davies did exactly that, coming into line with the increasingly anti-statist tone of Liberal opinion in the country. Horabin's commitment to state intervention was more deeply rooted, and during 1946 he resigned first as chief whip and then from the party in protest at its rightward drift.[14]

Like the advent of 'ownership for all' in the late 1930s, the reappraisal of Liberalism which took place after 1945 stemmed in part from a perception that Liberal policies were insufficiently distinctive. As the *Manchester Guardian* pointed out in an editorial, the policy reports which the party had produced during wartime 'were good technical essays, got together by experts in the several subjects, but no one could be sure that there was anything distinctively Liberal about them'. There was a pressing need for Liberals 'to go back to their basic principle of man's freedom and dignity and make sure they know on what it is

[10] Alan Wyburn-Powell, *Clement Davies: Liberal Leader* (2003), 140–3.

[11] Hansard, HC (series 5) vol. 413, cols 113–8 (16 August 1945).

[12] *Champion Redoubtable*, 294; British Library, Add. MS. 72735 (Harrod papers), fols 102–4, Dodds to Harrod, 3 September 1945, at fol. 102.

[13] Thurso papers, VII, 1/2, fols 9–10, Sinclair to Bonham Carter, 10 October 1946, at fol. 10; fols 32–4, Sinclair to W. R. Davies, 5 January 1946; and fols 39–40, Sinclair to W. R. Davies, 8 November 1945.

[14] Jaime Reynolds and Ian Hunter, 'Liberal class warrior', *JLDH*, no. 28 (2000), 17–21.

founded', and then to consider what policies were best suited to extending that freedom in the modern world.[15]

Elliott Dodds had argued this case throughout the war, and returned to the fray with a 1946 tract entitled *The Defence of Man*. Dodds took heart from the flowering of Christian Democracy in France and Italy, and argued that Liberalism was founded on the Christian doctrine of man as a person with infinite worth, natural rights, and reciprocal responsibilities. The full development of personality required not only the satisfaction of material needs but also opportunities for decision and choice—which would be extended by wider property ownership, but destroyed by wholesale planning.[16] The party at large was more receptive to these ideas than it had been in wartime, and the Christian basis of Liberal thought became a common theme.[17] Though the formation of the Liberal International in 1947 strengthened the party's links with its Liberal counterparts on the continent, some activists felt a closer kinship with Christian Democratic groups such as the Mouvement Républicain Populaire.[18]

The onset of the Cold War meanwhile gave greater currency to Hayek's warnings about the road to serfdom. Donald Wade thought that Hayek's thesis had 'never been convincingly answered', and Davies told Scottish activists that Liberalism was 'the only alternative to Totalitarianism whatever form that takes, be it the Totalitarianism of a dictator, a clique, a Socialist Commonwealth, or a Communis[t] state'.[19] Several of the Attlee government's policies were seized on as evidence that Britain was moving down this path, including the continuation of national service, the use of the Control of Engagement Orders to direct workers into key industries, and the assumption of wide discretionary powers to regulate prices and production. Davies accused the government of devaluing 'Personal Liberty and the dignity of Human Personality', whilst Ronald Walker regarded the inspectorate formed to enforce the National Insurance (Industrial Injuries) Act 1946 as 'an embryo gestapo'.[20] If some of these fears were alarmist, they nevertheless stemmed from a deeply felt commitment to individual freedom, which came to be symbolized by Viscount Samuel's

[15] *MG*, 27 November 1945, 4.

[16] Elliott Dodds, *The Defence of Man* (1946).

[17] Delegates at the 1947 Assembly even amended a policy statement to declare that 'political action should spring from principles based on the Christian ethic': *LM* (June 1947), 161–78, at 164.

[18] See, for instance, Alan Bullock in *LM* (August 1946), 346, and Peter Calvocoressi in *LM* (May 1947), 132–4.

[19] Donald W. Wade, *The Way of the West* ([1946]), 148; Clement Davies papers, K/1/35, 'Scottish Liberal Rally, Glasgow, 11th April, 1947'.

[20] Clement Davies papers, K/1/58, text of broadcast speech, 16 February 1950; LM (May 1946), 200–2, at 201.

efforts to pass a Liberties of the Subject Bill and by Liberal activist Harry Willcock's role in bringing an end to compulsory identity cards.[21]

The Liberals' renewed suspicion of planning was reinforced by their internationalism. Sinclair regarded the United States' commitment to reconstructing the world economy on liberal lines as the most promising development to emerge from the war, and was determined that Britain should participate fully in the new order. No other issue in post-war politics was 'at once so important and so distinctively Liberal'.[22] The party accordingly welcomed the Anglo-American Loan Agreement reached in December 1945—indeed, it was the only party which was united in support of it—but expressed concern that the government seemed to be resisting American pressure for trade liberalization.[23] Liberals also criticized the continuation of wartime import controls and bulk purchasing arrangements, and urged ministers to seize the opportunity which Marshall Aid provided to promote European integration.[24] When the Schuman Plan for a European Coal and Steel Community appeared in 1950, Davies welcomed it as an important step towards freer trade and European unity and protested at the government's decision not to join in.[25]

Concern at the direction of the Labour government's policies prompted some Liberals to advocate anti-socialist cooperation. After all, the Conservative Party had responded to its 1945 defeat by moving on to liberal terrain, confirming its commitment to an active employment policy and a mixed economy in the 'Industrial Charter', emphasizing the importance of competition and personal freedom, and reviving its interest in the creation of a 'property-owning democracy'.[26] Winston Churchill had even put himself at the forefront of the campaign for a United Europe. In February 1947, Juliet Rhys Williams and the Conservative MP Peter Thorneycroft launched the pamphlet *Design for Freedom*, which outlined a possible basis for centre-right cooperation and was signed by almost eighty Conservatives and more than thirty Liberal candidates and activists.[27] *Design for Freedom* was quickly repudiated by Liberal headquarters,

[21] Hansard, HL (series 5) vol. 167, cols 1041–55 (27 June 1950); Mark Egan, 'Harry Willcock: The forgotten champion of Liberalism', *JLDH*, no. 17 (1997–8), 16–17.

[22] Thurso papers, VII, 1/2, fols 32–4, Sinclair to W. R. Davies, 5 January 1946, at fol. 33.

[23] Hansard, HC (series 5) vol. 417, cols 736–9 (13 December 1945); Roy Harrod in *LM* (January 1946), 3–4.

[24] Hansard, HC (series 5) vol. 421, cols 633–7 (28 March 1946); Philip Fothergill in *LM* (March 1948), 96–101; *The Times*, 14 June 1947, 2.

[25] Hansard, HC (series 5) vol. 476, cols 1924–33 (26 June 1950).

[26] Nigel Harris, *Competition and the Corporate Society: British Conservatives, the State and Industry, 1945–1964* (1972).

[27] *The Times*, 19 February 1947, 2. The Liberal signatories included Oliver Smedley and Arthur Shenfield.

but the idea of an anti-socialist alliance remained a very live one, not least because Churchill privately indicated that he would be willing to give the Liberals a free run against Labour in thirty-five constituencies and would do his best to deliver electoral reform.[28] At the same time, Conservative Party chairman Lord Woolton sought to smother the Liberal Party's independent identity by promoting the formation of 'Conservative and Liberal Associations' in many constituencies.[29] In due course, Juliet Rhys Williams and Roy Harrod both gave up on the party and began to seek 'Conservative and Liberal' candidatures.[30]

Early in the 1945 Parliament, the Liberals had adopted a plan to fight the next general election on the broadest possible front, believing that voters would take the party more seriously if it offered an alternative government. It quickly became clear that this was a pipe-dream, but Davies and his colleagues nevertheless persevered with it and brushed off Conservative overtures. Though the Conservatives might have adopted liberal rhetoric, Davies argued in a 1949 radio broadcast, they were still 'the party of privilege, of class and section, yielding only when compelled to the claims of social justice and righteousness'; only Liberals really believed in spreading wealth and opportunity more widely.[31] As public opinion polarized over the Attlee government's record, however, the party struggled to get its message across, and when the votes were cast in February 1950 it suffered the worst rout in British parliamentary history. Four hundred and seventy-five Liberal candidates produced nine MPs, nine second places, and 319 lost deposits, against which the party had wisely taken out insurance with Lloyd's of London.

The 1950 election debacle emboldened Liberal advocates of anti-socialist cooperation and chastened many of those who had resisted it. Violet Bonham Carter warned that the party would soon become extinct unless it used pacts with the Conservatives to maintain a parliamentary presence and achieve electoral reform, and Philip Fothergill, Ronald Walker, and Sir Archibald Sinclair all endorsed this view.[32] A tacit non-aggression pact had

[28] Wyburn-Powell, *Clement Davies*, 172. Roy Harrod proposed an approach to the Conservatives at a Party Committee meeting in December 1947 but was defeated by four votes: Churchill Archives Centre, Churchill papers, 2/64/73, Rhys Williams to Churchill, 18 December 1947.

[29] Dutton, 'On the brink', 437–9. National negotiations over Liberal reunion had failed in 1946, although Liberal Nationals did return to the Liberal fold in London, Burnley and Huddersfield.

[30] BLPES, Rhys Williams papers, J/11/5, Rhys Williams to Churchill, 6 July 1948; Henry Phelps Brown, 'Sir Roy Harrod: A biographical memoir', *EJ*, xc (1980), 1–33, at 29.

[31] *MG*, 14 February 1949, 3.

[32] Bodleian Library, Oxford, MS. Bonham Carter 240, fols 1–5, 'Memorandum to Members of L.P.C.' by Violet Bonham Carter, n.d. [1950], and fols 157–9, 'Personal Notes on the Meeting of the Liberal Party Committee at the House of Commons on April 26th, 1950', unsigned; Clement Davies papers, J/3/23, Sinclair to Davies, 3 May 1950.

operated at Huddersfield in February, allowing Donald Wade to gain the town's West division from Labour in a straight fight, and Davies allowed Bonham Carter to negotiate with R. A. Butler during the spring and summer of 1950 about the possibility of making regional arrangements on these lines.[33] The talks eventually failed, partly because the Conservatives stalled on electoral reform and the allocation of seats, and any significant extension of the Huddersfield formula would almost certainly have aroused hostility from both rank-and-file activists and left-wing MPs.[34] (Indeed, Megan Lloyd George, Emrys Roberts, and Lancelot Spicer met with Herbert Morrison around this time to discuss the possibility of Lib–Lab cooperation.[35]) Even so, many leading Liberals continued to view local pacts as a necessary evil.[36] In the 1951 general election, which the party fought on a narrow front, Arthur Holt gained Bolton West on the basis of a Huddersfield-style arrangement, while Bonham Carter narrowly failed to win Colne Valley. Further conversations about reciprocal seats arrangements would take place in 1954–5.[37]

The Liberal Party's pursuit of local pacts in the early 1950s was clearly driven by a concern for electoral survival, and supporters of the Huddersfield and Bolton arrangements were at pains to stress that they involved no sacrifice of independence beyond a commitment to oppose socialist policies.[38] Yet the prevailing preference for dealing with the Conservatives rather than Labour showed how strongly many Liberals had reacted against the Attlee government's measures, and how far the party's wartime interventionism had dissipated. How did this 'drift to the right' reshape Liberals' attitudes to economic policy? The symbolic issue of nationalization is an obvious place to start.

NATIONALIZATION AND INDUSTRIAL POLICY

The 1945 Liberal manifesto committed the party to support public ownership wherever it was justified on economic grounds. In line with this approach, Liberal MPs voted for three of the government's nationalization measures during the first session of Parliament—the Bank of England, the coal mines, and civil aviation—and later for public ownership of electricity

33 See the extensive correspondence with Butler in MS. Bonham Carter 164.

34 Dutton, 'Oblivion', 442–3; *LN*, 6 October 1950, 1.

35 Ingham, 'Retreat', 41–3.

36 MS. Bonham Carter 168, fols 141–2, Bonham Carter to Davies, 27 October 1950.

37 TNA: PRO, PREM 11/1923/8–10, Woolton to Eden, 9 May 1955, and 14–15, Patrick Buchan-Hepburn to Churchill, 25 January 1954.

38 For instance, Elliott Dodds in *LN*, 6 October 1950, 1.

and gas.[39] The Coal Industry Nationalisation Bill, which came up for second reading in January 1946, predictably sparked most controversy. Roy Harrod circulated a strongly worded memorandum against the bill, and Rowntree's Coal Committee published a critical commentary, but Davies and his colleagues decided to support it on the grounds that the party had agreed the mines should be a 'public service'.[40]

Thereafter, Liberal attitudes towards the government's programme began to harden as legislation on transport and iron and steel came into prospect. The pre-election debate over the Rowntree report had convinced many Liberals that road transport was naturally competitive, while the party had never really considered iron and steel suitable for public ownership. Viscount Samuel declared in June 1946 that the government's proposals for steel went 'beyond reasonable limits', and Geoffrey Crowther told the Liberal Summer School that these two industries were best left in private ownership for economic reasons.[41]

A more ideological critique of nationalization came from Ronald Walker, who had written a pamphlet on *Transport: Freedom or Nationalisation?* in response to the Rowntree report. Walker argued that Liberals should view private ownership not as a matter for pragmatic judgment but as a question of principle:

> If we do not really mind whether men can run their own little businesses. If we do not really mind that power grows and concentrates in the hands of a few men at the centre of things; if we are quite uncertain whether personal property breeds self-reliance, industry and thrift or not; then, of course, we can fiddle about with minor matters. But if we are like that, why are we a Party? Above all, why are we called a LIBERAL Party? . . .
>
> I submit most urgently that except for broad and simple laws to prevent accident and to preserve public order and safety, it is of the highest importance that the Government should leave to the infinitely elastic adaptability of individual enterprise the whole business of the carriage of goods and of people. Any other proposal will swiftly entangle the Government and the industry in stiff, restrictive and harmful fetters.[42]

[39] Hansard, HC (series 5) vol. 415, cols 161–6 (29 October 1945) (Bank of England); vol. 418, cols 971–8 (30 January 1946) (coal mines); vol. 422, cols 727–32 (6 May 1946) (civil aviation); vol. 432, cols 1693–8 (4 February 1947) (electricity); and vol. 447, cols 485–90 (11 February 1948) (gas).

[40] Thurso papers, VII, 1/2, fols 27–9, copy of Roy Harrod to Clement Davies, 26 November 1945; *MG*, 14 January 1946, 3, and 23 January 1946, 5. Eight of the twelve Liberal MPs voted for the Coal Bill at second reading; Gwilym Lloyd George opposed it and Gruffydd, Granville, and Hopkin Morris did not vote.

[41] *MG*, 27 June 1946, 6; *LM* (August 1946), 340.

[42] Ronald Walker, *Transport: Freedom or Nationalisation? A Liberal View* (Leeds, [1945]), 2, 4.

Walker believed that competition in transport was economically justified, but he emphasized that 'something... much more important than good or bad transport' was at stake, since every measure of nationalization tended to 'narrow down the area of free and property-owning citizenship'.[43]

Walker's argument implied that the Liberal Party should revert to the policy of *Ownership for All*, seeking to promote competition wherever possible and resorting to nationalization only in exceptional cases. This was also the view of the party's Monopoly Committee, chaired by A. S. Comyns Carr, which had reported during the election campaign, and the party as a whole continued to espouse strong anti-trust measures.[44] In due course, Liberals would welcome the 1948 Monopolies and Restrictive Practices Act as a step in the right direction whilst complaining that it was too cautious.[45]

When the government's Transport Bill appeared at the end of 1946, the Liberals took a nuanced line. The Liberal Party Committee decided that rail nationalization deserved 'general but critical support', as suggested by the 1945 manifesto, but that long-distance road haulage was better left in private hands and deregulated so that it could provide competition for the railways.[46] This decision was endorsed by the party Council and received full support from the parliamentary party, which voted against the bill at both second and third reading.[47]

A 1947 policy statement on nationalization, prepared by the LPO executive and approved by the Council, showed that the party was moving away from the pragmatism of 1945 towards Walker's more anti-statist position. The Liberal Party, it declared, was 'inexorably opposed to collective ownership of all the means of production, distribution, and exchange', and believed that no industry should be nationalized until an impartial inquiry had shown it was necessary. Moreover, 'the benefit of State ownership in any given case must be great enough to overcome the special disadvantages which are inherent in it'.[48] On the basis of these criteria, the 1948 Iron and Steel Bill was clearly unsupportable, as Davies pointed out in the Commons: there had been no proper inquiry into the industry's needs, and the large increases in output achieved since 1939 suggested that it was already relatively efficient.[49] Megan Lloyd George and three other MPs were disposed to support the bill at second reading and amend it later, but

[43] Walker, *Transport*, 3.
[44] Liberal Party, *Monopoly* (1945).
[45] *LM* (June 1948), 213.
[46] *MG*, 11 December 1946, 6.
[47] *LM* (January 1947), 22; Hansard, HC (series 5) vol. 431, cols 2089–94 (17 December 1946), and vol. 437, cols 167–71 (5 May 1947).
[48] *MG*, 5 March 1947, 6, and 16 June 1947, 6.
[49] Hansard, HC (series 5) vol. 458, cols 251–62 (16 November 1948).

Davies and his new chief whip Frank Byers eventually persuaded them to join their colleagues in opposing it.[50] As an alternative to public ownership, a party committee recommended the creation of an independent Iron and Steel Authority, which would operate controls over steel prices and oversee the industry's development.[51]

By the 1950 general election, the party's attitude was clear:

> Monopoly where it is not inevitable is objectionable and should be broken up. If it cannot be broken up it should, if possible, be controlled in the public interest without a change of ownership; only when neither the restoration of competition nor control is possible should nationalisation be considered.[52]

A Liberal government, the manifesto promised, would return iron and steel and road transport to the private sector and impose a five-year moratorium on further nationalization. It would also 'free road transport' from licensing, establish a permanent commission of inquiry into monopolies and restrictive practices, and promote competition in the nationalized industries by 'decentralising control'.[53] This line was maintained with little controversy throughout the 1950s. The Liberals, then, accepted the nationalization of the most obvious 'natural monopolies' and the special case of coal, but otherwise returned to a market-oriented approach.

The Liberal Party's hardening opposition to nationalization was undoubtedly a triumph for the Liberal right and a reflection of the political atmosphere of the late 1940s. Growing middle-class hostility to the Attlee government had pushed the party's centre of gravity rightwards: government seemed to be the problem and the market the solution in a growing number of fields. At the same time, it is important to recognize that most left-wing Liberals were relatively indifferent towards nationalization once coal had been dealt with. Three reasons for this phenomenon may be noted. Firstly, there had always been a strand of left-Liberalism which cared much more about social reform than economics, and supported public ownership mainly because of what it symbolized. Megan Lloyd George more or less personified this tendency.[54]

Secondly, more constructive Liberals were impressed by the notion that ownership was irrelevant to the pursuit of greater efficiency in most industries. This argument had been implicit in the Yellow Book, but it gained a

[50] Wyburn-Powell, *Clement Davies*, 171.

[51] National Library of Scotland, Scottish Liberal Party papers, 46, 'Ad Interim Report of the Iron and Steel Committee', 1 September 1949.

[52] *Liberal Party General Election Manifestos, 1900–1997*, ed. Iain Dale (2000), 73.

[53] *Liberal Manifestos*, 73.

[54] Mervyn Jones, *A Radical Life: The Biography of Megan Lloyd George, 1902–66* (1991), 195.

more definite form in American managerialist writings such as Adolf Berle and Gardiner Means' *The Modern Corporation and Private Property* (1932) and James Burnham's *The Managerial Revolution* (1941). The Oxford economist Peter Wiles was the most significant Liberal exponent of this line. Since ownership had become 'divorced from management', Wiles wrote in the *Liberal Magazine* in 1948,

> five times out of ten, to change ownership is to change nothing of any importance: and another four times out of ten it is to make but the smallest dent on the vital problem of efficiency.[55]

Wiles argued that Liberals should therefore put the ownership question to one side and focus on improving the quality of management and production processes.[56]

Over time, the managerialist critique of nationalization became firmly embedded in Liberal thought and rhetoric. The idea of a moratorium, included in the 1950 manifesto, reflected the perception that nationalization plans brought instability, deterring private firms from investing in new plant. (Of course, this argument also implied that *denationalization* could be destabilizing—which may help explain Liberals' limited interest in dismantling the public sector.[57]) The party sought to capitalize on public fatigue with ownership changes by appealing to voters to 'get off that see-saw', a theme which it would continue to press for the following three decades.[58] Among other merits, the promise to stop further nationalization gave the Liberals an easily understood justification for seeking the balance of power; in a later generation it would also provide a basis for rapprochement with revisionist social democrats such as Roy Jenkins.

A third reason for left-wing Liberals' loss of interest in nationalization was the emergence of a radical alternative, in the form of proposals for compulsory co-ownership. The idea of 'ownership for all' was hardly new, but the 1938 report had concentrated on measures such as death duties and anti-trust legislation, which were likely to disperse ownership on a significant scale only in the relatively long run. During the 1940s, some Liberals came to the conclusion that a more radical approach was required if the party was to challenge Labour's appeal among the working class.

[55] *LM* (January 1948), 3–8, at 4, 5.

[56] Managerialist ideas also helped turn Labour revisionists such as Anthony Crosland against further nationalization: see Stephen Brooke, 'Atlantic crossing? American views of capitalism and British socialist thought 1932–62', *TCBH*, ii (1991), 107–36, and Ben Jackson, *Equality and the British Left: A Study in Progressive Political Thought, 1900–64* (Manchester, 2007), 155–7.

[57] Wiles argued this point particularly strongly: *LM* (January 1948), 6–7.

[58] Parliamentary Archives, Graham White papers, WHI/1/5/67, 'Giddy?' leaflet with cartoon by Naylor, n.d. [*c.*1951].

The appearance of 'property-owning democracy' as a Conservative slogan after the war made it all the more imperative to give 'ownership for all' a radical edge.

The promotion of profit-sharing and workers' participation in industry seemed to offer the best opportunity for action. Among other advantages, this policy applied directly to workers, fitted well with the post-war concern for raising productivity and sharpening work incentives, and allowed the party to occupy ground which Labour had abandoned. Despite the interest in workers' control which had existed in the early Labour movement, especially among guild socialists such as G. D. H. Cole, most Labour politicians in the 1940s and 1950s regarded trade union collective bargaining as the most appropriate form of representation for British workers—a view shared by industrial relations experts such as Hugh Clegg.[59]

Comyns Carr's Monopoly Committee proposed that firms with more than fifty employees or £50,000 in capital should be required to introduce co-ownership schemes which met four requirements: the payment of trade union or statutory wage rates, the encouragement of employee shareholding, elected representation for employees on the board of directors, and the division of profits between shareholders and employees.[60] A new Ownership for All Committee, chaired by Dodds, took up this idea and presented detailed plans to the 1948 Assembly. Advocates of compulsory co-ownership—including Dodds, who had changed his mind since 1938—argued that incentives would work too slowly, and pointed out that the state already set the terms on which firms engaged in business through the company law.[61] Conversely, opponents of compulsion, like Ronald Walker and Stephen Cawley, regarded it as an arbitrary interference in shareholders' rights and believed it would alienate businessmen from the party.[62] After a stormy debate, the former arguments won out, and the Ownership for All resolution was comfortably carried. Dodds fleshed out the party's vision in a pamphlet entitled *People in Industry*, and the principle of compulsion was later reaffirmed by the 1949 and 1952 Assemblies.[63]

[59] Peter Ackers, 'Collective bargaining as industrial democracy: Hugh Clegg and the political foundations of British industrial relations pluralism', *British Journal of Industrial Relations*, xlv (2007), 77–101.

[60] Donald Wade and Desmond Banks, *The Political Insight of Elliott Dodds* (Leeds, 1977), 36. The idea of compulsory profit-sharing had previously been floated in *The Liberal Way*: NLF, *The Liberal Way* (1934), 172–4.

[61] *LM* (June 1948), 209–13; Wade and Banks, *Political Insight*, 36–8.

[62] *LM* (June 1948), 209–13.

[63] Liberal Party, *People in Industry* (1949); *MG*, 26 March 1949, 3, and 17 May 1952, 5.

Compulsory co-ownership enjoyed a chequered history within the party, not least because Davies and other MPs were lukewarm towards it, and it would eventually be sidelined in the mid-1950s in favour of a policy based on tax incentives.[64] Nevertheless, its ideological significance was considerable. It shifted the main focus of the 'ownership for all' agenda from the market to the workplace and gave it an institutional form, bringing it closer to the Yellow Book than the 1938 report had been. Moreover, although co-ownership was frequently advocated on pragmatic grounds, many of its supporters also asserted that workers had a moral right to share in the profits created by their labour. As Stuart White has pointed out, this assertion carried radical implications for Liberals' understanding of what property ownership entailed.[65] At a more practical level, the adoption of compulsory co-ownership as Liberal policy helped the party maintain a radical identity at a time when its other policies were moving in a free-market direction.

As in the inter-war period, the corollary of Liberal support for an institutional form of industrial democracy was a lukewarm attitude towards the trade union movement. Liberals acknowledged that trade unions had an important role to play in representing workers' interests and organizing collective bargaining, but argued that the movement's adversarial culture and defensive attitude to economic change were no longer appropriate in an age of full employment. Davies and his colleagues opposed the 1946 Trade Disputes Act, which (*inter alia*) restored contracting-out, and strongly criticized the closed shop on civil liberties grounds; when the government refused to appoint a Royal Commission on the closed shop, the party set up its own Commission of Inquiry into the unions under the chairmanship of the barrister D. A. Scott Cairns, which reported in 1950.[66] Yet though the Liberals tried to develop a constructive agenda for reform, trade union leaders were deeply suspicious of their calls for a 'responsible' trade unionism geared towards industrial partnership. The establishment of the Association of Liberal Trade Unionists in 1947 did not help matters, since it spent much of its time encouraging breakaway unions and drawing attention to victimization cases.[67] This enduring attitudinal gulf between Liberals and mainstream

[64] Jorgen Scott Rasmussen, *The Liberal Party: A Study of Retrenchment and Revival* (1965), 129–30.

[65] Stuart White, '"Revolutionary Liberalism?" The philosophy and politics of ownership in the post-war Liberal Party', *British Politics*, iv (2009), 164–87, at 170–2.

[66] Hansard, HC (series 5) vol. 421, cols 1213–8 (2 April 1946), and vol. 430, cols 696–708 (19 November 1946); *MG*, 16 January 1950, 3.

[67] Matthew Cole, 'The Identity of the British Liberal Party, 1945–62' (Birmingham Ph.D. thesis, 2006), 158–66.

trade unionists almost certainly hampered the party's efforts to shed its rather middle-class image.

ECONOMIC MANAGEMENT UNDER LABOUR, 1945–51

Nationalization and trade unionism were central to political debate in the late 1940s, but in a sense they were incidental to the wider challenge of adjusting the British economy to post-war needs. After 1945, policy-makers were confronted not only by the domestic tasks of demobilization and reconstruction, but also by a world food and raw material shortage, a shortage of dollars resulting from high demand for North American goods, and sustained pressure from the United States to make sterling convertible and liberalize trade under the terms of the Loan Agreement. High import prices, rising money wages, and unfulfilled demand for consumer goods meant that the British economy was beset by inflationary pressures for most of this period, while balance of payments difficulties were recurrent, and sterling was eventually devalued from $4.03 to $2.80 in 1949.

As Alec Cairncross and Jim Tomlinson have shown, the Attlee government sought to manage the post-war transition mainly by maintaining the wartime apparatus of planning and control.[68] Manpower budgeting remained the main tool of macroeconomic policy until 1947, whilst import controls were used to reduce the balance of payments deficit, allocation systems channelled materials to key industries, and price controls, rationing, and food subsidies ensured 'fair shares' for all. Along with the high level of taxation required to finance the welfare state and ongoing defence commitments, these measures tended to suppress domestic consumption in favour of exports and investment. The government also retained some labour controls to ensure an adequate labour supply for basic industries like coal and agriculture, and persuaded the TUC to support a voluntary wage freeze in 1948–50.[69] The dollar shortage meanwhile gave urgency to the government's efforts to raise output and productivity through rationalization, an active investment policy, and the promotion of research and development.[70]

Though the decision to retain controls during the transition period initially enjoyed wide support, by 1947 several prominent economists were criticizing government policy on liberal Keynesian lines. According to this

[68] Alec Cairncross, *Years of Recovery: British Economic Policy 1945–51* (1985); Jim Tomlinson, *Democratic Socialism and Economic Policy: The Attlee Years, 1945–1951* (Cambridge, 1997).

[69] Cairncross, *Years of Recovery*, 23–8, 395–408.

[70] Tomlinson, *Democratic Socialism and Economic Policy*, 68–93.

critique, the use of controls and rationing to hold living costs down was merely suppressing inflation instead of dealing with its causes, whilst also restricting consumer choice and civil liberties. The lesson of Keynesianism seemed to be that inflation could be dealt with more effectively by reducing demand. This case was made within Whitehall by James Meade, who had succeeded Lionel Robbins as director of the Economic Section and urged ministers to adopt a national income and expenditure analysis which revealed an 'inflationary gap' between aggregate demand and supply. Meade was also keen that food subsidies should be reduced so that the price mechanism could operate more freely, a position backed by Treasury officials such as Sir Edward Bridges.[71] Outside government, a disinflationary fiscal policy was advocated by a wide spectrum of informed opinion, ranging from free-market Keynesians such as Roy Harrod and John Hicks through Dennis Robertson and Lionel Robbins to more orthodox commentators such as Oscar Hobson and Sir Hubert Henderson (who thought a balanced budget was 'the time-honoured remedy' for excess purchasing power).[72] Perhaps the most forceful version of the argument came from Harrod, whose October 1947 tract *Are These Hardships Necessary?* called for deep cuts in public investment to reduce total outlay by £500,000,000 and bring the economy into balance.[73]

The Labour government moved part-way towards a liberal Keynesian approach following the summer 1947 convertibility crisis. Dalton and Sir Stafford Cripps used their budgets in November 1947 and April 1948 to increase taxes, curb public investment, and cap food subsidies, whilst Harold Wilson at the Board of Trade presided over a steady removal of controls which ministers no longer considered necessary. However, the fiscal tightening undertaken in 1947–8 was less stringent than Harrod believed was required, and the exigencies of Korean War rearmament pushed the government back towards physical planning in 1950–1. Calls for the abolition of food and housing subsidies were resisted, and even the relatively liberal Hugh Gaitskell believed that some direct controls would always be necessary to maintain full employment.[74]

Although the Liberal Party's wartime flirtation with planning did not long outlast the war, there remained a current of Liberal opinion which sympathized with the Attlee government's approach and regarded its

[71] Alan Booth, *British Economic Policy, 1931–49: Was there a Keynesian Revolution?* (1989), 158–66.

[72] T. W. Hutchison, *Economics and Economic Policy in Britain, 1946–1966: Some Aspects of their Interrelations* (1968), 49–55, 60–2; *NC*, 3 March 1947, 3; for Henderson, see *Sunday Times*, 23 February 1947, 4.

[73] Roy Harrod, *Are These Hardships Necessary?* (1947), 66–102.

[74] Neil Rollings, 'Poor Mr Butskell: A short life, wrecked by schizophrenia?', *TCBH*, v (1994), 183–205, at 189–95.

failings as ones of practice rather than principle. At the beginning of the 1945 Parliament Davies endorsed the use of controls to prevent inflation, and he consistently argued that planning would be more effective if it were overseen by a small executive Cabinet on the wartime model.[75] Violet Bonham Carter took a similar line in her speech to the 1946 Assembly: 'Our Liberal cry should be "plan better", plan with greater foresight, courage, wisdom; and not "do not plan at all".'[76] Davies and Bonham Carter were also attracted by the idea of extending planning to include some sort of national wages policy, which was endorsed by the 1947 Assembly, whilst Megan Lloyd George and many left-leaning activists worried about the impact of decontrol on working-class living standards.[77]

From 1947 onwards, however, Davies became a consistent exponent of a liberal Keynesian policy, which fitted well with the party's renewed emphasis on competition and choice. The liberal Keynesian economists emphasized their debt to Keynes and their commitment to full employment (Harrod, of course, could gloss Keynes' legacy by writing his biography) and also benefited from the support of much of the quality press, including *The Economist*.[78] Davies' speeches on economic matters drew both on published criticisms of government policy—such as a *Lloyds Bank Review* article by Robbins which he quoted in the Commons—and on direct advice from sympathetic economists.[79] Harrod was a member of the Liberal Party Committee until 1948, when he resigned to pursue Liberal–Conservative cooperation, and Frank Paish joined the committee a year later.[80] The freelance journalist Graham Hutton was another influential voice, while Hobson was for some time a member of the party Council.[81] Several other free-market economists and journalists were more tangentially involved: thus W. Manning Dacey—a former editor of *The Banker*—moved a resolution on taxation at the 1947 Assembly, Stanley Dennison wrote

[75] Hansard, HC (series 5) vol. 414, cols 2051–7 (24 October 1945), and vol. 434, cols 1164–76 (11 March 1947).

[76] *LM* (June 1946), 242–5, at 243.

[77] *The Observer*, 23 February 1947, 7; *LM* (June 1947), 172–4; *LM* (June 1948), 218–9; *MG*, 26 March 1949, 5.

[78] *Economist*, 1 March 1947, 309–10. For a critical analysis of Harrod's *Life*, see Scott Newton, 'Deconstructing Harrod: some observations on *The Life of John Maynard Keynes*', *CBH*, xv (2001), 15–27.

[79] Lionel Robbins, 'Inquest on the crisis', *Lloyds Bank Review*, no. 6 (October 1947), 1–27; Hansard, HC (series 5) vol. 443, cols 384–97, at 384 (24 October 1947).

[80] Phelps Brown, 'Sir Roy Harrod', 29; *MG*, 23 December 1949, 6. Harrod also assailed government policy at the 1947 and 1948 Liberal Summer Schools: *MG*, 6 August 1947, 6, and 31 July 1948, 6.

[81] Clement Davies papers, H/4/1, typescript of 'The Economic Background to Britain's Crisis' by Hutton, 1952, and H/4/3, G[ilbert] Y. P[onsonby] to Davies, 19 February 1956; *LM* (September 1949), 385–403; *MG*, 12 April 1949, 6, and 29 May 1952, 5.

on 'Problems of Full Employment' for the *Liberal News*, and John Jewkes addressed the 1953 Liberal Summer School.[82] At grassroots level the accountant Guy Naylor and his wife Margot, who later became financial editor of *The Observer*, were among several London-based activists who pressed for a free-market approach.[83]

Davies began to articulate liberal Keynesian arguments in the wake of the February 1947 coal supply crisis, which shook public confidence in the effectiveness of planning. Speaking in a Commons economic debate in March, he accused the government of presiding over 'suppressed inflation' and argued that in such circumstances it was essential to balance the budget.[84] Since taxation was already very high, this had to be done by cutting expenditure, especially by abandoning conscription, shrinking the armed forces, and postponing the proposed increase in the school leaving age. Davies' call for spending cuts was subsequently endorsed by the party Council.[85]

The Liberal leader pushed this analysis further when he responded to Dalton's third budget in April 1947. He welcomed the fact that the Chancellor's speech had dealt with the whole economy rather than just the public finances, but argued that he should have produced a much larger surplus to deal with mounting inflationary pressures. Davies also urged a cut in the food and clothing subsidies, which had reached the 'appalling' figure of £400,000,000 per annum.[86] These points were elaborated in the July 1947 policy statement *Action Now*, issued in response to the convertibility crisis, which argued that only a major reduction in domestic demand and a shift towards production for export would ultimately solve the dollar problem. Demand could be reduced by raising indirect taxes and by a £500,000,000 cut in government spending, concentrated on investment programmes.[87] On this basis, the £200,000,000 cut in planned public investment which Dalton announced in his November 1947 budget would seem to Davies (as to Harrod) to be inadequate.[88]

The Liberal Party at large seems to have accepted the case for fiscal disinflation from 1947 onwards. Harrod's claim that this would facilitate rapid decontrol remained controversial—indeed, a resolution calling for

[82] *LM* (June 1947), 161–78, at 174–5; *LN*, 25 August 1950, 3, and 7 August 1953, 1, 4.

[83] *LM* (June 1948), 218–20; *LN*, 19 August 1949, 6.

[84] Hansard, HC (series 5) vol. 434, cols 1164–76, at 1168 (11 March 1947).

[85] *The Times*, 17 March 1947, 2.

[86] Hansard, HC (series 5) vol. 436, cols 226–35, at 233 (16 April 1947).

[87] *The Times*, 1 August 1947, 4. The Design for Freedom Committee offered a similar programme in its August 1947 pamphlet *Design for Survival*, written by Thorneycroft and Rhys Williams, and the January 1948 sequel *Design for Recovery*.

[88] Hansard, HC (series 5) vol. 444, cols 577–84, at 577–9 (13 November 1947); Roy Harrod, 'And still no plan', *Soundings* (December 1947), reprinted in Roy Harrod, *And So It Goes On: Further Thoughts on Present Mismanagement* (1951), 89–105.

the early abolition of controls and rationing was defeated at the 1948 Assembly after several young candidates denounced it as reactionary—but as inflation fell in 1948–9 Liberals seem to have become more confident that liberalization could be carried through.[89] The main economic resolution adopted by the 1949 Assembly, moved by Guy Naylor and entitled 'Programme for Recovery', confirmed the party's right turn. 'Programme for Recovery' declared that a Liberal government would use 'financial and budgetary control . . . to maintain full employment', restore 'free multilateral trade' at 'the earliest possible moment', and attack monopoly; it also promised 'searching scrutiny of Government expenditure', tax reductions, 'a progressive reduction in the Food subsidies', '[t]he removal of those industrial controls which prevent competition', and 'the abolition of restriction of output by the quota system'.[90] It was not suggested that all controls could be abolished immediately, but the ambition of Liberal policy was clear. The 1950 Liberal manifesto echoed this line, promising to 'budget for an excess of revenue over expenditure, until supply in every direction meets demand', and to abolish '[e]very control not imposed by the need for fair shares or scarcity'.[91] In 1951, Korean War bottlenecks made the Liberals more cautious, and prompted them to defer proposals for abolishing food subsides 'until the increased productivity campaign has brought down the cost of living', but the party's underlying approach remained the same.[92]

As well as criticizing controls and planning, Davies and his colleagues joined the Conservatives in challenging the Labour government's efforts to claim credit for full employment. As the 1950 Liberal manifesto pointed out, the American loan and Marshall Aid had allowed Britain to run large trade deficits which were unsustainable in the long run:

> Crisis after crisis comes upon us, because we are living beyond our means. The Liberal Party believes passionately in full employment in a free society, and in maintaining the social services. But unless we practise thrift and get full production, lower rations and mass unemployment are inescapable when American aid ends.[93]

Davies believed that the government was leading the nation 'to economic disaster', and Violet Bonham Carter regarded the situation as more serious than 1931.[94] Fears of a major economic crisis persisted even after a temporary improvement in the balance of payments allowed ministers to terminate

[89] *LM* (June 1948), 218–9.
[90] *LM* (April 1949), 186–7.
[91] *Liberal Manifestos*, 71, 72.
[92] *Liberal Manifestos*, 84.
[93] *Liberal Manifestos*, 71.
[94] Clement Davies papers, J/3/26i, Davies to Murray, 11 May 1950, and J/3/83, Bonham Carter to Davies, 2 October 1956.

Marshall Aid in December 1950, more than a year ahead of schedule. Further productivity improvements and more exports were required to put full employment and post-war living standards on a sustainable footing.[95]

Predictions of mass unemployment never came to pass, but taken as a whole the liberal Keynesianism of the late 1940s provided the Liberal Party with a relatively coherent economic message. Its main shortcoming, as *The Economist* noted, was that it placed the party in the same political space as the Conservatives, who had much better prospects of being able to carry out free-market policies.[96] Liberals could point to the discrepancy between the Conservatives' rhetoric and their inter-war record, but they could not plausibly deny the similarity between the two parties' stated views on economic management and public ownership.[97] Conversely, the policies which most distinguished the Liberals from the Conservatives, such as free trade, co-ownership, and proportional representation, were peripheral to the economic policy debate as Labour and the Conservatives defined it, and so were easy for the party's opponents to dismiss as 'faddist' obsessions.

With little compelling reason for voters to support the Liberals, the party was reduced in 1950–1 to nine and then six MPs. The collapse of the Labour government's majority to just five in 1950 should have put Davies in a strong position, but the parliamentary party proved unable to exploit the situation because it was so deeply divided. If the 1951 result had a silver lining, it was that three of the MPs who lost their seats—Megan Lloyd George, Emrys Roberts, and Edgar Granville—were vocal left wingers, so at least the embarrassment of Liberals voting in opposite division lobbies would subsequently become less common.

ECONOMIC MANAGEMENT UNDER THE CONSERVATIVES, 1951–6

When the Conservatives won the 1951 election with a majority of sixteen, Clement Davies turned down an invitation to become Minister of Education in the interests of the party's independence. Nevertheless, the Liberals promised to support 'measures clearly conceived in the interests of the country as a whole', and proceeded to vote with the government in most divisions during the 1951 Parliament.[98] Economic policy was

[95] *LN*, 13 January 1950, 2. [96] *Economist*, 11 February 1950, 305–6.

[97] MS. Bonham Carter 184, fols 103–8, 'Notes on Memorandum Issued by D. F. and M. Ll. G.', by Violet Bonham Carter, June 1950.

[98] *MG*, 29 October 1951, 9; Matt Cole, '"An out-of-date word": Grimond and the left', *JLH*, no. 67 (2010), 50–6, at 52. Davies even told Duncan Sandys that he was willing

perhaps the most important area of agreement. R. A. Butler's broad strategy as Chancellor—after the Cabinet rejected the 'Robot' convertibility plan—was to use Bank Rate and other monetary instruments to defend the external position of sterling, whilst boosting private consumption and investment through tax cuts and allowances as the economic situation permitted.[99] Davies and his colleagues welcomed the revival of an active monetary policy, voted for the Finance Bill which followed the tight 1952 budget, and supported the more expansionary 1953 one.[100] Indeed, the Liberals' main criticism was that Butler should have gone further and faster in reducing taxation, dismantling trade restrictions and controls, and encouraging private savings. At the same time, they continued to urge a close watch on inflation.[101] In practice, the apparent success of Butler's policy made it difficult to press these criticisms with much force. Up to the 1955 election, Liberal and Conservative policies stood within the same broad paradigm of fiscal and monetary fine-tuning combined with micro-economic liberalization, which seemed to be delivering long-awaited prosperity.

The year 1955 was a turning point for two reasons. Firstly, Butler's efforts to offset fiscal expansion with monetary restraint broke down in the context of buoyant demand and rumours that sterling would soon be made convertible. The income tax cuts which Butler introduced in his April budget stoked an election-year boom, which later had to be tamed by tightening credit and hire-purchase restrictions in July, curbing public investment, and raising taxes in a supplementary budget in October.[102] Eden, who had succeeded Churchill as Prime Minister, would move Butler from the Treasury at the end of the year and appoint Harold Macmillan in his place.

Secondly, inflation returned as a major political issue. Partly as a function of the boom, Retail Price Index inflation climbed rapidly from mid-1954 onwards, averaging 4.5 per cent in 1955 and peaking at 7.3

to join the government in 1954: Churchill Archives Centre, Sandys papers, 15/4, 'Prime Minister', note by Sandys, 1 October 1954.

[99] G. C. Peden, *The Treasury and British Public Policy, 1906–1959* (Oxford, 2000), 458–86.

[100] Hansard, HC (series 5) vol. 497, cols 1424–30 (12 March 1952); vol. 498, cols 2441–6 (7 April 1952); and vol. 514, cols 418–30 (16 April 1953).

[101] Subsidiary criticisms related to Butler's failure to extend family allowances to the first child, to reform the tax system, and to provide more assistance for pensioners: Hansard, HC (series 5) vol. 514, cols 418–30 (16 April 1953), and vol. 526, cols 395–9 (7 April 1954). Liberals tended to view convertibility as an important policy objective but not necessarily an immediate one: *LN*, 28 March 1952, 1, 27 March 1953, 2, and 25 March 1955, 4.

[102] J. C. R. Dow, *The Management of the British Economy, 1945–60* (Cambridge, 1964), 78–80, 85–90.

per cent in spring 1956. At the same time, economists, journalists, and politicians became more concerned about the consequences of a mild but persistent rise in prices. Sir Dennis Robertson warned in a March 1955 article that 'creeping inflation' undermined the basis of financial contracts and harmed those citizens who lacked the bargaining power to maintain their real incomes. Robertson believed that post-war governments had defined full employment too stringently, and had given too little priority to the task of maintaining the value of money.[103]

Both Frank Paish and Oscar Hobson shared Robertson's analysis, and Paish pressed the case for disinflationary measures on the Liberal leadership, which proved to be highly receptive.[104] The free-trade tradition, of course, had given the party a historic concern for cheapness, and the 'cost of living' rhetoric of the 1930s was ripe for revival, but many Liberals also raised moral and constitutional objections to the practice of steadily expanding the money supply. Nathaniel Micklem, the Congregationalist theologian who served as party president in 1957–8, thought a deliberate policy of inflation involved 'deceit, misrepresentation, breach of contract, [and] injustice', because it enabled government to inflate away the national debt at the expense of savers.[105] In similar vein, Fothergill claimed that it was 'a classic Liberal doctrine that it is the job of Government to maintain the value of our money', and argued that it was a 'down-right swindle' for politicians to introduce welfare benefits without stabilizing their value.[106]

These anti-inflationary arguments featured prominently in the Liberal Party's 1955 general election campaign. As the manifesto put it:

> By the inflationary policy of two Socialist Governments, continued in modified form by the Conservatives, pensioners and people living on small fixed incomes and the lowest wage scales have been most cruelly penalised. A constantly and rapidly depreciating pound strikes at the root of social justice. The Liberal Party, which made possible the Welfare Society by its early reforms, is maintaining its traditions by calling for a radical attack upon false economic policies which inevitably lead to ever-rising costs of living. Will either the Conservative or the Labour Party have the courage, on this side of disaster, to stem the tide of rising prices, subsidies and nominal wages?[107]

[103] D. H. Robertson, 'The problem of creeping inflation', *London and Cambridge Economic Bulletin*, new series, no. 13 (1955), ii–iv.

[104] Liberal Party papers, 16/27/10–12, 'The Revival of Inflation', memorandum by Paish, 22 February 1955; *NC*, 27 June 1955, 2.

[105] 'The morals of managed money', *Contemporary Review*, cxcv (1959), 57–72, at 57.

[106] Bodleian Library, Conservative Party Archive, CCO 3/4/74, text of election broadcast by Fothergill, 12 May 1955.

[107] *Liberal Manifestos*, 91.

Posters produced by Liberal headquarters echoed this theme, promising that Liberal MPs would fight for 'lower cost of living', 'reduced govt. spending' and 'freedom of the individual'.[108] Many candidates in the constituencies seem to have taken the same line.[109] As Garry Tregidga has noted, we might expect these arguments to have resonated particularly strongly among the small farmers, tradesmen, and non-unionized workers who bulked large in peripheral areas such as Devon and Cornwall.[110]

Bemoaning the persistence of inflation was an easy populist move, but the Liberals did try to articulate an alternative. Part of the solution lay in microeconomic reforms: abolishing tariffs, tackling monopolies and restrictive practices, and using co-partnership to improve productivity. Macroeconomic policy, however, was also an important part of the mix. The obvious implication of Robertson and Paish's arguments was that the government should restrain aggregate demand and accept a higher unemployment rate as the price of price stability. Paish argued that a modest rise in unemployment, perhaps to the 3 per cent rate which Beveridge had defined as 'full employment', would eliminate inflationary pressures and change workers' expectations.[111] This would later be understood as a downwards move along the Phillips Curve. Some Liberals were alarmed by the prospect, but Paish insisted that his policy did not require a return to the mass unemployment of the 1930s. Liberals could demand that inflation should have 'overriding priority in national economic policy'—as Paish, Graham Hutton, and Lawrence Robson did in their 1958 submission to the Radcliffe Committee on the Working of the Monetary System—only because a reasonably high level of employment was taken for granted.[112]

Paish's diagnosis of excessive demand was informed by the Keynesian concept of an 'inflationary gap', which could be closed by either fiscal or monetary measures, but he and other Liberals were also impressed by the extent to which inflation was a monetary phenomenon. Paish had 'no doubt' that inflation could be ended 'simply by action to ensure that the quantity of money does not rise further', whilst Jo Grimond believed that 'the root cause of it must be a continual tendency for too much credit and

[108] *LN*, 13 May 1955, 1.

[109] For instance, Richard Wainwright at Pudsey: *LN*, 13 May 1955, 5.

[110] Garry Tregidga, *The Liberal Party in South-West England Since 1918: Political Decline, Dormancy and Rebirth* (Exeter, 2000), 158.

[111] Paish revised his estimate of the rate of unemployment needed to conquer inflation downwards from 3–4% in the early 1950s, to 3% in 1955 and just over 2% by 1958. See *LN*, 21 March 1952, 4, and 4 March 1955, 4; and F. W. Paish, 'Progress, prices and the pound', *District Bank Review*, no. 125 (March 1958), 1–17.

[112] *Committee on the Working of the Monetary System: Principal Memoranda of Evidence. Volume 3* (1960), 189–93, at 192.

money to get into the system'.[113] The Liberal peer and insurance magnate Lord Grantchester (formerly Sir Alfred Suenson-Taylor) echoed the Currency School of the 1840s in arguing that this could be achieved by controlling the note issue, but Paish considered bank deposits much more important, and so preferred a wide-ranging credit squeeze involving Bank Rate, Treasury Deposit Receipts, and the funding of government debt, backed up by public spending restraint.[114] This was a more eclectic and discretionary approach than Milton Friedman and other monetarist economists were beginning to advocate, but it placed the Liberal leadership at the proto-monetarist end of policy debate in the 1950s alongside Peter Thorneycroft and other inflation hawks.[115]

The Liberal Party's approach to fiscal policy also took on a new form. Though Keynesian analysis suggested that tax increases could be just as effective as spending cuts in removing excess demand, Davies, Grimond, and their colleagues became increasingly adamant that spending cuts were preferable.[116] High taxes seemed to raise the cost of living directly and damage work incentives, whilst high government spending was liable to increase the monetary circulation.[117] Defence expenditure, government administration, and agricultural subsidies appeared to offer considerable scope for savings; so, too, did the idea of forcing the nationalized industries to raise capital on the market. Social service cuts, such as those sought by Thorneycroft as Chancellor in 1958, were consequently deemed unnecessary, although fiscal discipline was still needed here and public investment would have to be curtailed.[118]

The theoretical gap between the Liberal leadership and the Conservative government was not much larger after 1955 than it had been earlier in the decade: for instance, the credit squeeze of 1955–8 broadly took the form which Paish recommended.[119] Nevertheless, the Liberals made the most of

[113] F. W. Paish, 'Open and repressed inflation', *EJ*, lxiii (1953), 527–52, at 551; Hansard, HC (series 5) vol. 545, cols 1700–6, at 1705 (8 November 1955).

[114] Hansard, HL (series 5) vol. 202, cols 279–85 (6 March 1957); F. W. Paish, 'Inflation in the United Kingdom, 1948–57', *Economica*, new series, xxv (1958), 94–105; *Committee on the Working of the Monetary System: Principal Memoranda of Evidence. Volume 3*, 182–8.

[115] On Thorneycroft's relationship with monetarism, see Peden, *Treasury*, 486–93, E. H. H. Green, 'The Treasury resignations of 1958: A reconsideration', in E. H. H. Green, *Ideologies of Conservatism* (Oxford, 2002), 192–213, and Chris Cooper, 'Little local difficulties revisited: Peter Thorneycroft, the 1958 Treasury resignations, and the origins of Thatcherism', *CBH*, xxv (2011), 227–50.

[116] Rhys Hopkin Morris had always objected to the government running surpluses for macroeconomic reasons: R. Hopkin Morris, *Dare or Despair* ([1949]), 20.

[117] *The Times*, 17 April 1953, 9; Hansard, HC (series 5) vol. 545, cols 460–9, at 460 (27 October 1955).

[118] Hansard, HC (series 5) vol. 544, cols 1051–6 (26 July 1955); *LN*, 16 March 1956, 1, 4; Conservative Party Archive, CCO 3/5/94, 'The Penny Liberal', no. 2, n.d. [1958].

[119] F. W. Paish, 'Monetary policy and the control of the post-war British inflation', in F. W. Paish, *Studies in an Inflationary Economy: The United Kingdom, 1948–1961* (1962; second edition, 1966), 120–54.

the government's failings. Above all, the party argued that fiscal and monetary policy needed to be used together to conquer inflation, and complained that high government spending undermined monetary restraint. On this basis, Macmillan turned out to be a more satisfactory Chancellor than Butler, and Thorneycroft more satisfactory still.[120] Liberals claimed, however, that Thorneycroft's unpopular 'September measures' would not have been necessary if a tighter policy had been followed earlier on.[121]

Since the electoral ramifications of the Liberals' anti-inflation stance mostly followed Jo Grimond's succession to the party leadership in 1956, it makes most sense to consider these in the next chapter. For the time being, it is sufficient to note that anti-inflationary rhetoric was central to the Liberal Party's electoral identity during these years, and enabled the party to profit from the 'middle-class revolt' which developed during the 1955 Parliament. Whatever its flaws, the liberal Keynesianism of the 1950s thus deserves some credit for the first, tentative phase of Liberal revival.

THE STATE AND SOCIAL WELFARE

Across the fields of economic and social policy, the main trajectory of Liberal thought during Clement Davies' leadership reflected an increasingly cautious attitude towards the state. As good democrats and progressives, Liberals rarely questioned the legitimacy of state action in economic and social fields, but they were deeply aware of the dangers of arbitrary power. In pursuing full employment and social justice, Liberals felt, it was essential that the state should act within the rule of law, and that free enterprise and individual responsibility should be preserved. In respect of industrial organization and economic management, of course, this stance had been foreshadowed by Liberal policy during the late 1930s, but in matters of social welfare the caution which the party displayed after 1945 was rather newer.

Since at least the turn of the twentieth century, the Liberal Party had offered broad if conditional support for the piecemeal expansion of the state's welfare role. In unemployment insurance, national health insurance, and old age pensions it was the Asquith government that established the architecture of Britain's welfare system, whilst H. A. L. Fisher's 1918 Education Act built on the Forster Act of 1870 to extend compulsory schooling up to the age of fourteen. During the inter-war period the party

[120] *LN*, 18 January 1957, 1. [121] *LN*, 27 September 1957, 3.

had little opportunity to add to its record, but MPs like Ernest Simon, Percy Harris, and Graham White proved strenuous advocates of progressive policies such as council housing, the development of day nurseries, and the extension of unemployment insurance to 'black-coated' and agricultural workers. If Liberals tended to be more sensitive than Labour to the cost of social reforms, they could also be readier to support measures such as family allowances, which the trade unions initially opposed.[122] Certainly, it seemed natural that the Beveridge report and proposals for a national health service should be backed by most Liberals. 'Along the path of social reform,' Elliott Dodds could write in 1949, 'all progressives have marched together.'[123]

The Attlee government's flagship social legislation, the National Insurance Act and National Health Service Act of 1946, mostly received enthusiastic Liberal backing, but the party nevertheless expressed concern about several points of detail. Firstly, Liberals criticized the government's treatment of voluntary organizations, and especially its decision to exclude the friendly societies from the new social insurance system. Beveridge himself would emphasize the value of mutual provision in his 1948 report on *Voluntary Action*.[124] Secondly, Liberals pressed for 'a maximum amount of local interest and local responsibility' to be maintained in the NHS, and argued for Hospital Management Committees and regional boards to include elected representatives.[125] Thirdly, the party offered qualified support for the British Medical Association's campaign for General Practitioners to be paid mainly by capitation fees, instead of becoming salaried public employees. Finally, Liberals questioned whether the new welfare state was as comprehensive as the government claimed, since (for instance) the National Insurance Act treated employed and self-employed workers differently.[126] Over time, this criticism was augmented by concern about the quality and scope of provision for the elderly and mentally ill, and the growing number of pensioners who were reliant on National Assistance.[127] The Women's Liberal Federation was especially active in drawing attention to these 'Cinderellas of the Welfare State'.[128]

During the late 1940s, Liberals became increasingly sensitive to the danger that the continued expansion of state welfare provision would undermine individual responsibility and foster dependence. Hayek's *Road*

[122] John Macnicol, *The Movement for Family Allowances, 1918–45: A Study in Social Policy Development* (1980), 138–68.

[123] Elliott Dodds, 'The welfare state', *The Fortnightly* (September 1949), 172–8, at 172.

[124] Lord Beveridge, *Voluntary Action: A Report on Methods of Social Advance* (1948).

[125] *LM* (June 1946), 275.

[126] *LM* (March 1946), 128.

[127] *LM* (April 1948), 121–2; *LN*, 24 November 1950, 3; *MG*, 16 November 1953, 10.

[128] *LN*, 27 March 1953, 3.

to Serfdom contained warnings in this vein; so, too, did Wilhelm Röpke's treatise *Civitas Humana*, published in English in 1948, which contrasted the 'proletarianized society' with the liberal aim of a large property-owning middle class.[129] Even Beveridge pointed out that he believed in a welfare society rather than a welfare state.[130] In present circumstances the benefits of universal health-care and social insurance seemed to outweigh the disadvantages, but the Attlee government's policy of maintaining wartime food subsidies was a different matter entirely. Elliott Dodds thought food subsidies were a classic case of the state interfering with consumption patterns for well-meaning but misguided ends:

> Is it right that the State should appropriate so large a proportion of the citizens' incomes and spend it on their behalf, instead of leaving them to spend it according to their own free choices?[131]

Liberals' ethical objections to subsidies were backed up by economic ones. Not only did classical reasoning hold that subsidies concealed the true cost of goods and distorted resource allocation, but there were good reasons for thinking that they were an inefficient means of fighting poverty.[132] The same objections applied to government intervention in the housing market in the form of rent controls and council house subsidies. The abolition of subsidies also fitted neatly with the Liberals' macroeconomic stance.

Liberals, then, had good reasons for attacking food and housing subsidies. At the same time, it was clear that such an attack carried serious political risks, since—as James Hinton and Ina Zweiniger-Bargielowska have shown—questions of food, austerity, and welfare gave rise to sharply differing attitudes among the working and middle classes.[133] Indeed, this class division cut across the gendered dimension of austerity policies, which Zweiniger-Bargielowska considers more important but which most contemporaries seem to have taken for granted. From different perspectives, Dingle Foot, Elliott Dodds, and Peter Wiles all warned that criticism of the welfare state was likely to be seen as an assault on working-class interests.[134] At the very least, the Liberals would have to show that the

[129] Wilhelm Röpke, *Civitas Humana: A Humane Order of Society* (English edition, 1948).

[130] *LN*, 18 September 1953, 1, 3.

[131] Dodds, 'The welfare state', 173.

[132] For economic criticisms, see Dennis Robertson in *MG*, 30 August 1947, 3, and James Meade, *Planning and the Price Mechanism: The Liberal–Socialist Solution* (1948), 41.

[133] James Hinton, 'Women and the Labour vote, 1945–50', *Labour History Review*, lvii no. 3 (1992), 59–66; James Hinton, 'Militant housewives: the British Housewives' League and the Attlee Government', *History Workshop Journal*, xxxviii (1994), 129–56; Ina Zweiniger-Bargielowska, *Austerity in Britain: Rationing, Controls, and Consumption, 1939–1955* (Oxford, 2000), 60–98, 249–51.

[134] Dingle Foot to Megan Lloyd George, 15 August 1949, quoted in Jones, *A Radical Life*, 207; Dodds, 'The welfare state', 172–4; *LN*, 19 August 1949, 3. Wiles' argument drew

poorest citizens would be compensated in some way for the loss of benefits in kind.

Proposals for integrating social security with the income tax system offered a solution to this problem. Juliet Rhys Williams had canvassed a plan for universal cash allowances as an alternative to the Beveridge report during the Second World War, and had gained an enthusiastic reception from the Women's Liberal Federation, which recognized its value as a means of raising women's incomes.[135] After the war, Rhys Williams' scheme gained wider traction, and the 1949 Liberal Assembly approved the principle of tax-benefit integration as part of the 'Programme for Recovery'.[136] The party Council then established a committee, chaired by Guy Naylor, to work out plans in more detail, with expert input from Paish and his LSE colleague Alan Peacock. The Naylor Committee proposed a weekly cash allowance of 12/6 for each man, woman, and child, financed by a flat-rate income tax of 5/- on earned and 6/- on unearned income up to £600 per annum and the abolition of food subsidies.[137] This policy was approved by the 1950 Liberal Assembly, and later formed the basis of the party's submission to the Royal Commission on the Taxation of Profits and Income (1951–5).[138] In the short term it had little impact, but in a longer perspective it can be seen as a precursor of the negative income tax, tax credit, and basic income proposals which have figured prominently in social policy debate since the 1960s.

The problems of the housing market were if anything more difficult to unravel, though an ad hoc Liberal committee on rent restrictions, chaired by the London activist Granville Slack, was adamant that housing subsidies should be phased out. 'With full employment,' the committee argued, 'wages can be, and are in fact, sufficiently high for an economic rent to be paid, and subsidy by the taxpayer should be unnecessary.'[139] The committee also favoured the abolition of the patchwork of rent controls which had developed since the First World War, though this would have to await the

heavily on Honor Croome, 'Liberty, equality and full employment', *Lloyds Bank Review*, no. 13 (July 1949), 14–32.

[135] Juliet Rhys Williams, *Something to Look Forward To* (1943); Borthwick Institute for Archives, University of York, Rowntree papers, POV/3/18, Geoffrey Crowther to Seebohm Rowntree, 6 June 1944.

[136] *LM* (April 1949), 187.

[137] Surtax would be retained and a new supplementary tax imposed on incomes from £600 upwards: Liberal Party, *Reform of Income Tax and Social Security Payments: A Liberal Party Yellow Book* (1950).

[138] *LN*, 22 September 1950, 1; *MG*, 2 October 1950, 7; Cmd. 9015, *Royal Commission on the Taxation of Profits and Income. Second Report* (1954).

[139] Liberal Party, *Report of the Liberal Party Sub-Committee on the Rent Restrictions Acts and Housing Subsidies* (1948), 11.

resolution of the post-war housing shortage. In the longer term, Liberals were keen to promote owner-occupancy as part of their drive for 'ownership for all'. The 1948 Liberal Assembly approved proposals to give local authority tenants the right to buy their houses, and the party's Ownership for All Committee even suggested extending this right to private tenants.[140]

In social as in economic policy, the attitudes which the Liberal leadership developed in the late 1940s dovetailed with Conservative thinking—as expressed, for instance, in *One Nation* (1950)—and led the party to offer critical support to the Conservatives' conduct of affairs after 1951. Food subsidies were sharply reduced by R. A. Butler in his 1952 budget, with compensatory increases in family allowances and pensions, though (as some Liberals complained) he did not pursue a wider reform of the tax and benefit system.[141] Later in the decade the Liberals backed the 1956 Housing Subsidies Act, which restricted subsidies to slum clearance schemes, and the 1957 Rent Act, which decontrolled properties in England and Wales with a rateable value of more than £30 (£40 in London), though they made it clear that they would have preferred a more gradual and flexible approach to decontrol.[142]

The anti-statist trajectory of Liberal thinking on social welfare after 1945 culminated in the 1957 volume *The Unservile State*, in which a group of Liberal politicians and academics, organized by Elliott Dodds and including Grimond, Hutton, Peacock, and Wiles, pushed the idea of 'ownership for all' to its logical conclusion.[143] The book's tone was nuanced and realistic, but its implications radical and far-reaching. 'With the value they attach to self-direction', Dodds argued, Liberals should view the existing social services like 'crutches', which men and women could discard as they became able to provide 'welfare' for themselves.[144] In practice, as Wiles suggested, this meant that the welfare state could eventually be scaled back as real incomes and asset-ownership rose.[145] Peacock added that, in the

[140] *LM* (June 1948), 214; Scottish Liberal Party papers, 45, 'Report on Home-Ownership Submitted by the Ownership for All Committee', n.d. [November 1949].

[141] Hansard, HC (series 5) vol. 497, cols 1424–30 (12 March 1952); *LN*, 2 May 1952, 3.

[142] Hansard, HC (series 5) vol. 548, cols 2483–8 (15 February 1956); vol. 560, cols 1821–7 (21 November 1956); and vol. 567, cols 1477–82 (28 March 1957); *MG*, 4 February 1957, 4.

[143] Sir Alan Peacock has recalled that the Unservile State Group grew out of an unsuccessful meeting between Liberal politicians and economists at a Bayswater hotel in 1950: Alan Peacock, *Anxious to Do Good: Learning to be an Economist the Hard Way* (Exeter, 2010), 91–3.

[144] Elliott Dodds, 'Liberty and welfare', in George Watson (ed.), *The Unservile State: Essays in Liberty and Welfare* (1957), 13–26, at 18.

[145] Peter Wiles, 'Property and equality', in Watson (ed.), *Unservile State*, 88–109.

meantime, the state should focus on cash transfers wherever possible, and perhaps finance health and education through voucher systems.[146]

The Unservile State was an unofficial exercise in Liberal thought, not an official policy statement, but it was not wholly idiosyncratic, as this discussion has shown. Despite the Liberal Party's historic commitment to social reform, the limitations of state welfare provision had received sustained attention during the post-war decade. The extremes of poverty seemed to have been removed by full employment and social security; the task for the next generation, Jo Grimond thought in 1955, was to deal with the remaining pockets of poverty among pensioners and low earners, encourage wider home and share ownership, and generate the wealth needed to improve education and the other social services.[147] As the austerity of the 1940s gave way to growing affluence, Liberals hoped that the welfare state could soon be transformed into a more pluralistic welfare society.

THE FREE TRADE CONTROVERSY

Liberal Keynesian policies did not command universal assent within the Liberal Party during the late 1940s. As we have seen, many activists were alarmed by the prospect of removing controls and food subsidies, and left-wing Liberals such as Dingle Foot and Megan Lloyd George regarded the party's criticisms of the Attlee government as symptomatic of a right-ward drift. However, it was only after the 1950 general election that discontent and ill discipline gave way to concerted factional conflict over the party's direction. The catalyst for this conflict was a strident campaign against the party's support for the 1947 Agriculture Act, waged by diehard free traders.

The preamble to the party's 1936 constitution enshrined free trade as a central Liberal principle, but this left plenty of room for disagreement about what free trade meant. After 1945, the party revived its pre-war policy of removing all tariffs by stages over the lifetime of a five-year Parliament, starting with those on food and raw materials, and proposed to seek international agreement on the abolition or reduction of other trade restrictions—none of which was very controversial, though its feasibility was questioned by Liberal students such as Alan Share in the 1950s.[148] At Wilfrid Roberts' instigation, however, the parliamentary

[146] A. T. Peacock, 'Welfare in the Liberal state', in Watson (ed.), *Unservile State*, 113–30.

[147] National Library of Scotland, Jo Grimond papers (dep. 363), 15/10, untitled typescript by Grimond, n.d. [1955].

[148] *MG*, 5 March 1947, 6; for Share's campaign for a review of the free-trade policy see *LN*, 19 October 1956, 2, and correspondence in BLPES, McFadyean papers, 3/17.

party voted in favour of the system of guaranteed prices and assured markets embodied in the government's 1947 Agriculture Act. Roberts, as a farmer, was impressed by the Act's emphasis on nutritional needs, and felt that it pointed in 'the natural economic direction' by supporting livestock as well as cereal production.[149] Georgist and classical Liberal activists reacted with fury, and immediately began to agitate for a return to pure free-trade principles. By 1951, young candidates such as Bernard Dann were growing 'a little tired of the futile squabbling over whether we are a Free Trade Party'.[150] In fact, the squabbling had barely begun.

The campaign against guaranteed prices was initiated and run, not by the free traders of the 1930s, but by Oliver Smedley and S. W. Alexander—relative newcomers to the party who became parliamentary candidates in Saffron Walden and Ilford North respectively. Smedley was a highly effective platform orator, Alexander a financial journalist and owner of the *City Press* newspaper, and the two men complemented each other well. Smedley and Alexander espoused an extreme classical Liberalism, rejecting the welfare state, denouncing Keynesian policies, and demanding a return to the gold standard.[151] The United Nations and other international institutions were also repudiated. Smedley and his allies described themselves as 'radicals', since they resisted arbitrary power and went to the 'root' of social problems, and claimed to be more loyal Liberals than those who supported guaranteed prices.[152] At the same time, they also worked for free trade outside the Liberal Party, forming the Cheap Food League in August 1951 with Conservative and Labour allies.[153]

The core of Smedley and Alexander's support came from former members of the Liberal Liberty League, which merged into the Land Value Taxation League in the autumn of 1952, but they also drew backing from young candidates such as Roy Douglas and Peter Linfoot and developed a significant following within the London Liberal Party.[154] The economist Colin Clark provided valuable academic support, arguing that British agriculture could survive under free-trade conditions, though other neoliberals such as Arthur Seldon and Arthur and Barbara Shenfield seem to have kept their distance.[155]

[149] Hansard, HC (series 5) vol. 432, cols 657–65, at 659 (27 January 1947).

[150] *LN*, 9 February 1951, 3.

[151] See Oliver Smedley, *The Abominable No-Men: 'The Answer to Bevan, Beaverbrook, Beveridge and Butler'* (1952).

[152] *LN*, 24 July 1953, 2.

[153] *LN*, 31 August 1951, 4, and 13 March 1953, 2.

[154] For the demise of the Liberal Liberty League, see *L&L*, nos. 701–2 (October–November 1952), 122.

[155] For Clark, see *LN*, 8 January 1954, 2. The Shenfields were members of the committee which drafted the party's 'Radical Programme' in 1952, and Barbara Shenfield moved an official free-trade resolution at the 1952 Assembly which drew criticism from Smedley: *LN*, 4 April 1952, 1, and 23 May 1952, 3.

Mainstream Liberals meanwhile resented the way in which Smedley and Alexander had appropriated the free trade label. As Elliott Dodds protested in *Liberal News*,

> I was fighting for Free Trade long before Mr. Alexander attached himself to the Liberal Party. I shall continue to do so despite the handicap of propaganda which ignores both the difficulties that face us in restoring Free Trade and the problems that must arise in doing so.[156]

Other senior Liberals shared Dodds' view: Davies and Sinclair considered the Smedleyites extreme and misguided, and Fothergill warned that 'an exclusive sectional group' should not be allowed to dominate Liberal counsels.[157] In practice, there was never much risk that the faction would gain a general ascendancy. No Liberal Assembly was likely to vote for an end to economic management, a return to the gold standard, or withdrawal from the United Nations.

On the narrow issue of agricultural subsidies, however, the Smedleyites made a strong appeal to free-trade sentiment. All the classical criticisms of protection could be invoked: subsidies favoured one industry over others, sheltered inefficiency, and distorted the allocation of resources. 'If you really want guaranteed prices', Ronald Walker told delegates at one Assembly, 'you have no right to be here. All the arguments for them are protectionist.'[158] To this economic reasoning, the Smedleyites added civil libertarian concerns about the dispossession of farmers under the 1947 Act. The defenders of guaranteed prices, by contrast, emphasized the need to provide security for farmers and agricultural workers, argued that the world as a whole faced a growing food shortage, and claimed that the 1947 Act had kept retail prices down.[159] Perhaps unsurprisingly, the electoral implications of this debate were never far from the surface, as Liberal candidates for rural constituencies—especially in Devon and Cornwall—were alarmed by the prospect of fighting on an anti-subsidy platform.

The first set-piece debate over agriculture took place at the 1952 Assembly, and ended in defeat for the free traders. However, the executive agreed to sound out the opinions of the regional federations, six out of seven of which came down against guaranteed prices.[160] At the following year's Assembly in Ilfracombe, the executive backed a Reigate motion which called for guaranteed prices to be abolished, and after a stormy

156 *LN*, 13 November 1953, 2.

157 Clement Davies papers, J/3/13, Davies to Sinclair, 24 January 1950; *LN*, 24 April 1953, 3.

158 *LN*, 17 April 1953, 4.

159 *LN*, 12 October 1951, 2, and 23 May 1952, 3.

160 *MG*, 16 May 1952, 5.

debate this motion was carried, despite opposition from several MPs and candidates and a large delegation of Liberal students.[161] After the vote, Jeremy Thorpe seized the microphone to declare that West Country candidates could not accept a free-market agricultural policy; but repeated attempts to overturn it proved unsuccessful, and it would remain party policy for the rest of the decade.[162] In a sense, the Smedleyites' position was similar to that which the Georgists had faced for half a century: free trade and land value taxation could win wide support as stand-alone policies, but only a small minority of Liberals were prepared to accept the full implications of a classical or Georgist economic vision.

The divisions which emerged over free trade in the early 1950s were compounded by renewed controversy over co-ownership. Davies and other Liberal MPs had always been sceptical about the case for compulsion, whilst the Smedleyites were predictably hostile, and when the issue arose again in 1954 a majority of the LPO executive favoured a move to a more permissive approach.[163] The party's Economic Advisory Committee reinforced this scepticism with a provocative memorandum which argued that compulsory co-ownership would discourage entrepreneurship and investment.[164] An attempt to challenge compulsion at the 1954 Assembly narrowly failed, but Granville Slack was asked to chair a new, more representative committee, with a brief of reconciling conflicting views.

Though feelings ran high on both sides of the co-ownership debate, Slack's committee managed to produce a report which commanded broad acceptance within the party; this received almost unanimous endorsement from the Council and was adopted by the 1956 Assembly.[165] The compromise reached was that the party remained committed to the principle of compulsion, but would concentrate for the next five years on pressing for the removal of the obstacles to co-ownership which existed in the tax system and replacing them with positive incentives. Richard Wainwright, a Leeds accountant and future MP for Colne Valley, had proposed this course of action during the 1954 debate, and subsequently worked to develop proposals for Employee Savings Accounts—which would not be subject to income tax until money was withdrawn—into a main feature of

[161] *MG*, 9 April 1953, 2; *LN*, 17 April 1953, 3–4.

[162] *MG*, 11 April 1953, 1.

[163] Rasmussen, *Liberal Party*, 129–30.

[164] University of Bristol Special Collections, Mirfin papers, 6/11, 'Liberal Party and Co-Partnership', April 1954.

[165] *LN*, 16 December 1955, 1, and 5 October 1956, 2. The report was accompanied by a 'synopsis of agreement' signed by economists from both sides of the compulsion debate—George Allen, Graham Hutton, Frank Paish, and Peter Wiles—which set out the points on which they could agree: Liberal Party, *Interim Report of the Liberal Party Co-Ownership Committee* (1955).

Liberal policy.[166] From 1956 up to the early 1960s, Liberal MPs Donald Wade and Arthur Holt energetically sought to amend annual Finance Bills to introduce co-ownership incentives along these lines.[167]

The new approach to co-ownership which the Liberals took after 1956 was a sensible compromise which helped heal long-standing divisions over this issue. Even Dodds, indeed, was satisfied, since co-ownership could at last be preached without embarrassment by the Liberal leaders.[168] Nevertheless, the shift represented a clear retreat from the radicalism of 1948. Where compulsory co-ownership had held out the prospect of transforming capital–labour relations, tax incentives merely sought to nudge employers and workers towards greater cooperation.

THE RADICAL REFORM GROUP

One of the most striking characteristics of the Liberal Party in the late 1940s was the political and intellectual torpor of its left wing. With the partial exception of compulsory co-ownership, left-wing Liberals had little new to offer, and relied on a ritual anti-Conservatism and a selective reading of past policy statements to justify support for the Attlee government's policies. Megan Lloyd George and Dingle Foot, for instance, argued that the Yellow Book and *Full Employment in a Free Society* were 'the text books of modern Liberalism', and accused Davies of throwing over this accumulated wisdom in favour of 'ill-digested proposals' which could as easily have come from the Conservatives.[169] By the mid-1950s, most of the party's leading left wingers—Lloyd George, Foot, Wilfrid Roberts, and Edgar Granville—had defected to Labour, along with some rank-and-file activists who shared their views.

The Smedleyites' activities, however, had the unintended consequence of bringing a new Liberal left into being. Several weeks before the 1953 Assembly, a group of Liberal candidates from the Home Counties announced the formation of the Radical Reform Group, dedicated to defending 'the policy of social reform without socialism which Liberals have developed from 1908 onwards' against the advocates of 'pure laissez-faire'.[170] Peter Grafton, Desmond Banks, and

[166] Employee Savings Accounts were first proposed by George Copeman, editor of the journal *Business*. Wainwright summarized the party's proposals in *Own As You Earn: The Liberal Plan* (1958).

[167] See *LN*, 6 July 1956, 4; 10 July 1958, 4; 12 May 1960, 3; 16 June 1962, 3.

[168] *LN*, 8 June 1961, 4.

[169] MS. Bonham Carter 240, fols 160–3, 'Memorandum by Lady Megan Lloyd George & Mr Dingle Foot', 20 May 1950, at fol. 163.

[170] *MG*, 27 March 1953, 6.

A. J. F. Macdonald—who had briefly been MP for Roxburgh and Selkirk in 1950–1—were the group's driving spirits. As an early policy statement, *Radical Aims*, explained, its founders were

> concerned at the lack of enthusiasm in certain Liberal circles for the welfare society . . ., for full employment policies along the lines of that advocated by Lord Beveridge, for partnership in industry as set out in the 1948 Liberal Co-ownership proposals and for some form of assured prices for agriculture, approved in 1947 by all three political parties.[171]

Over time, the RRG would become the spearhead of the fight-back against Smedley and Alexander, but in its early days it found it difficult to rally left-Liberal opinion. One problem was that Liberal students such as Derick Mirfin and Timothy Joyce, who shared the RRG's hostility to the extreme free traders, thought it paid too little attention to the need for a competitive economy: as Mirfin wrote to Grafton,

> It is not enough to curse Smedley and still stagger on the blind Lady Megan tradition which imagines that it is enough to prate of progress and social welfare in order to be considered as a valid political theory.[172]

Others feared that the group would break the party's fragile unity and lead more of its members over to Labour.[173] Indeed, after losing the battle over guaranteed prices in 1953 and 1954, the RRG briefly became a non-party organization, and its first chairman, E. F. Allison, defected to Labour.[174] Only after it returned to the Liberal fold at the beginning of 1956 did the RRG really gain momentum. Under Desmond Banks' leadership, the RRG emphasized its loyalty to the Liberal cause, and won the confidence of senior figures such as Dodds, White, and Micklem; it also made a more consistent appeal to young candidates and students.[175] The group's standing in the party would be sealed in 1958, when Jo Grimond agreed to serve as its president.[176]

The ideological character of the RRG, like that of Radical Action a decade earlier, was always somewhat ambiguous, since its leaders were prone to conflate the Smedleyite campaign against state intervention with the free-market drift of party policy in general.[177] Mark Egan has

[171] Radical Reform Group, *Radical Aims: A Statement of Policy by the Radical Reform Group* (1954), 2.

[172] Mirfin papers, 1/11, Mirfin to Peter Grafton, 17 April 1953; see also *Ahead*, no. 20 (April 1954), 4.

[173] Mirfin papers, 3/1, Desmond Banks to Mirfin, 12 February 1956.

[174] *MG*, 18 April 1955, 3.

[175] Mirfin papers, 3/1, Banks to Mirfin, 12 February 1956. Dodds and Micklem had previously attended one of the RRG's first conferences: *MG*, 29 September 1953, 2.

[176] Mirfin papers, 3/1, RRG AGM minutes, 8 February 1958.

[177] For contemporary recognition of this ambiguity, see Paul Rose in *MG*, 23 April 1954, 8.

suggested that '[t]he RRG's ambitions were strictly limited to reaffirming Liberal Party policy, in the face of the laissez faire onslaught', and many Liberals seem to have viewed it in this light, as the involvement of Dodds, Micklem, and Deryck Abel implies.[178] Desmond Banks and some other leading members, however, had a more overtly left-Liberal agenda in mind. *Radical Aims* criticized 'Right-Wing Liberals' and *The Economist* for advocating policies which would produce higher unemployment, and argued that inflation should instead be restrained by winning the trade unions' confidence and introducing co-ownership.[179] Banks reiterated this point in later years, and felt that some members of the party were liable to exaggerate the deficiencies of the welfare state, a view which Derick Mirfin shared.[180] Banks was also discomfited by the emphasis which Frank Paish placed on the production of wealth rather than its distribution, and found the egalitarianism of Labour revisionists such as Anthony Crosland more appealing.[181]

The RRG was never a large organization—at its peak, it seems to have had about 200 members—and it had little impact on Liberal policy-making during the 1950s.[182] Nevertheless, it provided a significant indicator of ideological trends among the younger generation of Liberals. At a time when liberal Keynesian ideas shaped the thinking of the party leadership, the RRG helped to keep constructive and New Liberal arguments about the value of state action alive and to articulate a more radical reading of Keynes and Beveridge. The group thus prefigured the wider party's turn towards a more activist Liberalism in the 1960s.

CONCLUSION

The prevailing image of the Liberal Party under Clement Davies' leadership is one of division and confusion: a party without strategy or purpose, divided over its economic principles, and dominated by rival groups of 'faddists' who sought to impose unilateral free trade or compulsory co-ownership on the party's leaders. The evidence presented in this chapter shows that such an image is no more than half-accurate. Between the

[178] Mark Egan, *Coming into Focus: The Transformation of the Liberal Party, 1945–64* (Saarbrücken, 2009), 125.

[179] RRG, *Radical Aims*, 10–11, at 10. Significantly, the authors of this pamphlet acknowledged their debt to C. A. R. Crosland, *Britain's Economic Problem* (1953).

[180] *RRG Newsletter*, December 1957, 6–8; Mirfin papers, 3/1, Mirfin to Nathaniel Micklem, 23 April 1958.

[181] Mirfin papers, 3/1, Banks to Mirfin, 14 July 1956.

[182] Graham Lippiatt, 'Radical Reform Group', *JLH*, no. 67 (2010), 45–9.

extreme free traders and the RRG there stood a large centre ground, which included most of the party's MPs and office-holders, and in which libertarian and distributist arguments about the dangers of nationalization and planning became increasingly influential. The party's centre of gravity unquestionably moved rightward during the post-war decade, and its left wingers were justified in complaining of this. At the same time, it is important to emphasize that this 'drift to the right' took place within a broadly Keynesian policy framework, and that the Liberal leadership remained committed to demand-management policies, along with the retention—at least for the time being—of the welfare state and most of the nationalized industries. Liberal MPs, too, were generally committed to guaranteed agricultural prices, despite the agitation of grassroots free traders. There is no justification for conflating the free-market Keynesianism adopted by Clement Davies after 1947 with the dogmatic classical Liberalism of Smedley and Alexander.

The liberal Keynesianism of the late 1940s and early 1950s was a credible attempt to apply Liberal principles to Britain's post-war situation in the light of contemporary economic knowledge. If the Liberals had still been a major party this policy might have served them well, though we may question whether Roy Harrod fully appreciated the difficulty of the Attlee government's task and whether Frank Paish's remedy for inflation would have been effective. In electoral terms, however, liberal Keynesianism contributed relatively little to the party's pursuit of revival until after the 1955 general election. In one sense, of course, it is hard to see how any policy could have prevented the Liberals' marginalization in this period. The Attlee government's success in maintaining full employment and extending the welfare state enabled Labour to consolidate its working-class support, whilst the Conservatives rebuilt their predominantly middle-class coalition by stressing their moderation and modernity.[183] The close-fought elections of 1950 and 1951 seem to have marked the zenith of this class polarization. One does not need to believe that the Liberals were entirely at the mercy of the blind forces of electoral sociology to suspect that the conditions for a significant national revival lay outside the party's hands in these years.

In another sense, though, the content of Liberal policy necessarily shaped the party's political direction. If the Liberal Party had stuck with the interventionist Keynesianism of *Full Employment in a Free Society*, as its left wingers would presumably have preferred, it might have moved closer to Labour during the late 1940s and helped prolong the Attlee government's

[183] David Butler and Donald Stokes, *Political Change in Britain: Forces Shaping Electoral Choice* (1969), 247–74; John Bonham, *The Middle Class Vote* (1954).

existence. Instead, the Liberals' reversion to free-market policies after 1945 both reflected and reinforced the anti-planning mood of the austerity years, and helped legitimize the tendency for Liberals and ex-Liberals—including Gilbert Murray and Graham Hutton—to vote Conservative.[184] To progressive and working-class voters, meanwhile, the party's anti-statist rhetoric too often made it appear conservative and bourgeois, as Sir Percy Harris complained after failing to regain his seat in Bethnal Green.[185] Liberal candidates could win protest votes in by-elections, as the experience of the 1955 Parliament showed, but this hardly added up to a coherent political strategy. It would fall to Jo Grimond, who succeeded Davies as leader in the autumn of 1956, to articulate a more convincing vision of the party's purpose.

[184] MS. Bonham Carter 171, fols 146–7, Bonham Carter to Foot, 28 April 1950.

[185] Parliamentary Archives, Harris papers, HRS/22, 'The General Election of 1950', by Harris, n.d. [1950].

7

Jo Grimond and the Liberal Revival, 1956–64

The Liberal Party's revival under Jo Grimond's leadership during the late 1950s and early 1960s was a seminal episode in modern British politics. After years in the political wilderness, the Liberals returned to public prominence, gained new support, and started winning by-elections. Indeed, Eric Lubbock's sensational victory at Orpington in March 1962 raised hopes of regaining major-party status and returning to government. In practice, these ambitions proved wildly over-optimistic, as the party won just nine seats—though more than three million votes—at the 1964 general election. Nevertheless, the Grimond revival placed the Liberals back on the political map as a significant third party. A new generation of activists swelled membership from 76,000 in 1953 to 351,000 in 1963 and helped build a new local government base, especially in small-town and suburban England, and the party's organization and income grew correspondingly.[1] Grimond renewed the party's identity as a progressive movement, which aimed to supplant the Labour Party as the fulcrum of the centre-left, and abandoned the pacts with the Conservatives at Huddersfield and Bolton in the early 1960s. It is a commonplace of Liberal historiography that under his leadership 'social Liberalism' was reborn.

Jo Grimond was renowned for his belief that 'the content of politics' was 'all-important', and—as Geoffrey Sell has noted—stands out among twentieth-century Liberal leaders for his interest in ideas.[2] He used funding from the Rowntree Trust to establish a Liberal Research Department, and recruited a host of academics and outside experts to serve on policy panels; several of these, such as Michael Fogarty and Christopher Layton, later

[1] For membership, see William J. L. Wallace, 'The Liberal Revival: The Liberal Party in Britain, 1955–1966' (Cornell University D.Phil. thesis, 1968), 268, and *LN*, 19 March 1964, 1; for national organization, see Wallace, 'Liberal Revival', 180–244.

[2] Joseph Grimond, *The Liberal Challenge* (1963), 7; Geoffrey Sell, 'Liberal Revival: Jo Grimond and the Politics of British Liberalism, 1956–1967' (London Ph.D. thesis, 1996), 25.

became parliamentary candidates. The Unservile State Group, the Oxford Liberal Group (founded by Oxford dons in 1959), and the New Orbits Group (formed by students and Young Liberals in 1960) also produced a steady stream of ideas, some of which Grimond took up in his books *The Liberal Future* (1959) and *The Liberal Challenge* (1963).[3] Existing Liberal advisers and party committees remained important, but Grimond tended to be impatient with the party's policy-making process, and had a habit of flying kites which he assumed his colleagues would follow.

The contribution which policy made to the Liberal Party's revival should not, of course, be overstated, since a series of external factors—the mood of national (or elite) introspection which followed the Suez crisis, the growth of consumer affluence, and various Labour and Conservative missteps—helped create conditions in which the party could gain a better hearing. 'This new atmosphere', Grimond recognized, was 'much more congenial to Liberalism' than that of the early post-war years.[4] Local organization also played a significant role, as Mark Egan has shown, so it may not have mattered that the electorate's knowledge of Liberal policy was relatively low.[5] '[F]ew Liberal supporters', William Wallace has concluded from polling evidence, 'had much if any detailed knowledge of their party's policies, beyond a vague general image of a youthful and modern but moderate party'.[6] Nevertheless, policy fulfilled some important functions for Grimond's party. It helped shape the party's image, fleshing out its claims to be progressive and modern; it persuaded opinion-formers, including press commentators, to take the Liberals more seriously; and it aided the party's efforts to recruit and motivate grassroots activists.[7]

As leader, Grimond reshaped the Liberal Party's ideological orientation, marginalizing its extreme free traders and engaging sympathetically with contemporary social democratic thinking. Grimond and his colleagues embraced the 'soft left' diagnosis of Britain's relative economic decline popularized by journalists such as Andrew Shonfield and Michael Shanks, and sought to articulate a distinctively Liberal remedy, based on a reassessment of Britain's place in the world, greater investment in infrastructure and public services, and the promotion of competition and innovation in industry. Over time, the Liberals' left turn would pave the way for cooperation with moderate elements in the Labour Party under David Steel's leadership, in the form of the 1977–8 Lib–Lab Pact and the SDP–Liberal

[3] Tudor Jones, *The Revival of British Liberalism: From Grimond to Clegg* (Basingstoke, 2011), 9.

[4] Grimond, *Liberal Challenge*, 19.

[5] Mark Egan, *Coming into Focus: The Transformation of the Liberal Party, 1945–64* (Saarbrücken, 2009), 230–6.

[6] Wallace, 'Liberal Revival', 382.

[7] Egan, *Coming into Focus*, 143–5.

Alliance. However, there are some striking paradoxes here. One is that Grimond himself frequently viewed the state with suspicion, and never had much sympathy for Labour. The liberal Keynesianism of the 1950s certainly seems to have come more naturally to him than his 1960s enthusiasm for indicative planning. Another paradox is that it is not clear that the heavy involvement of experts necessarily made for better policy. As *The Times* noted, Liberal policy exercises in this period sometimes had 'a fly-paper quality': 'ideas which happen to be buzzing around at the time tend to get stuck on'.[8] With the benefit of hindsight, we can see that assumptions about the efficacy of indicative planning were liable to obscure both the difficulties which rapid growth would present—most obviously, for sterling—and the fact that hard spending choices would still need to be made.

This chapter explores the development of Liberal economic policy under Grimond's leadership, up to the 1964 general election. It shows that the liberal Keynesianism of the late 1940s and 1950s was supplanted after 1959 by a more planning-oriented policy, which was designed to reverse Britain's relative economic decline by promoting faster growth. The constructive tradition was partly rehabilitated, though Grimond also emphasized the value of competitive markets and argued that the state should seek to harmonize economic interests through persuasion rather than coercion. This shift had significant implications for wider political debate. In the late 1950s, the Liberals' improving by-election performances added to pressure on the Conservative government to conquer inflation and defuse a growing 'middle-class revolt'. By contrast, Liberal successes in the early 1960s amplified declinist concerns about slow growth and stagnation, and reinforced the policy imperatives which were already pushing the government towards indicative planning and higher public spending.[9]

THE ECONOMICS OF JO GRIMOND

From the very beginning of his political career, Jo Grimond possessed a strong sense of what political Liberalism ought to be. As Peter Barberis has pointed out, Grimond's educational background at Balliol College, Oxford—where he studied PPE in the 1930s—would have brought him

[8] *The Times*, 10 September 1963, 11.

[9] On the Conservative government's 'great reappraisal' after 1959, see Samuel Brittan, *The Treasury under the Tories, 1951–1964* (Harmondsworth, 1964); Hugh Pemberton, *Policy Learning and British Governance in the 1960s* (Basingstoke, 2004); and Glen O'Hara, *From Dreams to Disillusionment: Economic and Social Planning in 1960s Britain* (Basingstoke, 2007).

into close contact with T. H. Green's idealist Liberalism, with its emphasis on self-development, civic participation, and the common good.[10] Perhaps because of this, Grimond consistently regarded Liberalism as a humanitarian creed, informed by empirical judgments, and was impatient with attempts to define it in terms of economic principles. In a 1953 article for *Political Quarterly*, for instance, he argued that the Liberal Party had declined from the late nineteenth century onwards precisely because its members 'forgot that man is a social animal who has always lived in communities', and relaxed their efforts to ameliorate poverty and injustice by state action.[11] Unsurprisingly, then, Grimond was deeply hostile to the Smedleyites, and defended guaranteed prices at the 1953 Assembly on the grounds that Liberals should be concerned above all with the lives of human beings.[12] He was also keen to broaden the Liberal message beyond economic issues, and to identify the party more strongly with progressive positions on foreign policy, decolonization, and European integration.

Yet Grimond was far from indifferent towards economics. He had gained a decent foundation in the discipline at Balliol, and put this to good use in later life; as a young MP he often spoke on economic issues.[13] Grimond's dynamic conception of Liberalism meant that he was not opposed in principle to interventionist measures: in the mid-1940s he backed Beveridge's full employment policy, and later he pressed for the creation of a development board which would build roads, piers, and housing in the Highlands.[14] Nevertheless, his revulsion at Marxist doctrine made him receptive to anti-statist arguments, as he later recalled in his memoirs:

> I was convinced that Socialism as an all-embracing creed, and that is what it claims to be, was wrong—morally wrong and practically inefficient. . . I believed that only individuals had any ultimate value and that therefore any system such as communism, which treated them as means and subordinated them to the state, must be evil.[15]

During his years as Clement Davies' chief whip, Grimond became known for his forthright espousal of liberal Keynesian views, tinged with a belief in the significance of the money supply. This remained the case during the

[10] Peter Barberis, *Liberal Lion. Jo Grimond: A Political Life* (2005), 13.

[11] Joseph Grimond, 'The principles of Liberalism', *Political Quarterly*, xxiv (1953), 236–42, at 237.

[12] *MG*, 11 April 1953, 2.

[13] Michael McManus, *Jo Grimond: Towards the Sound of Gunfire* (Edinburgh, 2001), 26, 99–100.

[14] BLPES, Beveridge papers, VI/14/2/27, Grimond to C. P. Fothergill, 11 July 1945; McManus, *Jo Grimond*, 93–4.

[15] Jo Grimond, *Memoirs* (1979), 152.

early part of his leadership. Like his predecessor, he developed an effective working relationship with Frank Paish and broadly echoed Paish's policy recommendations. Grimond also met relatively frequently with journalists such as Donald Tyerman of *The Economist* and Donald McLachlan of the *Daily Telegraph*.[16] In economic matters, at least, these men seem to have exerted more influence on Grimond's thinking during the 1950s than his more progressive associates, such as Alastair Hetherington of the *Manchester Guardian* or the members of the Radical Reform Group.

Grimond's nuanced policy views enabled him to command support from the bulk of the Liberal Party, the Smedleyites being a predictable exception. Just as importantly, he was convinced that the times were ripe for a Liberal revival, since social changes were beginning to dissolve the class divisions on which the two-party system rested. The future of British politics, he argued, rested with 'the new technicians of the atomic era', who would 'live in a land between the old working and the old middle-classes'.[17] Grimond also floated from an early stage the idea of a party realignment. A conservative party, of course, would always exist, but there was no reason why socialists should dominate the British left in perpetuity. He hoped that the Liberal Party might become the core of a non-socialist progressive movement, which moderate Labour elements and progressive Conservatives could join. Ultimately, he declared, the Liberals aimed 'to replace the Labour Party as the Progressive wing of politics in this country'.[18]

In his first year as leader, Grimond worked to sharpen the Liberals' identity as 'the only Progressive Non-Socialist Party' (a slogan added to the *Liberal News*' masthead in July 1957) and develop his own public profile. At one level, he aimed to demonstrate the party's responsibility and moderation, providing 'an alternative which people who had voted Conservative could contemplate without alarm'.[19] At the same time, two bold policy moves were intended to underline the party's radicalism and relevance. Firstly, Grimond declared that Britain should abandon its independent nuclear deterrent in favour of participation in a shared western nuclear capability.[20] Quite apart from pacific motives, and the hope of stimulating multilateral disarmament, Grimond argued that abandoning the British H-bomb would save the Exchequer £200,000,000, and so help relieve inflation. Secondly, with encouragement from his mother-in-law

[16] National Library of Scotland, Jo Grimond papers (dep. 363), 1, engagement diaries of Jo Grimond, 1952–60.

[17] *LN*, 29 July 1955, 1.

[18] *LN*, 20 November 1958, 2.

[19] Grimond, *Memoirs*, 201.

[20] *LN*, 5 April 1957, 1. On Liberal attitudes to this policy, see Jorgen Scott Rasmussen, *The Liberal Party: A Study of Retrenchment and Revival* (1965), 123–8.

Violet Bonham Carter, Grimond steered the party towards support for British membership of the new European Common Market.[21] Free traders were alarmed by the Common Market's external tariff, but most of the party accepted the argument that political integration was intrinsically desirable, and that the grouping could become a first step towards wider trade liberalization if British Liberals were involved in it.[22] Over time, indeed, the prospect of Common Market membership provided a useful means of marginalizing the Smedleyites and reconciling the party as a whole to agricultural subsidies. The anti-Marketeers would eventually be routed at the 1960 Assembly.[23]

EXPLOITING THE 'MIDDLE-CLASS REVOLT', 1955–9

Grimond's vision of realignment required the Liberal Party to win 'converts' and 'allies' from liberal-minded voters across the political spectrum, but especially on the centre-left.[24] Grimond wanted to appeal to 'the frustrated idealists of the Labour Party', as well as to the 'many Tories who are horrified by Suez, Cyprus, Nyasaland and the treatment of [Nigel] Nicolson'—the Conservative MP for Bournemouth East and Christchurch who had been deselected after rebelling over Suez.[25] As nuclear weapons, decolonization, and Common Market entry became more salient, Grimond argued, the political agenda was moving on to Liberal terrain, while the Labour Party, obsessed with public ownership, was becoming a spent force.[26] Nevertheless, the Liberals had to gain electoral traction if they wanted to be taken seriously, so Grimond was happy to maintain a political posture during the 1955 Parliament which reaped its largest rewards among the discontented middle class.

The Economist and Oscar Hobson had both spotted the potential for the Liberals to exploit a middle-class revolt, and the party's 1955 election campaign seems to have been geared to this end.[27] Tellingly, its only television broadcast featured Mr and Mrs Hastings, a middle-aged, middle-class couple who had usually voted Conservative, putting questions to Frank

[21] Malcolm Baines, 'The Survival of the British Liberal Party, 1932–1959' (Oxford D.Phil. thesis, 1989), 117.

[22] For instance, Sir Arthur Comyns Carr in *LN*, 13 October 1960, 2.

[23] This episode is discussed in detail by Muriel Burton, 'The Making of Liberal Party Policy, 1945–1980' (Reading Ph.D. thesis, 1983), 230–322.

[24] *LN*, 22 April 1955, 1.

[25] *LN*, 24 September 1959, 6–7, at 6.

[26] *LN*, 9 July 1959, 1.

[27] *The Economist*, 1 May 1954, 355–6; *NC*, 13 June 1955, 2.

Byers and the cricket commentator (and Liberal candidate) John Arlott.[28] In by-elections, there was even more scope to harness protest votes against the rising cost of living. Grimond made this appeal most explicitly at the Torquay by-election in December 1955, where he spoke for Peter Bessell:

> Let there be no doubt that a continuance of a Conservative Government under the present leadership will mean the extinction of the middle classes and grave hardship to those who are not highly organised . . .
>
> A by-election gives the people an opportunity to express its dissatisfaction with the current behaviour of the Government even if they have not yet made up their minds that the Party in power should be changed. There is no question whatever of removing the Conservative Party from power. There is a wonderful opportunity, however, of saying to them in unmistakable language that if they want to retain the confidence of the people they must honour their pledges and bring some new thought on our vital problems.[29]

The Liberals' improving by-election performances during the 1955 Parliament are best understood in this frame. At Hereford in 1956, Gloucester and Ipswich in 1957, and Rochdale and Torrington in 1958, rising inflation figured as a major issue, and Liberal candidates criticized the government for failing to tame it.[30] A detailed NOP poll at Rochdale found that the Liberals' new support came mainly from ex-Conservatives and disproportionately involved female voters, who tended to be especially concerned about the cost of living.[31] Strikingly, too, as Figure 7.1 shows, the Liberals' Gallup Poll rating closely tracked the inflation rate from 1957 onwards. Conservative ministers and strategists certainly viewed the Liberals' success as part of a larger middle-class revolt, and noted that Liberal support fell away sharply in 1958–9 as inflationary pressures receded.[32]

The Liberals' crusade against inflation helped place the party back on the political stage. Mark Bonham Carter's victory at Torrington, especially, compensated for the 1957 loss of Carmarthen (which had been won for Labour by Megan Lloyd George following Hopkin Morris' death) and allowed Grimond to claim that the party was growing again. Clearly,

[28] *MG*, 20 May 1955, 16.

[29] *LN*, 9 December 1955, 1.

[30] *LN*, 3 February 1956, 1, 6 September 1957, 1, and 11 October 1957, 1; Bodleian Library, Oxford, MS. Balfour 30/4, 'Rochdale', 14 February 1958, and 'Torrington and a Liberal Revival', 27 March 1958.

[31] Bodleian Library, Conservative Party Archive, CRD 2/21/5, 'An Analysis of the Voting in the Rochdale By-Election', NOP report for Conservative Central Office, n.d. [February 1958].

[32] E. H. H. Green, 'The Conservative Party, the state and the electorate, 1945–64', in Jon Lawrence and Miles Taylor (eds), *Party, State and Society: Electoral Behaviour in Britain since 1820* (Aldershot, 1997), 176–200, at 192–3; Conservative Party Archive, CRD 2/21/5, 'Report of Public Opinion' by David Dear, 9 October 1958.

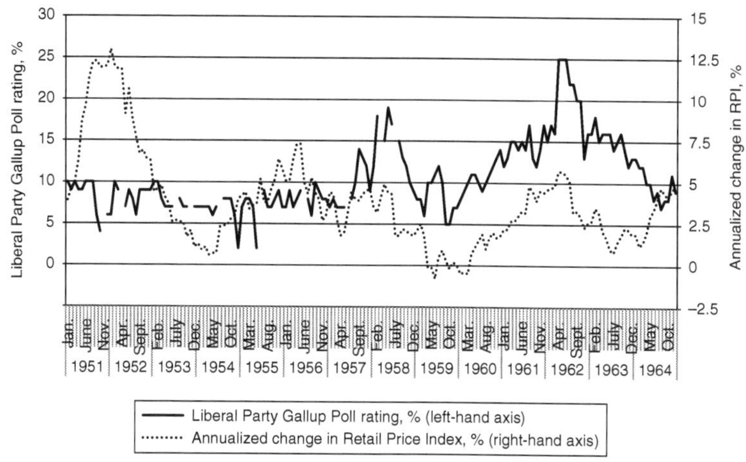

Fig. 7.1. Liberal Party Gallup Poll ratings and RPI inflation, 1951–1964.

however, there was no long-term future for Liberalism in appealing to the disaffected middle class, as Grimond readily acknowledged:

> The fact is that we are a progressive party or we are nothing. We shall never get and we do not want the die-hard Tory vote. They have a perfect right to their opinions, and they are invariably ignorant.[33]

As the 1959 general election approached, then, Grimond began a subtle repositioning, and stepped up his rhetoric about replacing the Labour Party. Although the Liberals remained concerned about the cost of living, they focussed increasingly on appealing to 'the left of the political rainbow' on issues like defence, the Common Market, and co-ownership in industry.[34] For this election, the party had two aims. Its tactical objective was to win more seats in Parliament by targeting winnable constituencies, mostly in rural areas, such as North Devon, North Cornwall, Anglesey, Hereford, and Inverness. Anti-inflationary rhetoric was likely to play relatively well in these areas, and Liberals privately seem to have hoped for six or seven gains.[35] The strategic objective, meanwhile, was to start winning over progressive voters more generally, and 'to assert ourselves'—as Frank Byers put it—'as the real, effective challenge to Toryism'.[36]

[33] *LN*, 24 September 1959, 7. [34] *LN*, 9 July 1959, 1.
[35] *LN*, 15 October 1959, 1, 3; Conservative Party Archive, CCO 3/5/94, A. Bowen-Gotham to C. F. R. Bagnall, 10 April 1959.
[36] *LN*, 15 October 1959, 3.

The Liberal campaign was a qualified strategic triumph but a tactical failure. With falling inflation, growing prosperity, and a huge publicity budget, the Conservatives were well placed to win a third term, but the Liberal vote more than doubled to 1,600,000. The Liberals made most progress in southern England, the Midlands, and the London and Manchester suburbs, where they seem to have taken votes away from Labour, and there is some evidence that the party profited from the spread of affluence.[37] Labour's emphatic defeat certainly appeared to confirm Grimond's argument that socialist policies had little appeal to the new middle class. However, the Liberals did worst in their target constituencies, and remained marooned on six seats overall, as Jeremy Thorpe's victory in North Devon was offset by the loss of Torrington to the Conservatives. *The Guardian* concluded that the Liberal revival had received a 'gentle push' from the electorate, rather than the 'catapult' for which Grimond had hoped.[38]

Despite this disappointment, Grimond moved on to the next stage in his plan. On the weekend after the election, he used an interview in *The Observer* to call on moderate Labour elements to join the Liberals in a new movement, in order to make progressive opinion 'more united and effective'.[39] As Labour descended into internecine conflict over Clause IV, Grimond reached out to that party's revisionist wing and began to advocate cooperation around a common programme. With Hugh Gaitskell as party leader, and the Liberals still electorally weak, most Labour politicians were unreceptive to these overtures, and no significant realignment would materialize for more than twenty years. Nevertheless, Grimond's desire to attract support from moderate progressives, both in the Labour Party and in the electorate at large, helped set the context for Liberal policy development in the 1960s.

PLANNING FOR GROWTH

By the late 1950s, the liberal Keynesianism which Liberals and Conservatives had espoused for the previous ten years was going out of fashion. If the overheating boom of 1955 had made R. A. Butler seem incompetent, the disinflationary policy that followed proved unpopular, and its most forthright proponent, Peter Thorneycroft, was easy to caricature as a reactionary. Butler, in his earlier optimism, had articulated the goal of doubling Britain's

[37] For suggestive evidence of Liberal progress among affluent workers, see *The Guardian*, 29 October 1959, 22, and 17 November 1959, 8; and Mark Abrams and Richard Rose, *Must Labour Lose?* (Harmondsworth, 1960), 43.

[38] *The Guardian*, 10 October 1959, 6.

[39] *The Observer*, 11 October 1959, 1.

living standards in twenty or twenty-five years, but industrial production stagnated between 1955 and 1958, and it seemed that economic growth was being sacrificed to the conquest of inflation and the maintenance of external stability. Relative economic decline emerged as a central theme of political debate in this period, as Jim Tomlinson has shown.[40] Economic journalists, led by Andrew Shonfield of *The Observer*, played an important role in this process by drawing attention to Britain's slow growth rate in comparison with her continental rivals.[41] By the turn of the 1960s these economic arguments were embedded in a wider 'state-of-the-nation' literature, typified by Michael Shanks' *The Stagnant Society* (1961), which linked slow growth with Britain's perceived social and cultural conservatism, the enduring dominance of the 'establishment', and the persistence of class divisions and restrictive practices in British industry.[42]

Among the first wave of declinist literature, Andrew Shonfield's 1958 analysis of *British Economic Policy Since the War* was perhaps particularly influential; like Shanks' book it was published as a Penguin Special. Shonfield attributed Britain's growth problem to the government's preoccupation with the defence of sterling, its habit of curtailing investment when faced with balance of payments crises, and the strain which large defence spending and other external payments placed on the economy. As a solution, he argued, the government should take a political decision to prioritize growth, and develop a five-year plan to double Britain's growth rate by raising productive investment and setting production targets for industry. Balance of payments difficulties would be prevented by reducing overseas commitments and reviving exchange controls; inflationary pressures could be dealt with through a wages policy, introduced for a defined period by agreement with the TUC.[43]

The idea of planning for growth gained currency most rapidly among Oxbridge-based economists and Labour politicians, who regarded inflation primarily as a cost-push phenomenon and had always been sceptical of monetary fine-tuning. The Labour Party, indeed, fought the 1959 election on a platform of 'planned expansion' which largely followed Shonfield's line.[44] However, young Liberal activists inside and outside the

[40] Jim Tomlinson, *The Politics of Decline: Understanding Post-War Britain* (Harlow, 2000), 9–29.

[41] Glen O'Hara, '"This is what growth does": British views of the European economies in the prosperous "golden age" of 1951–73', *Journal of Contemporary History*, xliv (2009), 697–718.

[42] Matthew Grant, 'Historians, the Penguin Specials and the "state-of-the-nation" literature, 1958–64', *CBH*, xvii (2003), 29–54.

[43] Andrew Shonfield, *British Economic Policy Since the War* (Harmondsworth, 1958).

[44] *Labour Party General Election Manifestos, 1900–1997*, ed. Iain Dale (2000), 91–101.

Radical Reform Group were also receptive to this analysis. As we have seen, the RRG's 1954 pamphlet *Radical Aims* criticized Frank Paish's deflationary approach, and urged that inflation should instead be tackled through co-ownership and wage restraint. When Peter Wiles judged essays on 'Inflation' in a competition for young Liberals in 1956, he found that these views were widespread:

> Certain Party circles should be dismayed at the emphasis on State control in almost all entries, to the neglect of the quantity of money and, even more so, Free Trade. If this is what the younger generation thinks, Liberal policy is in for a change.[45]

In similar vein, the young candidate Evan Richards argued that the true Liberal cure for inflation was to raise the national income and link wage rates to productivity.[46] Richards also advocated a twenty-year programme of 'specific industrial and social measures', focussing on fuel and power, rail electrification, road-building, and coastal defences, which would give the nation a positive purpose and revive 'the spirit of the great Yellow Book'.[47]

Shonfield's analysis involved a significant departure from the Liberal Party's existing policy, but it commended itself to Grimond and his colleagues for several reasons. Firstly, it fitted well with the party's geopolitical vision for Britain, which involved abandoning Great Power pretensions, reducing defence spending, and engaging with continental Europe. Secondly, many Liberals were already concerned by Britain's slow growth rate—the subject of Graham Hutton's lecture to the 1957 Liberal Summer School—and were impressed by suggestions that fine-tuning was not working.[48] The Radcliffe Committee's 1959 report seemed to provide authoritative support for the latter point, at least as far as monetary policy was concerned.[49] Thirdly, the Liberals were already committed to higher investment in several fields, such as road-building, on which a party committee chaired by Peter Bessell had recommended spending an extra £750,000,000 over the next decade.[50] The Shonfield approach suggested there was no reason to restrain this investment for macroeconomic reasons. Finally, a growth-oriented policy rescued Liberals from the uncomfortable position of advocating a deliberate rise in unemployment. This

[45] Parliamentary Archives, Graham White papers, WHI/15/4/70, 'Ramsay Muir Memorial Prizes', by P. J. D. Wiles, 15 July 1956.

[46] *LN*, 29 March 1957, 2.

[47] *LN*, 15 July 1955, 1.

[48] For Hutton's address, see *LN*, 9 August 1957, 1; for appreciation of the limits of fine-tuning, see Grimond, *Memoirs*, 211.

[49] Cmnd. 827, *Report of Committee on the Working of the Monetary System* (1959).

[50] *LN*, 15 November 1957, 3.

was the natural corollary of Paish's approach, but it had never been easy to stomach. When unemployment rose to more than 600,000—roughly 3 per cent of the workforce—in winter 1958–9, Liberal MPs took fright and called for measures to reduce it. Unemployment was 'a human tragedy', Mark Bonham Carter pointed out, as well as an economic problem.[51]

New political imperatives, a changing intellectual climate, and generational turnover within the Liberal Party together prompted Grimond to embrace the vogue for growth. During 1960 he began to emphasize the need for higher public investment, and used a pamphlet entitled *Let's Get On With It* to echo John Kenneth Galbraith's complaint that private opulence was coexisting with public squalor.[52] At the same time, Grimond recast his criticism of prestige projects like the British nuclear deterrent, arguing not that they caused inflation but that they took resources away from more necessary uses. The crucial shift to indicative planning, however, came in an April 1961 pamphlet, *Growth not Grandeur*, drafted for Grimond by the party's new research director, Harry Cowie.[53] The pamphlet proposed a 5 per cent growth target, an independent growth agency, and production targets for industry on the French model, as part of a general drive for modernization; Grimond apparently demurred at this interventionist approach, but signed the pamphlet anyway.[54] Young activists such as Frank Ware and Patrick Furnell joined Cowie in pressing indicative planning on Grimond, and acted as out-riders for the policy within the party, while more senior radicals like Desmond Banks, who chaired the LPO executive from 1961 to 1963, were also enthusiastic.[55] At the 1961 Assembly in Edinburgh, delegates approved a resolution calling for a five-year plan by an 'overwhelming majority', despite opposition from Heather Harvey, one of the party's treasurers, and the veteran electoral reformer Enid Lakeman.[56] With one bound, *The Guardian* enthused, the Liberals had 'moved decisively to the Left', and 'finally buried their unreconstructed Gladstonians'.[57]

From the Edinburgh Assembly up to the 1964 general election, and indeed for the rest of the 1960s, Liberal economic policy was framed around growth and indicative planning. The extent of the party's theoretical shift was rarely acknowledged, but it is significant that the

51 *LN*, 12 March 1959, 1; see also Arthur Holt in *LN*, 26 February 1959, 1.

52 *The Observer*, 29 May 1960, 8; Jo Grimond, *Let's Get On With It* (1960).

53 Interview with Harry Cowie, 26 September 2012.

54 Jo Grimond, *Growth not Grandeur* (1961); Barberis, *Liberal Lion*, 105.

55 Frank Ware, *5 Year Plan: Social Objectives, Industrial Growth, Taxation Reform* (1961); *LN*, 13 April 1961, 2, and 8 June 1961, 5.

56 *LN*, 28 September 1961, 4–5, 8, at 5.

57 *The Guardian*, 25 September 1961, 8.

Economic Advisory Committee was disbanded, and that Grimond named Christopher Layton, *The Economist*'s expert on European cooperation, as the party's new economic spokesman. The reservations about planning which Liberals had held since the 1940s seem to have evaporated. It is therefore worth considering in detail the character of the party's new programme.

THE DIMENSIONS OF LIBERAL PLANNING

On the centre and right of British politics, the memory of the Attlee government cast a long shadow over the idea of planning. Despite its superficial appeal, state planning in practice seemed to be austere, wasteful, and coercive, bearing out the theoretical criticisms offered by Hayek and others; Grimond, indeed, spent most of the 1950s encouraging this impression. When the Liberals turned back to planning in the 1960s, therefore, they took pains to emphasize how their plans differed from the socialist variant. Liberal plans would be oriented towards growth, rather than restriction; they would respect private enterprise and promote competition; and they would guide economic development along broad lines, instead of attempting detailed direction.[58]

The new Liberal planners self-consciously identified with earlier interventionists. 'Economic planning is not new to the Liberal party', Patrick Furnell pointed out. 'It was there in the Yellow Book of 1928; it re-appeared in Beveridge's "Full Employment in a Free Society". Now it needs to be brought up to date.'[59] In their emphasis on institutions, government's coordinating role, and the need to plan ahead, the new planners stood firmly in the constructive tradition, whilst the idea that the state should articulate the public interest, set positive goals for the community, and hold the ring between different sectional groups broadly echoed New Liberal thinking. Furnell, indeed, cited T. H. Green in support of the view that the 'community interest' required a national incomes policy.[60] At the same time, Grimond and his colleagues continued to conceive the state's role as one of providing a framework for economic activity, and many of the fields in which they advocated greater public spending, such as roads and education, had been acknowledged as suitable ones for state action by the classical economists. The planners' innovation lay in applying the concept of a framework to production and wage decisions. Lippmann and Hayek had argued that the state

[58] See especially Grimond, *Liberal Challenge*, 137–54.

[59] *LN*, 8 June 1961, 5.

[60] *LN*, 7 September 1961, 5.

should lay down rules of the road; Furnell now asked why it should not set 'a Highway code for incomes'.[61]

France, with its enviable growth record, provided the main model for the Liberals' planning proposals, although as Glen O'Hara has pointed out Britons often had a sketchy understanding of what French planning involved.[62] As one *Liberal News* contributor explained it, the French system of indicative planning was designed to focus the nation's attention on the need for higher output—'psychological factors are far more important than mere machinery'—and to persuade sectional interests 'to pool their efforts for the common good'.[63] At the heart of the system was the Commissariat du Plan, which organized the process of consultation between firms, government, and trade unions and set production targets in the light of a national target for economic growth. The French state backed up the plan by using its control of public investment, along with tax incentives, loans, and guarantees to private firms, to channel capital into priority sectors. Grimond called for a similar growth agency to be established in Britain, and welcomed the creation of the National Economic Development Council by Selwyn Lloyd, but emphasized that the government had to take responsibility for setting the growth target and for bringing management and unions together.[64] Later, Grimond and Layton called for NEDC to be developed into a fully fledged Ministry of Expansion.[65] Grimond's 5 per cent growth target, meanwhile, copied a different overseas model: it was the same as the one which President Kennedy had set for the United States.

The Liberals shared fully in the 'growthmanship' which Colin Clark diagnosed in this period.[66] Nevertheless, they were adamant that growth was desirable as a means to social ends, rather than an end in itself.[67] Higher industrial production would facilitate the modernization of Britain's infrastructure and a much-needed expansion of the welfare state. Galbraith's vision of a civilized society was influential here; so too was the emerging 'rediscovery of poverty' by social scientists such as Peter Townsend and Brian Abel-Smith. To their existing plan for road-building, the Liberals added a ten-year plan for education—including a doubling of full-time university places, a new school-building programme, and the promotion

[61] *LN*, 14 September 1961, 5.

[62] O'Hara, *From Dreams to Disillusionment*, 21.

[63] Geoffrey Warner in *LN*, 2 November 1961, 5.

[64] Grimond, *Growth not Grandeur*; Hansard, HC (series 5) vol. 651, cols 1029–36 (18 December 1961) and vol. 657, cols 1189–96 (10 April 1962).

[65] *LN*, 30 March 1963, 5, and 21 September 1963, 2.

[66] Colin Clark, *Growthmanship: A Study in the Mythology of Investment* (1961).

[67] Ware, *5 Year Plan*, 3.

of comprehensive schools—and a pledge to build 500,000 new homes each year. The party also promised to overhaul social security and increase the basic state pension to half average earnings, which would be paid for by a new payroll tax.[68] Of course, the Conservative government itself embarked on several ambitious new welfare projects in this period, including Sir Keith Joseph's Hospital Plan and the expansion of higher education envisaged by the Robbins report.[69] The Liberals, however, promised to go further and faster.

Tax reform was another element of the Liberals' modernization project. With such large spending commitments, the party could no longer promise overall tax cuts, but it could rationalize the tax system and sharpen incentives by shifting the burden from earnings to expenditure and capital. Grimond called for income tax and surtax to be merged, with a single graduated scale, and argued that a capital gains tax and land value taxation would offset any revenue loss.[70] (Indeed, partly in response to housing shortages and Rachmanism, land value taxation gained renewed prominence in these years.) The Liberal leader also advocated a flat-rate corporate tax in place of profits tax, and proposed to replace purchase tax with a general sales tax. These proposals were drawn together into a radical tax reform package by a party committee on taxation, chaired by Professor G. S. A. Wheatcroft, in 1961–2. The overall objective was to remove 'artificial complications' from the system, make it easier to use fiscal policy to regulate demand, and encourage innovation and competition.[71]

At the level of the product market, Grimond and his colleagues remained vocally committed to competition. Growth required that Britain should be internationally competitive, and both tariff cuts and Common Market membership were advocated as means of forcing British firms to reduce their costs.[72] The party also called for the abolition of retail price maintenance, which the Conservatives eventually carried through in 1963–4, and for stronger anti-trust measures, including powers for the Monopolies Commission to block mergers.[73] Trade unions' restrictive practices were equally damaging, and would need to be abandoned. Christopher Layton believed that cost and price reductions could help reduce wage inflation,

[68] *LN*, 16 March 1963, 5; *Liberal Party General Election Manifestos, 1900–1997*, ed. Iain Dale (2000), 112–4.

[69] Rodney Lowe, 'The replanning of the welfare state, 1957–1964', in Martin Francis and Ina Zweiniger-Bargielowska (eds), *The Conservatives and British Society, 1880–1990* (Cardiff, 1996), 110–35.

[70] Hansard, HC (series 5) vol. 639, cols 1686–91 (4 May 1961).

[71] Liberal Party, *Taxation: A Report to the Liberal Party* (1962), 3–6, at 6.

[72] *LN*, 11 August 1960, 4; Grimond, *Growth not Grandeur*.

[73] *Current Topics*, i, no. 9 (February 1962), 12–15; *LN*, 3 March 1962, 2.

and the NEDC's 1963 report on *Conditions Favourable to Faster Growth* provided semi-official support for these arguments.[74]

In relation to investment and incomes, the Liberals took a more interventionist approach. The idea of setting targets for particular industries and influencing the distribution of investment was a significant departure from free-market principles, but it aroused relatively little controversy, perhaps because the party did not really flesh out what its investment policy would involve. Wage determination enjoyed much greater prominence, as a result of Selwyn Lloyd's 1961–2 'pay pause' and the government's subsequent 'guiding light' policy. The Liberals advocated an incomes policy based on two 'guiding lights', an average and a ceiling, and insisted that rents, profits, and dividends should be included in it; they also suggested using the tax system to penalize firms and employees that exceeded the ceiling, an idea which Peter Wiles and the North Cornwall MP John Pardoe would develop into an 'inflation tax' in the 1970s.[75] Within this framework, the Liberals were keen to promote plant-level bargaining on the American model, and to link wage increases to productivity.[76] Grimond and his industrial relations expert, Michael Fogarty, believed that trade unions could be persuaded to accept these reforms if they were combined with measures to raise workers' status and security, for instance by making employment contracts obligatory, abolishing distinctions between manual and non-manual workers, and promoting workers' participation.[77] Profit-sharing was quietly downplayed—Fogarty did not like it—but the 1962 Assembly passed a resolution which called for all workers to have the right to elect company directors.[78]

Finally, the Liberals continued to support demand management within a national plan. Under a Liberal government committed to 5 per cent growth, of course, unemployment seemed unlikely to be a problem; but in 1962–3 it was a major political issue, as cautious Conservative policies and severe winter weather pushed joblessness to its highest level since the war. Christopher Layton and Arthur Holt, who served as economic spokesman in the House of Commons, recommended an immediate income tax cut to stimulate consumer spending.[79] In a return to Keynesian orthodoxy, fiscal policy was now the preferred demand-management tool. At the same time, Liberals recognized that unemployment was concentrated

[74] *LN*, 2 March 1963, 1.

[75] Michael Fogarty, *Opportunity Knocks* (1961); BLPES, Liberal Party papers, 2/1/170–8, LPO Council minutes, 25 May 1963, at fols 171–2.

[76] *Current Topics*, i, no. 9 (February 1962), 2–4.

[77] *Current Topics*, ii, no. 4 (November 1962), 19–23.

[78] *LN*, 15 June 1961, 5, and 29 September 1962, 2.

[79] *LN*, 9 March 1963, 1.

in Scotland, Northern Ireland, and northern England, and emphasized the need to attend to this regional dimension. Grimond called on the government to develop its 1960 Local Employment Act into a more comprehensive regional policy, using loans, grants, and investment allowances to broaden the industrial base of struggling regions.[80] Under a Liberal government these measures would form part of regional development plans, drawn up by elected regional authorities.[81]

Taken as a package, the planning proposals which the Liberal Party adopted during the early 1960s overlapped significantly with the modernization agenda that Harold Wilson evolved in the same period, first as Shadow Chancellor and then as Labour leader. Not only was Wilson's rhetoric very similar to Grimond's, but the large number of policies which both parties advocated—such as a national growth target, a capital gains tax, and higher public investment—reflected the extent to which they drew on common intellectual sources. Nevertheless, the ideological differences between 'Wilsonism' and Grimond's Liberalism should also be recognized. As Ilaria Favretto has shown, Wilson used declinist ideas to buttress views on planning, investment, and efficiency which he had held since the 1940s, and argued that scientific and technological developments had to be controlled by the state, if necessary through public ownership.[82] By contrast, Grimond and his colleagues placed much greater emphasis on competition and entrepreneurship as drivers of economic progress.

THE LIBERALS AND THE NEW RIGHT

Jo Grimond's new-found enthusiasm for indicative planning did not go wholly unchallenged in the Liberal ranks. Among veteran activists, especially, scepticism seems to have been quite widespread. Heather Harvey thought that the five-year plan policy was 'a staggering hotch-potch', riddled with 'vagueness and inconsistencies', which gave little indication of how faster growth could be achieved, whilst Ronald Walker regarded the party's new spending commitments as irresponsible vote-catching.[83] Leonard Behrens was alarmed by the prospect of a statutory incomes policy, and Nathaniel Micklem wondered how this could be reconciled with the party's historic commitment to the market.[84] Oliver Smedley and his allies predictably took

[80] *LN*, 15 December 1962, 1.

[81] Liberal Party papers, 2/2/8–14, LPO Council minutes, 26 October 1963, at fol. 9.

[82] Ilaria Favretto, '"Wilsonism" reconsidered: Labour Party revisionism 1952–64', *CBH*, xiv (2000), 54–80.

[83] *LN*, 28 September 1961, 5; Bodleian Library, MS. Bonham Carter 198, fol. 152, Ronald Walker to Bonham Carter, 17 September 1963.

[84] *LN*, 19 October 1961, 2, and 1 June 1963, 1, 8.

a similar line. In the party at large, however, these were isolated voices, which carried little weight with most Liberal members. Many new recruits had radical instincts, and others were simply prepared to trust Grimond's judgment, especially at a time when the party's electoral prospects were improving. In consequence, there was no concerted attempt to return the party to a liberal Keynesian line.

One significant cleavage did exist within the planning group, although it did not emerge into the open until after the 1964 election. This concerned the external implications of a growth strategy: in particular, whether sterling should be devalued to facilitate rapid expansion. Christopher Layton was adamant that Britain should 'put growth before the pound', but Grimond seems to have been sceptical towards devaluation, perhaps partly because Paish (whom he continued to consult) strongly opposed it.[85] Grimond and Layton floated the idea of devaluation during the 1966 election campaign, but the party remained divided on the issue, and a plan for 'creeping devaluation' devised by young Liberal economist John Williamson only partly resolved this.[86] Like both Labour and the Conservatives, then, the Liberals found it difficult to come to terms with the implications of a growth-oriented policy.[87] The failure to establish a clear line on this point is a serious indictment of the party's planning exercise.

The Liberals' conversion to planning also contributed to the breach between the party and some of its free-market supporters which took place during this period. After all, it was the Institute of Economic Affairs which published Colin Clark's *Growthmanship* (1961) and Paish's *Policy for Incomes?* (1964)—both critical of the assumptions of indicative planning—and which did most to propagate Milton Friedman's monetarist ideas in Britain. However, macroeconomic policy per se does not seem to have been a major cause of defections. Rather, frustration at the party's growing interventionism confirmed an existing tendency for neoliberals to distance themselves from party politics.

Although many classical Liberals and neoliberals were members of the Liberal Party during the 1940s and 1950s, they tended to devote most of their political energies to non-party organizations, in line with Hayek's strategy of trying to influence elite opinion across the political spectrum. Classical Liberals like Francis Hirst and S. W. Alexander were involved

[85] Liberal Party papers, 16/27/29–33, LPO press release of speech by Christopher Layton on 'Prices, Incomes and the Creation of Wealth', 3 September 1964, at fol. 33; for Paish's influence on Grimond, see Richard Lamb in *New Outlook*, no. 62 (March 1967), 3.

[86] *The Guardian*, 19 March 1966, 4; John Williamson, *How to Stop Stop-Go* (1966). Williamson's plan, which envisaged a 7% devaluation over three and a half years, was endorsed by the 1966 Assembly: *The Guardian*, 24 September 1966, 4.

[87] Interview with John Williamson, 13 July 2012.

in the Society of Individualists and the Cheap Food League, while free-market economists preferred the Mont Pèlerin Society. Frank Paish and Arthur Shenfield addressed MPS meetings in the early 1950s, and Lord Grantchester sought to promote neoliberal ideas in Britain through his journal *The Owl*.[88] When Oliver Smedley and the Conservative businessman Antony Fisher founded the IEA as an independent research institute in 1955, Grantchester donated funds, recommended Arthur Seldon for the post of editorial adviser (later editorial director), and joined its advisory council.[89] Post-war neoliberalism was thus as much of a Liberal milieu as a Conservative one. However, Liberals of this type were often sensitive to the danger that a Liberal revival would split the anti-socialist vote and let Labour back into office.[90] As Arthur Shenfield saw it, 'the defence of the liberal economy in Britain' had come to rest 'in Conservative hands', and neoliberals were most likely to achieve their goals by strengthening the Conservative Party's commitment to the free market.[91]

Shenfield seems to have cut his ties with the Liberal Party by the time he became economic director of the Federation of British Industries in 1955.[92] Seldon, who had been president of the Orpington Liberal Association, also scaled back his involvement in order to quell suspicions that the IEA was a 'Liberal front'.[93] Along with Alan Peacock, Seldon continued to hope that the party would build on *The Unservile State* by developing radical plans for public service reform, but these hopes steadily withered as Grimond 'bl[ew] hot and cold' on the issue.[94] The final straw came in the mid-1960s, when the party failed to adopt an education voucher scheme which Peacock had devised with his colleague Jack Wiseman.[95] Though Jo Grimond, Michael Fogarty, and John Pardoe were sympathetic to the idea, Liberal education spokesman Alec Peterson and party president Nancy Seear argued that the advantages of

[88] BLPES, Richard Cockett papers, 1/4, 'Programs of the Eight Meetings (1947–1957) of the MPS', 2 September 1957; *The Owl* (January 1951), 2.

[89] Richard Cockett, *Thinking the Unthinkable: Think-Tanks and the Economic Counter-Revolution, 1931–1983* (1994; paperback edition, 1995), 132–5.

[90] BLPES, McFadyean papers, 3/16, Geoffrey Acland to Sir Andrew McFadyean, 21 March 1956.

[91] *The Owl* (November 1952), 40–50, at 40.

[92] For Shenfield's career at the FBI see Neil Rollings, 'Cracks in the post-war Keynesian settlement? The role of organised business in Britain in the rise of neoliberalism before Margaret Thatcher', *TCBH*, xxiv (2013), 637–59, at 644–52.

[93] John Meadowcroft and Jaime Reynolds, 'Liberals and the New Right', *JLH*, no. 47 (2005), 45–51, at 48.

[94] *LN*, 24 August 1961, 4–5.

[95] Alan Peacock and Jack Wiseman, *Education for Democrats: A Study of the Financing of Education in a Free Society* (1964); Alan Peacock, *Anxious to Do Good: Learning to be an Economist the Hard Way* (Exeter, 2010), 145–200.

choice and competition would be outweighed by the instability which vouchers would create for schools and the risk of exacerbating social inequalities.[96] By the time Grimond resigned as Liberal leader in 1967, the Liberal Party's growing suspicion of free-market reforms contrasted sharply with the interest which Conservatives such as Enoch Powell and Sir Keith Joseph showed in the IEA's work. Grimond and Pardoe seem to have been almost alone in retaining links with the IEA into the 1970s.

The Smedleyites followed a similar route out of the party, though in their case the pivotal issue was the Common Market. As early as the late 1950s their influence within the party was on the wane, and they were reduced to fighting a rearguard action against Grimond's support for Common Market entry.[97] Smedley was also edged out of the IEA by Fisher, and taking control of the Free Trade Union in 1959 was not much compensation.[98] When the party backed Common Market membership in the early 1960s, Smedley resigned his candidature and threw his energies into the Keep Britain Out campaign which Alexander founded.[99] Though other anti-Marketeers such as Roy Douglas remained active Liberals, the party's classical individualist wing had essentially disintegrated.

The Liberal Party's left turn under Jo Grimond did not destroy the influence of classical ideas within the party, but it did closely circumscribe it. Most importantly, despite his personal sympathy with free-market ideas, Grimond was adamant that Liberals should view economics as a means to social and political ends.[100] Free trade was a policy, not a principle; the market had to be servant, rather than master. Many progressive Liberals, of course, had always taken this view, but until the 1960s there was sufficient ambiguity to allow classical and Georgist traditionalists to claim to be the party's purists. By the time Grimond retired as leader, the issue was no longer contested, as most of the party's new recruits were indifferent or hostile to classical economics. When the party constitution was revised in 1969, the commitment to free trade was removed from the preamble. The party had finally left behind the battles of 1846, 1906, and 1931.

[96] *New Outlook*, no. 50 (January 1966), 11–13, no. 54 (May 1966), 18–22, and no. 58 (October 1966), 28–30.

[97] For instance, Smedley was defeated for re-election as a vice-president of the party in 1957: *LN*, 4 October 1957, 4.

[98] Cockett, *Thinking the Unthinkable*, 137; BLPES, Cockett papers, 2/7, 'My Ten Years at Austin Friars', by Oliver Smedley, n.d. [*c.*1963].

[99] Smedley dramatically resigned his candidature at the 1961 Assembly: *LN*, 28 September 1961, 8.

[100] J. Grimond, *The Liberal Future* (1959), 54–6; Grimond, *Liberal Challenge*, 23.

'ORPINGTON MAN'

The years which followed the 1959 election were the heyday of Grimond's new Liberalism. Grimond himself became a major public figure, and the party in the country continued to strengthen. At first, the Liberals benefited from Labour's internal disputes over defence and nationalization; then, in 1961–2, the party successfully exploited discontent over the government's pay pause to erode the Conservative vote. Eric Lubbock's victory at Orpington in March 1962 placed the party in the limelight, and was followed by sweeping local election gains; one NOP poll even placed the Liberals narrowly ahead of both the other parties.[101] Fears of a Liberal breakthrough seem to have prompted Harold Macmillan to overhaul his Cabinet in the July 1962 'Night of the Long Knives', with Reginald Maudling replacing Selwyn Lloyd at the Treasury.[102] Between mid-1962 and the 1964 general election the Liberal bubble steadily deflated, as the Labour and Conservative parties encroached on the Liberals' terrain; when the election came, the party was confined to 11 per cent of the vote, and it gained seats only in the Highlands and the West Country. 'Orpington Man' nevertheless became shorthand for the Liberals' new appeal to the English suburbs, which paved the way for further advances in the 1970s and 1980s.

What did economic policy contribute to this second wave of Liberal revival? In so far as Liberal success was based on 'protest voting', it might be thought to have contributed relatively little.[103] Despite the party's turn away from anti-inflationary rhetoric, its Gallup rating continued to track the inflation rate until the end of 1963, suggesting that the party still served as a safety valve for disaffected Conservatives. The Orpington by-election took place with the Retail Price Index at 4.8 per cent, and Grimond promised voters there that Lubbock would act as a 'champion' for 'those being crushed between rising prices and rising taxation on the one hand, and the pay pause on the other'.[104] Clearly, too, many of the voters who supported the Liberals in this period were attracted by the party's general image, and did not develop any enduring attachment to the party's policies.

Such a negative verdict, though, is surely incomplete. For one thing, the protest vote of the early 1960s took a slightly different form to that of 1955–9. In the earlier period, disaffection resulted mainly from the

101 Ken Young, 'Orpington and the "Liberal revival"', in Chris Cook and John Ramsden (eds), *By-Elections in British Politics* (1973), 198–222.

102 D. R. Thorpe, *Supermac: The Life of Harold Macmillan* (2010), 516–23.

103 This is David Dutton's view: David Dutton, *A History of the Liberal Party since 1900* (second edition, Basingstoke, 2013), 186–7.

104 *The Guardian*, 6 March 1962, 3.

Conservatives' failure to cut spending and conquer inflation; in the later period, it was the government's efforts to curb wage increases (through the pay pause) and place the railways on a commercial footing that alienated voters in the commuter belt. Moreover, voters' grievances are themselves constructed through political argument, and perceptions that the pay pause was unjust and Britain's economy was growing too slowly presupposed that alternative policies could be pursued. As *The Spectator* recognized, Grimond and his colleagues offered 'an intelligent and sophisticated rationalisation' of voters' disaffection.[105]

From this perspective, the Liberal Party's conversion to planning and growth may have aided its electoral performance at two levels. Firstly, among suburban voters at Orpington and elsewhere, the party's commitment to growth burnished its 'modern' image and suggested that the rigours of the pay pause could be avoided by an expansionary policy. For the progressive middle class, especially, the Liberals offered rising living standards and an expanded welfare state, combined with a meritocratic and internationalist outlook which contrasted favourably with those of the Conservative establishment and the class-conscious Labour movement.[106] Data from the 1964 British Election Study suggest that the party performed particularly well not only among middle-class voters in general, owner-occupiers, and Nonconformists—which was quite predictable—but also among those aged 25–44, those who had been educated to sixth-form or degree level, and welfare and creative professionals.[107]

Secondly, the Liberals' new commitment to planning and regional development seems to have played well in their target seats on the Celtic fringe. The party promised to devolve power to the regions, create development agencies to oversee investment in infrastructure, and establish 'growth points' in under-developed areas. Suitable industries would be attracted to the peripheral regions, depopulation would be halted, and geographical disparities in education and service provision would be reduced. Liberals had called for action on these lines since the 1920s, but only under Grimond did regionalism and devolution become a major theme in the party's national campaign, especially during the 1964

[105] *Spectator*, 6 September 1963, 275.

[106] See especially Mark Abrams' survey, 'Who are the new Liberals?', in *The Observer*, 1 July 1962, 17–18. The distinctive relationship between the professional middle class and the state has been highlighted by Michael Savage and his collaborators: Michael Savage et al., *Property, Bureaucracy and Culture: Middle-Class Formation in Contemporary Britain* (1992).

[107] *The British Electorate, 1963–1987*, ed. Ivor Crewe, Neil Day, and Anthony Fox (Cambridge, 1991), 7–8, 19–21, 32–4, 37–9, 41; Anthony Heath et al., *Understanding Political Change: The British Voter, 1964–1987* (Oxford, 1991), 96.

election. The Liberals gained their reward with victories in Inverness, Ross and Cromarty, Caithness and Sutherland, and Bodmin. Peter Preston of *The Guardian* thought the Scottish seats had been won by the regionalist message, and more recently Garry Tregidga has underlined its enduring appeal in the West Country.[108]

The twin electoral pillars of post-Grimond Liberalism, namely progressive voters in the English suburbs and rural voters on the Celtic fringe, may therefore have been strengthened by the party's conversion to a more active role for the state. It certainly seems unlikely that the Liberals would have done as well in the early 1960s if they had remained wedded to anti-inflationary liberal Keynesianism. On the other hand, the party's new policy also had electoral limitations. Adopting moderate and fashionable positions could be a weakness as well as a strength in a three-party system: it left the Liberals vulnerable to a pincer movement as Labour and the Conservatives converged on the centre ground, and it meant that Liberal policy was rendered outdated as circumstances changed. By 1964 the Conservatives had embarked on a modernization programme, the economy was growing rapidly under Maudling's stewardship, and Harold Wilson was staking Labour's claim to the 'white heat' of the 'technological revolution'. Since the Liberals had only recently adopted their planning policy, it was difficult to claim that there was much that was intrinsically Liberal about it. After Labour returned to office in 1964, matters became even more difficult. 'Realignment of the left' was no longer a realistic possibility, despite Grimond's efforts to reach out to Harold Wilson, and the Liberals struggled to explain how their modernization programme differed from the government's ill-fated National Plan.[109]

CONCLUSION

The analysis of Liberal policy-making developed in this chapter allows us to assess Jo Grimond's leadership from a variety of perspectives. Grimond clearly enjoyed great success in reinvigorating the Liberal Party, reasserting its political relevance, and attracting new recruits; in this respect, he laid the foundations for its later development. He also showed considerable skill as a party manager, repositioning the party as a centre-left force

[108] *The Guardian*, 21 October 1964, 10; Garry Tregidga, *The Liberal Party in South-West England Since 1918: Political Decline, Dormancy and Rebirth* (Exeter, 2000), 205 and *passim*. Hugh Berrington pointed out that the party did unusually well in high-unemployment rural constituencies: H. B. Berrington, 'The general election of 1964', *Journal of the Royal Statistical Society*, series A, cxxviii (1965), 17–51, at 39.

[109] Barberis, *Liberal Lion*, 127–40; Jones, *Revival*, 43–7.

without serious internal dissension: as Muriel Burton has noted, he had a talent for convincing Liberals of almost all stripes that he was on their side.[110] In electoral terms, however, the picture was much more mixed, as the anticipated Liberal breakthrough failed to materialize and the party was left to make incremental progress in the constituencies; in 1970, indeed, the party would again be reduced to six MPs. William Wallace, Geoffrey Sell, and Tudor Jones have justifiably concluded that Grimond's strategy of 'realignment of the left' was intrinsically flawed, since it overstated the speed and political impact of *embourgeoisement* and understated the resilience of the Labour movement.[111] Only in the very different political climate of 1973–4 would the Liberals achieve wider electoral success, and only in the 1980s would disaffected social democrats ally themselves with the party. Even then, the SDP–Liberal Alliance struggled to break through the glass ceiling which geographically dispersed third parties face under Britain's electoral system.

As an exponent of Liberal philosophy, Grimond was arguably more effective than any party leader since Gladstone, convincing a generation of activists and voters that Liberalism provided a robust basis for political action. He breathed new life into historic Liberal principles such as internationalism and citizen participation, but also emphasized that the state had a dynamic role to play in stimulating growth, providing public goods and public services, and making good the shortcomings of the market. The activist impulse of the New Liberal and constructive traditions was thus rehabilitated. Depending on one's taste, this was either a necessary corrective to the anti-statism of the 1950s or a retreat towards what Grimond himself would later denounce as 'semi-dirigiste' moderation.[112]

The same can be said of Grimond's contribution to Liberal economic policy. On the one hand, he developed a relatively coherent and far-sighted prescription for improving Britain's economic performance, based on Common Market membership, higher investment, better education and skills, and a more competitive private sector. On the other hand, Grimond's heavy use of declinist arguments does not read well today, and it is hard to believe that a Liberal government would have avoided the difficulties which Harold Wilson and George Brown faced in putting planning into practice.[113] Expectations of faster growth and rising public spending had been raised so far by 1964 that they were almost

[110] Burton, 'Making', 154.

[111] Wallace, 'Liberal Revival', 170–9; Sell, 'Liberal Revival', 224–47; Jones, *Revival*, 47–50.

[112] *Spectator*, 31 January 1981, 11.

[113] On the intellectual deficiencies of declinism, see Tomlinson, *Politics of Decline*, 65–82.

unattainable, and the party's failure to consider the possibility of devaluation suggests that it would have struggled to resolve the tensions which planning raised between internal and external objectives and competing economic interests.

We might expect the Liberals to have reacted to the failure of the 1960s growth experiment by becoming more sceptical about state intervention, as the Conservative Party did under Ted Heath and Margaret Thatcher. In so far as this happened, however, the party's reaction took a post-materialist form more than a New Right one. As Andrew Gamble has shown, the party remained committed to economic modernization and reaffirmed its support for an incomes policy, tax reform, and industrial democracy.[114] At the same time, 'stagflation', the oil price spike, and the appearance of E. F. Schumacher's *Small is Beautiful* (1973) all raised doubts about the sustainability of economic growth, and prompted Liberals to shift their emphasis towards price stability and quality of life issues.[115] Advocates of 'community politics' sought a radical decentralization of power, while Jeremy Thorpe and David Steel responded to growing industrial turmoil by arguing that a more consensual political system was a prerequisite for effective and consistent policy-making. As the 1979 manifesto put it, 'Economic and industrial recovery can only follow from a radical programme of political and social reform.'[116] Liberal economic policy became more than ever intertwined with the party's plans for constitutional change.[117]

The Liberal Party's left turn during the Grimond years thus shaped the party's intellectual course for a generation, and helped ensure that the party would seek common ground with social democrats during the 1970s and 1980s instead of advocating monetarist and neoliberal policies alongside Margaret Thatcher.[118] Ironically, however, Grimond himself proved reluctant to claim much credit. After resigning the leadership in 1967, Grimond returned to the anti-statist emphases of his early years in Parliament and began to worry that the scale of government activity was crowding out personal initiative and community participation. He retained his personal links with free-market economists such as Alan Peacock and attended at least one Mont Pèlerin Society

[114] Andrew Gamble, 'Liberals and the economy', in Vernon Bogdanor (ed.), *Liberal Party Politics* (Oxford, 1983), 191–216, at 206–11.

[115] See especially the February 1974 manifesto, in *Liberal Manifestos*, 147–67, and Ralf Dahrendorf, *After Social Democracy* (1980).

[116] *Liberal Manifestos*, 188.

[117] Gamble, 'Liberals and the economy', 193–4.

[118] For a somewhat speculative counter-factual, see James Parry, 'What if the Liberal Party had broken through from the right?', in Duncan Brack and Iain Dale (eds), *Prime Minister Portillo and Other Things That Never Happened* (2003).

meeting.[119] In *The Common Welfare* (1978) and *A Personal Manifesto* (1983) Grimond urged his party to take New Right ideas more seriously and identify itself with the public reaction against the post-war consensus. Yet the logic of realignment of the left and Liberals' revulsion at the human cost of Thatcherism meant that this recantation had limited impact. Only in the 1990s and 2000s would the free-market strand in the Liberal inheritance begin to return to the fore.

[119] Ben Jackson, 'The think-tank archipelago: Thatcherism and neo-liberalism', in Ben Jackson and Robert Saunders (eds), *Making Thatcher's Britain* (Cambridge, 2012), 43–61, at 57.

Conclusion: Progressives, Distributists, and Neoliberals

In the course of this study, we have traced Liberal economic policy-making across three and a half decades—from the 1928 Yellow Book through the great depression, the Second World War, and post-war austerity and prosperity to the beginnings of Liberal revival under Jo Grimond. It should by now be clear that most Liberals in this period were neither wholly comfortable with the trend towards greater state intervention, nor remained shackled to an outdated Gladstonianism. Rather, what W. H. Greenleaf called 'the ambivalence of Liberalism' was still very much in evidence, as the party's zeal for full employment and social justice ran up against fear of an overweening state and an enduring commitment to internationalism and free markets.[1] If anything, the rise of state socialism and economic planning prompted Liberals to take their libertarian heritage more seriously. At the same time, Liberals sought to show how counter-cyclical economic management and social welfare policies could obviate the need for more direct interference with the market system. If the party sometimes seemed to be torn between mainstream progressive opinion and a more individualistic vision, there also remained some unifying elements in Liberal economic thought which helped hold it together. We are now in a position to flesh out this complex picture.

THE CHARACTER OF LIBERAL POLICY-MAKING

The mid-twentieth-century Liberal Party emerges from this study as a fragile but ultimately resilient political formation. Its fragility stemmed from the rise of the Labour Party as a class-based rival on the British left; the debilitating conflict between Asquith and Lloyd George, which hampered

[1] W. H. Greenleaf, *The British Political Tradition* (3 vols, 1983–7), ii, part two.

efforts to contain the Labour threat; and its inability to forge a distinctive role for itself after it became the third party. Were the Liberals the party of individual freedom and 'the small man', of the rural periphery against the centre, or of the progressive intelligentsia?[2] As a party in decline, the Liberals needed votes wherever they could get them, but tacking first to the left and then to the right made it harder to cultivate a distinct constituency of support. Voters and activists attracted at one election were liable to feel betrayed when the party changed direction, and MPs who owed their seats to local circumstances or their personal reputations had little incentive to toe the party line. As a result, it proved difficult to unite the party around a coherent vision of what a Liberal society would look like and how Liberal policies would bring it into being.

Despite these difficulties, the Liberal Party managed to survive for long enough to benefit from the slow unfreezing of class-based loyalties in the 1960s and 1970s and growing discontent with Labour and the Conservatives. The party's representative organs—the NLF and LPO—provided institutional continuity with the party of Gladstone and Asquith, whilst the survival of a small band of Liberal MPs prevented the party from withering into a pressure group. Other claimants to the Liberal heritage, such as the Liberal Nationals, were successfully warded off, and the stalwarts who had kept faith with the party during its inter-war decline were steadily augmented by new recruits who were repelled by Labour's socialism and the Conservatives' association with class privilege.

In common with their Victorian and Edwardian predecessors, mid-twentieth-century Liberals tended to take economic issues seriously. Many defined their Liberalism at least partly in economic terms, whether by a commitment to free trade or wider property ownership or 'social reform without socialism', and economic policy-making absorbed much greater time and energy than any other sphere of policy, with the possible exception of foreign affairs. Of course, this does not mean that economic issues were always well understood. Many Liberals' grasp of economic theory probably did not extend beyond a few basic concepts—classical, neoclassical, Keynesian, underconsumptionist, or Georgist—and the party's frequent use of economic experts may have stemmed as much from a lack of confidence in economic matters as from a rational, disinterested ethos. It is noteworthy that almost all of the party's macroeconomic policies were taken 'off the shelf' in one way or another, either from expert advisers (Keynes, Beveridge,

[2] On this point, see John Vincent, 'What kind of third party?', *New Society*, 26 January 1967, 120–1, and Ross McKibbin, 'Class and conventional wisdom: The Conservative Party and the "public" in inter-war Britain', in Ross McKibbin, *The Ideologies of Class: Social Relations in Britain, 1880–1950* (Oxford, 1990), 228–58, at 275–81.

Harrod, and Paish) or from newspapers like *The Economist*. Though Liberal leaders were usually the central figures in the policy-making process, their contribution lay largely in choosing which ideas to take up, relating them to the party's existing commitments, and then trying to sell them to Liberal activists and the electorate at large. This was a political exercise as much as an intellectual one. The party generally moved to the left when its leaders were confident about its political future and thought that radical ideas could capture the public imagination, and to the right when they felt they needed to retain traditional Liberal supporters and burnish the party's distinctiveness from Labour and the Conservatives.

No doubt the Liberal Party's efforts to develop relevant and up-to-date economic policies aided its political survival, but with the benefit of hindsight it is possible that some of the resources which Liberals invested in policy-making would have been better spent building up the party on the ground. Major-General W. H. Grey, treasurer of the Liberal Central Association, argued this case strongly in the 1950s.[3] It was too easy for Liberals to fall prey to the illusion that attractive policies would revive the party's fortunes; at best, as 1929, 1945, and 1964 showed, they tended to improve its national vote without making much impact on its representation. Since the Grimond era, the internal culture of the Liberal Party and Liberal Democrats has come to be shaped much more strongly by a commitment to constituency campaigning.

LIBERAL POLITICAL THOUGHT

Liberal economic policy-making naturally took place in the context of the party's political thought. This overlapped with the liberal ideological tradition anatomized by Michael Freeden and others, but the two were never coextensive. Liberal politicians were more interested in usable ideas than in philosophical originality, and did not necessarily regard the New Liberalism of Hobhouse and Hobson as an advance over the older Liberalism of Mill. Indeed, Liberals did not invoke any of these thinkers as frequently as we might expect, though Samuel took political philosophy seriously and Grimond recommended that all Liberals should read *On Liberty* once a year.[4] For most of the party, past political leaders such as Gladstone, Asquith, and Lloyd George and the policies which their governments had enacted were more important points of reference.

[3] National Library of Wales, Clement Davies papers, C/1/107, W. H. Grey to Frank Byers, 10 March 1958.

[4] Jo Grimond, *The Liberal Challenge* (1963), 35.

The dominant concept in Liberal political thought was liberty, enshrined after 1936 in the party's constitutional commitment to put freedom first. This prioritization had distinctly individualist and anti-paternalist overtones—liberty was more important than, say, equality or order—but Liberals recognized that liberty could only be fully realized in a social context. 'The Liberal ideal,' Elliott Dodds argued, 'is not a concourse of atoms, each concerned simply with its own advantage, but a commonwealth of self-respecting, self-directing citizens, in which the stronger accept their responsibility towards the weaker and all co-operate for the general good.'[5]

The vast majority of twentieth-century Liberals conceived of liberty in positive and expansive terms, including the freedom to develop and express one's personality unconstrained by 'poverty, ignorance or unemployment'. Michael Freeden has observed that practically all inter-war liberals were progressives in the sense that they wanted 'to improve and reform individuals and their social arrangements'; this was true of Liberal politicians as well as of liberal thinkers.[6] Although some more-or-less 'pure' classical Liberals can be identified, such as Francis Hirst, Rhys Hopkin Morris, and Oliver Smedley, they were always a minority element. Most of the party was more willing to believe that the state could pursue citizens' positive freedom without abrogating civil and political liberties.

The central ideological tension within British Liberalism after the First World War did not lie between classical and social forms of Liberalism; the advocates of a negative view of liberty were too weak for that. Rather, we may identify two different strands of social Liberalism, whose influence ebbed and flowed across our period. The first was the activist social Liberalism of Keynes and Beveridge, which sought to use state power to extend citizens' liberty by conquering visible social evils—unemployment, poverty, and economic stagnation—and reshaping the economic system around human needs. This strand drew its energy from Liberals' moral revulsion at the economic and social costs of free-market capitalism, and its ideological premisses somewhat diffusely from T. H. Green and the New Liberals (though in Freeden's terms it was more centrist-liberal than left-liberal); when it came to the fore in the 1920s, 1940s, and 1960s it helped the party appeal to mainstream progressive opinion and show that it could solve contemporary problems. Yet the exponents of this activist social Liberalism often struggled to convince their colleagues that the rather technocratic policies they favoured were distinctively Liberal ones.

[5] Elliott Dodds, *Let's Try Liberalism* (1944), 98.

[6] Michael Freeden, *Liberalism Divided: A Study in British Political Thought, 1914–1939* (Oxford, 1986), 12.

The idea of a social-democratic middle way hardly needed a party to champion it; it had plenty of advocates in pressure groups, leading newspapers, and the moderate wings of the Labour and Conservative parties.

The second strand of social Liberalism was the distributist tradition, in which a positive conception of liberty was combined with a republican commitment to an independent citizenry. Elliott Dodds and other distributist Liberals supported state action to remedy specific social and economic problems, but feared that reliance on the state for the necessities of life would destroy the independence, responsibility, and choice which true liberty required. This strong commitment to agency prompted Dodds to pursue what Stuart White has called 'an imagined dispersive utopia', in which a wide distribution of private property and employment opportunities would allow all citizens to make life choices *apart from* the state.[7] Distributists' sensitivity to the ways in which market competition, private savings, and voluntary action contributed to citizens' welfare could make them relatively cautious in policy terms, though at their most radical they sought to recast the whole basis of capital–labour relations. The strength of this dispersive social Liberalism was that it was unmistakeably Liberal, and formed a sharp contrast with the Labour Party's vision of social progress; it also anticipated the revival in republican political thought which Geoffrey Foote has identified in late-twentieth-century Britain.[8] Its weaknesses were that it could appear utopian, and thus complacent about contemporary British society, and that it lost much of its political purchase after 1945 when the Conservatives began to champion 'property-owning democracy'.

Part of Jo Grimond's achievement as party leader was that he held these two strands of social Liberalism together. His philosophy of Liberalism was a dispersive one, which centred on personal freedom, participatory citizenship, equality of opportunity, and the diffusion of power, yet he came to advocate an expansive role for the state in stimulating economic growth and providing education and social services. If this was an unwieldy hybrid, it could be justified on the grounds that a Liberal society required an active state and that civic participation was best served by decentralizing government rather than rolling it back. Grimond's portmanteau social Liberalism has been widely echoed within the party in subsequent decades.[9]

[7] Stuart White, '"Revolutionary Liberalism?" The philosophy and politics of ownership in the post-war Liberal Party', *British Politics*, iv (2009), 164–87, at 182.

[8] Geoffrey Foote, *The Republican Transformation of Modern British Politics* (Basingstoke, 2006), 89–113.

[9] See especially Donald Wade, *Our Aim and Purpose* (1961); Gordon Lishman and Bernard Greaves, *The Theory and Practice of Community Politics* (Hebden Bridge, 1980); and

THE MARKET AND THE STATE

Although economic policy was always a means, not an end, for Liberals, certain economic ideas embedded themselves firmly in Liberal thinking. The most important of these was the idea of the market. The party's long-standing commitment to free trade meant that each new generation of Liberals—at least up to the 1940s—learned to speak of the advantages of specialization, competition, and trade, and principles elaborated in an international context could hardly be ignored in a domestic one. Competition kept prices down, maintained a continual stimulus to innovation, and ensured that production responded quickly to a changing pattern of demand. Even radical Liberals found themselves defending the logic of the market against advocates of protectionism and socialism, both of which (as Keynes noted) had 'obvious scientific deficiencies'.[10] 'It seems to be the part of the Liberal Party,' one activist lamented in 1931, 'to hold aloft the banner of sound economic theory in a mad world.'[11]

Yet Liberals' appreciation for the dynamism and discipline of the market was balanced by recognition that the market alone would not deliver positive liberty for all citizens. Even Gladstone was not dogmatically committed to laissez-faire, and the New Liberal conception of the state as the instrument of the community and neoclassical economists' emphasis on the possibility of market failure together provided a powerful justification for state action in a variety of fields. The Campbell-Bannerman and Asquith governments' innovations—progressive taxation, old age pensions, unemployment and health insurance, special public investment funds, labour exchanges, and trade boards in sweated industries—were all carefully judged, but cumulatively added up to a significant extension of the state's economic role. The constructive Liberals of the 1920s sought to build on these measures by advocating a national system of industrial democracy and minimum wages, public supervision of monopolies, rationalization of the depressed basic industries, and an ambitious programme of national development works. Keynes argued that the party needed to complete its post-Gladstonian paradigm shift by dropping classical assumptions about the superior efficiency of markets and recognizing that a mature industrial economy required conscious management and coordination.

If the Liberal Party had remained a major party of government, its economic thought might well have developed further along these lines.

Duncan Brack, Richard Grayson, and David Howarth (eds), *Reinventing the State: Social Liberalism for the 21st Century* (2009).

[10] John Maynard Keynes, 'The end of laissez-faire', in *JMK*, ix, 272–94, at 286.

[11] A. P. Laurie in *NC*, 8 September 1931, 6.

However, Liberals found it harder to believe that Conservative and Labour governments would use economic power wisely and well, and the party's traditional suspicion of the state was reinforced by the rise of Communism and Fascism in Europe. Many Liberals were also impressed by the fragility of the market system; indeed, the economic malaise of the 1920s and 1930s seemed to show how easily markets could be destabilized by well-meaning interference. During the 1930s the party developed a sharp critique of wholesale economic planning and became more discriminating in its proposals for state intervention. The best forms of market regulation were those which were stable and predictable (like minimum wages), which dispersed economic power more widely (like industrial democracy), which policed competition (like anti-trust policies) instead of destroying it, and which retarded economic adjustment as little as possible. Liberals also continued to support public investment, both as a supply-side measure and as a means of countering the fluctuations of the trade cycle.

Enthusiasm for the idea of planning persisted on the Liberal left, as Liberal involvement in *The Next Five Years* showed, and party policy moved back in the direction of the Yellow Book—complete with rationalization and public ownership of key industries—during the Second World War. However, advocates of planning consistently struggled to allay suspicions that their schemes would be monopolistic, statist, and protectionist. It was only in the 1960s that the idea of an active state, going beyond demand management to promote growth and economic balance, finally emerged from the shadow of socialist planning. Although the limitations of indicative planning and growthmanship are clear in retrospect, Grimond, the Labour revisionists, and the Conservative modernizers of the 1960s deserve some credit for rehabilitating the notion that government had an expansive role to play in establishing the conditions for a successful market economy.

THE KEYNESIAN REVOLUTION

The Liberal Party's cautious attitude to direct state intervention helps explain the appeal of Keynesianism within the party: it offered a means of achieving full employment without abandoning private ownership or competitive markets. Though most Liberals declined to embrace the idea of a corporate economy, as Keynes had urged them to in 'The end of laissez-faire', they found the idea of discretionary economic management much more congenial. *We Can Conquer Unemployment* played an important role in launching Keynesian ideas into British political debate, and thereafter leading Liberals consistently argued that the state should use its control over public investment—and, for that matter, spending, taxation, and monetary policy—to stabilize the economic cycle. In the field of policy, as opposed to theory, there are grounds for regarding the Liberals as the first Keynesian party.

Yet if Keynesian ideas were easier to swallow than central planning, they still challenged Liberal orthodoxy in important ways. Until the *General Theory* appeared in 1936, many Liberals continued to subscribe to classical assumptions about the economy's long-term tendency towards self-adjustment, and to believe that the 'fundamental' solution to unemployment lay in the removal of barriers to trade and enterprise and the reduction of labour costs. Even those who championed public works tended to regard them as a short-term palliative, though with some ongoing stimulus and supply-side effects. More cautious Liberals warned that public borrowing was liable to destabilize business and financial confidence, and were reluctant to depart from the canons of public finance laid down by Gladstone and Asquith. The problem with the 1929 public works policy was not so much that Liberals were insincere in advocating it, as that they failed to integrate it with their broader economic analysis and to recognize the difficulty of carrying it out under a regime of free trade, free capital movements, and the gold standard. Given the theoretical immaturity of the Keynesian approach and a strong prior commitment to economic internationalism, it is hardly surprising that the party was pushed back towards orthodox policies by the depression and the 1931 financial crisis.

The theoretical and practical reservations about public works which Liberals expressed during the depression receded over the following decade, as the *General Theory* provided a theoretical basis for demand management and Keynes' policy ideas became more widely accepted. It is difficult to trace changes in politicians' economic thought with any precision, but by the Second World War only the party's individualist fringe was still speaking in terms of a self-regulating economic system. Thereafter, the question was what kind of Keynesianism the party favoured. Moderate and right-leaning Liberals, such as Sinclair and Dodds, inclined towards a liberal Keynesianism which relied as far as possible on fiscal and monetary techniques, but left wingers doubted whether this would be sufficient to maintain full employment. The ascendancy of the latter view during wartime helps explain the party's support for *Full Employment in a Free Society*.

The long world boom which followed 1945 settled fears of mass unemployment, and allowed the party to revert to liberal Keynesianism. Most Liberals followed Roy Harrod's lead in seeing Keynes as an internationalist economic technician rather than a radical critic of markets. '[W]hat is likely to survive in his economic teaching', Alan Peacock argued in *Liberal News*,

> is not his analysis of the causes of unemployment, important though it is, but his general method of approach, which is equally applicable to conditions of deflation and inflation.[12]

In the post-war era, the issue of budgeting for a deficit never really arose, and demand management instead became a means of trading off 'over-full' employment for greater price stability at the margins. In common with Conservative politicians and Treasury officials, Liberals tended towards a hawkish position on inflation and ignored Keynes' strictures against using monetary policy as an instrument of fine-tuning. Indeed, Frank Paish and Jo Grimond even took a proto-monetarist interest in the money supply, before concern about slow growth and relative economic decline pushed the party towards more expansive 'Keynesian-plus' policies in the 1960s. Liberal policies, then, were eclectic and frequently reflected intellectual and political fashion. Although the party remained proud of its links with Keynes, it showed no greater fidelity to the *General Theory* than Labour or the Conservatives.

LIBERALS AND NEOLIBERALS

Historians have long recognized that Keynesianism is a malleable economic idea, which has been interpreted in diverse ways and harnessed to a variety of political agendas, yet the assumption that Keynesianism and neoliberalism are intrinsically antithetical has proved a difficult one to shake. This study should reinforce the growing body of work which seeks to dispel it. In the case of the Liberal Party, it would be truer to say that two economic languages were mutually reinforcing. Liberals were able to accept neoliberal arguments against detailed economic planning partly because they believed that mass unemployment could be defeated without it.

The Liberal Party's engagement with the early neoliberal movement went beyond the overlap in personnel which Richard Cockett highlights in *Thinking the Unthinkable*. Just as important as the involvement of Arthur Seldon and Arthur Shenfield in Liberal policy-making was the way in which neoliberal ideas chimed with the party's identity and sense of purpose. During the 1930s, Liberal politicians and free-market economists were similarly bewildered by the growth of nationalism, protectionism, and class warfare, and similarly prone to blame the world's woes on the collapse of the liberal world order which had existed up to 1914. Both groups saw the

[12] *LN*, 23 February 1951, 2.

contemporary political struggle as a clash between internationalist and nationalist policies, and were highly suspicious of the contemporary cult of planning; indeed, many felt that the fortunes of Liberal politics and free-market economics were tied together. This essentially neoliberal narrative went into eclipse during the Second World War, but regained its force in the Cold War atmosphere of the late 1940s and 1950s. One did not have to be a classical individualist to identify with the idea of a 'libertarian counter-revolution' against 'collectivist, *dirigiste* and mercantilist thinking'.[13]

Most British Liberals would have found it difficult to accept neoliberal ideas if they had entailed a wholesale rejection of all forms of state intervention. Walter Lippmann's *The Good Society* was so influential because it combined a critique of planning with a positive agenda for reform which included many of the party's existing commitments. Liberals could champion the market system whilst continuing to advocate social insurance and demand management; they could also offer even-handed criticism of business and trade union restrictive practices. On this reading, the true alternative to socialism was neither a negative defence of the status quo nor a laissez-faire regime but a progressive Liberalism which sought to temper the instability of the market, curb its excesses, and redistribute economic power.

The intellectual and political divergence between the Liberal Party and the neoliberal movement which took place from the mid-1950s onwards stemmed in part from the Liberal Party's left turn. In contrast to the post-war liberal Keynesians, the young activists who joined the Liberal Party during the 1950s and 1960s tended to take a radical view of Keynes, a sceptical view of monetary policy, and a highly optimistic view of planning and the welfare state. Under Grimond's leadership, the party left behind the anti-statism of the Clement Davies years and made its peace with mainstream progressivism. At the same time, however, neoliberalism also changed, as Lippmann and Hayek's efforts to legitimate the market system gave way to the more confident anti-interventionism of Milton Friedman.[14] Friedman and other monetarists questioned the effectiveness of demand management, public choice theory and empirical research by Alan Peacock and Jack Wiseman prompted warnings about a 'ratchet effect' in public spending, and Arthur Shenfield became a vocal critic of anti-trust policies.[15] By the time the interventionist social and economic

[13] Deryck Abel in *LN*, 8 January 1954, 3–4, at 3.

[14] Angus Burgin, *The Great Persuasion: Reinventing Free Markets since the Depression* (Cambridge, Mass., 2012).

[15] David Smith, *The Rise and Fall of Monetarism* (1987); Alan T. Peacock and Jack Wiseman, *The Growth of Public Expenditure in the United Kingdom* (Princeton, 1961); G. C. Peden, 'Economists and the British Welfare State from New Liberalism to the New

policies of the 1960s gave way to the 'stagflation' of the 1970s, neoliberals were much more uniformly critical of Keynesianism and the welfare state than they had been in an earlier period. If free-market economists increasingly regarded the Liberals as woolly-minded moderates, younger Liberals tended to view the IEA and its contributors as reactionary. The parting of the ways between the Liberal Party and neoliberalism thus involved not the betrayal of one by the other, but movement by both away from positions they had once held in common.

THE ROAD TO 2010

This study ends with the 1964 general election, which can be seen in retrospect as the high point of the post-war settlement. Over the next fifteen years British governments found themselves engaged in almost continual crisis management, struggling to combine growth with price and exchange stability in the face of rising trade union militancy and a volatile world economy. Though the misjudgments of Harold Wilson and Edward Heath opened up new opportunities for the Liberals, Conservative critics of Keynesian economic management were the ultimate beneficiaries, and the internationalist, post-industrial free-market settlement established by the Thatcher government has persisted in modified form to the present day. It would be impossible to do justice to the development of Liberal and Liberal Democrat economic policy in the half century since 1964 in just a few pages, but we can nevertheless end with some general comments on the trajectory of the party's thought.[16] Among other things, this helps set the Cameron–Clegg coalition in context.

There is much to be said for seeing the 1960s as an intellectual watershed for British Liberalism as well as a political one, in which the party broke out of its Gladstonian inheritance, tempered its suspicion of the state, and reasserted its progressive credentials. If younger Liberals in the

Right', paper for International Workshop on 'Cambridge, LSE, and the Foundations of the Welfare State: New Liberalism to Neo-Liberalism', Hitotsubashi University, Tokyo, 13–14 March 2010; Norman Barry, 'Arthur Asher Shenfield, 1909–1990: An appreciation', in *Limited Government, Individual Liberty and the Rule of Law: Selected Works of Arthur Asher Shenfield*, ed. Norman Barry (Cheltenham, 1998), 1–13.

[16] The following discussion draws extensively on Andrew Gamble, 'Liberals and the economy', in Vernon Bogdanor (ed.), *Liberal Party Politics* (Oxford, 1983), 191–216; Duncan Brack, 'Liberal Democrat policy', in Don MacIver (ed.), *The Liberal Democrats* (Hemel Hempstead, 1996), 85–110; Duncan Brack, 'Political economy', in Kevin Hickson (ed.), *The Political Thought of the Liberals and Liberal Democrats since 1945* (Manchester, 2009), 102–17; Tudor Jones, *The Revival of British Liberalism: From Grimond to Clegg* (Basingstoke, 2011); and *Liberal Party General Election Manifestos, 1900–1997*, ed. Iain Dale (2000).

1950s were sceptical about free trade, later recruits tended to regard it as a historical curiosity.[17] Since Liberalism was basically about human values and the distribution of power, Grimond argued, the party's support for market economics was pragmatic and contingent; indeed, if a workable form of libertarian socialism could be devised it would have to be taken seriously.[18] Liberal politicians and activists increasingly emphasized how different the British social Liberal tradition was to the classical Liberalism espoused by some continental Liberal parties and the neoliberalism of New Right think-tanks. David Steel thought Grimond had made it clear that 'as far as modern Liberalism was concerned, Keynes and Beveridge were the father figures. Not Adam Smith or anybody else who might have been around.'[19] It might be added that economic policy in general became less central to Liberal identity in this period, as both Jeremy Thorpe and David Steel were more interested in foreign affairs, racial and sexual equality, and constitutional reform.

The Liberal Party's left turn meant that the subsequent rise of the New Right largely passed it by. Instead, Thorpe and Steel remained avowedly Keynesian, seeking to tame the rapid inflation of the 1970s through a statutory incomes policy and the mass unemployment of the early 1980s through a targeted increase in public spending and investment. Both of these policies helped establish common ground with the Social Democratic Party, and though support for free capital movements and Bank of England independence has since constrained the Liberal Democrats' Keynesianism, it has not destroyed it. Alongside macroeconomic management, Liberals and Liberal Democrats have emphasized the need for government to work in partnership with private firms to promote investment, research and development, vocational training, and workplace participation, and have responded to the growth of inequality since 1979 by highlighting the importance of redistributive taxation and high-quality public services. This commitment to an active role for the state in promoting growth, employment, and social justice has received ideological reinforcement from the merger with the SDP, and sociological reinforcement from the prominence of middle-class professionals within the Liberal Democrats. It has also fitted well with the main thrust of the party's electoral strategy, namely the capture of rural and suburban seats from the Conservatives.

We have already noted Jo Grimond's concern that the Liberal Party of the 1970s and 1980s was too closely aligned with the defence of the

[17] Mark Egan, *Coming into Focus: The Transformation of the Liberal Party 1945–64* (Saarbrücken, 2009), 151–2.

[18] J. Grimond, *The Liberal Future* (1959), 54–60.

[19] 'The importance of being Liberal', *Marxism Today* (October 1986), 25–33, at 27.

post-war settlement. Many Liberal activists shared this fear, but they tended to ground their critique of social democracy in a post-materialist perspective rather than a free-market one. 'Community politics' practitioners such as Michael Meadowcroft, Gordon Lishman, and Bernard Greaves believed that the collapse of the long post-war boom paved the way for a transition to a post-capitalist society, geared to the satisfaction of human needs rather than continual economic growth. Workers would become full partners with capital through cooperatives and co-ownership, small-scale production would become more common, and non-material sources of well-being would assume much greater significance.[20] This perspective challenged the assumptions of the modern capitalist system at least as much as it did those of revisionist social democracy.

Support for market economics nevertheless endured within the party, especially at parliamentary level. Besides Grimond, Liberal economic spokesmen John Pardoe and Richard Wainwright emphasized the importance of a profitable private sector and sought to contest Margaret Thatcher and Sir Keith Joseph's claim to be the heirs of Gladstonian Liberalism. Pardoe proposed a radical shift in the tax burden from income to expenditure and wealth (an idea which partially anticipated Sir Geoffrey Howe's 1979 budget) and the Liberals supported most of the Thatcher government's trade union reforms, along with several early privatization measures. This commitment to competitive and flexible markets was matched within the SDP by David Owen's espousal of a 'social market economy', and Paddy Ashdown and Alan Beith sought to underline the Liberal Democrats' free-market credentials after 1988 by advocating private competition for British Rail and opposing plans for a national minimum wage. However, party conference rebellions in 1992 and 1994 suggested that most activists were more interested in dealing with the disruptive social legacy of Thatcherism than in pushing privatization and deregulation further.

If ideological tensions within British Liberalism never wholly went away, they have been brought into much sharper relief in the new millennium. The publication of *The Orange Book* (2004) marked the appearance of a new and more self-confident Liberal Democrat right wing, which sought to reassert the centrality of 'economic liberalism' to the party's identity and vision. Yeovil MP David Laws complained that the Liberal Party's free-market heritage had been 'progressively eroded by forms of soggy socialism and corporatism' during the twentieth century, and argued that Liberal Democrats ought to champion the expansion of choice and

[20] Michael Meadowcroft, *Liberal Values for a New Decade* (second edition, Manchester, 1981); Lishman and Greaves, *Theory and Practice*.

competition within the public services.[21] Laws' emphasis on the efficiency of markets and the limits of the state has since become increasingly influential, especially under Nick Clegg's leadership. Left-leaning Liberal Democrats have responded by reiterating the importance of democratic participation, universal health and education provision, and a more equal distribution of wealth and income.[22] Although the differences between 'Orange Bookers' and 'social Liberals' are liable to be exaggerated, the party is undoubtedly more factionalized than it was in the Ashdown years.

The formation of the coalition government in 2010 has meanwhile been a salutary reminder of how Liberals' support for an integrated global economy can constrain their progressive instincts. Nick Clegg and his colleagues turned to coalition and austerity after the 2010 general election partly because they feared that the crisis of financial confidence in the Eurozone would spread to Britain in the absence of a credible deficit-reduction strategy.[23] If some Liberal Democrats were ideologically sympathetic to public spending cuts, most of the party regarded them as a necessary evil: the large structural deficit which had developed after the 2007–8 banking crisis could not be sustained indefinitely, and putting off the need for cuts seemed likely to push up interest rates. The parallels with 1931 are striking, though the economic and political contexts and the details of government policy were rather different.

Within the constraints imposed by deficit reduction, Liberal Democrat ministers have put some long-standing Liberal concerns on the coalition government's agenda, including tax reform, infrastructure investment, employee ownership, and the need to rebalance the British economy away from its over-reliance on the City of London. All of these policies have been widely supported within the party. Controversies over the coalition's economic strategy and public sector reforms, however, point to an underlying difference of opinion over what the party's longer-term vision should be. Should Liberal Democrats accept the free-market settlement established by the Thatcher government, and indeed extend the scope of market forces, whilst maintaining a social safety net and promoting social mobility?[24] Or should the party seek to use state power more energetically

[21] David Laws, 'Reclaiming Liberalism: a liberal agenda for the Liberal Democrats', in Paul Marshall and David Laws (eds), *The Orange Book: Reclaiming Liberalism* (2004), 18–42, at 29.

[22] Brack et al. (eds), *Reinventing the State.*

[23] Rob Wilson, *5 Days to Power: The Journey to Coalition Britain* (2010), 36–45, 165–70; Vince Cable, 'Keynes would be on our side', *New Statesman*, 17 January 2011, 30.

[24] David Laws, '*The Orange Book*: Eight years on', *Economic Affairs*, xxxii no. 2 (2012), 31–5.

to reduce the instability and inequality of the capitalist system and preserve a non-market public sphere?[25]

This debate is a new and discomfiting one for many Liberal Democrats, but the inter-war and early post-war Liberals studied in this book would probably find it rather familiar. Twentieth-century Liberals grappled at length with the issues thrown up by the party's complex political and economic heritage: the nature of freedom, the strengths and limitations of the market, and the proper role of the state. The translation of Liberal values into policy was a recurring subject of controversy, and in an interventionist age the party frequently found itself making the case for competitive markets. Only in the 1960s did the party break its links with free-market economists and place itself firmly in the progressive mainstream. This triumph of the Liberal left shaped the character of the party's post-war revival. How today's Liberal Democrats interpret their creed may have similarly far-reaching implications for the party's political fortunes and policy impact in the twenty-first century.

25 Prateek Buch, *Plan C—Social Liberal Approaches to a Fair, Sustainable Economy* (2012) <http://planc.socialliberal.net/social-liberal-approaches-to-a-fair-sustainable-economy> accessed 9 October 2013.

Bibliography

All books and pamphlets are published in London unless otherwise stated.

MANUSCRIPT AND ARCHIVAL SOURCES

Bodleian Library, Oxford
MSS. Balfour
MSS. Bonham Carter
Conservative Party Archive
Eighty Club papers (MSS. Eng. c. 2000–9, d. 2000–24, e. 2000–10)
Hirst papers
Maclean papers (dep. a. 49–50, c. 465–71, c. 473, e. 171)
MSS. Macmillan
MSS. Simon
Union of University Liberal Societies papers (MSS. Eng. d. 2025–7)

Borthwick Institute for Archives, University of York
Seebohm Rowntree papers

British Library
Viscount Gladstone papers (Add. MSS. 45985–6118 and 46474–86)
Roy Harrod papers (Add. MSS. 71181–97, 72727–818, and 71609–20)
Reading private papers (MSS. Eur. F118)

British Library of Political and Economic Science, London School of Economics
Ashmore papers
Beveridge papers
Cannan papers
Cockett papers
Henderson papers
Johnson papers
Josephy papers
Liberal Party papers
McFadyean papers
Frank Paish papers
Sir George Paish papers
Robbins papers
Rhys Williams papers
Wainwright papers

Churchill Archives Centre, Cambridge
Mark Abrams papers
Churchill papers
Dingle Foot papers
Sandys papers
Thurso papers

Flintshire Record Office, Hawarden
Flintshire Liberal Association papers

Lancashire Record Office, Preston
Darwen Liberal Association papers

London Metropolitan Archives
London Liberal Party papers

Manchester Archives
Lancashire, Cheshire, and North Western Liberal Federation papers
Ernest Simon papers

The National Archives: Public Record Office
Cabinet and War Cabinet papers (CAB)
Ministry of Housing and Local Government papers (HLG)
Prime Minister's Office papers (PREM)
Treasury papers (T)

National Archives of Scotland
Lothian papers (papers of Philip Kerr, 11th Marquess of Lothian, GD40/17)

National Library of Scotland
Jo Grimond papers (dep. 363)
Scottish Liberal Party papers (Acc. 11765)

National Library of Wales, Aberystwyth
Roderic Bowen papers
Clement Davies papers
Sir Henry Haydn Jones papers
Megan Lloyd George papers

Parliamentary Archives
Harris papers
Lloyd George papers
Samuel papers
Graham White papers

Tower Hamlets Local History Library and Archive
Lydia Benoly diary and scrapbook

Trinity College Library, Cambridge
Layton papers

University of Bristol Special Collections
Liberal Council papers
Mander papers
Mirfin papers
National League of Young Liberals papers
Women's Liberal Federation papers

University of Sheffield Special Collections
Elliott Dodds papers

University of Sussex
Mass Observation Archive

West Yorkshire Archive Service, Kirklees (Huddersfield)
William Mabane papers

West Yorkshire Archive Service, Leeds
Yorkshire Liberal Federation papers

Private collection
David Penwarden papers

NEWSPAPERS AND PERIODICALS

Ahead
The British Weekly
Contemporary Review
Daily Herald
The Economist
Huddersfield Daily Examiner
Land & Liberty
Liberal Council Notes
The Liberal Forward
Liberal Magazine
Liberal News
Liberal Party Organisation Bulletin
The Liberal Year Book
Manchester Guardian (*The Guardian* from 1959)
The Nation and Athenaeum

National Liberal Federation Proceedings
New Outlook
New Statesman (*New Statesman and Nation*, 1931–64)
News Chronicle
The Observer
The Owl
Radical Reform Group Newsletter
The Scotsman
The Spectator
The Times
Westminster Newsletter

OFFICIAL PAPERS

Cmd. 3897, *Report of Committee on Finance and Industry* (1931).
Cmd. 6527, *Employment Policy* (1944).
Cmd. 9015, *Royal Commission on the Taxation of Profits and Income. Second Report* (1954).
Cmnd. 827, *Report of Committee on the Working of the Monetary System* (1959).
Committee on the Working of the Monetary System: Principal Memoranda of Evidence. Volume 3 (1960).
Parliamentary Debates (Hansard).

BOOKS AND ARTICLES

Abel, Deryck, *Free Trade Challenge* (1953).
Abel, Deryck, *Ernest Benn: Counsel for Liberty* (1960).
Abrams, Mark, and Rose, Richard, *Must Labour Lose?* (Harmondsworth, 1960).
Ackers, Peter, 'Collective bargaining as industrial democracy: Hugh Clegg and the political foundations of British industrial relations pluralism', *British Journal of Industrial Relations*, xlv (2007), 77–101.
Acland, Sir Richard, *Only One Battle* (1937).
Acland, Sir Richard, *Unser Kampf: Our Struggle* (Harmondsworth, 1940).
Addison, Paul, *The Road to 1945: British Politics and the Second World War* (1975).
Alden, Percy, *The Unemployed: A National Question* (1905).
Allen, G. C., 'Economic advice for Lloyd George', in G. C. Allen, *British Industry and Economic Policy* (1979), 196–207.
Ayerst, David, *Guardian: Biography of a Newspaper* (1971).
Backhouse, Roger, *A History of Modern Economic Analysis* (Oxford, 1985).
Barberis, Peter, *Liberal Lion. Jo Grimond: A Political Life* (2005).
Barry, Norman, 'Arthur Asher Shenfield, 1909–1990: An appreciation', in *Limited Government, Individual Liberty and the Rule of Law: Selected Works of Arthur Asher Shenfield*, ed. Norman Barry (Cheltenham, 1998), 1–13.
Bentley, Michael, *The Liberal Mind, 1914–1929* (Cambridge, 1977).
Bentley, Michael, *The Climax of Liberal Politics: British Liberalism in Theory and Practice 1868–1918* (1987).

[Bernays, Robert], *The Diaries and Letters of Robert Bernays, 1932–1939: An Insider's Account of the House of Commons*, ed. Nick Smart (Lampeter, 1996).

Berrington, H. B., 'The general election of 1964', *Journal of the Royal Statistical Society*, series A, cxxviii (1965), 17–51.

Beveridge, Sir William (Lord Beveridge), *Planning under Socialism and Other Addresses* (1936).

Beveridge, Sir William (Lord Beveridge), *Full Employment in a Free Society* (1944).

Beveridge, Sir William (Lord Beveridge), *Why I am a Liberal* (1945).

Beveridge, Sir William (Lord Beveridge), *Voluntary Action: A Report on Methods of Social Advance* (1948).

Beveridge, Sir William (Lord Beveridge) et al., *Tariffs: The Case Examined. By a Committee of Economists under the Chairmanship of Sir William Beveridge, K.C.B.* (1931).

Biagini, Eugenio F., *Liberty, Retrenchment and Reform: Popular Liberalism in the Age of Gladstone, 1860–1880* (Cambridge, 1992).

Birch, A. H., *Small-Town Politics: A Study of Political Life in Glossop* (Oxford, 1959).

Blaazer, David, *The Popular Front and the Progressive Tradition: Socialists, Liberals, and the Quest for Unity, 1884–1939* (Cambridge, 1992).

Black, Lawrence, *The Political Culture of the Left in Affluent Britain, 1951–1964: Old Labour, New Britain?* (Basingstoke, 2003).

Black, Lawrence and Pemberton, Hugh (eds), *An Affluent Society? Britain's Post-War 'Golden Age' Revisited* (Aldershot, 2004).

Blackburn, Sheila, *A Fair Day's Wage for a Fair Day's Work? Sweated Labour and the Origins of Minimum Wage Legislation in Britain* (Aldershot, 2007).

Bogdanor, Vernon, 'Conclusion: The Liberal Party, the Alliance, and the future', in Bogdanor (ed.), *Liberal Party Politics*, 275–84.

Bogdanor, Vernon (ed.), *Liberal Party Politics* (Oxford, 1983).

Bonham, John, *The Middle Class Vote* (1954).

[Bonham Carter, Violet], *Champion Redoubtable: The Diaries and Letters of Violet Bonham Carter, 1914–1945*, ed. Mark Pottle (1998).

[Bonham Carter, Violet], *Daring to Hope: The Diaries and Letters of Violet Bonham Carter, 1946–1969*, ed. Mark Pottle (2000).

Booth, Alan, 'The 'Keynesian revolution' in economic policy-making', *Economic History Review*, second series, xxxvi (1983), 103–23.

Booth, Alan, *British Economic Policy, 1931–49: Was there a Keynesian Revolution?* (1989).

Booth, Alan, 'Inflation, expectations, and the political economy of Conservative Britain, 1951–1964', *HJ*, xliii (2000), 827–47.

Boyce, Robert W. D., *British Capitalism at the Crossroads, 1919–1932: A Study in Politics, Economics, and International Relations* (Cambridge, 1987).

Boyd Orr, Sir John, *Food, Health and Income* (1936).

Brack, Duncan, 'Liberal Democrat policy', in MacIver (ed.), *The Liberal Democrats*, 85–110.

Brack, Duncan, 'Political economy', in Hickson (ed.), *Political Thought of the Liberals and Liberal Democrats since 1945* (Manchester, 2009), 102–17.

Brack, Duncan, Grayson, Richard, and Howarth, David (eds), *Reinventing the State: Social Liberalism for the 21st Century* (2009).

Briggs, Asa, *Social Thought and Social Action: A Study in the Work of Seebohm Rowntree, 1871–1954* (1961).

The British Electorate, 1963–1987, ed. Ivor Crewe, Neil Day, and Anthony Fox (Cambridge, 1991).

Brittan, Samuel, *The Treasury under the Tories, 1951–1964* (Harmondsworth, 1964).

Broadberry, S. N., and Crafts, N. F. R., 'Britain's productivity gap in the 1930s: Some neglected factors', *Journal of Economic History*, lii (1992), 531–58.

Broadberry, S. N., and Crafts, N. F. R., 'British economic policy and industrial performance in the early post-war period', *Business History*, xxxviii, no. 4 (1996), 65–91.

Brooke, Stephen, 'Atlantic crossing? American views of capitalism and British socialist thought 1932–62', *TCBH*, ii (1991), 107–36.

Brooke, Stephen, *Labour's War: The Labour Party and the Second World War* (Oxford, 1992).

Buch, Prateek, *Plan C—Social Liberal Approaches to a Fair, Sustainable Economy* (2012) <http://planc.socialliberal.net/social-liberal-approaches-to-a-fair-sustainable-economy> accessed 9 October 2013.

Bullock, Alan, and Shock, Maurice (eds), *The Liberal Tradition from Fox to Keynes* (1956).

Burgin, Angus, *The Great Persuasion: Reinventing Free Markets since the Depression* (Cambridge, Mass., 2012).

Butler, David, and Stokes, Donald, *Political Change in Britain: Forces Shaping Electoral Choice* (1969).

Butler, J. R. M., *Lord Lothian (Philip Kerr), 1882–1940* (1960).

Cairncross, Alec, *Years of Recovery: British Economic Policy 1945–51* (1985).

Calder, Angus, *The Myth of the Blitz* (1991).

Campbell, John, 'The renewal of Liberalism: Liberalism without Liberals', in Peele and Cook (eds), *The Politics of Reappraisal*, 88–113.

Campbell, John, *Lloyd George: The Goat in the Wilderness, 1922–1931* (1977).

[Churchill, Sir Winston, and Sinclair, Sir Archibald], *Winston and Archie: The Collected Correspondence of Winston Churchill and Archibald Sinclair, 1915–1960*, ed. Ian Hunter (2005).

Clark, Colin, *Growthmanship: A Study in the Mythology of Investment* (1961).

Clarke, Peter, *Liberals and Social Democrats* (Cambridge, 1978).

Clarke, Peter, *The Keynesian Revolution in the Making, 1924–1936* (Oxford, 1988).

Close, D. H., 'The realignment of the British electorate in 1931', *History*, lxvii (1982), 393–404.

Cockett, Richard, *Thinking the Unthinkable: Think-Tanks and the Economic Counter-Revolution, 1931–1983* (1994; paperback edition, 1995).

Cole, Matt, '"An out-of-date word": Grimond and the left', *JLH*, no. 67 (2010), 50–6.

Cole, Matt, *Richard Wainwright, the Liberals and Liberal Democrats: Unfinished Business* (Manchester, 2011).

Collini, Stefan, *Liberalism and Sociology: L. T. Hobhouse and Political Argument in England, 1880–1914* (Cambridge, 1979).

Cook, Chris, *The Age of Alignment: Electoral Politics in Britain, 1922–1929* (1975).

Cook, Chris, 'Liberals, Labour and local elections', in Peele and Cook (eds), *The Politics of Reappraisal*, 166–188.

Cooper, Chris, 'Little local difficulties revisited: Peter Thorneycroft, the 1958 Treasury resignations, and the origins of Thatcherism', *CBH*, xxv (2011), 227–50.

Cowie, Harry, *Why Liberal?* (Harmondsworth, 1964).

Cragoe, Matthew, and Readman, Paul (eds), *The Land Question in Britain, 1750–1950* (Basingstoke, 2010).

Croome, Honor, 'Liberty, equality and full employment', *Lloyds Bank Review*, no. 13 (July 1949), 14–32.

Crosland, Anthony, *Britain's Economic Problem* (1953).

Crosland, Anthony, *The Future of Socialism* (1956).

Cyr, Arthur, *Liberal Party Politics in Britain* (New Brunswick, NJ, 1977).

Dahrendorf, Ralf, *After Social Democracy* (1980).

Daunton, Martin, *Trusting Leviathan: The Politics of Taxation in Britain, 1799–1914* (Cambridge, 2001).

Daunton, Martin, *Just Taxes: The Politics of Taxation in Britain, 1914–1979* (Cambridge, 2002).

Davies, Sam, and Morley, Bob, *County Borough Elections in England and Wales, 1919–1938: A Comparative Analysis* (3 vols to date, Aldershot, 1999–).

Davis, John, 'Primrose, Archibald Philip, fifth earl of Rosebery and first earl of Midlothian (1847–1929)', *Oxford Dictionary of National Biography* (60 vols, Oxford, 2004), xlv, 370–83.

Dawson, Michael, 'The Liberal land policy, 1924–1929: Electoral strategy and internal division', *TCBH*, ii (1991), 272–90.

Design for Freedom Committee, *Design for Freedom* (1947).

Design for Freedom Committee, *Design for Survival* (1947).

Design for Freedom Committee, *Design for Recovery* (1948).

Dimsdale, Nicholas H., 'Employment and real wages in the inter-war period', *National Institute Economic Review*, no. 110 (November 1984), 94–103.

Dodds, Elliott, *Liberalism in Action: A Record and a Policy* (1922).

Dodds, Elliott, *Let's Try Liberalism* (1944).

Dodds, Elliott, *The Rights of Men as Persons* (1945).

Dodds, Elliott, *The Defence of Man* (1946).

Dodds, Elliott, 'The welfare state', *The Fortnightly* (September 1949), 172–8.

Dodds, Elliott, 'Liberty and welfare', in Watson (ed.), *The Unservile State*, 13–26.

Douglas, Roy, *The History of the Liberal Party, 1895–1970* (1971).

Douglas, Roy, *Land, People and Politics: A History of the Land Question in the United Kingdom, 1878–1952* (1976).

Douglas, Roy, *Liberals: A History of the Liberal and Liberal Democratic Parties* (2005).

Dow, J. C. R., *The Management of the British Economy, 1945–60* (Cambridge, 1964).

Doyle, Barry M., 'Urban Liberalism and the "lost generation": Politics and middle class culture in Norwich, 1900–1935', *HJ*, xxxviii (1995), 617–34.

Dudley Edwards, Ruth, *The Pursuit of Reason: The Economist, 1843–1993* (1993).

Durant, Henry W., *Political Opinion: Four General Election Results* (1949).

Durbin, Elizabeth, *New Jerusalems: The Labour Party and the Economics of Democratic Socialism* (1985).

Dutton, David, 'On the brink of oblivion: The post-war crisis of British Liberalism', *Canadian Journal of History*, xxvii (1992), 425–50.

Dutton, David, *Simon: A Political Biography of Sir John Simon* (1992).

Dutton, David, *A History of the Liberal Party since 1900* (Basingstoke, 2004; second edition, Basingstoke, 2013).

Dutton, David, 'William Mabane and Huddersfield politics, 1931–1947: "By any other name a Liberal"', *Northern History*, xliii (2006), 137–53.

Dutton, David, *Liberals in Schism: A History of the National Liberal Party* (2008).

Duverger, Maurice, *Political Parties: Their Organization and Activity in the Modern State* (1954).

Dwyer, Terence M., 'Henry George's thought in relation to modern economics', *AJES*, xli (1982), 363–73.

Egan, Mark, 'Harry Willcock: The forgotten champion of Liberalism', *JLDH*, no. 17 (1997–8), 16–17.

Egan, Mark, *Coming into Focus: The Transformation of the Liberal Party, 1945–64* (Saarbrücken, 2009).

Egan, Mark, 'Radical Action and the Liberal Party during the Second World War', *JLH*, no. 63 (2009), 4–17.

Eichengreen, Barry, *Sterling and the Tariff, 1929–32* (Princeton, 1981).

Eichengreen, Barry and Uzan, Marc, 'The 1933 World Economic Conference as an instance of failed international cooperation', in Peter B. Evans, Harold K. Jacobson, and Robert D. Putnam (eds), *Double-Edged Diplomacy: International Bargaining and Domestic Politics* (Berkeley, Calif., 1993), 171–206.

Eltis, Walter, 'Growth without inflation', in Watson (ed.), *Radical Alternative*, 69–91.

Emy, H. V., 'The Land Campaign: Lloyd George as a social reformer, 1909–14', in A. J. P. Taylor (ed.), *Lloyd George: Twelve Essays* (1971), 35–68.

Emy, H. V., *Liberals, Radicals and Social Politics, 1892–1914* (Cambridge, 1973).

Favretto, Ilaria, '"Wilsonism" reconsidered: Labour Party revisionism 1952–64', *CBH*, xiv (2000), 54–80.

Fielding, Steven, 'What did "the people" want? The meaning of the 1945 general election', *HJ*, xxxv (1992), 623–39.

Fielding, Steven, Thompson, Peter, and Tiratsoo, Nick, *'England Arise!' The Labour Party and Popular Politics in 1940s Britain* (Manchester, 1995).

Finn, Margot, *After Chartism: Class and Nation in English Radical Politics, 1848–1874* (Cambridge, 1993).

Fletcher, Gordon, *Dennis Robertson* (Basingstoke, 2008).

Fogarty, Michael, *Opportunity Knocks* (1961).

Fogarty, Michael, *My Life and Ours* (Oxford, 1999).

Foot, Dingle, *Despotism in Disguise* (1937).

Foot, Isaac, *Liberty & the Liberal Heritage: The Ramsay Muir Memorial Lecture, 1947* (1948).

Foote, Geoffrey, *The Republican Transformation of Modern British Politics* (Basingstoke, 2006).

Fourcade, Marion, *Economists and Societies: Discipline and Profession in the United States, Britain, and France, 1890s to 1990s* (Princeton, 2009).

Freeden, Michael, *The New Liberalism: An Ideology of Social Reform* (Oxford, 1978).

Freeden, Michael, *Liberalism Divided: A Study in British Political Thought, 1914–1939* (Oxford, 1986).

Freeden, Michael, *Ideologies and Political Theory: A Conceptual Approach* (Oxford, 1996).

Fulford, Roger, *The Liberal Case* (Harmondsworth, 1959).

Gamble, Andrew, 'Liberals and the economy', in Bogdanor (ed.), *Liberal Party Politics* (Oxford, 1983), 191–216.

Gamble, Andrew, 'Ideas and interests in British economic policy', *CBH*, x (1996), 1–21.

Garside, W. R., *British Unemployment, 1919–1939: A Study in Public Policy* (Cambridge, 1990).

George, Henry, *Progress and Poverty: An Inquiry into the Cause of Industrial Depressions and of Increase of Want with Increase of Wealth, The Remedy* (Garden City, NY, 1879).

Gilbert, Bentley, 'Third parties and voters' decisions: The Liberals and the general election of 1945', *Journal of British Studies*, xi (1972), 131–41.

Gliddon, Paul, 'The political importance of provincial newspapers, 1903–1945: The Rowntrees and the Liberal press', *TCBH*, xiv (2003), 24–42.

Goldman, Lawrence, *Science, Reform, and Politics in Victorian Britain: The Social Science Association, 1857–1886* (Cambridge, 2002).

Grant, Matthew, 'Historians, the Penguin Specials and the "state-of-the-nation" literature, 1958–64', *CBH*, xvii (2003), 29–54.

Grayson, Richard S., *Liberals, International Relations, and Appeasement: The Liberal Party, 1919–1939* (2001).

Grayson, Richard S., 'Social democracy or social liberalism? Ideological sources of Liberal Democrat policy', *Political Quarterly*, lxxviii (2007), 32–9.

Greaves, Julian, *Industrial Reorganization and Government Policy in Interwar Britain* (Aldershot, 2005).

Green, Ewen, 'The Conservative Party, the state and the electorate, 1945–64', in Jon Lawrence and Miles Taylor (eds), *Party, State and Society: Electoral Behaviour in Britain since 1820* (Aldershot, 1997), 176–200.

Green, Ewen, *Ideologies of Conservatism: Conservative Political Ideas in the Twentieth Century* (Oxford, 2002).

Green, Ewen, 'Conservatism, the state, and civil society in the twentieth century', in Green, *Ideologies of Conservatism*, 240–79.

Green, Ewen, 'The Treasury resignations of 1958: A reconsideration', in Green, *Ideologies of Conservatism* (Oxford, 2002), 192–213.

Green, Ewen, 'The Conservative Party and Keynes', in Green and Tanner (eds), *Strange Survival*, 186–211.

Green, Ewen and Tanner, Duncan (eds), *The Strange Survival of Liberal England: Political Leaders, Moral Values and the Reception of Economic Debate* (Cambridge, 2007).

Green, Ewen and Tanner, Duncan, 'Introduction', in Green and Tanner (eds), *Strange Survival*, 1–33.

Greenleaf, W. H., *The British Political Tradition* (3 vols, 1983–7).

Griffiths, Clare, *Labour and the Countryside: The Politics of Rural Britain, 1918–1939* (Oxford, 2007).

Grimond, Joseph, 'The principles of Liberalism', *Political Quarterly*, xxiv (1953), 236–42.

Grimond, Joseph, *The New Liberal Democracy* (1958).

Grimond, Joseph, *The Liberal Future* (1959).

Grimond, Joseph, *Let's Get On With It* (1960).

Grimond, Joseph, *Growth not Grandeur* (1961).

Grimond, Joseph, *The Liberal Challenge* (1963).

Grimond, Joseph, *The Common Welfare* (1978).

Grimond, Joseph, *Memoirs* (1979).

Grimond, Joseph, *A Personal Manifesto* (Oxford, 1983).

de Groot, Gerard J., *Liberal Crusader: The Life of Sir Archibald Sinclair* (1993).

Harris, José, *Unemployment and Politics: A Study in English Social Policy, 1886–1914* (Oxford, 1972).

Harris, José, *William Beveridge: A Biography* (1977; second edition, Oxford, 1994).

Harris, José, 'Political ideas and the debate on state welfare, 1940–45', in Harold L. Smith (ed.), *War and Social Change: British Society in the Second World War* (Manchester, 1986), 233–63.

Harris, Nigel, *Competition and the Corporate Society: British Conservatives, the State and Industry, 1945–1964* (1972).

Harris, Sir Percy, *Forty Years in and out of Parliament* (1947).

Harrod, Roy, *Tory Menace: What is Article 7?* (1945).

Harrod, Roy, *Are These Hardships Necessary?* (1947).

Harrod, Roy, 'And still no plan', *Soundings* (December 1947), reprinted in Roy Harrod, *And So It Goes On: Further Thoughts on Present Mismanagement* (1951), 89–105

Harrod, Roy, *The Life of John Maynard Keynes* (1951).
[Harrod, Roy], *The Collected Interwar Papers and Correspondence of Roy Harrod*, ed. Daniele Besomi (3 vols, Cheltenham, 2003).
Hayek, F. A. (ed.), *Collectivist Economic Planning: Critical Studies on the Possibilities of Socialism* (1935).
Hayek, F. A., *Freedom and the Economic System* (Chicago, 1939).
Hayek, F. A., *The Road to Serfdom* (1944).
Heath, Anthony, Jowell, Roger, and Curtice, John, *How Britain Votes* (Oxford, 1985).
Heath, Anthony, et al., *Understanding Political Change: The British Voter, 1964–1987* (Oxford, 1991).
Hicks, J. R., 'Mr Keynes and the classics: A suggested interpretation', *Econometrica*, v (1937), 147–59.
Hickson, Kevin (ed.), *The Political Thought of the Liberals and Liberal Democrats since 1945* (Manchester, 2009).
Hilson, Mary, and Melling, Joseph, 'Public gifts and private identities: Sir Richard Acland, Common Wealth, and the moral politics of land ownership in the 1940s', *TCBH*, xi (2000), 156–82.
Hinton, James, 'Women and the Labour vote, 1945–50', *Labour History Review*, lvii, no. 3 (1992), 59–66.
Hinton, James, 'Militant housewives: the British Housewives' League and the Attlee Government', *History Workshop Journal*, xxxviii (1994), 129–56.
Hirst, Francis W., *Gladstone as Financier and Economist* (1931).
Hirst, Francis W., *Economic Freedom and Private Property* (1935).
Hirst, Francis W., *Liberty and Tyranny* (1935).
Hirst, Francis W., *Pressing Problems and Fashionable Fallacies of Political Economy* (1942).
Hirst, Francis W., *Principles of Prosperity* (1944).
Hobhouse, L. T., *Liberalism* (1911).
Hobhouse, L. T., *The Metaphysical Theory of the State: A Criticism* (1918).
Hobson, J. A., 'The impact of Henry George in England', *Fortnightly Review*, lxviii (1897), 835–44.
Hobson, J. A., *The Social Problem* (1902).
Hobson, J. A., *Confessions of an Economic Heretic* (1938).
Hobson, J. A. and Mummery, A. F., *The Physiology of Industry: An Exposure of Certain Fallacies in Existing Theories of Economics* (1889).
Holt, Arthur, 'The Liberal attitude to contemporary problems', *Political Quarterly*, xxiv (1953), 249–58.
Hopkin Morris, R., *Dare or Despair* ([1949]).
Howe, Anthony, *Free Trade and Liberal England, 1846–1946* (Oxford, 1997).
Howe, Anthony, 'The Liberals and the City 1900–1931', in Ranald Michie and Philip Williamson (eds), *The British Government and the City of London in the Twentieth Century* (Cambridge, 2004), 135–52.
Howson, Susan, *Lionel Robbins* (Cambridge, 2011).
Hubback, David, *No Ordinary Press Baron: A Life of Walter Layton* (1985).

Hutchison, T. W., *A Review of Economic Doctrines, 1870–1929* (Oxford, 1953).

Hutchison, T. W., *Economics and Economic Policy in Britain, 1946–1966: Some Aspects of their Interrelations* (1968).

Hutchison, T. W., *On Revolutions and Progress in Economic Knowledge* (Cambridge, 1978).

Hutton, D. Graham, 'Our economic discontents', *Lloyds Bank Limited Monthly Review*, no. 76 (June 1936), 286–303.

Hyde, H. Montgomery, *Strong for Service: The Life of Lord Nathan of Churt* (1968).

Ingham, Robert, 'Clement Davies: A brief reply', *JLDH*, no. 26 (2000), 24–5.

Ingham, Robert, 'Battle of ideas or absence of leadership? Ideological struggle in the Liberal Party in the 1940s and 1950s', *JLH*, no. 47 (2005), 36–44.

Ingham, Robert, 'A retreat from the left? The Liberal Party and Labour 1945–55', *JLH*, no. 67 (2010), 38–44.

Ingham, Robert, and Brack, Duncan (eds), *Peace, Reform and Liberation: A History of Liberal Politics in Britain 1679–2011* (2011).

Jackson, Ben, *Equality and the British Left: A Study in Progressive Political Thought, 1900–64* (Manchester, 2007).

Jackson, Ben, 'At the origins of neo-liberalism: The free economy and the strong state, 1930–1947', *HJ*, liii (2010), 129–51.

Jackson, Ben, 'Freedom, the common good, and the rule of law: Lippmann and Hayek on economic planning', *Journal of the History of Ideas*, lxxiii (2012), 47–68.

Jackson, Ben, 'The think-tank archipelago: Thatcherism and neo-liberalism', in Ben Jackson and Robert Saunders (eds), *Making Thatcher's Britain* (Cambridge, 2012), 43–61.

Jackson, Ben, 'Socialism and the New Liberalism', in Ben Jackson and Marc Stears (eds), *Liberalism as Ideology: Essays in Honour of Michael Freeden* (Oxford, 2012), 34–52.

Jefferys, Kevin, *The Churchill Coalition and Wartime Politics, 1940–1945* (Manchester, 1991).

Jevons, W. S., *The State in Relation to Labour* (1882).

Johnson, Donald, *Bars and Barricades* (1952).

Joint Political Committee of the National League of Young Liberals and the Union of Liberal Students, *New Orbits* (1959).

Jones, J. Graham, 'Wales and the New Liberalism, 1926–1929', *National Library of Wales Journal*, xxii (1981–2), 321–46.

Jones, J. Graham, 'The Liberal Party and Wales, 1945–79', *Welsh History Review*, xvi (1993), 326–55.

Jones, Mervyn, *A Radical Life: The Biography of Megan Lloyd George, 1902–66* (1991).

Jones, Tudor, 'Liberal Democrat thought', in MacIver (ed.), *The Liberal Democrats*, 63–83.

Jones, Tudor, *The Revival of British Liberalism: From Grimond to Clegg* (Basingstoke, 2011).

Joyce, Peter, *The Liberal Party and the 1945 General Election* (Dorchester, 1995).

Joyce, Peter, *Realignment of the Left? A History of the Relationship between the Liberal Democrat and Labour Parties* (Basingstoke, 1999).

Kerr, Philip (Marquess of Lothian), *Liberalism in the Modern World* (1933).

Keynes, John Maynard, 'Does unemployment need a drastic remedy?' [1924], reprinted in *JMK*, xix, 219–23.

Keynes, John Maynard, 'Am I a Liberal?' [1925], reprinted in *JMK*, ix, 295–306.

Keynes, John Maynard, 'The end of laissez-faire' [1926], reprinted in *JMK*, ix, 272–94.

Keynes, John Maynard, 'Liberalism and Labour' [1926], reprinted in *JMK*, ix, 307–11.

Keynes, John Maynard, *A Treatise on Money* (2 vols, 1930).

Keynes, John Maynard, 'The means to prosperity' [1933], reprinted in *JMK*, ix, 335–66.

Keynes, John Maynard, 'National self-sufficiency' [1933], reprinted in *JMK*, xxi, 233–46.

Keynes, John Maynard, *The General Theory of Employment Interest and Money* (1936).

Keynes, John Maynard, 'The general theory of employment', *Quarterly Journal of Economics*, li (1937), 209–23.

Keynes, John Maynard, 'How to avoid a slump' [1937], reprinted in *JMK*, xxi, 384–95.

Keynes, John Maynard, and Henderson, H. D., *Can Lloyd George Do It? An Examination of the Liberal Pledge* (1929).

[Keynes, John Maynard], *The Collected Writings of John Maynard Keynes*, ed. D. E. Moggridge and Elizabeth S. Johnson (30 vols, 1971–89).

Kirby, M. W., 'Government intervention in industrial organization: Coal mining in the nineteen thirties', *Business History*, xv (1973), 160–73.

Koss, Stephen, *Sir John Brunner: Radical Plutocrat, 1842–1919* (Cambridge, 1970).

Koss, Stephen, 'Lloyd George and Nonconformity: the last rally', *EHR*, lxxxix (1974), 77–106.

Koss, Stephen, *The Rise and Fall of the Political Press in Britain* (2 vols, 1981–4).

Labour Party General Election Manifestos, 1900–1997, ed. Iain Dale (2000).

Laidler, David, *Fabricating the Keynesian Revolution: Studies of the Inter-war Literature on Money, the Cycle, and Unemployment* (Cambridge, 1999).

Land Enquiry Committee, *The Land: The Report of the Land Enquiry Committee* (2 vols, 1913–14).

Laws, David, 'Reclaiming Liberalism: a liberal agenda for the Liberal Democrats', in Paul Marshall and David Laws (eds), *The Orange Book: Reclaiming Liberalism* (2004), 18–42.

Laws, David, *22 Days in May: The Birth of the Lib Dem–Conservative Coalition* (2010).

Laws, David, '*The Orange Book*: Eight years on', *Economic Affairs*, xxxii, no. 2 (2012), 31–5.

Lee, Bradford A., 'The miscarriage of necessity and invention: Proto-Keynesianism and democratic states in the 1930s', in Peter A. Hall (ed.), *The Political Power of Economic Ideas: Keynesianism across Nations* (Princeton, 1989), 129–70.

Leijonhufvud, Axel, *On Keynesian Economics and the Economics of Keynes* (1968).

Liberal Council, *Safeguarding under the Searchlight: An Enquiry into the Origin and Results of the Safeguarding Duties Separately Examined* (*c.*1928).

Liberal Council, *Report of the Annual Meeting, held on Wednesday, 10th April, 1929* (1929).

Liberal Council, *Report of the Annual Meeting, held on Tuesday, 14th January, 1930* (1930).

Liberal Council, *Report of the Annual Meeting, held on Tuesday, 14th April, 1931* (1931).

Liberal Council, *The Right Way with the Rates* (1937).

Liberal Council, *The Time for Economy* (1938).

Liberal Industrial Inquiry, *Britain's Industrial Future: Being the Report of the Liberal Industrial Inquiry* (1928).

Liberal Party, *We Can Conquer Unemployment: Mr Lloyd George's Pledge* (1929).

Liberal Party, *Constitution of the Liberal Party* (1936).

Liberal Party, *Ownership for All: The Liberal Party Committee's Report on the Distribution of Property* (1938).

Liberal Party, *Liberal Policy: Being the resolutions adopted at the meeting of the Assembly of the Liberal Party Organisation, at Scarborough May 11th & 12th, 1939* (1939).

Liberal Party, *Food and Agriculture* (1943).

Liberal Party, *International Trade* (1943).

Liberal Party, *Land and Housing* (1943).

Liberal Party, *Money and Banking* (1943).

Liberal Party, *The Relation of the State to Industry* (1943).

Liberal Party, *Remuneration of the Worker* (1943).

Liberal Party, *Status of the Worker* (1943).

Liberal Party, *The Government's Employment Policy Examined: An Interim Report of the Liberal Party Committee on Full Employment* (1944).

Liberal Party, *The Future of British Transport: Proposals of a Liberal Party Committee under the Chairmanship of B. Seebohm Rowntree, C.H.* (1945).

Liberal Party, *The Liberal Charter* (1945).

Liberal Party, *Monopoly: The Report of a Liberal Party Committee* (1945).

Liberal Party, *The Radical Programme of the Liberal Party* (1945).

Liberal Party, *Reorganisation of the Coal Industry: Report of a Liberal Committee* (1945).

Liberal Party, *Report of the Liberal Party Sub-Committee on the Rent Restrictions Acts and Housing Subsidies* (1948).

Liberal Party, *People in Industry: A Report on the Liberal Co-ownership Proposals* (1949).

Liberal Party, *Reform of Income Tax and Social Security Payments: A Liberal Party Yellow Book* (1950).

Liberal Party, *The Liberal Party Housing Committee: Interim Report* (1951).
Liberal Party, *A Radical Programme: Commentary on the Official Resolution to be Submitted to the Assembly Meeting, Hastings* (1952).
Liberal Party, *Report of the Liberal Co-Ownership Committee* (1953).
Liberal Party, *Monopoly: Being a Second Report, presented to the Liberal Party Assembly at Buxton, April, 1954* (1954).
Liberal Party, *Interim Report of the Liberal Party Co-Ownership Committee* (1955).
Liberal Party, *Liberal Candidates' and Speakers' Handbook, 1959* (1959).
Liberal Party, *Taxation: A Report to the Liberal Party* (1962).
Liberal Party General Election Manifestos, 1900–1997, ed. Iain Dale (2000).
Liberal Women's Unemployment Enquiry Group, *Unemployment: Report of the Liberal Women's Unemployment Enquiry Group* (1934).
Lippiatt, Graham, 'Radical Reform Group', *JLH*, no. 67 (2010), 45–9.
Lippmann, Walter, *The Method of Freedom* (New York, 1934).
Lippmann, Walter, *The Good Society* (1937; second edition, New York, 1943).
Lishman, Gordon, and Greaves, Bernard, *The Theory and Practice of Community Politics* (Hebden Bridge, 1980).
Lloyd George, David, the Marquess of Lothian, and Rowntree, B. Seebohm, *How to Tackle Unemployment: The Liberal Plans as laid before the Government and the Nation* (1930).
Lowe, Rodney, 'The Second World War, consensus, and the foundation of the welfare state', *TCBH*, i (1990), 152–82.
Lowe, Rodney, 'The replanning of the welfare state, 1957–1964', in Martin Francis and Ina Zweiniger-Bargielowska (eds), *The Conservatives and British Society, 1880–1990* (Cardiff, 1996), 110–35.
Lowe, Rodney, 'Modernizing Britain's welfare state: The influence of affluence, 1957–1964', in Black and Pemberton (eds), *An Affluent Society?*, 35–51.
McCallum, R. B., and Readman, Alison, *The British General Election of 1945* (Oxford, 1947).
McCarthy, Helen, 'Parties, voluntary associations, and democratic politics in interwar Britain', *HJ*, l (2007), 891–912.
McCarthy, Helen, *The British People and the League of Nations: Democracy, citizenship and internationalism,* c.*1918–48* (Manchester, 2011).
McFadyean, Sir Andrew, *Government and Industry* (1944).
McFadyean, Sir Andrew, *The Liberal Case* (1950).
McFadyean, Sir Andrew, *Recollected in Tranquillity* (1964).
MacIver, Don (ed.), *The Liberal Democrats* (Hemel Hempstead, 1996).
McKibbin, Ross, 'The economic policy of the second Labour government, 1929–1931', *Past and Present*, lxviii (1975), 95–123.
McKibbin, Ross, 'Class and conventional wisdom: The Conservative Party and the "public" in inter-war Britain', in Ross McKibbin, *The Ideologies of Class: Social Relations in Britain, 1880–1950* (Oxford, 1990), 228–58.
McKibbin, Ross, *Classes and Cultures: England, 1918–1951* (Oxford, 1998).
McKibbin, Ross, *Parties and People: England, 1914–1951* (Oxford, 2010).

Macleod, Iain, and Maude, Angus, *One Nation: A Tory Approach to Social Problems* (1950).

McManus, Michael, *Jo Grimond: Towards the Sound of Gunfire* (Edinburgh, 2001).

Macnicol, John, *The Movement for Family Allowances, 1918–45: A Study in Social Policy Development* (1980).

Markwell, Donald, *John Maynard Keynes and International Relations* (Oxford, 2006).

Marquand, David, *Ramsay MacDonald* (1977).

Marshall, Alfred, *The Present Position of Economics: An Inaugural Lecture Given in the Senate House at Cambridge, 24 February 1885* (1885).

Marwick, Arthur, 'Middle opinion in the Thirties: Planning, progress and political "agreement"', *EHR*, lxxix (1964), 285–98.

Mason, D. M., *Monetary Policy, 1914–1928* (1928).

Matthew, H. C. G., *The Liberal Imperialists: The Ideas and Politics of a Post-Gladstonian Elite* (Oxford, 1973).

Matthew, H. C. G., 'Disraeli, Gladstone, and the politics of mid-Victorian budgets', *HJ*, xxii (1979), 615–43.

Matthews, R. C. O., 'Why has Britain had full employment since the war?', *EJ*, lxxviii (1968), 555–69.

Meade, James, 'Sir William Beveridge's *Full Employment in a Free Society* and the White Paper on Employment Policy (Command 6527)', in *The Collected Papers of James Meade*, ed. Susan Howson and Donald Moggridge (4 vols, 1988–90), i, 233–64.

Meade, James, *Planning and the Price Mechanism: The Liberal–Socialist Solution* (1948).

Meadowcroft, John, and Reynolds, Jaime, 'Liberals and the New Right', *JLH*, no. 47 (2005), 45–51.

Meadowcroft, Michael, *Liberal Values for a New Decade* (second edition: Manchester, 1981).

Meston, James (Lord Meston), 'At the N.L.F.', in *Ramsay Muir*, 194–8.

Micklem, Nathaniel, *The Box and the Puppets (1888–1953)* (1957).

Micklem, Nathaniel, *Honest Politics for a New World* (1957).

Micklem, Nathaniel, *My Cherry-Tree* (1966).

Middleton, Roger, *Towards the Managed Economy: Keynes, the Treasury, and the Fiscal Policy Debate of the 1930s* (1985).

Middleton, Roger, *Charlatans or Saviours? Economists and the British Economy from Marshall to Meade* (Cheltenham, 1998).

Middleton, Roger, 'Economists and economic growth in Britain, *c.*1955–65', in Black and Pemberton (eds), *An Affluent Society?*, 129–47.

Middleton, Roger, 'British monetary and fiscal policy in the 1930s', *Oxford Review of Economic Policy*, xxvi (2010), 414–41.

Middleton, Roger, 'Macroeconomic policy in Britain between the wars', *Economic History Review*, second series, lxiv (2011), special virtual issue on Macroeconomic Policy in Britain between the Wars, 1–31.

Mill, John Stuart, *Principles of Political Economy with Some of Their Applications to Social Philosophy* (1848).

Mirowski, Philip, 'Postscript: Defining neoliberalism', in Mirowski and Plehwe (eds), *The Road from Mont Pèlerin*, 417–55.

Mirowski, Philip, and Plehwe, Dieter (eds), *The Road from Mont Pèlerin: The Making of the Neoliberal Thought Collective* (Cambridge, Mass., 2009).

von Mises, Ludwig, 'Economic calculation in the Socialist Commonwealth' in Hayek (ed.), *Collectivist Economic Planning* (1935), 87–130.

Mitchell, Ashley, *Memoirs of a Fallen Political Warrior* (1974).

Mitchell, B. R., and Deane, Phyllis, *Abstract of British Historical Statistics* (Cambridge, 1962).

Moggridge, D. E., *British Monetary Policy, 1924–1931: The Norman Conquest of $4.86* (Cambridge, 1972).

Morgan, Kenneth O., *Consensus and Disunity: The Lloyd George Coalition Government, 1918–1922* (Oxford, 1979).

Morris, June, *The Life and Times of Thomas Balogh: A Macaw among Mandarins* (Brighton, 2007).

Morris-Jones, Sir Henry, *Doctor in the Whips' Room* (1955).

Muir, Ramsay, *Liberalism and Industry* (1920).

Muir, Ramsay, *Unemployment: How to Deal with It* (1930).

Muir, Ramsay, *The Faith of a Liberal* (1933).

Muir, Ramsay, *The Record of the National Government* (1936).

[Muir, Ramsay], *Ramsay Muir: An Autobiography and Some Essays*, ed. Stuart Hodgson (1943).

Murray, Bruce K., *The People's Budget 1909/10: Lloyd George and Liberal Politics* (Oxford, 1980).

Murray, Gilbert, et al., *F. W. Hirst: By His Friends* (1958).

National League of Young Liberals, *A Declaration of Liberal Faith* (York, 1932).

National League of Young Liberals, *Planning* (1935).

National Liberal Federation, *The Liberal Way: A Survey of Liberal Policy, Published by the Authority of the National Liberal Federation. With a Foreword by Ramsay Muir* (1934).

New Orbits Group, *High Time for Radicals* (1960).

Newton, Bernard, 'The impact of Henry George on British economists, I', *AJES*, xxx (1971), 179–86.

Newton, Bernard, 'The impact of Henry George on British economists, II', *AJES*, xxx (1971), 317–27.

Newton, Bernard, 'The impact of Henry George on British economists, III', *AJES*, xxxi (1972), 87–102.

Newton, Scott, 'A "visionary hope" frustrated: J. M. Keynes and the origins of the postwar international monetary order', *Diplomacy and Statecraft*, xi (2000), 189–210.

Newton, Scott, 'Deconstructing Harrod: some critical observations on *The Life of John Maynard Keynes*', *CBH*, xv (2001), 15–27.

Newton, Scott, and Porter, Dilwyn, *Modernization Frustrated: The Politics of Industrial Decline in Britain since 1900* (1988).

The Next Five Years: An Essay in Political Agreement (1935).

O'Brien, D. P., *The Classical Economists Revisited* (Princeton, 2004).

O'Hara, Glen, *From Dreams to Disillusionment: Economic and Social Planning in 1960s Britain* (Basingstoke, 2007).

O'Hara, Glen, '"This is what growth does": British views of the European economies in the prosperous "golden age" of 1951–73', *Journal of Contemporary History*, xliv (2009), 697–718.

Owen, Frank, *Tempestuous Journey: Lloyd George, His Life and Times* (1954).

Packer, Ian, 'The Liberal cave and the 1914 budget', *EHR*, cxi (1996), 620–35.

Packer, Ian, *Lloyd George, Liberalism and the Land: The Land Issue and Party Politics in England, 1906–1914* (Woodbridge, 2001).

Packer, Ian, *Liberal Government and Politics, 1905–15* (Basingstoke, 1996).

Paish, Frank, *The Post-War Financial Problem and Other Essays* (1950).

Paish, Frank, 'Open and repressed inflation', *EJ*, lxiii (1953), 527–52.

Paish, Frank, 'Progress, prices and the pound', *District Bank Review*, no. 125 (March 1958), 1–17.

Paish, Frank, 'Inflation in the United Kingdom, 1948–57', *Economica*, new series, xxv (1958), 94–105.

Paish, Frank, 'Monetary policy and the control of the post-war British inflation', in F. W. Paish, *Studies in an Inflationary Economy: The United Kingdom, 1948–1961* (1962; second edition, 1966), 120–54.

Parry, James, 'What if the Liberal Party had broken through from the right?', in Duncan Brack and Iain Dale (eds), *Prime Minister Portillo and Other Things That Never Happened* (2003).

Parsons, Wayne, *The Power of the Financial Press: Journalism and Economic Opinion in Britain and America* (Aldershot, 1989).

Pasinetti, Luigi, *Keynes and the Cambridge Keynesians: A 'Revolution in Economics' to be Accomplished* (Cambridge, 2007).

Patinkin, Don, 'In defense of IS–LM', *Banca Nazionale del Lavoro Quarterly Review*, xliii (1990), 119–34.

Peacock, Sir Alan, *The Economics of National Insurance* (Edinburgh, 1952).

Peacock, Sir Alan, 'Welfare in the Liberal state', in Watson (ed.), *The Unservile State*, 113–30.

Peacock, Sir Alan, *The Welfare Society* (1961).

Peacock, Sir Alan, 'LSE and postwar economic policy', *Atlantic Economic Journal*, x (1982), 35–40.

Peacock, Sir Alan, *Anxious to Do Good: Learning to be an Economist the Hard Way* (Exeter, 2010).

Peacock, Sir Alan, and Wiseman, Jack, *The Growth of Public Expenditure in the United Kingdom* (Princeton, 1961).

Peacock, Sir Alan, and Wiseman, Jack, *Education for Democrats: A Study of the Financing of Education in a Free Society* (1964).

Peck, Jamie, *Constructions of Neoliberal Reason* (Oxford, 2010).

Peden, G. C., 'Sir Richard Hopkins and the "Keynesian revolution" in employment policy, 1929–1945', *Economic History Review*, second series, xxxvi (1983), 281–96.

Peden, G. C,, 'The road to and from Gairloch: Lloyd George, unemployment, inflation, and the "Treasury view" in 1921', *TCBH*, iv (1993), 224–49.

Peden, G. C,, 'Economic knowledge and the state in modern Britain', in S. J. D. Green and R. C. Whiting (eds), *The Boundaries of the State in Modern Britain* (Cambridge, 1996).

Peden, G. C., *The Treasury and British Public Policy, 1906–1959* (Oxford, 2000).

Peele, Gillian, and Cook, Chris (eds), *The Politics of Reappraisal, 1918–1939* (1975).

Pemberton, Hugh, *Policy Learning and British Governance in the 1960s* (Basingstoke, 2004).

Perkin, H. J., 'Land reform and class conflict in Victorian Britain', in J. Butt and J. F. Clarke (eds), *The Victorians and Social Protest: A Symposium* (Newton Abbot, 1973), 177–217.

Peterson, A. D. C., 'A policy for education', in Watson (ed.), *Radical Alternative*, 95–119.

Peterson, A. D. C., *Investment in People: A Liberal Design for Education* (1962).

Phelps Brown, Henry, 'Sir Roy Harrod: A biographical memoir', *EJ*, xc (1980), 1–33.

Phillips, Hubert, et al., *Whither Britain? A Radical Answer* (1932).

Pigou, A. C., *The Economics of Welfare* (1920).

Pinder, John (ed.), *Fifty Years of Political & Economic Planning: Looking Forward, 1931–1981* (1981).

Pinto-Duschinsky, Michael, *British Political Finance, 1830–1980* (1981).

Plehwe, Dieter, 'Introduction', in Mirowski and Plehwe (eds), *The Road from Mont Pèlerin*, 1–42.

Pollard, Sidney, *The Development of the British Economy, 1914–1950* (1962).

Public Opinion, 1935–1946, ed. Hadley Cantril (Princeton, 1951).

Pugh, Martin, 'The Liberal Party and the popular front', *EHR*, cxxi (2006), 1327–50.

Radical Reform Group, *Radical Aims: A Statement of Policy by the Radical Reform Group* (1954).

Rasmussen, Jorgen Scott, *The Liberal Party: A Study of Retrenchment and Revival* (1965).

Rattue, James, *Kissing Your Sister: A History of the Oxford University Liberal Club and its Successors, 1913–1993* (privately published, 1993).

Readman, Paul, *Land and Nation in England: Patriotism, National Identity, and the Politics of Land, 1880–1914* (Woodbridge, 2008).

Reynolds, Jaime, '"Jimmy": The career of James de Rothschild, MP', *JLDH*, no. 32 (2001).

Reynolds, Jaime, and Hunter, Ian, '"Crinks" Johnstone', *JLDH*, no. 26 (2000), 14–18.

Reynolds, Jaime, and Hunter, Ian, 'Liberal class warrior', *JLDH*, no. 28 (2000), 17–21.

Rhys Williams, Juliet, *Something to Look Forward To* (1943).

Rhys Williams, Juliet, *Taxation and Incentive* (1953).

Riccio, Barry D., *Walter Lippmann: Odyssey of a Liberal* (1994).

Ritschel, Daniel, *The Politics of Planning: The Debate on Economic Planning in Britain in the 1930s* (Oxford, 1997).

Robbins, Lionel, *The Great Depression* (1934).

Robbins, Lionel, 'The planning of British agriculture', *Lloyds Bank Limited Monthly Review*, no. 57 (November 1934), 458–69.

Robbins, Lionel, *The Economic Problem in War and Peace* (1947).

Robbins, Lionel, 'Inquest on the crisis', *Lloyds Bank Review*, no. 6 (October 1947), 1–27.

Robbins, Lionel, *The Theory of Economic Policy in English Classical Political Economy* (1952).

Robertson, D. H., 'The problem of creeping inflation', *London and Cambridge Economic Bulletin*, new series, no. 13 (1955), ii–iv.

Robertson, J. M., *The Fallacy of Saving* (1892).

Robinson, Colin, *Arthur Seldon: A Life for Liberty* (2009).

Rollings, Neil, 'Poor Mr Butskell: A short life, wrecked by schizophrenia?', *TCBH*, v (1994), 183–205.

Rollings, Neil, 'Cracks in the post-war Keynesian settlement? The role of organised business in Britain in the rise of neoliberalism before Margaret Thatcher', *TCBH*, xxiv (2013), 637–59.

Rooth, Tim, *British Protectionism and the International Economy: Overseas Commercial Policy in the 1930s* (Cambridge, 1992).

Röpke, Wilhelm, *Civitas Humana: A Humane Order of Society* (English edition, 1948).

Rowntree, B. Seebohm, *Poverty: A Study of Town Life* (1901).

Rowntree, B. Seebohm, *The Price of Full Employment* (1944).

Rowntree, B. Seebohm, *Poverty and the Welfare State* (1951).

Russell, Conrad, *An Intelligent Person's Guide to Liberalism* (1999).

Samuel, Sir Herbert (Viscount Samuel), *Liberalism* (1902).

Samuel, Sir Herbert (Viscount Samuel), *The Political Situation. Being the Inaugural Address to the Liberal Summer School, Cambridge, August 1st, 1935* (1935).

Samuel, Sir Herbert (Viscount Samuel), *Belief and Action: An Everyday Philosophy* (1937).

Samuelson, Paul, 'Lord Keynes and the General Theory', *Econometrica*, xiv (1946), 187–200.

Savage, Michael, Barlow, James, Dickens, Peter, and Fielding, Tony, *Property, Bureaucracy and Culture: Middle-Class Formation in Contemporary Britain* (1992).

Schumacher, E. F., *Small is Beautiful: A Study of Economics as if People Mattered* (1973).

Schumpeter, Joseph, *History of Economic Analysis* (1954).

Searle, G. R., *The Quest for National Efficiency: A Study in British Politics and Political Thought, 1899–1914* (Oxford, 1971).

Searle, G. R., 'The Edwardian Liberal Party and business', *EHR*, xcviii (1983), 28–60.

Seldon, Arthur (ed.), *Not Unanimous: A Rival Verdict to Radcliffe's on Money* (1960).

Seldon, Arthur, 'Economic scholarship and political interest: IEA thinking and government policy', in *The Collected Works of Arthur Seldon*, vii, 43–68.

[Seldon, Arthur], *The Collected Works of Arthur Seldon*, ed. Colin Robertson (7 vols, Indianapolis, 2004–5).

Seymour-Ure, Colin, 'The press and the party system between the wars', in Peele and Cook (eds), *The Politics of Reappraisal*, 232–57.

Shackle, G. L. S., *The Years of High Theory: Invention and Tradition in Economic Thought, 1926–1939* (Cambridge, 1967).

Shakespeare, Sir Geoffrey, *Let Candles Be Brought In* (1949).

Shonfield, Andrew, *British Economic Policy Since the War* (Harmondsworth, 1958).

Sidgwick, Henry, *The Principles of Political Economy* (1883).

Simon, E. D., 'Some questions about free trade', *Political Quarterly*, i (1930), 479–95.

Simons, Henry, *A Positive Program for Laissez Faire: Some Proposals for a Liberal Economic Policy* (Chicago, 1934).

Sinclair, Sir Archibald, *Liberal Policy: A Speech Delivered to the Council of the Liberal Party Organisation on the 15th March, 1939* (1939).

Skidelsky, Robert, *Politicians and the Slump: The Labour Government of 1929–1931* (1967).

Skidelsky, Robert, *John Maynard Keynes* (3 vols, 1983–2001).

Sloman, Peter, 'Rethinking a progressive moment: The Liberal and Labour parties in the 1945 general election', *Historical Research*, lxxxiv (2011), 722–44.

Smart, Nick, 'Constituency politics and the 1931 election', *Southern History*, xvi (1994), 122–51.

Smart, Nick, *The National Government, 1931–40* (Basingstoke, 1999).

Smedley, Oliver, *The Abominable No-Men: 'The Answer to Bevan, Beaverbrook, Beveridge and Butler'* (1952).

Smith, David, *The Rise and Fall of Monetarism* (1987).

Smith, Julie, *A Sense of Liberty: The History of the Liberal International, 1947–1997* (1997).

Stacey, Margaret, *Tradition and Change: A Study of Banbury* (1960).

Stannage, Tom, *Baldwin Thwarts the Opposition: The British General Election of 1935* (1980).

[Steel, David], 'The importance of being Liberal', interview with Malcolm Rutherford and Martin Jacques, *Marxism Today* (October 1986), 25–33.

Tanner, Duncan, *Political Change and the Labour Party, 1900–1918* (Cambridge, 1990).

Tanner, Duncan, 'The strange death of Liberal England', *HJ*, xxxvii (1994), 971–9.

Thane, Pat, 'Women, liberalism and citizenship, 1918–1930', in Eugenio F. Biagini (ed.), *Citizenship and Community: Liberals, radicals, and collective identities in the British Isles, 1865–1931* (Cambridge, 1996), 66–92.

Thompson, James, 'Political economy, the labour movement and the minimum wage, 1880–1914', in Green and Tanner (eds), *Strange Survival*, 62–88.

Thompson, James, 'The Liberal Party, Liberalism and trade unions, 1906–24', *Cercles*, xxi (2011), 27–38.

Thompson, Noel, *Political Economy and the Labour Party: The Economics of Democratic Socialism, 1884–2005* (1994; second edition, 2006).

Thorpe, Andrew, *The British General Election of 1931* (Oxford, 1991).

Thorpe, Andrew, 'The membership of the Communist Party of Great Britain, 1920–1945', *HJ*, xliii (2000), 777–800.

Thorpe, Andrew, 'Reasons for 'progressive' disunity: Labour and Liberal politics in Britain, 1918–45', *Socialist History*, xxvii (2005), 21–42.

Thorpe, Andrew, *Parties at War: Political Organisation in Second World War Britain* (Oxford, 2009).

Thorpe, D. R., *Supermac: The Life of Harold Macmillan* (2010).

Tomlinson, Jim, *Problems of British Economic Policy 1870–1945* (1981).

Tomlinson, Jim, 'A 'Keynesian revolution' in economic policy-making?', *Economic History Review*, second series, xxxvii (1984), 258–62.

Tomlinson, Jim, *Employment Policy: The Crucial Years, 1939–1955* (Oxford, 1987).

Tomlinson, Jim, *Public Policy and the Economy since 1900* (Oxford, 1990).

Tomlinson, Jim, 'Planning: Debate and policy in the 1940s', *TCBH*, iii (1992), 154–74.

Tomlinson, Jim, *Democratic Socialism and Economic Policy: The Attlee Years, 1945–1951* (Cambridge, 1997).

Tomlinson, Jim, *The Politics of Decline: Understanding Post-War Britain* (Harlow, 2000).

Toye, Richard, *The Labour Party and the Planned Economy, 1931–1951* (Woodbridge, 2003).

Toye, Richard, *Lloyd George and Churchill: Rivals for Greatness* (2007).

Toye, Richard, '"I am a Liberal as much as a Tory": Winston Churchill and the memory of 1906', *JLH*, no. 54 (2007), 38–44.

Toye, Richard, 'The Labour Party and Keynes', in Green and Tanner (eds), *Strange Survival*, 153–85.

Toye, Richard, 'Winston Churchill's "crazy broadcast": Party, nation, and the 1945 Gestapo speech', *Journal of British Studies*, xlix (2010), 655–80.

Tregidga, Garry, *The Liberal Party in South-West England Since 1918: Political Decline, Dormancy and Rebirth* (Exeter, 2000).

Tregidga, Garry, 'Turning of the tide? A case study of the Liberal Party in provincial Britain in the late 1930s', *History*, xcii (2007), 347–66.

Trentmann, Frank, *Free Trade Nation: Commerce, Consumption, and Civil Society in Modern Britain* (Oxford, 2008).

Tribe, Keith, 'Liberalism and neoliberalism in Britain, 1930–1960', in Mirowski and Plehwe (eds), *The Road from Mont Pèlerin*, 68–97.

Vincent, John, 'What kind of third party?', *New Society*, 26 January 1967, 120–1.

Vincent, John, 'Chamberlain, the Liberals and the outbreak of war, 1939', *EHR*, cxiii (1998), 367–83.

Wade, Donald W., *The Way of the West* ([1946]).

Wade, Donald W., *Our Aim and Purpose* (1961).

Wade, Donald W., and Banks, Desmond, *The Political Insight of Elliott Dodds* (Leeds, 1977).

Wainwright, Richard, *Own As You Earn: The Liberal Plan* (1958).

Walker, Ronald, *Transport: Freedom or Nationalisation? A Liberal View* (Leeds, [1945]).

Ware, Frank, *5 Year Plan: Social Objectives, Industrial Growth, Taxation Reform* (1961).

Wasserstein, Bernard, *Herbert Samuel: A Political Life* (Oxford, 1992).

Watkins, Alan, *The Liberal Dilemma* (1966).

Watson, George (ed.), *The Unservile State: Essays in Liberty and Welfare* (1957).

Watson, George (ed.), *Radical Alternative: Studies in Liberalism by the Oxford Liberal Group* (1962).

West, Gordon, *Lloyd George's Last Fight* (1930).

White, Stuart, '"Revolutionary Liberalism?" The philosophy and politics of ownership in the post-war Liberal Party', *British Politics*, iv (2009), 164–87.

Whitehead, Sarah, and Brack, Duncan, 'Party organisation from 1859', in Ingham and Brack (eds), *Peace, Reform and Liberation*, 373–86.

Wiles, Peter, 'In defence of "big business"', *Encounter* (December 1954), 29–34.

Wiles, Peter, 'Property and equality', in Watson (ed.), *The Unservile State*, 88–109.

Wiles, Peter, 'The economy and the cold war', in Watson (ed.), *Radical Alternative*, 43–66.

Williamson, John, *How to Stop Stop-Go* (1966).

Williamson, Philip, '"Safety first": Baldwin, the Conservative Party, and the 1929 general election', *HJ*, xxv (1982), 385–409.

Williamson, Philip, *National Crisis and National Government: British Politics, the Economy and Empire, 1926–1932* (Cambridge, 1992).

Williamson, Philip, *Stanley Baldwin: Conservative Leadership and National Values* (Cambridge, 1999).

Wilson, Rob, *5 Days to Power: The Journey to Coalition Britain* (2010).

Wilson, Trevor, *The Downfall of the Liberal Party, 1914–1935* (1966).

Winch, Donald, *Economics and Policy: A Historical Study* (1969).

Winch, Donald, '"A composition of successive heresies": The case of J. A. Hobson', in Donald Winch, *Wealth and Life: Essays on the Intellectual History of Political Economy in Britain, 1848–1914* (Cambridge, 2009), 297–331.

Women's National Liberal Federation, *Children's Allowances. Final Report of the Family Endowment Enquiry Committee of the Women's National Liberal Federation* (1927).

Wood, Barbara, *Alias Papa: A Life of Fritz Schumacher* (1984).

Worswick, G. D. N., 'The sources of recovery in the UK in the 1930s', *National Institute Economic Review*, no. 110 (November 1984), 85–93.

Wyburn-Powell, Alun, *Clement Davies: Liberal Leader* (2003).

Young, Ken, 'Orpington and the "Liberal Revival"', in Chris Cook and John Ramsden (eds), *By-Elections in British Politics* (1973), 198–222.

Zweiniger-Bargielowska, Ina, *Austerity in Britain: Rationing, Controls, and Consumption, 1939–1955* (Oxford, 2000).

THESES AND DISSERTATIONS

Baines, Malcolm, 'The Survival of the British Liberal Party, 1932–1959' (Oxford D.Phil. thesis, 1989).

Burton, Muriel, 'The Making of Liberal Party Policy, 1945–1980' (Reading Ph.D. thesis, 1983).

Calder, A. L. R., 'The Common Wealth Party, 1942–1945' (Sussex Ph.D. thesis, 1967).

Cole, Matthew, 'The Identity of the British Liberal Party, 1945–62' (Birmingham Ph.D. thesis, 2006).

Doyle, Barry M., 'Middle Class Realignment and Party Politics in Norwich, 1900–1932' (East Anglia Ph.D. thesis, 1990).

Egan, Mark, 'The Grass-roots Organisation of the Liberal Party, 1945–1964' (Oxford D.Phil. thesis, 2000).

Faulkes, Stewart, 'The Strange Death of British Liberalism: The Liberal Summer School Movement and the Making of the Yellow Book in the 1920s' (London Ph.D. thesis, 2000).

Fox, Ruth, 'The Liberal Party 1970–1983: Its Philosophy and Political Strategy' (Leeds Ph.D. thesis, 1999).

Hart, Michael, 'The Decline of the Liberal Party in Parliament and in the Constituencies, 1914–1931' (Oxford D.Phil. thesis, 1982).

Howard, Jason G., 'The British General Election of 1929' (Cambridge Ph.D. thesis, 1999).

Jones, Brendon, 'Manchester Liberalism 1918–1929: The electoral, ideological and organisational experience of the Liberal Party in Manchester with particular reference to the career of Ernest Simon' (Manchester Ph.D. thesis, 1997).

Jones, Sian, 'The Political Dynamics of North East Wales, with special reference to the Liberal Party, 1918–1935' (Bangor D.Phil. thesis, 2003).

Roberts, David M., 'Clement Davies and the Liberal Party, 1929–56' (University of Wales M.A. thesis, 1974).

Rowe, E. A., 'The British General Election of 1929' (Oxford B.Litt. thesis, 1959).

Sell, Geoffrey, 'Liberal Revival: Jo Grimond and the Politics of British Liberalism, 1956–1967' (London Ph.D. thesis, 1996).

Sommer, Ronald M., 'The Organization of the Liberal Party, 1936–1960' (London D.Phil. thesis, 1962).

Wallace, Jonathan, 'The Political Career of Walter Runciman, 1st Viscount Runciman of Doxford (1870–1949)' (Newcastle upon Tyne Ph.D. thesis, 1995).

Wallace, William J. L., 'The Liberal Revival: The Liberal Party in Britain, 1955–1966' (Cornell University D.Phil. thesis, 1968).

Ward, John, 'The development of the Labour Party in the Black Country (1918–1939)' (Wolverhampton D.Phil. thesis, 2004).

UNPUBLISHED PAPERS

Leeson, Robert, 'The rise and fall of the Phillips curve in British policy-making circles', Murdoch University, Department of Economics, Working Paper no. 133, 1995.

Peden, G. C., 'Economists and the British Welfare State from New Liberalism to the New Right', paper for International Workshop on 'Cambridge, LSE, and the Foundations of the Welfare State: New Liberalism to Neo-Liberalism', Hitotsubashi University, Tokyo, 13–14 March 2010.

INTERVIEWS AND CORRESPONDENCE

Mr Harry Cowie (interview), 26 September 2012.
Mr Derick Mirfin (interview), 6 May 2014.
Sir Alan Peacock (correspondence), 1 April 2012.
Mr David Penwarden (interview), 3 October 2011.
Mr George Watson (interview), 13 June 2011.
Professor John Williamson (interview), 13 July 2012.

Index

Printed and bound by CPI Group (UK) Ltd, Croydon, CR0 4YY